Leadership & Management Strategies for Education

Volume 2
Managing key institutional processes

David Hall • Nicholas Bowskill • Ben Hayes • Sue Ellis

Leadership & Management Strategies for Education
Volume 2: Managing key institutional processes
© DHP 2025. All rights reserved.
First edition.

No part of this publication may be reproduced, distributed, or transmitted in any form or by any means, including photocopying, recording, or other electronic or mechanical methods, without the prior written permission of the publisher, except in the case of brief quotations embodied in critical reviews and certain other non-commercial uses permitted by copyright law.

For permission requests, write to the publisher, addressed "Attention: Permissions Coordinator", at the address below:

David Hall Publishing (DHP)
Carlisle, Cumbria
Email: dhp@davidhall.uk
Website: davidhall.uk/dhp

This book is a work of nonfiction. The events, situations, and dialogue described are based on the author's experiences, and while the intent is to provide accurate and reliable information, the author and publisher make no representations or warranties with respect to the completeness, accuracy, or timeliness of the content within this book.

Published by David Hall Publishing (DHP)
Printed in the United Kingdom

ISBN: 978-1-917541-11-4

Cover design by DHP / chatGPT

First Printing, 2025

 DHP Books

CONTENTS

List of illustrations	vii
Acknowledgments	viii
Foreword	ix
Chapter 1 - Shaping the curriculum	1
The concept of curriculum	2
Curriculum components	4
The curriculum design cycle	6
Curriculum leadership and management	10
Curriculum design	16
The product model	16
The process model	18
Curriculum frameworks	21
Curriculum organisation	23
Chapter 2 - Effective assessment strategies	32
The foundations of assessment	33
Managing assessment	37
Key assessment bodies and standards	47
Designing fit-for-purpose assessments	55
Assessment formats	60
Grading and feedback	65
Technology enhanced assessment	71
Future trends in assessment	73
Chapter 3 - Enhancing teaching and learning	77
Strategic vision for teaching and learning	78
Building collaborative teaching communities	87
Promoting pathways into teaching	92
Teacher leadership	93
Leading inclusive and equitable learning	94

Chapter 4 - Cultivating future leaders — 100

    Developing the leaders of tomorrow — 101
    Formal training and education — 102
    Experiential learning — 103
    Reflective practice — 105
    Shared leadership opportunities — 105
    Collaborative learning — 106
    Coaching and mentoring in leadership development — 108
    Coaching and mentoring models and frameworks — 111
    The role of leadership in coaching and mentoring — 117
    Measuring the impact of coaching and mentoring — 121
    Developing a coaching and mentoring strategy — 123

Chapter 5 - Inspiring and engaging staff — 127

    Fostering inspiration and engagement — 128
    Principles of people leadership — 129
    Understanding the people in educational settings — 130
    Understanding yourself as a leader — 132
    A leader's relationship with staff — 136
    Organisational issues in managing people — 152

Chapter 6 - Developing human resources — 156

    Overview of human resource management (HRM) — 157
    Strategic HRM in education — 158
    Recruitment and selection — 159
    Staff development and training — 161
    Performance management — 164
    Staff well-being and work-life balance — 167
    Reward and recognition systems — 170
    Legal and ethical considerations in HR — 172
    HR leadership in differing educational contexts — 174
    Technology and HR in education — 177

Chapter 7 - Evidence-based decision making — 182

    The growing role of data in educational excellence — 183
    Foundations of data-driven decision making — 185
    The data cycle — 186
    Data analysis techniques in education — 188
        Qualitative data analysis — 188
        Quantitative data analysis — 190

Data sources and technology in education	192
Using data to drive pedagogical innovation	197
The role of leadership in data-driven cultures	199
Challenges in implementing data-driven decision making	200
Ethical considerations in data use	202
Stakeholder engagement with data	205

Chapter 8 - Harnessing E-Leadership and AI   212

Introducing E-Leadership and AI	212
Using readymade prompts as pedagogical tools	213
The readymade prompt as a learning resource	217
The readymade prompt in course design	219
The readymade prompt in an adaptive learning system	221
Enhancing leadership and management with AI prompts	224
AI generated prompts in establishing an institute's vision	225
AI generated prompts in strategic decision-making	226
Enhancing communication through AI generated prompts	228
Streamlining administrative efficiency with AI	229
AI driven learning design for critical decision making	229
AI driven coaching and leadership reflection	229
Automated policy guidance through AI	230
Personalising leadership training with AI	232

Chapter 9 - Raising standards   235

The importance of quality in education	235
Historical perspectives on quality in education	238
Quality control - ensuring consistency	240
Quality assurance - a proactive approach	244
Continuous improvement in education	246
Data-driven improvement	251
Total Quality Management	256
Adoption of TQM in education	259
Six Sigma	260
Future directions in quality management	262
Quality in action - bridging theory and practice	265
Managing quality in education	266

Chapter 10 - Bringing it all together - Tom's story   270

Meet Tom Bennett	270
Shaping the curriculum	271
Effective assessment strategies	272

Harnessing E-Leadership and AI　　　　　　　　　　273
　　Cultivating future leaders　　　　　　　　　　　　274
　　Managing professional development　　　　　　　275
　　Quality and standards　　　　　　　　　　　　　　276
　　Enhancing teaching and learning　　　　　　　　277
　　Inspiring and engaging staff　　　　　　　　　　　277
　　Evidence-based decision making　　　　　　　　278
　　Developing human resources　　　　　　　　　　279

Appendix 1 - Establishing learning objectives and learner needs　282

Appendix 2 - The assessment cycle　292

Appendix 3 - Teaching and learning　294

Appendix 4 - Data-driven decision making　304

Appendix 5 - Readymade prompts　320

Appendix 6 - Gathering quality assurance data　322

References　326

Index　359

LIST OF ILLUSTRATIONS

Figures

Figure 1.1	-	The curriculum design cycle	7
Figure 1.2	-	Improved curriculum design cycle	8
Figure 1.3	-	Tyler's rationale for curriculum design	17
Figure 2.1	-	The assessment cycle	40
Figure 2.2	-	Observation rubric	61
Figure 3.1	-	Our values infographic	83
Figure 4.1	-	The GROW model	112
Figure 4.2	-	The CLEAR model	113
Figure 4.3	-	The OSKAR model	114
Figure 5.1	-	Maslow's Hierarchy of Needs	137
Figure 5.2	-	Thomas-Kilmann Conflict Model	147
Figure 7.1	-	Data cycle in education	187
Figure 7.2	-	School Management Information System (SIMS)	195
Figure 8.1	-	Prompts within the pedagogical framework	223
Figure 8.2	-	The PromptFrame shell (UK History)	224
Figure 9.1	-	The Plan-Do-Check-Act cycle	247
Figure 9.2	-	Cause-and-effect diagram	253
Figure 9.3	-	Pareto chart for a history test	255
Figure 9.4	-	The flipped TQM structure	258
Figure 9.5	-	Continuous improvement	259

Tables

Table 1.1	-	Components of the total curriculum	5
Table 1.2	-	Curriculum design support systems	9
Table 1.3	-	Practical strategies for fostering curriculum leadership	12
Table 1.4	-	Distinctions between teaching and facilitating	19
Table 1.5	-	Typical elements of a curriculum framework	22
Table 1.6	-	Key skills competencies	27
Table 2.1	-	Assessment types	35
Table 2.2	-	Bloom's taxonomy and associated question types	61
Table 4.1	-	The mentoring cycle	117
Table 5.1	-	Principles for leading and managing people	130
Table 6.1	-	HR leaders across educational contexts	175
Table 8.1	-	A prototype taxonomy of readymade prompts	217

ACKNOWLEDGMENTS

I would like to express my sincere gratitude to the many educators, leaders, and institutions whose experiences have informed the case studies and insights presented in this book. While their identities remain anonymous to respect their privacy, their real-world contributions have been invaluable in shaping the content and providing practical relevance. Their willingness to share their experiences has greatly enriched this work, and I am deeply appreciative of their support and cooperation.

A particular mention goes to ChatGPT, whose creative assistance in the generation of a number of the book's images, helps to catch people's attention and visualise the book's content.

FOREWORD

Leadership & Management Strategies for Education: Volume 2 - Managing key institutional processes is an essential guide for today's educational leaders. This volume builds on the principles established in Volume 1 and explores the practical and often complex areas that every institution must manage to ensure success, sustainability, and continued growth.

This book offers a deep dive into the core institutional functions that shape the day-to-day operations and long-term vision of educational environments. From curriculum development to human resources management, the chapters in this volume are designed to address the multifaceted nature of educational leadership, providing comprehensive insights into the systems and processes that keep schools, colleges and universities running smoothly.

One of the great strengths of this volume is its balanced approach to management and leadership. Each chapter not only outlines the operational aspects but also integrates them with leadership theory, providing a dynamic interplay between management responsibilities and leadership vision. Whether discussing financial management, diversity and inclusion, or assessment and evaluation, the book demonstrates how strategic leadership can transform these areas from routine functions into catalysts for institutional improvement.

Drawing from a broad range of both contemporary and classic research, this book offers educational leaders practical tools and proven strategies that can be applied in real-world settings. Each chapter is meticulously researched, blending evidence-based practices with innovative thinking to ensure that leaders are well-prepared for the challenges of today's fast-paced and ever-evolving educational landscape.

Perhaps the most valuable aspect of this volume is its ability to connect leadership with key institutional functions in a way that encourages both operational excellence and personal growth. For instance, chapters on coaching and mentoring, professional development, and staff wellbeing not only address the mechanics of management but also highlight the importance of cultivating a supportive and empowering environment for both students and staff.

In a world where educational institutions face growing pressures to perform, this book serves as a crucial resource for leaders who are committed to creating high-performing, inclusive, and sustainable learning environments. Whether you are new to leadership or an experienced professional seeking fresh insight, *Managing key institutional processes* offers the knowledge and inspiration needed to guide your institution through the complexities of modern education with confidence and skill.

Chapter 1 - Shaping the curriculum: Curriculum management is at the heart of educational success, shaping the experiences of learners and ensuring alignment with institutional and societal goals. This chapter provides a comprehensive exploration of the processes and principles that guide curriculum design, implementation, and evaluation. Drawing on research and practical case studies, it bridges theoretical frameworks with real-world application, offering valuable insights for educators, leaders, and policymakers. By delving into the complexities of the management cycle, this work inspires a deeper understanding of how thoughtful curriculum leadership drives meaningful and lasting impact in education.

Chapter 2 - Effective assessment strategies: Assessment is a cornerstone of education, driving learning, guiding teaching, and shaping institutional strategies. Its effectiveness depends on strong leadership and management at all levels. Leaders must design fair and reliable systems, meet diverse learner needs, and align assessment with institutional goals while addressing external demands.

This chapter explores the principles and strategies of effective assessment, emphasising the critical role of leadership in fostering collaboration, innovation, and continuous improvement. By blending theory with practical guidance, it aims to equip educators and leaders to harness assessment as a powerful tool for enhancing teaching, learning, and institutional success.

Chapter 3 - Enhancing teaching and learning: Effective teaching and learning are driven by leaders who deeply understand both the structure and essence of the learning process within their educational contexts. These leaders relentlessly seek insights into what drives meaningful outcomes, asking vital questions: How can we achieve better results? What practices should become routine? And, equally important, what practices should be discarded for lack of impact? At the core of these efforts is a simple truth: the quality of teaching and learning experiences is critical. This chapter explores the essential role of educational leaders in attracting, developing, supporting, and retaining exceptional teachers, who are the cornerstone of a thriving learning community.

Chapter 4 - Cultivating future leaders: In a world where leadership is constantly evolving, the ability to guide and nurture future leaders has become more important than ever. The significance of coaching and mentoring in leadership and management development cannot be overstated. These practices offer powerful ways to support the growth and transformation of leaders at all levels of an organisation. In this chapter, we explore the principles and practices that underpin effective coaching and mentoring strategies. Through insightful examples, theoretical frameworks, and practical tips, this chapter equips educators, managers, and leaders with the tools necessary to cultivate leadership capability within their organisations. Whether you are an experienced leader looking to enhance your coaching skills or an organisation aiming to integrate coaching and mentoring into your leadership development programmes, the ideas presented here will help you unlock the full potential of your leadership teams.

Chapter 5 - Inspiring and engaging staff: Effective leadership in education hinges on the ability to manage people with empathy, insight, and vision. This chapter highlights the relational core of leadership, illustrating how strong interpersonal skills and emotional intelligence can transform educational institutions into thriving communities. By addressing the needs of teachers, staff, students, and stakeholders, this chapter equips leaders with the tools to foster collaboration, navigate challenges, and build a culture of trust and growth.

Chapter 6 - Developing human resources: Human Resource Management (HRM) is at the heart of educational institutions, influencing everything from the recruitment of qualified staff to the ongoing development of teachers and administrative teams. This chapter explores the multifaceted role of HRM in education, emphasising its critical importance in creating a supportive and effective learning environment. From aligning HR strategies with educational goals to fostering a culture of collaboration and well-being, HRM plays a pivotal role in shaping the success of an institution.

Chapter 7 - Evidence-based decision making: Accountability and evidence-based practices are key to defining educational success. This chapter explores the critical importance of data in education, examining its role in classroom decisions and strategic institutional planning. It offers a clear understanding of qualitative and quantitative data and how it is analysed in order to drive meaningful improvements. By exploring diverse data sources, ethical considerations, and innovative technologies, this chapter equips educators and leaders with the tools to harness data responsibly and effectively. It also highlights the pivotal role of leadership in evidence-based decision-making, offering practical solutions to overcome common challenges.

Chapter 8 - Harnessing E-Leadership and AI: The introduction of AI into leadership development brings with it a unique opportunity to redefine how leaders grow, learn, and guide their organisations. As we transition further into a digital-first world, e-leadership becomes crucial in helping leaders adapt to the changing landscape. This chapter provides insights into how leaders can effectively harness the power of AI, especially through the use of ready-made prompts, to elevate their leadership capabilities. It not only explores the mechanics of these tools but also addresses the critical role that human judgment, empathy, and ethics continue to play in the age of artificial intelligence.

Chapter 9 - Raising standards: Education is the bedrock of societal progress, and the pursuit of quality within it is a journey that demands both vision and precision. As educational institutions evolve to meet the challenges of an interconnected world, the ability to manage and sustain quality has never been more critical. Raising standards is not just about compliance with standards or meeting benchmarks; it is about fostering a culture of excellence where every learner thrives, every educator feels empowered, and every stakeholder sees the value of education as transformative. This chapter offers a comprehensive exploration of quality management, equipping readers with the historical context, theoretical frameworks, and practical tools necessary to navigate this complex terrain. By integrating insights from diverse educational settings, it provides a roadmap for leaders committed to making quality a defining feature of their institutions.

Chapter 10 - Bringing it all together - Tom's story: In the final chapter of this volume, we turn to a story that brings theory to life. Tom Bennett's journey offers a grounded, insightful perspective on how the key institutional functions explored in this book - curriculum, assessment, staff development, and more - come together in the lived experience of school leadership. Tom's approach is thoughtful and people-focused. He shows that effective leadership is not just about systems or strategies, but about relationships, values, and a commitment to growth - for students, colleagues, and the school as a whole. His story reflects how leadership can be both strategic and deeply human. Tom's experience invites us to consider not just what we do as leaders, but how - and why - we do it.

Each chapter includes case studies, activities, pertinent factual information and opportunities for reflection:

Case Study
Case studies, drawn from real-life experiences in educational institutions, provide practical insights and illustrate key leadership and management concepts in action.

Activity
Activities encourage readers to apply their learning in practical contexts, promoting critical thinking and skill development. They help bridge theory and practice.

Information Factual information boxes present clear, concise summaries of key theories and research. They serve as quick reference points and ground broader discussions in concrete evidence.

Question Question boxes prompt deeper thinking, reflection and self-assessment, helping readers connect theory with their own experiences and contexts.

Example boxes highlight instances of specific theories and concepts in action in educational institutes.

1 SHAPING THE CURRICULUM

David Hall

Introduction

Leading the design of effective curriculum requires a clear educational vision, a deep understanding of learners' needs, and the ability to align purpose with practice. It goes beyond managing content - it involves shaping meaningful learning journeys that are coherent, inclusive, and future-focused. Effective curriculum leadership brings together pedagogy, policy, and innovation to create frameworks that not only meet current standards but also inspire lifelong learning and adaptability in a changing world.

This chapter provides an overview of curriculum leadership, introducing key definitions, elements, and management approaches. It discusses the curriculum cycle as a means to enhance practice and outcomes, and outlines how intent, implementation, and impact can be defined and evaluated. It also considers leadership roles in curriculum development, emphasising clarity and collaboration, and applies design principles using recognised frameworks and taxonomies. Organisational strategies are explored to support structured and adaptable curriculum planning.

This chapter:

- Outlines curriculum concepts, including definitions, components, and management models.
- Examines the concept of a management cycle to refine curriculum practices.
- Defines the principles and measures of curriculum intent, curriculum implementation and curriculum impact.
- Analyses the roles and responsibilities of those charged with leading curriculum development.
- Applies curriculum design principles, emphasising frameworks and taxonomies.
- Explores effective curriculum organisation strategies and structural approaches.

The concept of curriculum

Curriculum Studies has emerged relatively recently as an independent field of research in education. In the UK, its development was marked by an increased focus on the systematic planning and preparation of learning, particularly in schools, during the second half of the 20th century. Before this time, curriculum development was often fragmented and inconsistent. However, educators recognised that if learning was to keep pace with societal changes - such as technological advancements, shifting economic demands, and evolving cultural expectations - the curriculum needed to be deliberately designed and managed across all educational contexts.

In schools, the Ministry of Education responded by establishing the *Curriculum Study Group* and the *Secondary Schools Examination Council*, which were replaced in 1964 by the *Schools Council* following recommendations from the Lockwood Committee (Gillard, 2011). The *Schools Council* took responsibility for curriculum development and examinations in England and Wales, marking the beginning of a more research-informed and strategic approach to curriculum planning. Although this council has since been succeeded by other organisations, it laid the foundation for contemporary curriculum development in primary and secondary education.

In further and higher education, curriculum development has also evolved significantly. In FE, the focus has often been on preparing learners for the workplace, with curricula that adapt to vocational and technical needs. In HE, curriculum development typically emphasises academic rigor, research integration, and the preparation of learners for advanced societal contributions. Across these sectors, the importance of aligning the curriculum with societal and technological changes remains central.

If curriculum development is fundamentally about meeting the current and future needs of learners, it should evolve at a pace that reflects societal changes - favouring gradual evolution over abrupt revolution and adopting proactive strategies rather than reactive adjustments. This principle applies not only to schools but also to post-compulsory education, and other educational contexts, such as adult and informal education, where flexibility and responsiveness are crucial to meeting diverse learner needs. This raises important questions about the approaches taken by policymakers and the legitimacy of centralised, politically driven control of the curriculum across all sectors.

Definition of curriculum

Educational practitioners are all familiar with the term *curriculum*, yet defining the concept remains challenging due to its evolving and multifaceted nature. Over time, the term has taken on a range of meanings, reflecting varying theoretical, cultural, and practical perspectives.

Doll (1992) proposed a broad definition of curriculum as the formal and informal content and methods through which learners acquire knowledge and understanding, build skills, and shape their attitudes, perceptions, and values. This expansive view highlights the complexity of curriculum as not only a collection of content but also an interactive process shaped by context, pedagogy, and learner experiences. However, such a comprehensive definition may be impractical for management purposes. Lumby (1995) contended that if the definition encompasses all aspects of the institute, then curriculum management risks becoming indistinguishable from managing the institution itself. Conversely, if the definition is too narrow, curriculum management may be reduced to curriculum development, sidelining broader issues specific to management, such as resource allocation, staff development, and quality assurance.

To manage the curriculum effectively, it is critical for institutions to adopt a clear, context-specific definition. As Lofthouse (1995, p. 9) observed, "It is critically important that you know where you stand". This clarity provides a foundation for aligning curriculum goals with institutional vision, learner needs, and societal demands.

Definitions of curriculum vary significantly, reflecting differences in emphasis and scope. Marsh & Willis (2003) provide several examples that highlight this diversity. For instance, some definitions emphasise content, while others focus on the process, outcomes, or even the hidden curriculum - the implicit lessons learned through institutional culture and practice.

More recent research supports the idea that curriculum definitions must evolve to remain relevant in rapidly changing educational landscapes. Kelly (2009) underscores the importance of balancing traditional academic knowledge with skills for the 21st century, including critical thinking, creativity, and digital literacy. Young & Muller (2015) propose a curriculum model that balances disciplinary knowledge with responsiveness to societal needs, emphasising the importance of teacher professionalism and local adaptability over rigidly centralised frameworks.

Ultimately, an institution's chosen definition of curriculum should reflect its mission, values, and the specific needs of its learners while maintaining flexibility to adapt to future challenges. This adaptability ensures that curriculum management remains both relevant and effective in fostering meaningful learning experiences.

Formal definitions of curriculum can vary enormously, both in their breadth and emphasis. Here are a number of examples taken from Marsh & Willis (2003).

1. Curriculum is such 'permanent' subjects as grammar, reading, logic, rhetoric, mathematics, and the greatest books of the Western world that best embody essential knowledge.

2. Curriculum is those subjects that are most useful for living in contemporary society.

3. A curriculum comprises all the activities that students undertake in order to develop their intellectual, personal, social and physical growth.

4. Curriculum is all the experiences learners have under the guidance of the school.

5. Curriculum is the totality of learning experiences provided to students so that they can attain general skills and knowledge at a variety of learning sites.

6. Curriculum is anything and everything that effects the intended learning.

Curriculum components

Kelly (2009) explains that the curriculum is composed of various components that collectively form the 'total curriculum'. Table 1.1 includes a number of components that, together, make up the total curriculum. It refers to the components of the formal curriculum - those activities for which an institute schedules specific periods of teaching time, and other, informal, voluntary activities that take place before and after normal hours.

These activities - breakfast clubs, sports clubs, educational visits, school, college or university societies, and similar initiatives - are often referred to as 'extra-curricular,' a term that implies they exist entirely outside or beyond the main curriculum. This label can be misleading, as it suggests a clear division between formal education and other learning experiences. However, in the context of thoughtful and inclusive curriculum planning, it would be prudent to recognise and incorporate this broad spectrum of activities, many of which are intentionally designed and implemented with specific educational aims in mind. These undertakings are rarely accidental; rather, they are carefully structured to support student development, social engagement, and a richer educational experience. In fact, there are educators and theorists who argue that such activities hold just as much educational significance as the formal lessons and structured programmes provided by the institution. Perhaps, then, any comprehensive definition of curriculum should take into account not only the formal teaching and learning that occurs during scheduled classroom hours but also the informal and co-curricular learning that happens in parallel - whether inside or beyond the official timetable.

The Total Curriculum

1. Official (planned) curriculum	The official curriculum is the intended curriculum as devised by those responsible for its design and development. For example, the Government, the Department for Education, local education authorities, Ofsted, Quality Assurance Agency for Higher Education (QAA), individual institutes of education and private sector training departments. It is the learning (and learning experience) that is meant to take place and that which is laid down in syllabuses and prospectuses.
2. Taught (operational, actual) curriculum	The taught curriculum is the learning that actually takes place and is the reality of the learning experience. It would ideally be the same as the official curriculum but, more often than not, it differs (for a variety of reasons). It is what teachers actually teach, as opposed to what they are supposed to teach.
	The disparity between the official and the taught curriculum may be deliberate or unintentional. For example, it could be an attempt by teachers or others to deceive, to make what they offer appear more attractive than it really is, or merely the fact that any course will never match the hopes and intentions of those who planned it.
3. Learned (observed) curriculum	This is what students actually take away from the classroom. It is the words, sounds, images, ideas, themes, etc. that make it into the students' minds and memories. For a number of reasons, they may not learn everything they are taught. This may stem from a teacher's inability to achieve certain learning outcomes, a student's lack of capacity to grasp key concepts, or flaws in the learning experience itself (poor attendance, inadequate learning facilities, a lack of resources, and teaching to the assessment, i.e., when teaching is heavily focused on preparing students to pass the exams etc.).

4. Tested (evaluated) curriculum	The tested curriculum consists of that portion of the curriculum over which a student is tested. It may fall short of the curriculum, either by design or by the inability of test instruments to measure the full range of learning outcomes. As a result, teachers may emphasise the tested curriculum to the detriment of the rest of the curriculum. The tested curriculum sometimes becomes an inaccurate measure of the institute's success. Teachers are often encouraged to teach to the objectives of the test rather than to the objectives of curriculum standards.
5. Hidden (unplanned) curriculum	Hidden curriculum refers to a range of things (attitudes, opinions, values) that pupils learn, not from the formal curriculum, but simply from the experience of being in the institute. These derive from the implicit messages conveyed through the structure and organisation of the institution, the relationships between teachers and pupils, the disciplinary regime, the assessment system and the various subcultures that exist. Hidden curriculum may come about by design or by accident and may have a positive or a negative influence on learners. Some would say that the hidden curriculum transmits the true ideals and goals of the institution, and this may be dangerous because often we do not know it exists.
6. Null (excluded) curriculum	Null curriculum refers to that portion of the curriculum that should be taught but, in fact, isn't. It may result from time constraints, teacher preferences, unavailable resources etc. It may be an unintended outcome, or it may happen by design.

Table 1.1 - Components of the total curriculum
Source: Kelly (2009)

The curriculum design cycle

The curriculum design cycle is an iterative process that ensures educational programmes remain relevant, coherent, and impactful. It comprises four key stages: needs analysis, course design, implementation, and evaluation (Figure 1.1).

Needs analysis: Focuses on identifying the knowledge, skills, and attributes learners require. This includes reviewing societal, institutional, and learner-specific needs, ensuring alignment with educational goals and standards (Kelly, 2009). For example, a vocational programme might analyse industry trends to define its curriculum focus.

Course design: Translates these needs into a structured curriculum. This stage includes selecting content, sequencing topics, and aligning objectives with outcomes

(Tyler, 1949). Approaches like Wiggins & McTighe's (2005) backward design emphasise starting with desired outcomes to ensure coherence. This phase also considers frameworks, such as Bloom's taxonomy, to scaffold learning progression.

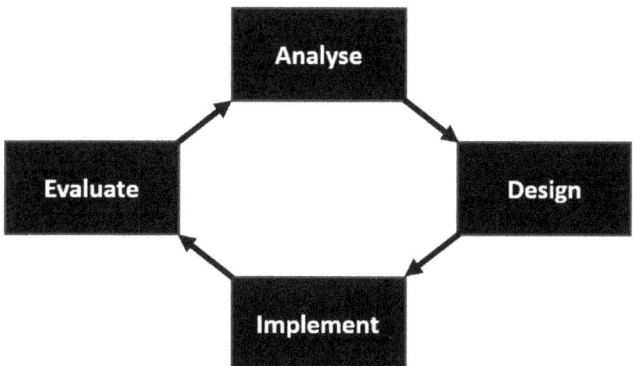

Figure 1.1 - The curriculum design cycle

Course implementation: Involves delivering the curriculum in classrooms or other learning environments. Teachers' expertise, pedagogical approaches, and resource availability are critical factors influencing successful implementation. Effective teacher training and ongoing professional development can enhance fidelity to curriculum intent (Bromley, 2023).

Course evaluation: Assesses the programme's impact, focusing on whether learners achieve desired outcomes. Evaluation models such as *Tyler's Objectives Evaluation* or *Stufflebeam's CIPP Model* provide structured frameworks for assessing relevance, implementation, and effectiveness (Ashbee, 2021). Feedback from evaluations informs future curriculum updates, completing the cycle.

On the second and subsequent cycles, *Needs Analysis* becomes *Review*, and *Design* becomes *Update*. The cycle is not linear but dynamic, requiring continuous reflection to adapt to changing needs. This iterative approach ensures that curricula remain responsive, preparing learners for future challenges.

Intent, implementation and impact

Evaluation of the curriculum has recently developed to include intent, implementation and impact. Since 2019, these quality measures have become core elements of the UK *Ofsted Education Inspection Framework* (Ofsted, 2023).

Intent: Refers to a judgement of the potential effectiveness of a curriculum *before* it is implemented. By evaluating intent first, institutes can identify potential gaps or misalignments in curriculum design, preventing issues during implementation. A clear intent helps teachers align their teaching practices with the curriculum's goals.

Implementation: Examines how the curriculum is delivered in classrooms, focusing on teaching strategies, learning experiences, and assessments. This ensures that teaching methods are effective and meet the planned intent.

Impact: Measures the outcomes of the curriculum, including student progress, attainment, and readiness for future learning or employment.

As a result, the curriculum design cycle can be modified as shown in Figure 1.2.

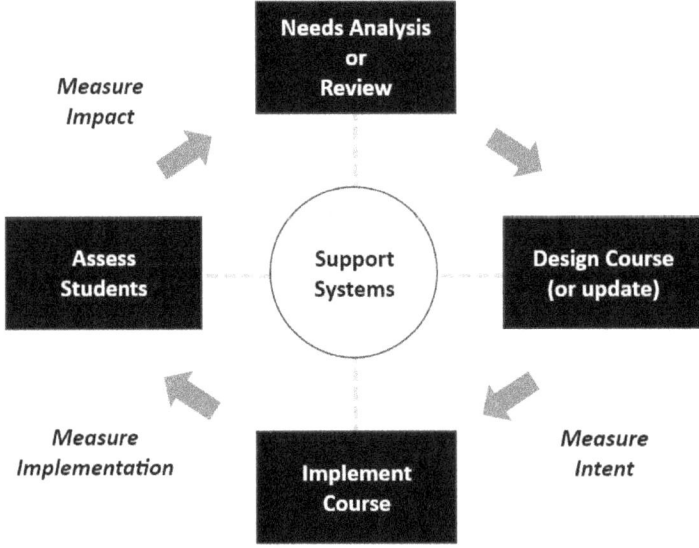

Figure 1.2 - Improved curriculum design cycle

Support systems

In the revised curriculum design cycle, the *support systems* encompass the essential infrastructure, resources, and processes that form the foundation of each phase of the design process. These systems, outlined in detail in Table 1.2, play a pivotal role in ensuring that the curriculum design is not only effective but also sustainable and adaptable to the evolving needs of stakeholders. By providing a robust framework, the support systems facilitate seamless transitions between phases, uphold quality standards, and enable the curriculum to remain dynamic and responsive in a constantly changing educational landscape.

Design phase	Support system components
1. Needs Analysis (or review)	**Data collection tools**: Surveys, interviews, and analytics to assess learner needs and institutional priorities. **Stakeholder engagement**: Mechanisms for consulting teachers, students, parents, and employers. **Access to standards**: Guidelines or frameworks such as national curriculum requirements, higher education subject benchmarks and sector-recognised standards. *Note: The needs analysis is often simplified by deferring to subject matter experts or to established curriculum frameworks (such as the national curriculum).*
2. Course Design (or Update)	**Curriculum development teams**: Experts in pedagogy, subject matter, and instructional design. **Design tools**: Software for curriculum mapping (e.g., EduPlanet21, CMAP). **Professional development**: Training for staff on curriculum theories like backward design or the Tyler model. **Research resources**: Access to recent academic studies and exemplars of effective curriculum models.
3. Course Implementation	**Teaching resources**: Instructional materials, lesson plans, and digital platforms. **Teacher training**: Ongoing support in implementing new teaching methods or assessments. **Monitoring mechanisms**: Classroom observations, feedback systems, and data collection during delivery. **IT infrastructure**: Tools for blended or online learning, such as learning management systems (e.g., Moodle, Blackboard).
4. Course Evaluation	**Assessment frameworks**: Evaluation tools like formative and summative assessments to gauge effectiveness. **Data analysis tools**: Software to analyse student performance and curriculum impact (e.g., Tableau, Excel). **Feedback loops**: Systems for gathering and acting on feedback from teachers, students, and stakeholders. **Evaluation models**: Structured approaches such as Stufflebeam's CIPP model or Kirkpatrick's model of evaluation.

Cross-cutting support systems	Across all phases, institutes benefit from overarching systems, including: **Leadership support:** Guidance and endorsement from senior leaders and curriculum managers. **Budget and funding:** Adequate financial resources for materials, training, and implementation. **Policy frameworks:** Clear policies that align curriculum design with broader institutional or national goals.

Table 1.2 - Curriculum design support systems

Curriculum leadership and management

Curriculum leadership is central to institutional success and learner achievement. It encompasses the strategic planning, implementation, and review of the curriculum to ensure relevance, coherence, and high-quality outcomes. Effective curriculum leadership and management guide the organisation's direction and influence the experiences of both staff and students. This depends on the strong leadership role of principals, the benefits and challenges of shared curriculum leadership, and the importance of aligning curriculum with institutional goals.

Key concepts and theoretical foundations

Curriculum leadership involves the processes of designing, implementing, evaluating, and revising educational programmes to meet learner needs and institutional goals. It requires strategic thinking and collaborative decision-making.

Two dominant curriculum models guide curriculum leaders:

- **Product model** (Tyler, 1949): Emphasises defined learning objectives, outcomes, and assessment standards. It is linear, focusing on measurable end goals.
- **Process model** (Stenhouse, 1975): Centres on the learning experience and development of understanding, offering flexibility and adaptability in pedagogy and content delivery.

Effective curriculum leadership must often blend these models and align them with broader institutional missions. Leadership theories relevant to curriculum management include:

- **Transformational Leadership** (Leithwood & Jantzi, 2006): Inspires and motivates staff through vision and empowerment.

- **Instructional Leadership** (Hallinger & Murphy, 1985): Focuses on teaching and learning as core priorities.
- **Distributed Leadership** (Spillane, 2006): Involves multiple actors in leadership roles, sharing responsibility for curriculum outcomes.

Leadership roles in curriculum management

The role of the principal

The principal's role in curriculum management is foundational. As strategic leaders, principals must articulate a clear vision, foster curriculum leadership at all levels, and balance accountability demands with innovation in pedagogy.

Vision-setting and aligning the curriculum with institutional goals

A compelling vision ensures curricular coherence and relevance. As Harris (2011) notes, vision-setting shapes curriculum direction and delivery. Principals who provide a strategic roadmap help align teaching practices and subject content with institutional aspirations.

"At Greenfield Academy, our vision is to provide a dynamic, inclusive curriculum that fosters academic excellence and personal growth. We aim to equip students with skills and values to thrive in a changing world, ensuring the curriculum is challenging, engaging, and accessible. By promoting collaboration, critical thinking, and creativity, we prepare students for success and lifelong learning. Through strategic partnerships and ongoing professional development, we keep the curriculum relevant and aligned with student needs and educational goals".

This vision underscores a strategic commitment to both excellence and innovation.

Supporting curriculum leadership across all levels

Principals must nurture leadership capacity within their teams, ensuring that curriculum development becomes a shared and sustainable endeavour. Table 1.3 outlines practical strategies for fostering curriculum leadership through professional development, collaborative planning, and clearly defined leadership roles.

Strategy	Description	Examples/Actions
Professional development opportunities	Provide ongoing training to enhance leadership skills and curriculum knowledge across all levels of staff.	• Offer workshops on curriculum design and assessment methods. • Organise conferences and seminars with educational experts.
Collaborative planning	Encourage teachers and leaders to collaborate on curriculum development and refinement.	• Set up regular team meetings for curriculum review and planning. • Use collaborative tools (e.g., Google Docs, shared drives) for planning.
Mentorship and coaching	Pair experienced leaders with less experienced staff to guide and support curriculum leadership development.	• Assign senior teachers to mentor new teachers or middle leaders. • Provide instructional coaching to support curriculum leadership.
Clearly defined leadership roles	Establish specific roles for curriculum leaders at all levels to ensure clear ownership and accountability.	• Designate department heads, subject coordinators, or grade-level leads. • Create job descriptions outlining curriculum leadership responsibilities.
Shared leadership	Share leadership responsibilities across the staff to create a collective approach to curriculum management.	• Involve teachers in curriculum design and decision-making processes. • Empower middle leaders to take charge of key areas (e.g., assessment or pedagogy).
Evidence-based decision making	Use student performance data to inform curriculum decisions and leadership actions.	• Regularly analyse assessment data to adjust curriculum delivery. • Hold data meetings with teachers to discuss strategies based on student outcomes.

Regular feedback and reflection	Create a system for feedback and self-reflection to promote continuous improvement in curriculum leadership.	• Conduct regular staff surveys on curriculum effectiveness. • Hold reflection sessions after curriculum implementation to discuss challenges and successes.
Cross-institute collaboration	Encourage collaboration with other institutes or departments to expand ideas and approaches to curriculum leadership.	• Establish partnerships with neighbouring institutes for curriculum sharing. • Invite guest speakers or external educators for cross-institute discussions.
Recognition and incentives	Acknowledge and reward staff contributions to curriculum leadership and innovation.	• Implement staff awards for curriculum innovation. • Provide professional development grants or opportunities for outstanding leaders.

Table 1.3 - Practical strategies for fostering curriculum leadership

Such strategies encourage staff engagement, distribute responsibility, and build institutional resilience.

Balancing accountability with innovation

Accountability frameworks often prioritise measurable outcomes. However, fostering innovation requires flexibility. Harris (2011) identifies the principal as a mediator between these forces - upholding standards while enabling creative curriculum practices.

Case Study: Curriculum accountability
A secondary school implemented a cross-curricular project that integrated English, geography, and design technology to explore environmental sustainability. Students researched a local environmental issue, proposed solutions, and created physical or digital models to present their ideas. Through this approach, they developed critical skills such as research, collaboration, and creativity while meeting national curriculum standards for each subject.

> To maintain accountability, school leaders established clear objectives aligned with the curriculum. For instance, in English, students focused on persuasive writing to advocate for their solutions, while in geography, they analysed local data and proposed environmentally sound actions. In design technology, they applied principles of engineering and creativity to create prototypes. Traditional assessments such as written assignments and tests were complemented by innovative evaluations including group presentations, design reviews, and peer feedback sessions.
>
> The principal supported teachers in implementing this approach by providing professional development on interdisciplinary teaching methods, assessment strategies, and collaboration techniques. She also allocated time during planning periods for teachers from different departments to coordinate their lessons. Regular progress checks ensured that students met the required standards in all subjects while benefiting from a richer, more integrated learning experience.
>
> By encouraging innovation within the framework of national accountability systems, this secondary school principal has created opportunities for students to connect their learning across disciplines, preparing them for the complex, interconnected challenges of the modern world.

Strategies for building shared leadership

Shared curriculum leadership ensures that leadership is distributed across roles and functions. This not only improves curriculum relevance but also builds ownership among staff and promotes innovation.

Building leadership capacity at multiple levels

Spillane's (2006) distributed leadership model sees leadership as a collective endeavour. By identifying emerging leaders, principals can support professional growth through training, mentorship, and project-based leadership opportunities. Lambert (2002) advocates for teacher leadership as a foundation for shared responsibility in student achievement.

Enhancing ownership and engagement among staff

When staff contribute to curriculum design and review, they are more committed to its success. Participatory decision-making - highlighted by Fullan (2015) - improves both staff morale and curriculum quality.

A primary school rolling out a new literacy programme held co-design workshops where teachers collaborated on lesson plans. Their contributions were reflected in practice, fostering a sense of ownership and improving curriculum outcomes.

Strategies for effective delegation and support

Bush & Glover (2003) stress the importance of role clarity in leadership. Effective delegation involves not only assigning responsibility but also providing professional learning, time, and resources. Kotter (1996) highlights the need for a supportive environment to enable change.

Case Study: Shared curriculum leadership

Skeldale Primary, a large, multiple-entry primary school, implemented a collaborative approach to improve its science curriculum. Recognising the need for innovation, the head teacher established a curriculum leadership team comprising representatives from each year group.

The leadership team was tasked with reviewing the existing science curriculum, identifying gaps, and proposing changes to align it with the school's vision of fostering inquiry-based learning. Members attended professional development workshops on curriculum design and collaborated during weekly meetings to draft new lesson plans and assessment strategies. Teachers were encouraged to trial these lessons and provide feedback, creating a dynamic process of refinement.

To support the team, the head ensured access to resources such as science kits, training sessions, and dedicated planning time. Delegated responsibilities were clearly defined, with specific staff members leading on aspects like resource selection, lesson evaluation, and parent engagement. This collaborative effort resulted in a curriculum that not only met national standards but also sparked greater student interest in science.

The success of this initiative highlights the importance of building leadership capacity, enhancing ownership, and providing effective support for staff involved in curriculum management.

Challenges and considerations

Navigating resistance and conflict

Resistance to change and overlapping responsibilities can challenge shared leadership. Principals must establish clear communication channels, role definitions, and norms for collaboration. Change management literature (e.g., Kotter, 1996) advises cultivating trust and shared vision to overcome inertia.

Time constraints and capacity

Balancing teaching and leadership requires time management and institutional support. Principals can allocate protected time for planning and coordination, ensuring staff capacity for curriculum engagement.

Recognising existing curriculum leadership

Curriculum leadership is often inherently shared in many institutions - led by programme managers, module leaders, subject heads, and coordinators. These individuals already ensure curriculum quality and innovation. While formal distributed leadership models can enhance practice, they are not always essential. Many institutions achieve excellence without explicitly adopting such models. As Harris (2012) warns, poorly managed distributed leadership can lead to fragmentation. A context-sensitive approach is key: where staff leadership capacity is still growing or coherence is essential, a more centralised leadership model may be more effective.

Curriculum design

Curriculum design is a multi-layered process that involves the careful consideration of numerous elements, including objectives, content, pedagogy, assessment, and the needs of diverse learners. It is not a task reserved for a single individual or team; rather, it requires the collaborative input of curriculum leaders and stakeholders at all levels. Senior management sets the strategic vision and ensures alignment with institutional goals and external frameworks. Middle managers and subject or programme leaders operationalise this vision by shaping the curriculum to meet contextual needs, while teachers bring it to life in the classroom through their expertise and creativity. Effective curriculum design is therefore a shared responsibility, requiring ongoing dialogue, reflection, and adaptation to ensure that it is both practical and responsive to the ever-changing educational landscape.

The product model

The *product model,* also referred to as the *behavioural* or *objective model*, has become a dominant approach to curriculum development. This model follows a scientific process where objectives are defined, a plan is formulated, and outcomes (products) are measured. Originating from the works of Franklin Bobbitt and Ralph W. Tyler, it has gained significant influence in the UK since the late 1970s, particularly with the rise of vocationalism and an emphasis on competencies. This approach underpinned much of the debate around the National Curriculum in the 1980s and 1990s, where attention was often directed at objectives and content.

This model emphasises that curriculum planning must identify the abilities, attitudes, habits, appreciations, and knowledge that learners require. These elements become the objectives, and the curriculum consists of a series of experiences designed to meet these goals.

Tyler's rationale

Tyler's rationale for curriculum design (Figure 1.3) involves four key steps: diagnosing learner needs, creating learning experiences, organising them for maximum effect, and evaluating the process for continuous improvement (Tyler, 2009).

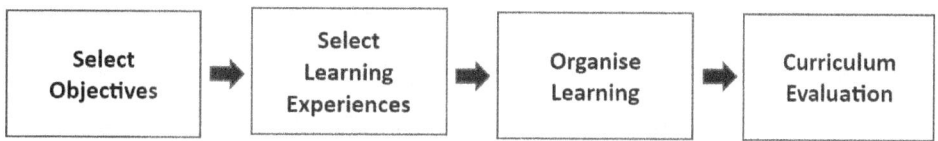

Figure 1.3 - Tyler's rationale for curriculum design

Select objectives

In this stage, objectives are obtained by examining the subject matter, the needs of the learner and contemporary life. Once objectives are identified, they are filtered through a philosophical screen before they are selected for inclusion in the curriculum.

Appendix 1 provides more detail on objectives and learner needs.

Select learning experiences

Tyler emphasises that learning experiences should be both motivating and achievable for learners. They must capture interest, encourage engagement, and be suited to the learner's level and prior knowledge. This makes learning meaningful, builds confidence, and supports deeper understanding.

Organise learning

Once selected, experiences must be organised in such a way as to maximise the effectiveness of the combined experiences. Sequencing of experiences, as well as the potential for subject integration, is considered in this stage.

Curriculum evaluation

This stage serves as a check to ensure the original objectives, as specified by the curriculum, were achieved. If not, then the previous stages can be revisited and adjusted as required.

In practice, senior managers may oversee the evaluation and alignment of institutional objectives with national or vocational standards. Middle managers, such as subject leaders, design competency-based learning experiences, while teachers contribute by delivering curriculum elements and providing feedback for improvement.

Other models of curriculum design include: *Taba's model of curriculum development*; *Bruner's spiral curriculum*; *Stenhouse's process model*; the *Constructivist approach* (Vygotsky and Piaget); the *Humanistic Model*; *Problem-Based Learning* (PBL); *Freire's critical pedagogy*; *UbD* (Understanding by Design); and the *Integrated Curriculum Model* (ICM).

While systematic and structured, the product model has limitations. Learners often have minimal input in shaping their educational experiences, which may stifle creativity and critical thinking. Teachers may also feel constrained by rigid objectives, as noted during early discussions of the National Curriculum under Prime Minister Jim Callaghan in 1976.

The process model

The *process* model, also called the *developmental* or *progressive model*, was first advanced by Lawrence Stenhouse (1975) as an alternative to the product model. It emphasises the experiences of teachers and learners, focusing on how learning occurs rather than what specific outcomes are achieved.

Senior management plays a role in promoting a culture where learner-centred approaches are valued and supported institutionally. Middle managers, such as heads of departments, facilitate professional development for teachers and ensure resources are available for flexible, responsive teaching. Teachers act as facilitators, guiding learners through participatory and exploratory activities that promote critical thinking and collaboration.

In this model, learning activities are central, and learners are encouraged to participate in decisions about the nature of these activities. Such an approach is particularly suited for curricula focused on social and life skills, but it also has relevance across other subject areas.

The strengths of the process model include its emphasis on active engagement from both teachers and learners, its focus on life skills, and its ability to adapt to learners' needs. However, it can neglect content specificity, making it challenging to apply in disciplines requiring precise knowledge.

Assessment in the process model is formative and diagnostic, occurring continuously throughout the learning process. Teachers, supported by middle management, play a critical role in designing and administering assessments that provide feedback to guide learning.

Learner-centred education

The process model calls for a shift from traditional teaching to facilitation, which has implications for teachers and institutional leaders alike.

- **Senior management**: Promotes institutional policies that value facilitation over didactic teaching, ensuring professional development for staff.
- **Middle management**: Develops frameworks for participatory learning and supports teachers in adopting these methods.
- **Teachers**: Transition from delivering pre-set curricula to facilitating learner-driven activities. They create an environment of trust and collaboration, using group discussions and practical activities to foster diverse viewpoints and shared learning experiences.

The distinctions between teaching and facilitating are outlined in Table 1.4.

Pedagogy	Teaching approach	Facilitating approach
Content delivery	Teachers follow a pre-set curriculum.	Facilitators adapt to learners' needs and contexts.
Methodology	Teaching often involves information flowing from teacher to student.	Facilitators build equal, trust-based relationships with learners.
Relationship dynamics	Teachers maintain formal relationships based on authority.	Facilitators build equal, trust-based relationships with learners.

Table 1.4 - Distinctions between teaching and facilitating

By valuing learners' input and encouraging different perspectives, the process model supports a more inclusive, adaptive educational experience, which requires contributions from all levels of management and teaching staff to succeed effectively.

 **Examples of product and process models in use**

The product model

1. *Vocational training programmes, such as courses certifying electricians:* Specific competencies, like wiring circuits or interpreting electrical codes, are identified as objectives. The curriculum is structured to deliver necessary knowledge and skills through workshops, simulations, and assessments. Outcomes are measured against standardised criteria to confirm learners meet required competencies, reflecting the systematic, outcome-focused nature of the product model.

2. *Secondary school mathematics courses preparing students for standardised exams like GCSEs or SATs:* Objectives, such as mastering skills like solving quadratic equations or calculating probabilities, guide curriculum design. Lessons are structured step-by-step with exercises and tests to measure progress against predefined criteria. Success is evaluated through summative assessments, aligning with the product model's emphasis on measurable objectives and results.

The process model

1. *Social and emotional learning (SEL) programmes aim to develop students' interpersonal and self-regulation skills:* Instead of fixed outcomes, the curriculum emphasises meaningful experiences, such as group discussions, role-playing, and reflective journaling. Teachers facilitate activities that encourage exploration and collaboration. Assessment is formative, providing feedback to deepen understanding and real-world application, prioritising engagement and growth over predefined results.

2. *Primary school project-based learning activities on environmental awareness:* Pupils could explore reducing school waste collaboratively. Instead of a rigid curriculum, teachers facilitate curiosity and guide topics like recycling or composting. Activities might include visiting recycling centres, creating posters, or presenting findings. Formative assessments with ongoing feedback refine ideas and develop problem-solving and teamwork skills, emphasising the learning process over fixed objectives.

Question — How do you decide whether product or process is more important? Do you think that curriculum design sometimes, emphasises the wrong model? For example, a secondary school might prioritise the process model over the product model. As a result, methods like group discussions and project-based learning can overshadow clear academic goals and outcomes. While engaging, these methods may leave students unsure about what they need to achieve, complicating progress assessment for teachers.

Curriculum leaders, such as subject coordinators, play a key role in balancing engaging strategies with defined objectives. They must align the curriculum with clear outcomes and regularly review it to ensure effective learning and measurable results. As Suskie (2009, p155) argues, "Every assignment should help students achieve important learning goals ".

The backward design process

Many educators plan lessons by relying on textbooks, familiar activities, and long-standing practices, rather than aligning these tools with specific goals or standards. However, the most effective curricular approaches utilise *backward design* (Wiggins & McTighe, 2005), which prioritises starting with the end in mind. A classic example of this approach is Tyler's Rationale.

In backward design, the process begins by identifying the desired learning outcomes or goals. From these, the curriculum is systematically developed to ensure those goals are met. Educational objectives serve as the foundation for selecting materials, organising content, designing instructional strategies, and creating assessments, ensuring every component supports the targeted outcomes.

Curriculum frameworks

What is a curriculum framework?

In designing curriculum, educational institutions often use curriculum frameworks to streamline and standardise the process. These frameworks may encompass an entire programme of study or address specific components, ensuring consistency in what learners are taught across different contexts.

Curriculum frameworks primarily serve as structured guides to assist teachers and curriculum managers in making informed decisions. They provide a cohesive structure that integrates various curriculum elements, ensuring alignment with learning objectives and improving educational outcomes. Frameworks also play a critical role in curriculum review and development, ensuring that content remains relevant and effective.

Senior management, such as heads of education or policymakers, often oversee the adoption of curriculum frameworks, ensuring alignment with institutional goals and compliance with regional or national guidelines. Middle management, including programme and subject leaders, typically use these frameworks to design or revise course structures. Teachers, supported by curriculum managers, apply the framework in their lesson planning and classroom delivery, tailoring it to meet learners' needs.

Composition of curriculum frameworks

A curriculum framework encompasses a group of related subjects, themes, or topics within a specific domain, structured according to predetermined criteria to cover the area of study comprehensively. These frameworks provide:

- *Structure and guidance* for subject design.
- *Rationale and policy context* for curriculum development.

Frameworks are often statutory documents produced at national or regional levels to ensure consistency in general education, establish benchmarks for academic standards in further and higher education, and guide vocational qualification standards.

Typical elements of a curriculum framework document are presented in Table 1.5.

Element	Composition
Rationale	Principles and assumptions upon which the framework is based.
Scope and parameters	Outlining the breadth of the curriculum area.
Goals and purposes	Broad objectives for subjects.
Guidelines for course design	Practical tools for middle managers and teachers.
Content	Key subject matter.
Teaching and learning principles	Pedagogical strategies for classroom application.
Evaluation guidelines	Criteria for assessing subjects.
Accreditation and certification criteria	Standards for subject recognition.
Future developments	Forward-looking recommendations for the curriculum area.

Table 1.5 - Typical elements of a curriculum framework

Effective frameworks link theory with practice, ensuring the inclusion of relevant pedagogy, contemporary learning strategies, and appropriate resources. They enable senior management to maintain strategic alignment, middle management to implement operational goals, and teachers to deliver meaningful learning experiences to students.

Examples of UK national frameworks
- Statutory Framework for the Early Years Foundation Stage.
- National Curriculum.
- Higher Education Subject Benchmarks.

Levels of understanding

When discussing the statutory curriculum for primary and secondary schools, Male (2012a, 2012b) argues that curriculum design goes beyond simply listing what pupils are expected to learn. It encompasses the entire set of learning experiences that they engage with as they progress through school. He identifies three *levels of understanding* the curriculum:

1. The curriculum set out by the nation: the national expectations of what young people should learn.
2. The curriculum set out by the school or teacher: how national expectations are adapted to be relevant to the specific pupils in a school or class.
3. The curriculum as experienced by the pupils, which can vary from pupil to pupil, even within the same class.

Male's framework can also be loosely applied to other learning contexts, such as post-16 education and private sector training, where national influence may be less pronounced, especially in the latter. Therefore, when designing curriculum, the application of a rationale like Ralph Tyler's will differ based on the institution's nature and the role of each practitioner.

Curriculum organisation

Learning should not be seen merely as the achievement of isolated objectives but as the cumulative attainment of outcomes that result from interconnected objectives. It also involves fostering changes in attitudes and behaviour, making learning a long-term process rather than a short-term event. Effective learning unfolds over time, emphasising the need for careful planning and organisation of educational experiences.

For educational experiences to have a meaningful cumulative impact, they must be systematically organised to reinforce one another. This organisation plays a critical role in curriculum development and implementation, influencing both the efficiency and effectiveness of teaching and learning.

Vertical and horizontal relationships

The organisation of learning experiences involves two key types of relationships: *vertical* (across time) and *horizontal* (across areas of study). Vertical relationships refer to the progression of learning within a subject over time - for example, the way KS4 Science builds on KS3 Science in UK secondary schools. Horizontal relationships, by contrast, concern the connections between different subjects taught at the same stage, such as KS3 History and KS3 Geography.

Both types of relationships are essential for achieving a coherent and cumulative educational impact. A well-designed vertical relationship ensures that later learning builds logically on earlier content without unnecessary repetition, allowing students to deepen and extend their knowledge and skills. Care must be taken to avoid excessive overlap in vertical progression, which can lead to disengagement or a sense of redundancy.

Similarly, strong horizontal links between subjects can enhance understanding and foster interdisciplinary thinking. When History and Geography at KS3 are thoughtfully connected, they can reinforce each other, contributing to a more integrated and meaningful educational experience. In contrast, weak or absent connections - whether vertical or horizontal - can fragment students' learning and diminish the overall effectiveness of the curriculum.

Effective organisation

To create an effectively organised curriculum, three key criteria must be addressed: *continuity*, *sequence*, and *integration*.

Continuity: Involves the repeated emphasis of major curriculum elements over time. For example, if a Science objective is to "develop a meaningful concept of energy," this concept should be revisited and reinforced across consecutive stages of the Science curriculum. This ensures that foundational ideas are consistently built upon, making continuity a critical factor in effective vertical organisation.

Sequence: Builds on continuity by ensuring that each new learning experience progresses logically from the previous one. Instead of mere repetition, the focus is on deepening and expanding understanding. For instance, in Mathematics, KS2 students develop number skills by solving problems involving three-digit numbers using number facts, place value, and complex addition or subtraction. This builds upon the simpler two-digit problem-solving skills learned in KS1.

Integration: Focuses on the horizontal relationship between curriculum experiences. It aims to help students develop a unified understanding and consistent application of their learning across subjects. For example, spoken language skills taught in KS3 and KS4 English can also be applied in other subjects like History or Geography, as well as in real-life situations. This cross-curricular approach enhances the overall coherence of the educational programme.

Organising threads

An essential step in curriculum organisation is identifying the overarching elements, or *organising threads*, that weave through the curriculum. These threads highlight core concepts and skills deemed fundamental and are revisited with increasing complexity as students progress.

Examples

- **Mathematics**: Number; Addition and subtraction; Multiplication and division; Fractions, decimals, percentages, ratio, and proportion; Algebra; Statistics; Measurement; and Geometry.
- **History**: Historical enquiry; Interpretations of history; Change and continuity; Cause and consequence; Diversity; and Significance.
- **Music**: Performance; Composing; Listening and appraising; Musical notation; Musical forms and structures; and Cultural and historical context.

Students are introduced to these threads early in their education, and their understanding deepens as they move through successive stages of learning.

Organising threads can also foster *reinforcement*. For instance, the concept of place value in Mathematics can extend into its applications in Science or Design and Technology, as well as in practical, everyday scenarios. This reinforces learning across disciplines, creating a cohesive educational experience.

Subject-based or integrated curricula?

Curriculum design can take various forms, each with distinct approaches to organising learning experiences. Three notable models - Subject-Based, Coordinated, and Integrated Curricula - offer contrasting methods for structuring content and fostering student understanding.

Subject-based curriculum centres on individual disciplines, maintaining clear boundaries between them. Each subject is taught independently, with its own distinct objectives, content, and methods. For example, Mathematics, History, and Biology are delivered as separate entities in schools, emphasising depth and mastery within each domain. This traditional model prioritises specialised knowledge but may limit opportunities for students to see connections across fields.

In contrast, *coordinated curriculum* seeks to create connections between subjects while preserving their individual identities. Different disciplines are linked by a shared theme or topic, fostering interdependence and mutual reinforcement. For instance, a study on climate change might coordinate Geography, Science, and Economics, allowing students to explore the topic through multiple disciplinary lenses. While retaining subject-specific boundaries, this model promotes complementary relationships and helps learners develop a more holistic understanding of complex issues.

Integrated curriculum takes a step further by merging subjects into a unified area of study. Individual disciplines lose their distinct identities, and learning revolves around interdisciplinary themes or projects. For example, a unit on "Sustainable Living" might blend aspects of Science, Technology, and Social Studies into a seamless learning experience. Integration can occur at various levels - intra-disciplinary (within a field), inter-disciplinary (across fields), or multi-disciplinary (drawing from multiple domains). This approach emphasises collaboration, critical thinking, and real-world application but may risk diluting the depth of subject-specific knowledge.

Modularisation and credit transfer

Integration of subjects may also be influenced by *modularisation*. Most universities and colleges group their learning into stand-alone modules, which each carry a currency of credits (typically 20 credits per standard module in higher education). The idea is that credits can be transferred between learning institutes, or between programmes within the same institute, so that students are not committed to any one single programme, college or university (or indeed to a single country). For example, the UK has a *Credit Accumulation and Transfer Scheme* (CATS) and accumulated credits are referred to as *CATS credits* or *CATS points*.

Whilst the modular approach has many advantages, it can make it very difficult to integrate learning across boundaries which are effectively dynamic.

Key skills

Many programmes of study include a set of key skills which serve to augment the subject areas and act also as life skills. They go by many names which differ from one context to another and from one country to another. Some of the familiar ones are *core skills*, *functional skills* and *transferable skills*. They tend to be grouped into personal skills (such as self-awareness, relating to others, communication, working with others, decision-making and social awareness) and learning skills (such as critical thinking, problem-solving, creativity, application of number and technology).

You will find these skills embedded into the frameworks of the National Curriculum and into programmes of further and higher education in many countries. The competencies are often spread across a number of subjects as depicted in Table 1.6.

	English	Maths	Science	History	Geography	Art	Music
Problem Solving		X	X				
Teamwork				X			X
Critical Thinking	X	X	X		X		
Creativity	X					X	X
Communication	X			X	X		X

Table 1.6 - Key skills competencies

The problem, then, is deciding for which subject each competency is best covered without the competencies themselves becoming isolated from each other. For example, it is surely difficult to be in a team without communicating with each other. One solution would be to adopt a multi-disciplinary, integrated approach to learning and include a number of projects, each of which involve all of the competencies. Indeed, the projects themselves could be integrated in order to further reinforce learning and to help 'knit' a complete course or programme together.

Case Study: Introducing a Communication Skills curriculum

Conniston Secondary School followed the curriculum design process to introduce a new Communication Skills curriculum for its Year 9 students.

1. Needs analysis

The school identified a gap in students' ability to express ideas effectively, collaborate, and participate in group discussions - skills critical for academic and career success.

- *Stakeholder input:* Feedback was gathered from teachers, students, parents, and local employers, highlighting a lack of emphasis on soft skills in the current curriculum.
- *Data collection:* A review of student outcomes in group-based projects, written assignments, visual displays (such as posters) and oral presentations showed below-average performance in some aspects.

- *Policy review:* The National Curriculum's emphasis on preparing students for work and life underpinned the decision to prioritise communication skills.

2. Course design

A multidisciplinary team was formed to design the Communication Skills course.

- *Objectives:* The course aimed to enhance verbal and non-verbal communication, active listening, and digital communication etiquette.
- *Frameworks:* Tyler's model guided the design, focusing on clear objectives, aligned teaching methods, and assessments (Tyler, 2009).
- *Content development:* Modules included public speaking, teamwork exercises, persuasive writing, and conflict resolution.

3. Measuring intent

The school outlined the course's purpose and success criteria in a curriculum intent document:

- *Vision statement:* To equip students with essential communication skills for academic success, future employment, and personal growth.
- *Alignment:* Objectives aligned with the school's broader mission of developing well-rounded individuals.
- *Success indicators:* Indicators included improved student confidence, higher engagement in discussions, and positive feedback from stakeholders.
- *Stakeholder review:* Drafts were reviewed by teachers and external partners to ensure relevance and feasibility. Two potential issues were identified and addressed: vagueness in success indicators making progress difficult to assess; and misalignment with practical needs - overlooking specific priorities such as digital communication or cultural relevancy.

4. Course implementation

- *Teacher training:* Teachers attended workshops on active learning strategies and communication skill pedagogy.
- *Pilot phase:* The course was piloted with Year 9 students over one term, using a blended learning approach.
- *Resource allocation:* Classrooms were equipped with audiovisual tools to support presentation and discussion activities.

5. Measuring implementation

The school monitored delivery to ensure fidelity to the course design:

- *Observation:* Senior leaders conducted classroom observations to assess teaching quality.
- *Feedback mechanisms:* Regular surveys collected input from teachers and students on course delivery challenges.
- *Issues identified:* A number of issues arose including the competence of teachers in using certain technologies. Many teachers felt intimidated by students who were more aware and more adept at using current software.

- *Intervention:* Adjustments were made, such as providing additional training for teachers struggling with the new methods and involving students themselves in the teaching process.

6. Assessing students

- *Formative assessments:* A range of activities, including peer-reviewed presentations, collaborative projects, quizzes, and reflective journals, provided opportunities for ongoing feedback and skill development.
- *Summative assessments:* Students were evaluated through their usual range of assessments in other subjects including group debates, written reports, presentations and multimedia projects, all graded against standardised rubrics.
- *Additional metrics:* Participation in class discussions, self-assessment surveys, and peer evaluations offered further insights into student progress, ensuring a comprehensive understanding of learning outcomes.

7. Measuring impact

The school evaluated the course's effectiveness:

- *Student outcomes:* Analysis showed a marked improvement in written and oral communication skills, as evidenced by assessment results.
- *Stakeholder feedback:* Parents and teachers noted increased confidence in students' communication abilities.
- *Evaluation frameworks:* Stufflebeam's CIPP model guided the evaluation, emphasising both process and outcomes (Madaus et al., 1983).
- *Long-term tracking:* The school plans to monitor how the skills transfer to other subjects and extracurricular activities.

The case study illustrates how Conniston School successfully introduced a bespoke Communication Skills curriculum for Year 9 students, responding to a clearly identified need for enhanced soft skills, as highlighted through stakeholder consultations and analysis of student performance data. The course was thoughtfully developed using Tyler's model of curriculum design, ensuring that the content and objectives were relevant, purposeful, and aligned with both school priorities and broader national educational goals.

Implementation was strategic and inclusive, beginning with a pilot phase and dedicated teacher training. Initial challenges - particularly around teacher confidence in integrating technology - were met with timely support measures and proactive student involvement, which helped to build momentum and ownership among both staff and learners.

A balanced approach to assessment, incorporating both formative and summative methods, along with ongoing feedback from key stakeholders, provided robust evidence of improved student communication skills and increased self-confidence. Underpinned by the *CIPP evaluation model*, the initiative was marked by careful planning, flexible delivery, and a clear, measurable impact - demonstrating a successful blend of theory-informed practice and responsive educational leadership.

Activity: Curriculum design in action

The purpose of this activity is to apply the principles and strategies covered in this chapter to a practical scenario.

Identify a subject area or course you are familiar with. Consider the effectiveness of the existing curriculum design / update process and how you might improve it. Questions to consider include:

1. What are the key components of the curriculum, and are they clearly identified?
2. How effective is the current curriculum design cycle in this context?
3. How well does the curriculum address *intent*, *implementation*, and *impact*?
4. What support systems are in place to aid curriculum design and implementation?
5. Who manages the curriculum, and how effective are they in their role(s)?
6. How do national-level policies or guidelines influence the curriculum?
7. What role do local authorities play in shaping or supporting the curriculum?
8. How does institutional leadership influence the curriculum design process?
9. What role does departmental leadership play in curriculum management?
10. How do individual educators contribute to the curriculum's design and success?
11. What external influences (e.g., policies, assessments, global trends) impact curriculum decisions?
12. What internal constraints (e.g., resources, staff, culture) affect curriculum design?
13. How do global influences shape the curriculum in this subject or course?
14. How do you balance external influences and internal constraints in the curriculum?
15. What role does the principal or institutional leader play in curriculum management?
16. How is curriculum management shared among staff and stakeholders?
17. Is the curriculum design based on a product model, process model, or a mix?
18. How effectively does the curriculum follow Tyler's rationale or other frameworks?
19. How well do curriculum frameworks support clarity and coherence?
20. How is the curriculum organised, and does this meet the needs of learners?

Summary

The concept of curriculum encompasses the planned learning experiences provided to learners. Its definition extends beyond content, incorporating purpose, delivery, and outcomes. Key components include objectives, content, teaching methods, and assessment strategies, all integral to the curriculum design cycle. This cycle ensures a coherent process from intent to implementation and impact, supported by systems that enable effective delivery and evaluation.

Curriculum leadership involves various stakeholders across different levels. At the national level, governments and policymakers set overarching goals, while local authorities provide regional support. Institutional leadership, particularly principals, plays a pivotal role in adapting these goals to the school context, ensuring alignment with broader objectives. Departmental leaders translate these into subject-specific frameworks, and individual educators contribute to effective delivery through their expertise and creativity.

Curriculum leaders operate within a web of influences and constraints. External influences include policy changes, examination requirements, and global trends, while internal constraints may involve resource limitations, staff capacity, and organisational culture. Balancing these factors requires strategic decision-making to maintain coherence and relevance in the curriculum.

Two primary curriculum design models guide this process: the product model, exemplified by Tyler's rationale, emphasises clear objectives and measurable outcomes, whereas the process model values flexibility, focusing on learner experiences and development. Curriculum frameworks provide structure, ensuring consistency and clarity. Organising the curriculum effectively, whether through traditional subjects or interdisciplinary approaches, is essential for meeting diverse learner needs.

Principals play a key role in shared curriculum leadership, fostering collaboration and distributing leadership. By integrating institutional vision with the practicalities of curriculum design and implementation, they create a dynamic system that supports continuous improvement. Overall, effective curriculum leadership requires balancing global trends, local needs, and individual contributions to achieve impactful educational outcomes.

2 EFFECTIVE ASSESSMENT STRATEGIES

David Hall

Introduction

Assessment is a key component of educational practice. It influences how learners engage with their studies, how educators design and deliver their teaching, and how institutions define and measure success. But assessment is not simply a technical exercise - it is a deeply human process that reflects the values, priorities, and aspirations of an educational community. When thoughtfully led, assessment becomes a powerful tool to promote learning, enhance equity, and inform improvement at every level.

Leading assessment in education involves navigating complex challenges. Leaders must balance the demands of external accountability with the needs of individual learners, manage tensions between consistency and innovation, and ensure that assessment practices remain fair, inclusive, and meaningful. Strong leadership in this area requires a clear educational vision, an understanding of both formative and summative approaches, and the ability to build trust and shared responsibility among staff.

This chapter:
- Investigates the purpose, principles, and types of assessment, including formative, summative, diagnostic, and dynamic approaches.
- Describes the design and implementation of effective assessment strategies that align with learning objectives and cater to diverse learner needs.
- Critiques the quality of assessment tools and methods, ensuring validity, reliability, and fairness.
- Analyses the development and leadership of assessment policies and processes, including standardisation, moderation, and feedback systems.
- Evaluates the use of technology in enhancing assessment design, delivery, and analysis while addressing accessibility challenges.
- Investigates the role of leadership in fostering a culture of continuous improvement and innovation in assessment practices.
- Examines the navigation of external assessment frameworks, policies, and standards in order to meet institutional and accreditation requirements.
- Discusses how to engage with stakeholders effectively, balancing their roles and expectations in the assessment process.

The foundations of assessment

Assessment is a critical component of the educational landscape, influencing both teaching and learning processes. It is the process by which educators measure students' progress, understanding, and achievements. The purpose of assessment extends beyond simply assigning grades; it is integral in shaping instructional strategies, informing curriculum design, and driving continuous improvement in educational practices.

What is assessment?

Assessment refers to the process of gathering, interpreting, and utilising information about learners' achievements to make informed decisions about their educational progress. In UK education, assessment serves both as a tool for gauging student performance and as a means to support learners in their development. It involves a range of activities, from formal examinations to more informal methods such as observation and feedback (Black & Wiliam, 2009). The UK educational system has placed a significant emphasis on assessment at all stages of learning, from primary education through to higher education, with a focus on ensuring that assessments accurately reflect students' knowledge and skills.

Why do we assess?

The primary purposes of assessment are to monitor progress, support learning, and inform educational decisions. For students, assessments help identify areas of strength and areas requiring further development, thereby guiding their learning journey. For educators, assessments inform teaching strategies, enabling them to adapt and tailor instruction to meet the needs of individual learners. At a broader level, assessments help to ensure that educational standards are met and maintained, providing stakeholders such as parents, school leaders, and policymakers with valuable insights into the quality of education being delivered (Murchan & Shiel, 2024). In addition, assessments play a role in accountability, ensuring that learners meet the required standards for progression and qualifications, such as GCSEs or A-levels.

Principles of effective assessment

To be effective, assessment must adhere to several key principles that underpin its effectiveness, ensuring it is fair, accurate, and supportive of student learning. These principles guide educators in designing assessments that not only measure student progress reliably, but also provide valuable insights for improving teaching and learning. By adhering to these principles, educators can create an inclusive and transparent assessment process that meets the diverse needs of all learners and fosters their development. Here is a summary of the key principles:

Suitability: An assessment should align with its intended purpose and be straightforward to administer. It must suit the subject matter, the context, and the learners' developmental level, ensuring it is neither too simple nor overly complex. For example, a diagnostic assessment might focus on identifying gaps in knowledge, while a summative assessment evaluates overall achievement.

Reliability, validity, and objectivity: Effective assessments must be reliable (consistent results over time and across assessors), valid (accurately measuring what they are intended to measure), and objective (free from personal biases). Clear criteria and standardised administration procedures contribute to maintaining these qualities.

Inclusivity: Assessments should accommodate the diversity of learners, ensuring they are accessible to all, including students with special educational needs or disabilities. This involves using plain language, providing alternative formats where needed, and avoiding cultural or linguistic biases.

Evaluation: Assessments should be used to regularly review and analyse student performance across a variety of assessment methods to identify potential biases or inequities. This helps to ensure that no particular group of students is disadvantaged due to the format, content, or delivery of the assessment.

Feedback: Feedback should be timely, specific, and constructive, offering students clear guidance on their strengths and areas for improvement. It plays a critical role in helping students understand their progress and how they can meet their learning objectives.

Information

Too much feedback can be negative because it may overwhelm students, decrease motivation, blur focus, and create dependency on external input rather than promoting self-assessment. A more proactive approach would be to offer specific, constructive guidance for future improvement, focusing on actionable suggestions to help students enhance their performance moving forward. This is often termed *feedforward*.

Evidence: Assessment serves as a tool to gather meaningful evidence about students' knowledge, skills, and understanding. This information allows educators to make informed decisions about teaching strategies and adjust the curriculum to better meet the needs of their learners. Assessments should provide ample data to make well-founded judgments about a student's abilities or competencies. A single test or task may not be sufficient; combining multiple forms of evidence often yields a more accurate picture.

Integrated: Assessment should not be seen as a separate process but integrated seamlessly within the teaching and learning cycle. Ongoing formative assessments can guide instruction and ensure that learning activities are responsive to student progress and needs.

Communication: Assessment results should be communicated transparently and ethically, ensuring that students understand their performance. Clear reporting fosters trust and allows students and their guardians to engage meaningfully with the learning process.

Types of assessment

Assessment methods can be broadly categorised into several types, each serving distinct purposes and yielding different kinds of data. These include *summative, formative, diagnostic, dynamic, synoptic,* and others such as *criterion-referenced* and *norm-referenced* assessments. These are summarised in Table 2.1.

Assessment type	Characteristics
Summative assessment *(Assessment of learning)*	Evaluations that occur at the end of an instructional period to determine whether learning objectives have been achieved. Often called *assessment of* learning. Common examples include final exams, end-of-year tests, or summative coursework. The primary purpose of summative assessment is to provide a final judgement on students' performance, usually resulting in grades or scores that contribute to their overall academic record. In the UK, summative assessments such as GCSEs and A-levels play a crucial role in determining a student's future educational path (Murchan & Shiel, 2024).
Formative assessment *(Assessment for learning)*	Conducted during the learning process they are intended to provide feedback that helps students improve. Often referred to as *assessment for learning*, these assessments can take many forms, including quizzes, peer assessments, and teacher observations. Formative assessment is often used to identify areas where learners may need additional support or intervention. In the UK, the use of formative

	assessment strategies such as ongoing teacher feedback has been shown to improve learning outcomes, particularly when students are provided with clear guidance on how to improve (Black & Wiliam, 2009).
Baseline assessment	Establishes a starting point for measuring progress by providing a general overview of students' skills, knowledge, or abilities at the beginning of a course, term, or academic year. It is often used to set benchmarks or to evaluate the effectiveness of teaching by comparing results later (e.g., with formative or summative assessments). For example, testing pupils' reading levels at the start of the school year.
Diagnostic assessment	Used to identify learners' existing knowledge, skills, and misconceptions before new learning begins. These assessments can help educators tailor their teaching to better meet the needs of their students. For example, diagnostic tests at the beginning of a course can help identify gaps in knowledge that may need to be addressed before moving on to more complex content.
Dynamic assessment	Refers to a form of assessment that integrates both evaluation and support within the same process. It is often used to assess the potential for learning rather than just measuring current abilities. Dynamic assessment focuses on the processes involved in learning, allowing educators to gauge how well students can learn with guidance. This approach aligns with the theory of Vygotsky (1978), who emphasised the importance of the *Zone of Proximal Development* (ZPD) in shaping learning experiences.
Synoptic assessment	Involves assessing students' ability to integrate and apply knowledge and skills from different areas of study. This type of assessment encourages students to make connections between previously learned material and demonstrate their ability to synthesise information from various domains. It is often used in higher education contexts, where students are required to analyse and apply a broad range of knowledge.
Criterion referenced	Measures a student's performance against a fixed set of criteria or learning objectives. The focus is on whether the learner has achieved specific goals or standards. For example, in GCSE and A-level examinations, students are assessed based on how well they meet predefined criteria, with a clear distinction between different levels of achievement.

Norm referenced	Compares a student's performance to that of a larger group or population. This approach is often used in standardised testing and aims to rank students in relation to each other. In the UK, this method is used in various contexts, such as in university admissions or the use of percentile rankings in certain national assessments.
Value-added assessment	Focuses on measuring the progress that students make over time, rather than just their final level of achievement. This approach takes into account the starting point of each student and evaluates how much they have learned during a specific period. Value-added models are increasingly used in the UK to assess the effectiveness of schools or educational programmes, as they consider student progress rather than just achievement (Rivkin et al., 2005).

Table 2.1 - Assessment types

Manging assessment

Assessment management is integral to the effective operation of educational institutions, ensuring that assessment processes are clear, fair, and contribute to continuous improvement in student learning. It ensures that assessments are aligned with curriculum goals and contribute to the overall quality of education.

Assessment managers

The management of assessments varies significantly between educational organisations depending on their size and type. In large institutions, such as universities, multi-campus schools, the military and public services such as the NHS, assessment management often involves centralised offices with dedicated teams overseeing policy development, quality assurance, and logistical coordination.

In contrast, smaller organisations, such as primary schools, secondary schools or small colleges, often rely on a more localised, teacher-led approach with fewer administrative layers and simpler systems.

Regulatory requirements, stakeholder expectations, and available resources all influence how assessments are designed, delivered, and reviewed. As a result, practices vary widely - from standardised, centralised systems in larger organisations to more flexible, locally managed approaches in smaller settings. This diversity highlights the need for assessment to be both purposeful and adaptable to each organisation's specific goals and context.

Assessment management in a large organisation

Managing assessments in a large organisation requires a structured approach involving multiple levels of administration, clear roles, and robust processes. Below is an outline of a typical setup:

Centralised assessment office

Usually led by an *Assessment Officer*, the office coordinates, assures quality, and ensures the smooth execution of assessments. The team establishes the assessment strategy, aligning it with institutional goals and external standards (e.g., government policies and accreditation requirements). Procedures, ethical considerations, and quality measures are clearly defined. All assessment-related activities (including exam supervision) are overseen to ensure policy adherence. The office also manages the receipt, logging, and secure storage of assessments. Assessment data is handled, statistical analyses conducted, and reports produced to support decision-making. Scheduling, venues, and materials are efficiently coordinated.

On completion of an assessment process, the centralised assessment office validates, approves and communicates results, ensuring consistent and fair grading practices and handling disputes regarding assessment outcomes. It also endeavours to achieve continuous improvement by reflecting on and refining assessment practices (based on data collected from students, staff, and external stakeholders).

Faculty/department-level management

At faculty/department level, heads of department and programme leaders are responsible for the implementation and customisation of assessments. They adapt centralised policies to fit specific programmes, ensuring assessments align with curriculum objectives. They monitor assessment quality, ensure consistency across modules, and handle disputes or anomalies. They design, deliver, and coordinate the marking of assessments, providing grades and formative feedback to students.

Faculty/department assessment managers also play their part in the quality assurance process. They maintain assessment standards and integrity through internal moderation and external examination and monitor for plagiarism, cheating, and other violations.

Technology support

Larger organisations typically use advanced technologies, such as Learning Management Systems (LMS) and data analytics, to handle high volumes of assessments and provide detailed insights. The technology support team facilitates and administrates the use of digital tools. It manages platforms like *Blackboard*, *Canvas*, or *Moodle*, where assessments are delivered and graded. It ensures technological infrastructure supports online assessments, secure submission, and plagiarism detection tools.

Support services

Support services assist staff and students in navigating assessment processes. They provide guidance on assessment policies. They ensure accessibility through accommodations such as extra time, alternative formats, or assistive technologies. They equip students with strategies for exam preparation and academic writing.

Assessment management in a small organisation

Assessment management in a small educational organisation will differ significantly in complexity, resources, and approach. The principal or head teacher often takes a hands-on role in managing assessments, supported by a minimal leadership team. They ensure alignment with national standards such as the Early Years Foundation Stage (EYFS) Framework and Key Stage 1 (KS1) / Key Stage 2 (KS2) statutory assessments. They collaborate on setting priorities for formative and summative assessments. The main differences for small organisations are summarised as follows:

- Teachers are heavily involved in all aspects of assessment, from design to grading. They often collaborate informally with peers for quality assurance. In primary schools, *class teachers* lead assessment processes within their classrooms, including designing formative assessments and implementing summative evaluations such as SATs (Standard Assessment Tests). *Subject leads* (in larger primary schools) may oversee specific curriculum areas, ensuring assessments align with subject goals and national expectations.
- They are flexible and can quickly adapt assessment practices to meet student needs.
- They excel in personalised feedback and direct communication with students and parents, thanks to close teacher-student relationships.
- They may have reduced access to technology and rely on basic tools like spreadsheets or Google Classroom. IT support is limited.
- They will rely more on statutory assessment instruments such as *Reception Baseline Assessment* (RBA) and *Statutory SATs*.
- Administrative tasks such as scheduling and record-keeping are managed by generalist staff using systems like *SIMS* (School Information Management System).
- Quality assurance relies on informal peer moderation with occasional external reviews.

The assessment cycle

The assessment cycle (Figure 2.1) is a fundamental component of educational practice, encompassing baseline, formative, and summative assessments.

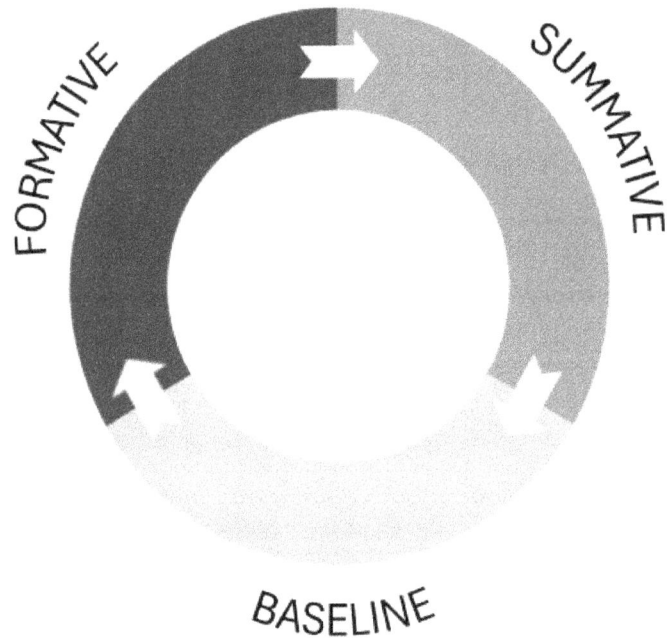

Figure 2.1 - The assessment cycle

While predominantly used in schools, this simple cycle is equally valuable in other contexts such as further and higher education, professional training, corporate settings, healthcare, and military or aviation training (see Appendix 2).

Its adaptability lies in its structured approach to: establish starting points by identifying prior knowledge or skills; provide ongoing feedback to guide improvement; and to evaluate cumulative outcomes for grading, certification, or performance reviews. Each stage of the cycle serves a distinct purpose in evaluating and enhancing student learning.

Baseline assessment

Baseline assessment, also known as *placement* or *initial assessment*, is conducted before instruction begins to determine students' existing knowledge and skills. This diagnostic tool enables educators to tailor teaching strategies to meet individual needs, ensuring that instruction is appropriately challenging and supportive. Baseline assessment is essential for positioning students at the correct point in an instructional sequence, thereby facilitating effective learning pathways (Meechan et al., 2022).

Formative assessment

Formative assessment occurs during the instructional process and is designed to monitor student learning, providing ongoing feedback that can be used by instructors to improve their teaching and by students to enhance their learning. This type of assessment is integral to adaptive teaching methods, allowing for real-time adjustments to address learning gaps. Black & Wiliam (1998) emphasise that formative assessment, or *assessment for learning*, is crucial for raising educational standards through active engagement with student progress.

Summative assessment

Summative assessment or *assessment of learning* takes place at the end of an instructional period, such as the conclusion of a unit, course, or academic term. Its primary purpose is to evaluate student learning by comparing it against a standard or benchmark. Summative assessments are typically *high stakes*, i.e., they carry significant consequences for students. They include final exams or major projects, and are used to assign grades or determine proficiency. While they provide a comprehensive overview of student achievement, they are less effective for informing day-to-day instructional adjustments. Stake (1967) illustrates the distinction between formative and summative assessments with the analogy: "When the cook tastes the soup, that's formative; when the customer tastes the soup, that's summative."

Integration of assessment types

Effective educational practice requires the integration of all three assessment types within the assessment cycle. Baseline assessments inform the starting point for instruction, formative assessments guide ongoing teaching strategies, and summative assessments evaluate the overall effectiveness of the instructional programme. McTighe & O'Connor (2005) advocate for the use of varied assessment practices to support student learning, emphasising the importance of clear criteria and continuous feedback.

> **Case Study: Assessing mathematics in a secondary school**
> Riverwood Secondary School is an urban school with a diverse student body. The school employs a range of assessment strategies in its mathematics department to ensure that students develop a deep understanding of

> mathematical concepts and are prepared for further education. The department uses baseline, formative, and summative assessments to monitor and support student progress throughout the academic year.
>
> **Baseline assessment**: At the start of the year, the Year 7 mathematics teacher administers a baseline assessment to understand each student's prior knowledge in areas such as basic arithmetic, fractions, and simple algebraic concepts. This initial assessment helps identify gaps in knowledge following transition from primary school and allows the teacher to plan lessons that cater to students' individual learning needs. The results are also used to group students into different ability levels, ensuring that everyone is taught at a pace that suits their understanding.
>
> **Formative assessment**: Throughout the year, formative assessments are used regularly to track student progress. These include quizzes, quick-fire questions at the start or end of lessons, homework, and interactive problem-solving activities that help the teacher gauge student understanding. The teacher also uses peer assessments during group work, where students give feedback to each other on problem-solving methods or mathematical explanations. These assessments provide immediate feedback, allowing students to address misconceptions and improve their understanding before more formal assessments take place.
>
> **Summative assessment**: At the end of each term, students take a summative assessment, usually a written test that covers the key topics taught during the term, such as basic algebra, geometry, and arithmetic. The test includes a mix of multiple-choice, short-answer, and longer problem-solving questions that assess both knowledge and the ability to apply mathematical concepts. These summative assessments contribute to students' term grades and provide an overall measure of their progress. They also help the teacher assess how effectively the curriculum has been delivered and identify any areas that may need to be revisited.

Assessment design decisions

Assessment design is a structured, sequential process where decisions must be carefully made at each stage to ensure the assessment aligns with learning objectives, curriculum requirements, and student needs. Here is a six-step process, derived from Bearman et al. (2014).

Step 1: Purpose of assessment

Assessment activities serve various purposes, including supporting learning, helping students achieve learning outcomes, contributing to final grades, and enabling students to assess their own work. While all these purposes are important, assessment design often prioritises grading over supporting learning or developing students' ability to self-assess.

Example: The use of peer assessments in a writing or design course.

Rationale: Peer assessments promote learning by encouraging students to review each other's work, fostering critical thinking and self-reflection. While they can contribute to final grades, their main purpose is to support learning and help students assess their own work.

Step 2: Context of assessment

Assessment practice is deeply interconnected with various aspects of education. It is shaped by factors such as the learners, the educators, the institution, and the discipline. The context in which assessment occurs is crucial for understanding its implementation and impact. Vocational standards, institutional policies, and departmental cultures all influence how assessments are designed. Learners' prior experiences and backgrounds affect their approach to assessment and feedback. The overall programme, team dynamics, and learning environments also play a role in shaping the assessment experience. Successful assessment design requires educators to adapt assessments to meet these specific needs, often through collaboration and effective communication with colleagues and students.

Example: The use of group projects in a business studies course.

Rationale: Group projects in a business studies course reflect the discipline's focus on teamwork, helping students develop skills like communication and problem-solving. They prepare students for similar tasks in future modules or professional settings and make assessment more manageable in large classes. This approach aligns with both the programme goals and students' development needs.

Step 3: Learning outcomes

Assessment must align with the intended learning outcomes, ensuring that students meet course requirements and any relevant external standards. While grading and accreditation are key concerns, assessment tasks also interact with student development throughout the course and programme. New learning outcomes should be introduced, developed through formative assessment, and confirmed via summative assessment. Additionally, assessments are often designed to foster broader skills, such as writing or applying scientific arguments, which extend beyond specific learning outcomes to support students' overall academic and professional growth.

Example: The use of case study analysis in a healthcare or business course.

Rationale: A case study assessment introduces new learning outcomes by applying theoretical knowledge to real-world situations. It is developed through formative assessments, such as discussions and feedback, to enhance critical thinking. The summative assessment, through a final case study report, ensures students meet learning outcomes while fostering transferable skills like analytical thinking and decision-making.

Step 4: Assessment format

The assessment format is fundamental to assessment design, as it involves evaluating a learner's performance, typically through grades or feedback. The chosen format (e.g., essay, presentation, observation, etc.) will require students to demonstrate their understanding of content and allow for skill development and error correction. A well-designed assessment aligns with the overall teaching goals and learning outcomes, offers opportunities for practice and feedback, and enables fair judgements of the learner's performance. The assessment will contain a set of criteria against which students are judged and a rubric that includes a description of different levels of performance for each criterion.

Example: The use of portfolios in a creative arts or education course.

Rationale: Portfolios allow students to demonstrate their understanding and growth over time by showcasing their work and receiving iterative feedback. This format supports both the final product and the development process, encouraging self-reflection and evaluative skills. It offers a sustainable way for educators to assess ongoing development rather than relying on a single high-stakes task, ensuring alignment with learning outcomes.

Assessment formats are covered in more detail later in this chapter.

Step 5: Feedback processes

Feedback should be seen as an ongoing process where students submit work for evaluation, receive feedback, and then apply what they've learned in subsequent iterations. This process is crucial for assessments that aim to foster learning. To ensure feedback is effective, educators must design assessments that encourage students to engage with and respond to feedback. Providing multiple opportunities for work completion and feedback helps students develop over the duration of a course or programme. Additionally, feedback can come from peers, which can be valuable for both the giver and the recipient, but it requires careful management to maximise its effectiveness.

Example: In the case of the portfolios example, feedback might take the form of both formative and summative comments throughout the process.

Formative feedback provides guidance for improvement throughout the process, such as suggesting additional sources or encouraging deeper analysis and reflection on progress.

Summative feedback assesses overall development, highlighting strengths and areas for refinement, like enhancing conclusions to better link to the research question.

Step 6: Interactions

Assessment design is an ongoing and interactive process that requires educators to engage with various stakeholders, including colleagues and learners, to ensure its effectiveness. Educators must communicate, negotiate, and evaluate the design to ensure it is understood, valued, and continually refined. This process can involve strategic discussions to align stakeholders, or adapting the assessment based on learner performance and feedback. It is essential to recognise that assessment is not a standalone event but interacts dynamically with other teaching and learning activities.

Example: The design of the portfolio assessment would involve ongoing interactions with colleagues and students. Educators collaborate with colleagues to align the assessment with programme goals and ensure consistency in evaluation criteria. They also share best practices for giving feedback. With students, educators clarify the portfolio's structure and purpose, offer formative feedback on drafts, and encourage self-reflection. Adjustments to the assessment design may be made based on student performance and feedback. These interactions ensure that the assessment is responsive, aligns with learning outcomes, and supports continuous improvement.

Information — Not all assessments require design. Statutory assessments, such as the SATs at Key Stages 1 and 2, GCSEs and A-Levels, are standardised and mandated by the government. These come with pre-determined frameworks, test formats, and scoring systems, leaving little scope for local adaptation.

Assessment implementation

Once assessments are designed, the next step is implementation, which involves managing the logistics of administering the assessments. This might involve: coordinating assessment dates (hand-in, feedback, referrals, etc.); arranging for invigilators, moderators and second markers; setting up electronic submission points; ensuring that exam venues are prepared; and ensuring that students are properly informed about assessment requirements.

One important consideration of assessment implementation is piloting. Piloting involves testing an assessment on a small scale before full deployment. This step allows educators to identify potential challenges, refine the assessment design, and ensure its reliability and validity. For example, a newly developed rubric for evaluating critical thinking might be trialled in a single class to gather feedback from both students and instructors. Insights from the pilot can inform revisions, enhancing the clarity of criteria and the alignment of performance descriptors with learning outcomes. The piloting process also fosters stakeholder buy-in. Involving educators and learners in the development and testing phases promotes a shared understanding of the assessment's purpose and benefits, while addressing concerns about fairness, workload, or practical feasibility. Educators can use the pilot to evaluate whether the assessment provides meaningful data to support instructional decisions and learner growth.

Finally, in the evaluation phase, assessment managers are responsible for ensuring that the results are accurately recorded, analysed, and communicated. For instance, Assessment Coordinators may oversee the grading process, ensuring that faculty use consistent grading standards. They also facilitate the generation of reports on student performance, which may be used for internal assessments or external accountability purposes (Winstone & Boud, 2019). In addition, these results are reviewed to determine whether any improvements are needed in future assessments.

Communicating assessment results

Effective communication of assessment results is essential. Results should be communicated clearly and fairly to students, faculty, and other stakeholders. Feedback should be both timely and constructive. Clear communication of assessment results not only informs students of their performance but also provides them with actionable insights for future improvement (Bloxham & Boyd, 2007).

In some cases, there may be a need for external reporting. For example, submitting assessment data to accrediting bodies or regulatory agencies, ensuring that the institution meets accreditation standards and that the assessment process is transparent.

Evaluating and improving assessment practices

Continuous evaluation and improvement are essential to maintaining the effectiveness and relevance of assessment practices, ensuring that assessments align with learning outcomes, support student development, and adhere to institutional and professional standards. To refine assessment practices further, programme and course evaluations are regularly conducted and feedback from both faculty and students is gathered to identify strengths and areas for improvement (Ramsden, 2003).

Benchmarking may also be carried out to compare an institution's assessment practices with those of similar organisations or against established standards. This ensures alignment with best practices in the field (Biggs & Tang, 2022).

Evaluation data from benchmarking and internal reviews are used to make evidence-based improvements, such as revising assessment designs, grading criteria, or feedback mechanisms, fostering a culture of continuous improvement (Torrance, 2012).

Key assessment bodies and standards

Assessment bodies in the UK are tasked with overseeing educational standards and providing frameworks for effective assessment, from early education through to higher education and beyond. Each of these bodies works together to establish a system of accountability and continuous improvement, which helps to ensure that learners receive an education that is rigorous, equitable, and aligned with societal and workforce needs.

UK schools

In the UK, primary and secondary schools are significantly influenced by key assessment bodies, including the *Office for Standards in Education, Children's Services and Skills* (Ofsted), the *Office of Qualifications and Examinations Regulation* (Ofqual), and the *Standards and Testing Agency* (STA). These bodies shape the assessment frameworks, standards, and accountability mechanisms that underpin the educational landscape.

Ofsted

Ofsted inspects and regulates educational institutions in England, evaluating the quality of teaching, learning, and assessment. Its role spans both primary and secondary education, providing accountability and supporting school improvement. Ofsted inspections include a thorough review of assessment practices, ensuring they align with curriculum goals and support student progress (Ofsted, 2023). Reports generated from inspections are pivotal for schools to identify areas of strength and improvement, often influencing pedagogical and assessment strategies across all key stages.

Ofqual

Ofqual oversees qualifications, examinations, and assessments across England. While Ofqual's focus is more pronounced in secondary education due to its regulation of GCSEs and A-Levels, its standards impact primary education indirectly by shaping the transition to secondary school.

Standards and Testing Agency (STA)

The STA is specifically focused on primary education, overseeing statutory assessments such as the Key Stage 1 and Key Stage 2 SATs. Its responsibilities include developing test content and ensuring consistency and fairness in administration. The STA plays a critical role in measuring student progress and informing educational policy, providing essential data to support school improvement efforts (STA, 2022).

Integrative impact on schools

Together, these bodies establish a cohesive system of standards and accountability. In primary schools, the STA ensures early assessment accuracy, setting a foundation for secondary education. Ofsted's inspections drive continuous improvement in assessment practices across all school phases, while Ofqual's regulation ensures consistency and fairness in secondary examinations. Collectively, these organisations contribute to a robust framework that supports educational equity and excellence in the UK.

Further education

Further Education (FE) in the UK, encompassing post-16 education such as A-levels, vocational qualifications, and apprenticeships, is shaped by several key assessment and regulatory bodies. These organisations ensure the quality and fairness of assessment practices, maintain accountability, and align qualifications with national standards and workforce needs.

FE, like schools, is significantly influenced by Ofsted and Ofqual. Ofsted inspects and regulates FE institutions, focusing on the quality of teaching, learning, and assessment, as well as leadership and learner outcomes. Its inspection framework emphasises the alignment of curriculum design with local labour market needs to ensure learners are well-prepared for further education, training, or employment. Similarly, Ofqual oversees the regulation of vocational and technical qualifications in FE, ensuring assessments are fair, reliable, and consistent. Through initiatives like the regulation of T Levels, Ofqual plays a key role in maintaining public confidence and shaping the vocational education landscape.

Education and Skills Funding Agency (ESFA)

The ESFA oversees funding and accountability for FE and apprenticeship providers. Its role includes ensuring that public funds are used effectively to deliver high-quality education and training. The ESFA also monitors learner outcomes, which indirectly influences assessment practices by encouraging alignment with funding requirements and performance metrics (ESFA, 2024).

Institute for Apprenticeships and Technical Education (IfATE)

The IfATE is a key player in developing and maintaining apprenticeship standards and technical qualifications. It ensures that qualifications meet employer needs, promoting workforce readiness. The IfATE works closely with Ofqual to guarantee that assessments for technical qualifications, such as T Levels, are rigorous and aligned with industry requirements. Its approach emphasises collaboration with employers to ensure that qualifications remain relevant in an evolving economic landscape (IfATE, 2023).

Collectively, these bodies shape the FE landscape, fostering a system that balances academic rigor with practical relevance. Recent developments, such as the rollout of T Levels and the growing emphasis on apprenticeships, underscore the critical role of these organisations in adapting FE to meet contemporary challenges and opportunities (City & Guilds, 2024).

Higher education

Higher education (HE) in the UK operates under the influence of several key assessment bodies that ensure the quality, consistency, and credibility of academic standards. Among these, the Quality Assurance Agency (QAA) and the Office for Students (OfS) play pivotal roles, supported by professional, statutory, and regulatory bodies (HEBRG, 2011).

The Quality Assurance Agency (QAA)

The QAA is the primary body overseeing quality assurance in UK higher education, ensuring institutions meet established academic standards. It operates the UK *Quality Code for Higher Education*, a comprehensive framework that sets expectations for programme design, student assessment, and learning outcomes. The QAA conducts periodic reviews to evaluate institutional quality, providing guidance and recommendations for improvement (QAA, 2024).

Recently, the QAA's focus has shifted towards enhancing inclusivity and ensuring that assessments accommodate diverse student needs. This aligns with broader national strategies for widening participation in higher education. The QAA has also been instrumental in supporting institutions to adapt assessment practices to meet the challenges posed by the digital transformation of learning environments.

The Office for Students (OfS)

As the regulator for English higher education, the OfS focuses on accountability, value for money, and ensuring high-quality experiences for students. It oversees the *Teaching Excellence Framework* (TEF), which evaluates and rewards institutions for outstanding teaching and assessment practices (OfS, 2023). The TEF has a significant influence on shaping institutional strategies, particularly regarding assessment design and student satisfaction.

The OfS also ensures that institutions meet their responsibilities for academic standards and fairness in assessment, particularly concerning the integrity of degree classifications. Its recent initiatives include addressing grade inflation and enhancing transparency in assessment processes.

Professional, Statutory, and Regulatory Bodies (PSRBs)

PSRBs oversee the accreditation of degree programmes in disciplines such as medicine, law, and engineering. These bodies ensure that assessments meet the standards required for professional practice. For instance, the *General Medical Council* (GMC) and the *Solicitors Regulation Authority* (SRA) prescribe specific assessment criteria for degrees leading to professional qualifications, ensuring alignment with industry requirements (GMC, 2023; SRA, 2024).

Apprenticeships and work-based learning

Apprenticeships and work-based learning programmes play a critical role in bridging education and employment, equipping individuals with practical skills that align with industry needs. These pathways are governed by a range of key assessment bodies and frameworks to ensure their quality and effectiveness.

Ofqual and standards regulation

Ofqual oversees the regulation of qualifications linked to apprenticeships and work-based learning in England. It works closely with apprenticeship awarding organisations to set clear standards for end-point assessments (EPAs), which test whether an apprentice is fully competent in their role (Ofqual, 2023). EPAs often include practical demonstrations, professional discussions, and written exams tailored to specific industries.

Sector Skills Councils and employer involvement

Sector Skills Councils (SSCs) and professional bodies contribute to shaping apprenticeship standards and assessments. For instance, organisations such as *Skills for Care* and the *Construction Industry Training Board* (CITB) provide expertise in aligning training with sector-specific needs. Their involvement ensures that apprenticeship programmes address current and future workforce demands. Employer engagement is also crucial, as businesses often co-design apprenticeship frameworks and serve as key assessors of on-the-job performance.

Funding and monitoring by ESFA

The *Education and Skills Funding Agency* (ESFA) plays a vital role in funding and monitoring apprenticeships in England. The ESFA ensures that training providers meet the required standards and that public funding is used effectively. It also enforces compliance with apprenticeship frameworks and the Apprenticeship Levy, promoting accountability across the system (ESFA, 2023).

Recent developments in standards and assessment

The introduction of T Levels and the growing emphasis on skills-based education have highlighted the importance of robust assessment practices in work-based learning. These developments reflect a shift towards integrating technical qualifications and apprenticeships into a cohesive skills strategy, enabling learners to transition smoothly into the workforce (DfE, 2021). The emphasis on quality assurance has also led to increased scrutiny of training providers and assessment organisations, ensuring alignment with national and international benchmarks (OECD, 2023b).

Information

As of April 2025, the UK apprenticeship system is being reformed to improve flexibility, reduce bureaucracy, and better meet workforce demands. A new Growth and Skills Levy will replace the Apprenticeship Levy, funding a wider range of training options. From August 2025, the minimum apprenticeship duration will drop from 12 to 8 months, speeding up training in key sectors. Entry requirements are also easing, with those aged 19 and over no longer needing prior English or maths qualifications to begin. Administrative processes are being streamlined for employers and training providers. However, concerns remain about ensuring equitable access, particularly for small businesses and disadvantaged groups. A review of construction training has also recommended major changes to the Construction Industry Training Board, including a possible merger with the ECITB.

Other education and training

Assessment plays a crucial role across diverse sectors, including corporate settings, health and social care, and specialised fields such as military and aviation training. These fields rely on various bodies and standards to ensure robust evaluation practices aligned with their unique requirements.

Corporate settings

In corporate environments, assessments are guided by structured standards and frameworks to maintain consistency and quality. Key contributors include awarding organisations, professional bodies, and international standards agencies. Awarding organisations such as *Pearson*, *City & Guilds*, and *ILM* provide standardised qualifications, including NVQs, leadership certifications, and professional diplomas. These qualifications use modular and competency-based assessments to validate both theoretical knowledge and practical skills.

Professional organisations like the *Chartered Institute of Personnel and Development* (CIPD) set industry-specific standards, as seen in HR certifications that blend theoretical and practical assessments (CIPD, 2024). The *International Standards Organisation* (ISO) offers frameworks such as ISO 9001 and ISO 29993 to promote uniformity and efficiency in workplace training (Brown et al., 2021).

Digital platforms, including *Credly* and *LinkedIn Learning*, have emerged as key players, enabling corporations to issue micro-credentials and track skill development through digital badges. These innovations bridge traditional qualifications with workplace demands.

Health and social care training

Assessment in health and social care is essential for ensuring professional competence and high-quality care delivery. Regulatory bodies like the *Nursing and Midwifery Council* (NMC) and *Health and Care Professions Council* (HCPC) establish standards for training and practice.

The NMC integrates theoretical and practical assessments, including *Objective Structured Clinical Examinations* (OSCEs) and reflective portfolios, to ensure practitioners meet its stringent code of practice (NMC, 2023). Similarly, the HCPC mandates clinical simulations and direct observations to evaluate practitioner competency in over 15 regulated professions (HCPC, 2023). *Skills for Care* supports adult social care workers through workplace-based assessments aligned with its *Care Certificate Standards*, focusing on practical competencies like safeguarding and infection control (Skills for Care, 2023).

Awarding organisations such as City & Guilds and NCFE further enhance the sector with qualifications ranging from Level 2 diplomas to advanced leadership certifications. Their assessment strategies balance case studies, written assignments, and in-situ observations (City & Guilds, 2023).

Military and aviation training

Military and aviation training rely on stringent assessment standards to ensure personnel meet safety and operational requirements. In the UK, the *Ministry of Defence* (MOD) oversees military training, embedding evaluations in high-pressure, realistic environments to test technical proficiency, leadership, and decision-making.

These assessments align with national defence policies and international standards for military cooperation.

The Civil Aviation Authority (CAA) regulates aviation training, ensuring compliance with both national and international standards, such as those set by the *International Civil Aviation Organisation* (ICAO) and the *European Union Aviation Safety Agency* (EASA). Aviation assessments combine theoretical knowledge (e.g., aerodynamics, regulations) with practical evaluations, including simulations and real-world tests. Regular reassessments ensure ongoing competency for pilots, air traffic controllers, and other personnel (CAA, 2024; EASA, 2024).

Information

Outside the UK, a variety of key assessment bodies and standards help shape educational quality and consistency. In the United States, the *Department of Education* provides federal oversight, while accreditation is managed by independent bodies like the *Higher Learning Commission* and the *Middle States Commission on Higher Education*. In Australia, the *Tertiary Education Quality and Standards Agency* (TEQSA) oversees higher education, with the *Australian Qualifications Framework* (AQF) ensuring consistency across learning levels. Canada uses provincial assessment bodies such as the *Ontario College Quality Assurance Service*, reflecting its decentralised system.

The *International Baccalaureate* (IB), *Cambridge Assessment International Education*, and the OECD's *PISA* provide widely adopted frameworks across many countries, enabling comparative benchmarking and consistent quality standards globally. These bodies collectively contribute to setting and maintaining assessment practices that are aligned with local and international expectations.

Assessment policies in practice

Clearly, assessment bodies play a critical role in shaping assessment design by establishing frameworks and standards that ensure consistency, fairness, and relevance. However, their influence can simultaneously limit educators' autonomy in crafting assessments tailored to their unique educational contexts.

Benefits of key assessment bodies

Consistency and standardisation: Standards provided by assessment bodies create a consistent baseline for measuring learners' competencies. This is particularly beneficial in professional and vocational contexts, where qualifications need to be recognised across industries and geographies. For instance, frameworks like the NVQs and ISO certifications ensure that skills are transferable and comparable.

Alignment with industry needs: Many assessment bodies work closely with industries to ensure that qualifications remain relevant. For example, the *Chartered Institute of Personnel and Development* (CIPD) ensures that HR certifications align with current practices, which equips learners with skills that employers value.

Quality Assurance: The structured guidelines provided by these organisations help maintain high-quality assessment practices. Regulatory bodies such as the *Nursing and Midwifery Council* (NMC) ensure that assessments are rigorous and meet safety and professional standards, fostering public trust in professionals.

Innovation through research: Some bodies invest in research and development to enhance assessment methods. For example, digital credentialing platforms like *Credly*, endorsed by professional bodies, incorporate real-time analytics, which helps track granular competencies and adapt assessments to evolving needs.

Weaknesses and challenges of external influence

Restricted flexibility: The standardisation enforced by key assessment bodies often limits educators' ability to innovate or contextualise assessments. For instance, a rigid adherence to predefined rubrics may prevent educators from tailoring assessments to local, cultural, or organisational needs.

Overemphasis on compliance: Educators may focus excessively on meeting assessment criteria, sometimes at the expense of fostering creativity, critical thinking, or exploration in learners. The focus on compliance can make assessments feel like box-ticking exercises rather than meaningful evaluations of learning.

Time and resource constraints: Designing assessments that adhere to external standards can be time-consuming and resource-intensive. This is particularly challenging in underfunded educational settings, where educators may struggle to meet external demands without sacrificing other priorities.

Potential stagnation: While these bodies ensure consistency, they may inadvertently stifle innovation by promoting traditional assessment methods over more progressive, learner-centred approaches. For example, reliance on standardised tests in primary schools may overlook the benefits of alternative formats such as project-based or experiential assessments.

Misalignment with emerging needs: The frameworks established by key bodies are often slow to adapt to emerging trends or technologies. For instance, in rapidly evolving fields like digital marketing or AI, the assessments provided by awarding organisations may lag behind current industry requirements.

Balancing compliance and autonomy

Educators can navigate these constraints by integrating external standards with their creative expertise. For example:

- *Contextualising assessments:* Incorporating local examples and scenarios within the broader framework provided by the assessment body.
- *Advocating for change:* Collaborating with assessment bodies to highlight the need for updated or more flexible criteria.
- *Blending approaches:* Combining standardised assessments with innovative, formative methods that promote deeper learning.

While key assessment bodies ensure accountability and consistency, it is crucial for educators to balance these frameworks with contextualised, innovative approaches. This balance fosters learner engagement and ensures that assessments remain relevant, meaningful, and aligned with the goals of education.

Designing fit-for-purpose assessments

Over the past decade, there has been increasing focus on designing assessments that are not only valid and reliable but also fit for the diverse needs of learners. This includes the design of fit-for-purpose assessments, focusing on product versus process assessment, the domains of learning, aligning assessments with learners' needs, and approaches to group assessment. Assessment should also include the *Accreditation of Prior Experiential Learning* (APEL), highlighting the importance of flexible and inclusive assessment practices.

Product and process assessment

Product assessment evaluates the end result of learning, typically through summative methods such as final exams or essays. These assessments focus on the output of the learning process, measuring how well learners have achieved the intended outcomes. This aligns with the *Tyler Rationale* of curriculum design and assessment (Tyler, 2009).

Process assessment, on the other hand, concentrates on how learners engage with the learning journey, often using formative assessment methods like portfolios, projects, and observations. Process assessments provide ongoing feedback to both students and educators, helping to guide the learning process and allowing for adjustments to be made in real-time. This aligns with *Stenhouse's Process Model* of curriculum design and assessment (Stenhouse, 1975) and *Dewey's Progressive Education Philosophy* (Dewey, 1986).

Both types of assessment are essential for a comprehensive evaluation of student learning. While product assessments are often used to judge the final outcomes of educational programmes, process assessments enable the tracking of progress and the development of skills over time (Nicol & Macfarlane-Dick, 2006). A balanced assessment strategy that integrates both product and process assessments ensures that the full scope of student achievement is captured, promoting continuous improvement and more accurate learning outcomes.

The product-process dilemma

The final grade for an educational course is often determined by a single, end-of-course assessment. Such assessments are deemed to measure the extent to which learners have achieved the intended learning outcomes for the course. This is all well and good provided that the learning outcomes are detailed and comprehensive.

Question

Consider the following learning outcomes for a course.
1. Develop an understanding of design principles and technology.
2. Students will apply their knowledge to create design solutions.
What do you think is the title of this course?
Could the learning outcomes alone be used as assessment criteria?

You would be correct to have identified the course as Design & Technology. However, the learning outcomes are quite broad and lack specific details about what exactly students should learn or how they should demonstrate their understanding and skills.

Hopefully, the course specification would include more detailed objectives such as:

> 1. Students will demonstrate an understanding of key design principles, including form, function, and aesthetics, by analysing existing products and identifying how these principles are applied.
> 2. Students will research and evaluate different materials and their properties (e.g., strength, durability, sustainability) and explain how these influence material selection in design.
> 3. Students will use sketching and computer-aided design (CAD) software to create detailed design proposals for a product, showing an understanding of scale, proportions, and design specifications.
> 4. Students will plan and construct a prototype using appropriate tools and techniques, applying knowledge of manufacturing processes and safety procedures.
> 5. Students will conduct testing of their prototype, evaluating its performance against design criteria such as functionality, usability, and durability, and suggest improvements based on their findings.

6. Students will reflect on the environmental and ethical implications of product design, demonstrating an understanding of sustainable design practices and considering factors such as resource efficiency and lifecycle impact.

7. Students will communicate their design ideas effectively through written reports, presentations, and visual diagrams, demonstrating the ability to explain the rationale behind their design choices to a range of audiences.

8. Students will collaborate in teams to solve a design problem, applying problem-solving skills, critical thinking, and effective teamwork strategies to develop and refine a design solution.

9. Students will analyse the impact of technological advancements on the design process, exploring how new tools, materials, and technologies can be incorporated into modern design solutions.

10. Students will critique and evaluate their own designs and those of peers, using relevant design terminology and providing constructive feedback for improvement.

These learning objectives are more specific and measurable, ensuring that students can demonstrate both their theoretical understanding and practical skills gained during the course. Therefore, the objectives themselves should be used as the basis for the assessment criteria rather than just the learning outcomes.

Information | It is generally better to assess learning objectives progressively throughout a course, using results toward the final grade. This approach offers advantages like regular feedback, a more comprehensive view of student progress, increased motivation, reduced pressure, and clearer grading based on specific assessment criteria.

Domains of learning

The domains of learning refer to different areas in which learners develop during the educational process. *Bloom's Taxonomy*, originally divided learning into three primary domains: *cognitive*, *psychomotor*, and *affective* (Gershon, 2015). Understanding these domains is essential for designing assessments that are aligned with the diverse nature of learning.

Cognitive domain: This domain involves intellectual skills and knowledge acquisition. It is traditionally the primary focus of academic assessments, where learners demonstrate their ability to recall information, analyse concepts, and apply learned material to new contexts. Cognitive assessments are designed to measure the depth and breadth of understanding in a particular subject (Anderson, 2000).

Psychomotor domain: This domain encompasses physical skills and the ability to perform tasks that require coordination and fine motor skills. Assessing psychomotor abilities is critical in subjects like physical education, vocational training, and healthcare, where practical performance is an essential part of learning

(Viscione et al., 2017). Psychomotor assessments often involve observation of skills in action, as well as practical tests and demonstrations.

Affective domain: This domain relates to the emotional aspects of learning, including attitudes, values, and motivation. Assessing affective learning requires different methods than cognitive and psychomotor assessments, as it focuses on measuring students' personal growth, self-awareness, and emotional intelligence. While difficult to assess with traditional methods, educators can measure affective outcomes through self-reports, peer assessments, and reflective writing (Krathwohl, 2009).

To design fit-for-purpose assessments, it is crucial to ensure that all three domains of learning are considered. In the UK, where vocational education, practical skills, and personal development are increasingly emphasised, educators must use a range of assessment methods to capture progress in all three areas (Boud & Falchikov, 2007).

Fitting assessment to learners' needs

In the modern educational landscape, assessments must be designed to meet the diverse needs of learners, ensuring that all students are given an equitable opportunity to demonstrate their learning. Two key approaches to achieving this are *individualisation* and *differentiation*, fostering equality and inclusivity in assessment.

Differentiation and individualisation

Differentiation and individualisation are crucial strategies for meeting the unique needs of learners.

Differentiation involves tailoring the content, process, and assessment methods to accommodate the varying learning styles, abilities, and interests of students. For instance, students with additional learning needs, such as dyslexia, might benefit from extended time for assessments or alternative formats, such as oral presentations instead of written exams (Tomlinson, 2001).

Individualisation goes one step further, allowing students to have a more personalised learning and assessment experience, often involving the use of learning plans or adaptive technologies.

By designing assessments that provide options for students to demonstrate their knowledge in various formats, educators can ensure that all learners have a fair chance to succeed (Guskey & Bailey, 2010).

Equality and inclusivity

Equality and inclusivity are central to ensuring that assessments are accessible to all learners, regardless of their background or abilities. According to the *UK Equality Act 2010*, educational institutions are required to provide reasonable adjustments for learners with disabilities or specific learning needs, ensuring that assessments are not discriminatory (UK Government, 2010). For example, students with visual impairments may require assessments to be provided in braille or audio formats. Similarly, students from different cultural backgrounds may benefit from assessments that are mindful of linguistic diversity, avoiding bias in question design.

Inclusive assessment practices also promote a fairer representation of students' achievements and competencies, especially in diverse classrooms. Ensuring that assessments do not disadvantage particular groups is a key component of fit-for-purpose assessment design (Race, 2019).

Group assessment

Group assessments have become increasingly common in education, as they encourage collaborative learning and the development of teamwork skills. Group assessments typically involve collective projects or presentations, where students are required to work together to achieve a shared goal.

Benefits and challenges

The main benefit of group assessments is that they simulate real-world work environments, where collaboration is often necessary for success. Additionally, group assessments encourage students to engage with peers, which can deepen understanding and foster a sense of community within the classroom (Cohen, 1994). However, group assessments come with challenges, particularly in the fair distribution of effort among group members. Often, some students contribute less than others, which can lead to inequities in the final grades (Boud & Falchikov, 2007). This can be problematic in ensuring that all students are held accountable for their learning.

Strategies for fair assessment of group work

To address the challenges of group assessments, educators can implement strategies to ensure fairness and equity. These include the use of peer evaluations, where students assess each other's contributions to the project, and the provision of individual assessments alongside group tasks (Topping, 2009). Clear guidelines and expectations, along with structured group roles, can also help ensure that all students contribute meaningfully to the assessment.

Accreditation of Prior Learning and Experience (APEL)

Accreditation of Prior Learning (APL) and *Accreditation of Prior Experiential Learning* (APEL) are processes that recognise the value of knowledge and skills acquired outside formal education. APEL is especially relevant in lifelong learning contexts, where learners bring diverse experiences to their studies.

Through APEL, learners can gain academic credit for their prior experiences, which can then contribute to their progression in formal qualifications. This process involves the assessment of non-academic achievements such as work experience, volunteering, or informal learning. APEL requires the use of clear, structured assessment criteria and can involve the submission of reflective portfolios or assessments designed to match the learner's previous experiences with curriculum requirements.

Assessment formats

A diverse range of tools and techniques can be employed to assess students across educational stages, reflecting both traditional and innovative practices.

Assessment instruments

Observations

Observation is a qualitative assessment tool used to monitor and evaluate student behaviour, participation, and skill application in real-time settings. It is particularly effective in early years education, where structured and unstructured observation techniques help assess developmental milestones (Tickell, 2011). Observational frameworks, such as those outlined by Ofsted (2019), provide guidance for assessing aspects like social interaction and practical skills. While observation offers rich contextual insights, its subjective nature necessitates standardised criteria to ensure reliability and validity.

Example

An example of standardised criteria in a primary school setting is the use of an observation rubric to assess pupils' participation in collaborative group work during a structured activity (Figure 2.2).

The teacher systematically observes each group in action, recording scores against pre-determined criteria that ensure consistency and fairness in assessment. Following the activity, detailed feedback is provided to each group and to each individual pupil, highlighting their strengths and pinpointing areas for growth. This feedback not only fosters self-awareness but also encourages skill development in key areas.

In practice, the rubric might encompass a range of essential competencies such as effective communication, constructive cooperation, and timely task completion, ensuring a holistic evaluation of the pupils' collaborative skills.

	Participation
4	Actively engages in discussion and tasks, contributing ideas and solutions.
3	Participates consistently but with occasional prompting or guidance.
2	Engages minimally, with little initiative or contribution.
1	Rarely participates or disrupts the group's efforts.

Figure 2.2 - Observation rubric
(Where: 4=Excellent, 3=Good, 2=Fair, 1=Needs improvement)

Questioning techniques and taxonomies

Questioning is a ubiquitous assessment technique, and frameworks like *Bloom's Taxonomy* remain foundational in designing questions that target various cognitive levels. Recent adaptations, such as Anderson & Krathwohl's (2001) revision, emphasise higher-order thinking skills like analysing and creating.

Effective questioning strategies, including Socratic questioning and diagnostic questioning, are central to formative assessment practices (Wiliam, 2011). They encourage deeper engagement with subject matter but require skilful implementation to avoid superficial responses. Table 2.2 illustrates Bloom's Taxonomy along with examples of questions that might be asked at each level.

Oral assessments and interviews

Oral assessments, including viva voce and structured interviews, allow students to articulate knowledge and reasoning verbally. They are frequently employed in disciplines like language learning and professional training (Reimann & Yates, 2020). These methods assess not only content knowledge but also communication skills and critical thinking. Challenges include ensuring standardisation and minimising examiner bias, which recent studies address through rubrics and digital recording for moderation (Boud & Falchikov, 2019).

Level	Examples of assessment questions
6. Create	Can you design an experiment to test the effects of sunlight on plant growth? Can you write a short story that incorporates the themes we discussed in class. How would you create a campaign to promote recycling in your school?
5. Evaluate	Do you agree with the author's argument? Why or why not? Which solution to the problem do you think is the most effective? Justify your answer. How would you assess the credibility of this news source?
4. Analyse	What evidence supports the character's decision in the story? Can you compare and contrast the roles of the legislative and executive branches of government? Why do you think this experiment produced these results?
3. Apply	How would you use what you've learned about fractions to double this recipe? Can you apply the laws of motion to explain how a car accelerates? How would you solve this math problem using the formula we learned?
2. Understand	Can you describe the main idea of the story? How would you explain photosynthesis in your own words? What's the difference between a democracy and a monarchy?
1. Remember	What are the key points discussed in today's lesson? Can you list the steps in the water cycle? Who wrote *Romeo and Juliet*?

Table 2.2 - Bloom's taxonomy and associated question types

Portfolios, journals, and log books

Portfolios are versatile tools that showcase a learner's progress, achievements, and reflections. They can include academic work like essays, reports, and presentations, as well as creative outputs such as artwork, creative writing, or multimedia projects. Practical and vocational evidence, like photographs of tasks or skill checklists, can also be included. Reflections, self-evaluations, and feedback responses highlight personal growth, while certificates, awards, and professional skills documentation demonstrate competencies. Portfolios may also feature collaborative work, prior learning evidence, digital projects, and learning plans, offering a comprehensive view of a learner's journey and achievements.. They are widely used in creative disciplines and professional qualifications (Quality Assurance Agency, 2024).

Journals and logbooks encourage reflective learning, allowing students to document their experiences and analyse their development. These tools foster autonomy and metacognition but require clear guidelines to ensure consistency in content and assessment criteria (Moon, 2013).

Essays, reports, and objective tests

Essays and reports are traditional assessment tools used to evaluate critical thinking, synthesis, and academic writing skills. They remain integral to summative assessments, particularly in higher education (HEFCE, 2017).

Objective tests, such as multiple-choice questions, provide an efficient way to assess factual knowledge and application skills. Advances in automated marking technology have enhanced the scalability and reliability of objective tests (Nicol, 2020). However, these tools must balance assessing surface-level knowledge with deeper learning outcomes.

Seminars and presentations

Seminars and presentations assess students' ability to research, organise, and communicate information effectively. These methods are especially valuable in fostering soft skills like public speaking and teamwork (Kivunja, 2015). Peer evaluation during presentations can enhance engagement but must be managed carefully to ensure fairness and constructive feedback (Falchikov & Goldfinch, 2021).

Role-play and problem-solving tasks

Role-playing and problem-solving tasks engage students in experiential learning, simulating real-world scenarios to assess practical skills and decision-making abilities. These methods are particularly relevant in professional training programmes, such as teacher education and healthcare (Boud et al., 2021). They foster creativity and collaboration but require significant preparation and facilitation to be effective.

Digital simulations and games

Technology-enhanced assessments, including digital simulations and serious games, have gained traction in recent years. Simulations, such as virtual labs and case studies, allow students to practise skills in a controlled environment (Laurillard, 2012). Games engage learners through interactive and immersive experiences, promoting problem-solving and critical thinking (Gee, 2007). In the UK, initiatives like JISC's *Digital Capabilities Framework* encourage the integration of such tools in higher education (JISC, 2023). Challenges include ensuring accessibility and aligning these methods with learning outcomes.

Peer and self-assessments

Peer and self-assessments involve students evaluating their own or their peers' work, fostering a deeper understanding of assessment criteria and promoting reflective practices. These methods align with constructivist theories of learning, emphasising active participation (Vygotsky, 1978). Peer assessment is widely used in collaborative projects, while self-assessment supports personal goal-setting and accountability (Boud et al., 2018). Recent studies highlight the importance of providing clear rubrics and training to enhance the reliability of these approaches (Tai et al., 2018).

Application and impact

Integrating multiple methods

Effective assessment strategies often combine multiple tools to address diverse learning objectives and student needs. For instance, a programme might use observations for formative feedback, essays for summative evaluation, and digital simulations for skill development. Integrating traditional and innovative methods ensures a comprehensive assessment framework that caters to cognitive, affective, and psychomotor domains.

Addressing equity and inclusivity

Assessment design must thoughtfully integrate principles of equity and inclusivity, ensuring that every learner is afforded a fair opportunity to demonstrate their knowledge and skills. While digital tools offer innovative possibilities, they must be carefully selected and adapted to remain accessible to students with disabilities and those from disadvantaged backgrounds, avoiding the risk of widening existing gaps. Inclusive assessment practices - such as providing alternative formats, accommodating diverse learning needs, and embedding cultural relevance - are not just supplementary measures but essential components of a supportive and empowering learning environment. These practices promote not only fairness but also a sense of belonging, enabling all students to engage fully and succeed (Hockings, 2010).

Adapting to evolving educational needs

The COVID-19 pandemic significantly accelerated the adoption of online and hybrid assessment methods, compelling educators worldwide to re-evaluate and transform traditional approaches to evaluation (Crawford et al., 2020). This abrupt shift illuminated the vast potential of technology to introduce greater flexibility, enhance student engagement, and expand access to innovative assessment practices. However, it also exposed critical challenges, such as the pressing need for robust digital infrastructure, equitable access to devices and connectivity, and comprehensive digital literacy for both educators and students. These insights have reshaped the discourse on assessment, emphasising the importance of preparedness and inclusivity in using technology for education.

Grading and feedback

Grading and feedback are essential components of the educational process, providing mechanisms for evaluating student performance, maintaining standards, and fostering learning. These elements must be thoughtfully designed and implemented to ensure they are equitable, valid, and effective in enhancing student outcomes.

Developing grading systems

Grading systems provide a structured framework for assessing and communicating student achievement. They involve designing marking schemes and rubrics, as well as developing level and grade descriptors to ensure clarity and consistency.

Marking schemes and rubrics

Marking schemes and rubrics are foundational tools for grading. A marking scheme provides specific criteria for evaluating an assignment, while rubrics offer a detailed breakdown of performance levels for each criterion. Research highlights the effectiveness of rubrics in promoting transparency and fairness (Brookhart, 2013). For instance, a rubric for an essay might assess clarity of argument, evidence use, and writing mechanics, assigning distinct descriptors for performance levels ranging from "excellent" to "needs improvement". By aligning grading with clear criteria, rubrics reduce subjectivity and enhance reliability.

Level and grade descriptors

Level and grade descriptors articulate the expectations for student performance at different stages of education. These descriptors align with national frameworks, such as the UK's *Regulated Qualifications Framework* (RQF), ensuring consistency across institutions (Ofqual, 2020). For example, a Level 3 descriptor might specify that students must demonstrate analytical skills, while a Level 6 descriptor might require critical evaluation. Clear descriptors help students understand what is required to achieve specific grades, promoting self-directed learning.

Maintaining assessment standards

Ensuring validity, reliability, standardisation, and moderation are key to maintaining high assessment standards. These processes uphold the integrity of grading and ensure that outcomes are fair and meaningful.

Validity

Validity refers to the extent to which an assessment accurately measures what it is intended to measure. It ensures that the content and objectives of the assessment align with the intended learning outcomes. For example, if a mathematics test is designed to assess problem-solving skills, including an excessive number of language-heavy word problems could reduce its validity for non-native speakers or students with reading difficulties. This is because the assessment might inadvertently test language comprehension rather than mathematical reasoning.

There are several types of validity to consider:
- **Content validity:** Ensures the assessment content adequately represents the subject matter. For instance, an English literature exam that focuses only on poetry would lack content validity if the curriculum also covers novels and plays.
- **Construct validity:** Refers to how well the assessment aligns with the theoretical constructs it aims to measure. For example, a test designed to measure critical thinking skills should include tasks that require analysis, evaluation, and synthesis, rather than just recalling facts.
- **Criterion-related validity:** Indicates how well an assessment correlates with an external criterion. For instance, a vocational skills test's results should align with actual performance in a real-world work environment.

An assessment with poor validity can lead to misleading results, potentially disadvantaging learners or failing to identify gaps in knowledge and skills accurately. To improve validity, educators should align assessments closely with learning objectives, review test items for bias, and pilot assessments with diverse groups of students.

Reliability

Reliability refers to the consistency of assessment outcomes over time, across different assessors, or within the same test. A reliable assessment yields stable and consistent results, minimising the influence of external factors such as variations in marking or test conditions.

Key factors influencing reliability include:
- **Clear criteria**: Detailed rubrics or marking schemes help ensure consistency in grading. For example, a rubric for evaluating student essays might specify criteria

for coherence, evidence use, grammar, and structure, with clear descriptors for each performance level.
- **Assessor training**: Ensuring that all assessors have a shared understanding of the grading criteria enhances reliability. For instance, in GCSE English exams in the UK, assessors undergo standardised training to ensure consistency in marking.
- **Test-retest reliability**: Refers to the stability of assessment results over time. If students take the same test under similar conditions on two occasions, their scores should be comparable, barring significant changes in their knowledge or skills.
- **Inter-rater reliability**: Ensures consistency between different assessors grading the same work. This can be achieved through moderation processes, where multiple assessors review and discuss a sample of work to align their grading standards.

Balancing validity and reliability

While both validity and reliability are essential, they can sometimes conflict. A highly reliable multiple-choice test may lack validity if it only measures recall, while an open-ended project may offer high validity but be harder to grade reliably. To strike a balance, educators can use mixed methods - such as combining multiple-choice questions for factual knowledge with essays to assess critical thinking and argumentation.

Improving validity and reliability requires careful design, regular review, and iterative testing of assessments. Incorporating feedback from students, peer reviews, and expert consultations can further enhance the quality of assessment tools, ensuring they meet the diverse needs of learners and the intended educational goals.

Standardisation and moderation processes

Standardisation and moderation processes are vital mechanisms for ensuring consistency, fairness, and credibility in assessment practices. These processes address potential discrepancies in grading that may arise due to subjective interpretations, diverse institutional practices, or contextual differences in how assessments are administered.

Standardisation refers to the development and application of consistent procedures, grading criteria, and benchmarks to ensure uniformity in assessment outcomes across assessors and settings. It typically involves creating detailed rubrics, conducting training sessions for assessors, and establishing clear guidelines for marking. In schools, standardisation might include aligning teachers' understanding of national curriculum standards through professional development workshops or collaborative meetings. For example, in primary education, teachers may engage in moderation meetings to compare and standardise the grading of writing samples using agreed rubrics.

In higher education, standardisation ensures that assessments across modules and programmes reflect comparable levels of academic rigor and learning outcomes. For instance, a university offering similar courses across multiple campuses might use standardised marking guides and grading policies to ensure that students' work is assessed consistently, regardless of location.

Moderation refers to the quality assurance processes used to review and verify assessment decisions to uphold standards and address any inconsistencies. Moderation can occur at various stages, including pre-assessment (e.g., reviewing the validity of assessment tasks), during assessment (e.g., collaborative marking), or post-assessment (e.g., reviewing grading outcomes). Moderation techniques include:

- **Cross-marking:** Work is independently graded by multiple assessors to compare and align interpretations. For example, in teacher education programmes, two assessors might independently grade a student teacher's lesson observation to ensure a consistent evaluation of teaching competencies. In higher education, a student dissertation will likely be graded by moderating the scores of two independent markers.
- **Moderation through sampling:** A moderator selects a sample of student submissions that is representative of the entire cohort. The size of the sample often follows a statistical model, such as the square root of the total number of submissions, ensuring that the sample is neither too small to miss significant discrepancies nor too large to become inefficient. This process allows moderators to focus on identifying patterns of inconsistency or bias rather than reviewing every individual submission.
- **Review panels:** Panels of experts or educators meet to discuss and agree on the grading of a sample of assessments. In vocational training, for example, industry professionals might join educators to moderate assessments to ensure they align with workplace standards.
- **External reviews:** Independent external examiners or auditors evaluate assessment practices and grading to ensure they meet institutional or national standards. In UK higher education, the external examiner system plays a crucial role in this process. External examiners review samples of graded work, assessment tasks, and marking criteria to verify that academic standards are being upheld and applied consistently across institutions (Quality Assurance Agency, 2024).

In further education (FE), moderation processes might include partnerships with awarding bodies, which require standardisation meetings and external verification visits to maintain the credibility of vocational qualifications. Similarly, in adult education settings, moderation helps ensure that assessments for non-formal certifications are fair and aligned with recognised standards.

In international contexts, such as *International Baccalaureate* (IB) schools or institutions delivering transnational education, moderation processes are essential for ensuring consistency across diverse cultural and linguistic contexts. For instance, IB teachers worldwide participate in moderation activities coordinated by the IB Organisation, including the review of coursework and examinations by global panels to maintain equity across regions (IBO, 2024).

Moderation fosters confidence in the fairness and credibility of assessments for all stakeholders. For students, it reassures them that their grades reflect equitable standards. For educators, it provides a framework to ensure their judgments align with best practices. For external stakeholders, such as employers or accrediting bodies, moderation enhances the trustworthiness of qualifications and certifications.

Assessing group work

Group work is increasingly used in education to develop collaborative skills, but assessing group work presents unique challenges. Key approaches include shared group grades and peer review mechanisms.

Shared group grades

Assigning a shared grade for group work can encourage collective responsibility and collaboration, as it reflects the output of the group as a whole. However, this approach often raises concerns about fairness, particularly when individual contributions are unequal. Disputes over effort and participation can affect group dynamics and outcomes. Recent research advocates for hybrid approaches that combine group grades with individual assessments to address these challenges (Chiriac, 2014). For example, a group project might be graded on the overall quality of the final product, such as a report or presentation, while individual contributions are assessed separately. This could involve reflective reports, self-assessments, peer evaluations, or individual presentations that highlight each member's role and input. Rubrics that clearly define expectations for both group and individual components can help manage discrepancies and ensure transparency in grading.

Hybrid approaches are particularly beneficial in diverse educational contexts. For instance, in vocational education, group projects may simulate workplace tasks, and individual performance is often evaluated to ensure alignment with professional competencies. In online learning environments, individual assessments can help monitor engagement and contribution in virtual teams. These methods recognise the value of teamwork while mitigating potential conflicts, leading to fairer and more comprehensive evaluations of students' skills and efforts.

Peer review and assessment

Peer assessment enables students to evaluate their peers' contributions, fostering accountability, self-regulation, and critical thinking. When students assess each other's work, they engage more deeply with assessment criteria and develop a better understanding of quality standards. Tools like online peer evaluation platforms, such as *Peergrade* and *FeedbackFruits*, have enhanced the feasibility of implementing peer review in group assessments by streamlining the process and providing anonymity. These tools allow instructors to collect, review, and integrate peer feedback effectively, even in large classes.

To ensure fairness and reliability in peer assessments, it is crucial to provide students with training on giving constructive feedback and using the assessment criteria appropriately. Clear guidance on how to evaluate peers, examples of effective feedback, and calibration exercises can improve the quality of peer reviews (Topping, 2017). Anonymous mechanisms, where students do not know whose work they are evaluating or who has evaluated their work, can reduce bias and alleviate concerns about interpersonal conflicts.

In practice, peer assessment is widely used across disciplines. For example, in engineering education, students might evaluate each other's contributions to a design project, providing feedback on technical accuracy and teamwork. In creative disciplines, such as arts or media studies, students may assess peers' portfolios or performances, offering critiques that contribute to iterative improvement. However, peer assessment requires careful implementation, as students may lack the expertise or confidence to provide accurate evaluations. Combining peer feedback with instructor moderation can address these limitations and enhance the overall assessment process.

Feedback strategies

Feedback is a powerful tool for learning, but its effectiveness depends on how it is delivered. Strategies for providing timely, constructive feedback and managing feedback in high-stakes contexts are critical for supporting student growth.

Timely and constructive feedback

Timeliness is crucial for feedback to be effective. Research indicates that feedback is most impactful when provided soon after the assessment, allowing students to act on it while the learning experience is still fresh (Hattie & Clarke, 2019). Constructive feedback should focus on specific strengths and areas for improvement, using clear language to guide students toward actionable steps. For example, instead of stating, "This argument is unclear", feedback might specify, "Clarify your argument by providing more evidence to support your claim ".

Managing feedback in high-stakes contexts

High-stakes assessments, such as final exams or capstone projects, pose additional challenges for feedback delivery. In these contexts, feedback should not only address performance but also support emotional resilience and future learning. Studies highlight the importance of balancing critical and positive comments to maintain motivation and self-efficacy (Carless, 2020). Additionally, institutions should provide opportunities for follow-up, such as one-to-one meetings or workshops, to help students interpret and apply feedback effectively.

Technology-enhanced assessment

Technology-Enhanced Assessment (TEA) has transformed educational evaluation by integrating digital tools to enhance assessment design, implementation, and feedback. This evolution has been particularly significant in online and blended learning environments, where traditional assessment methods may not fully capture student learning and engagement. While TEA offers significant opportunities to enrich educational evaluation through innovative methods that cater to diverse learning environments, it also presents challenges that require careful consideration to ensure accessibility, validity, and ethical use. Ongoing research and thoughtful implementation are essential to harness the full potential of TEA in enhancing student learning outcomes.

Technology in assessment design

Online and blended learning contexts: In online and blended learning settings, technology facilitates diverse assessment strategies that accommodate various learning styles and provide immediate feedback. The increasing adoption of online assessments has highlighted the need for valid, reliable, and fair evaluation methods in virtual environments. Research on technology-enhanced assessment emphasises the importance of selecting appropriate online assessment formats to maintain educational standards (Khan & Jawaid, 2020).

Digital portfolios and e-assessments: Digital portfolios and e-assessments enable students to showcase their work and reflect on their learning over time. These tools support formative assessment by allowing continuous monitoring of student progress and providing opportunities for self-assessment. Research in higher education indicates that digital technologies in assessment can enhance student engagement and provide more comprehensive evaluations of student competencies (Nkomo et al., 2021).

Methods in tech-based assessment

Automated testing and AI tools: Artificial Intelligence (AI) has introduced automated testing systems capable of evaluating complex student responses efficiently. AI-driven assessments can provide instant feedback, adapt to individual learning needs, and reduce the grading burden on educators. A systematic review highlighted the potential of AI in automating the assessment of text-based responses, enhancing the scalability and consistency of evaluations (Gao et al., 2024).

Interactive learning activities: Interactive assessments, such as simulations and gamified quizzes, engage students actively, promoting deeper learning and retention. These activities can be tailored to individual learner profiles, providing personalised learning experiences. The integration of interactive assessments in technology-enhanced learning environments has been shown to improve student motivation and achievement (Duterte, 2024).

Synchronous and asynchronous assessments: Technology enables both synchronous (real-time) and asynchronous (time-independent) assessments, offering flexibility to accommodate diverse student schedules and learning paces. Synchronous assessments, such as live quizzes, facilitate immediate feedback and interaction, while asynchronous assessments, like discussion boards and recorded presentations, allow thoughtful reflection and self-paced learning. The choice between synchronous and asynchronous assessment methods should align with learning objectives and student needs.

Challenges and opportunities

Ensuring accessibility: While technology-enhanced assessments offer numerous benefits, ensuring accessibility for all students remains a critical challenge. Factors such as internet connectivity, digital literacy, time zones, and accessibility must be considered to provide equitable assessment opportunities. Institutions need to implement inclusive design principles and provide necessary support to address these disparities.

Balancing innovation with validity: Innovative assessment methods must maintain validity and reliability to ensure that they accurately measure intended learning outcomes. The rapid integration of AI and other technologies in assessments raises concerns about academic integrity and the potential for misuse. Educators are advised to develop clear guidelines and ethical frameworks to govern the use of AI in assessments, ensuring that technology serves as a tool for learning enhancement rather than a shortcut for students.

Future trends in assessment

The evolution of assessment practices is increasingly shaped by advancements in technology, the growing emphasis on personalised learning, and the interconnectedness of the global community, alongside ethical imperatives. Emerging trends indicate a paradigm shift toward adaptive systems that are globally relevant and grounded in principles of equity, integrity, and sustainability. Personalised learning and adaptive assessments hold the potential to enhance learner engagement and outcomes, while global frameworks stress the importance of skills relevant to a connected world. Addressing ethical and sustainability challenges remains crucial to ensuring that these innovations uphold principles of equity. As these trends continue to evolve, collaborative efforts among educators, policymakers, and technologists will be essential to shape assessment practices that are both innovative and responsible.

Personalised learning and adaptive assessments

One significant trend is the rise of personalised learning, underpinned by adaptive assessments. These assessments utilise artificial intelligence (AI) and data analytics to tailor questions and feedback to individual learners' abilities, ensuring a customised learning experience. Adaptive assessments can identify gaps in knowledge more efficiently than traditional methods, allowing educators to provide targeted interventions. These systems use algorithms that adjust the difficulty level of questions in real-time, promoting both engagement and mastery.

Personalised assessments are transforming formative and summative evaluations. Platforms such as *Duolingo* and *Khan Academy* demonstrate the efficacy of adaptive tools in assessing language proficiency and mathematical skills. These innovations are not confined to academics but extend to professional training, where competency-based assessments align with industry standards. However, the widespread adoption of adaptive assessments requires careful calibration to avoid biases embedded in algorithms, necessitating ongoing research and monitoring. Relying too heavily on AI in assessments poses a risk, highlighting the need for human oversight to guarantee a fair evaluation process (Vorecol, 2024).

Global trends in assessment practices

Globally, assessment practices are shifting to emphasise skills relevant to the 21st century, such as critical thinking, creativity, collaboration, and digital literacy. Organisations like the *Organisation for Economic Co-operation and Development* (OECD) have pioneered frameworks such as the *PISA for Schools* initiative, which evaluates problem-solving and global competencies alongside traditional academic skills.

Cross-national assessments are increasingly incorporating technology to ensure scalability and inclusivity. The transition to digital platforms enables seamless administration, scoring, and reporting across borders. In higher education, micro-credentials and digital badges are gaining traction as alternative forms of assessment that recognise specific skills and competencies. These credentials align with lifelong learning paradigms, allowing learners to showcase their achievements in a flexible, modular manner (Brown et al., 2021).

Ethical considerations and sustainability

As assessment practices evolve, ethical considerations and sustainability are becoming central to their design and implementation. Ethical challenges include ensuring data privacy, preventing algorithmic biases, and maintaining transparency in automated scoring systems. As Williamson (2021) argues, the increasing reliance on data-driven assessments necessitates robust governance frameworks to protect student rights and ensure accountability.

Sustainability in assessment encompasses both environmental and social dimensions. Digital assessments reduce the environmental impact associated with paper-based testing but raise concerns about electronic waste and energy consumption. Social sustainability requires that assessment systems be equitable and accessible, addressing disparities in technology access and digital literacy.

Information

Electronic waste (e-waste) is unwanted or broken electronic devices, like old computers, laptops, iPads, phones, or TVs. It can harm the environment if not recycled properly.

Activity: Designing an assessment plan

The purpose of this activity is to apply the concepts from the chapter on effective assessment strategies by designing an assessment plan that aligns with learning objectives, promotes fairness, and integrates technology, while addressing diverse learner needs.

Choose a specific learning objective from a course or programme you are familiar with (e.g., a unit from one of your own courses).

Based on this objective, design a formative and summative assessment plan. Explain why each type of assessment is appropriate for this learning objective and how they support different stages of the learning process.

> Identify the key stakeholders in the assessment process (e.g., students, faculty, administrators, accreditation bodies, etc.). Describe how you would engage each stakeholder group in the assessment process, balancing their roles and expectations. How would you ensure clear communication and collaboration between them?
>
> Select one assessment format (e.g., essay, quiz, portfolio, project, exam, observation) and critically evaluate its validity, reliability, and fairness. Reflect on how you would adapt this tool to meet the diverse needs of learners, ensuring that it accommodates different learning styles and abilities.
>
> Discuss how technology could enhance the design, delivery, and analysis of your assessments. Consider tools such as learning management systems (LMS), digital platforms, or AI-powered assessments. How will you address accessibility challenges to ensure that all learners can engage with the assessments?
>
> Describe how feedback will be provided to students and how this feedback will be used to inform future assessments and improve the learning experience.
>
> Discuss how assessment data will be analysed to identify areas for institutional improvement.
>
> Create a brief action plan for implementing your assessment strategy, including the timeline, resources needed, and any steps for involving leadership and other stakeholders.
>
> After completing the activity, reflect on the importance of having a strategic approach to assessment and how leadership plays a crucial role in fostering continuous improvement in assessment practices.

Summary

Assessment is a cornerstone of education, guiding learners, educators, and institutions toward achieving meaningful outcomes. It serves as both a tool for measuring progress and a driver for improving teaching and learning. However, the success of assessment hinges on effective leadership and management at all levels.

Leaders play a critical role in designing and overseeing assessment systems that are valid, reliable, and equitable. They must balance the needs of learners with institutional objectives, align assessment strategies with educational goals, and respond to external pressures such as accreditation standards and policy reforms. Effective leaders foster a culture of collaboration and continuous improvement, ensuring that assessment not only measures achievement but also enhances the learning experience.

Through strategic planning, thoughtful implementation, and the integration of innovative tools, leaders can transform assessment into a powerful mechanism for supporting student success and institutional growth.

3 ENHANCING TEACHING & LEARNING

David Hall

Introduction

The most effective teaching and learning is almost always driven by those who truly understand both the structure and the essence of a strong learning process within their specific context. These leaders are constantly working to better understand what happens behind the scenes in education. They continually ask how they can achieve better outcomes, what practices they should integrate into regular routines, and what should be discarded because it isn't contributing enough.

The key to success lies in the quality of teachers and the learning experiences they provide. Therefore, leaders must focus on the critical tasks of attracting, developing, supporting, and retaining excellent teachers. Leadership is not merely a secondary influence; it is central to the learning process and the success of the entire educational community.

This chapter:

- Explores the development and communication of a clear, shared vision that aligns teaching priorities with institutional goals and inspires collective action.
- Examines strategies to encourage and support educators in adopting innovative teaching practices, including integrating new technologies and fostering creative approaches.
- Discusses how to foster collaboration through professional learning communities and peer networks, enabling the exchange of best practices and resources to enhance teaching.
- Highlights ways to promote reflective practices and professional development that drive ongoing improvement in teaching and learning processes.
- Addresses how to identify and tackle common challenges, such as resistance to change, resource limitations, and varying student needs, with proactive and adaptive strategies.
- Explores efforts to create inclusive and equitable learning environments, addressing disparities and fostering success for all students through culturally responsive leadership.
- Considers the promotion of pathways into teaching by raising awareness and facilitating various entry routes.

- Outlines the potential of teacher leadership as a strategy to empower teachers to take on leadership roles within their institutes and add additional value to teaching and learning.

Strategic vision for teaching and learning

Teaching and learning are shaped by practices that respond to the diverse needs of learners across age ranges and are underpinned by robust theoretical frameworks (Biggs & Tang, 2022). High-quality education thrives when curricula align with both national and international standards, and when diverse teaching methods enrich the learning experience. However, the effectiveness of these practices depends on strong leadership and a clear strategic vision. Leaders play a crucial role in guiding institutions by fostering alignment with educational goals, ensuring effective communication, and creating an environment where teaching excellence can flourish. By extending their vision to embrace innovative and inclusive approaches, leaders empower both teachers and students to achieve success in a complex, interconnected world.

Setting and communicating a clear vision

A well-defined vision serves as a compass, guiding educators toward common objectives and fostering a sense of purpose. Leaders who effectively communicate this vision ensure that all stakeholders understand and are committed to the shared goals. Fostering high-quality teaching and dynamic educational experiences empowers all students to achieve their aspirations. This clarity enables educators to align their teaching methods with the overarching mission of the institution, creating a cohesive and focused learning environment. Leaders must ensure that their vision resonates across all levels of the organisation, allowing for consistent progress towards shared educational objectives.

Here are a number of practical examples that illustrate the relationship between *vision and strategy* and *teaching and learning*:

Example 1: Creating a professional development programme

To communicate and reinforce the vision, a head of department organises workshops and ongoing professional learning sessions. For example, if the institution prioritises integrating technology into teaching, training on tools such as interactive whiteboards, and learning management systems (LMS) like Moodle, Blackboard or Canvas ensures staff are equipped to align with this goal. Additionally, training on collaborative platforms like *Google Classroom* or *Microsoft Teams* can empower educators to create more engaging, interactive learning experiences. These sessions may also include best practices for utilising data analytics to monitor student progress, thereby supporting teachers in making informed decisions to enhance learning outcomes.

Example 2: Developing a unified teaching framework

A school principal implements a clear instructional model - such as *direct instruction* or *project-based learning* - as the foundation for teaching across all grade levels. This model aligns with the school's mission of fostering critical thinking and creativity, ensuring that educators have a shared understanding of how to deliver lessons effectively.

Question — You might question whether leaders should impose strict instructional models. Would it not prove more effective for institutions to draw on a variety of instructional models, depending on their philosophy, priorities, and student needs? *Some commonly used models are shown in Appendix 3, Part 1.*

Example 3: Setting institution-wide academic goals

Senior leaders define clear targets, such as raising literacy rates by 10% within three years. By communicating these goals to teachers, parents, and students, everyone understands their role in achieving them. Progress is monitored through regular assessments and reviews, maintaining alignment with the institution's vision.

Example 4: Empowering students as stakeholders

Leaders involve students in decision-making, such as forming a student council to provide input on teaching strategies, curriculum changes or extra-curricular programmes. This ensures that the vision is inclusive and resonates with all members of the community.

Information — Many institutions regularly gather feedback from students on their learning experiences using their *student voice* - the active participation and contribution of students in decisions related to their learning experiences, institutional policies, and the overall educational environment. This empowers students to express their opinions and preferences, giving them a sense of agency in shaping their education.

Example 5: Establishing cross-department collaboration

A deputy head organises monthly interdisciplinary meetings where science and English teachers, for instance, collaborate on projects that integrate STEM and literacy. This fosters a cohesive learning experience and aligns with the vision of holistic education.

For further examples see Appendix 3, Part 2.

Aligning strategies with goals and standards

Aligning teaching strategies with institutional goals and educational standards is essential for maintaining consistency and ensuring that educational objectives are met. Constructive alignment, as described by Biggs & Tang (2022), involves designing teaching and assessment activities that directly address the intended learning outcomes. This approach ensures that all components of the educational process are interconnected and purpose-driven. Aligning instructional practices with education quality standards enhances student engagement and achievement, as it provides clarity and consistency in educational experiences.

Example: A collaborative group project, where students research and present a topic, helps develop skills in teamwork, communication, and problem-solving. This is followed by a group presentation and report, which evaluates students' ability to apply knowledge, analyse data, and communicate findings. These activities align with institutional goals focused on improving employability by fostering essential skills.

Fostering a shared understanding of teaching excellence

Senior leaders play a crucial role in cultivating a shared understanding of teaching excellence within an institution. By promoting reflective practices and professional development, leaders encourage continuous improvement in teaching and learning processes. The Center for Transformative Learning (2023) emphasises that when principals develop and communicate a clear, actionable vision for teaching and learning, it sets the foundation for student success. This shared understanding fosters a culture of collective efficacy, where educators collaborate and support each other in striving for excellence. Senior leaders help to ensure that the vision for teaching and learning permeates throughout the school, establishing a unified approach to instructional improvement and innovation.

Example teaching and learning vision:

> "To provide an inclusive, innovative, and student-centred learning environment that prepares all learners for success in their future careers and further education. We will achieve this by fostering a culture of high expectations, integrating modern technologies, and encouraging active participation in both academic and vocational courses. Through personalised learning pathways, collaborative teaching, and continuous professional development, we will ensure that all students are supported to reach their full potential, equipped with the skills, knowledge, and confidence to succeed in their intended vocation and thrive in an ever-changing world."

In order that the vision is not merely rhetoric, the included intentions must form part of the institute's strategic plan (see Appendix 3, Part 3).

>  **Case Study: Innovating for the future**
> Riverside Secondary School, located in a diverse suburban area, serves 1,200 students aged 11 to 18. The school is committed to providing an inclusive, student-centred learning environment that prepares students for future careers and further education. Over the past five years, Riverside has transformed its teaching practices to align with its vision: "To provide an inclusive, innovative, and student-centred learning environment that prepares all learners for success". The vision has been translated into the following actions:
>
> 1. **Inclusive learning:** Riverside offers personalised learning pathways with both academic and vocational options. Support mechanisms such as mentoring and differentiated instruction ensure that all students, including those with special needs, succeed.
> 2. **High expectations:** The school promotes a culture of high expectations, encouraging students to take responsibility for their learning. Teachers set challenging goals and provide regular feedback, celebrating progress and effort.
> 3. **Technology integration:** Classrooms are equipped with interactive whiteboards and students have access to tablets and laptops. The school uses a learning management system (LMS) for assignments and communication. Apps like *Kahoot!* and *Google Classroom* foster active participation.
> 4. **Active participation in courses:** Riverside combines academic and vocational courses, using project-based learning (PBL) to engage students in real-world tasks. This approach develops problem-solving, teamwork, and communication skills.
> 5. **Collaborative teaching:** Teachers collaborate to deliver high-quality, integrated lessons across subjects. Co-teaching models ensure a cohesive curriculum that prepares students for both higher education and the workforce.
> 6. **Continuous Professional Development (CPD):** Staff engage in ongoing CPD, focusing on new technologies and teaching strategies. Partnerships with universities and industry leaders ensure teachers stay up-to-date.
>
> **Outcomes:** Riverside has improved student engagement, academic performance, and vocational success. More students now progress to higher education or apprenticeships. Collaboration has boosted teaching effectiveness, and stronger community ties offer valuable work experience.

Integrating theories of learning into strategic vision

A comprehensive strategic vision incorporates an understanding of various learning theories to inform teaching practices. Behaviourism, cognitivism, constructivism, and connectivism offer diverse perspectives on how students learn, each with implications for instructional design:

Behaviourism: Focuses on observable behaviours and how they are influenced by stimuli in the environment. It emphasises the role of reinforcement and punishment in shaping behaviour. According to behaviourist theory, learning occurs through conditioning - either classical or operant (Miller & Rollnick, 2013).

Cognitivism: Emphasises the role of mental processes, such as attention, memory, and problem-solving, in learning. It posits that learners actively process information, build mental models, and use existing knowledge to make sense of new experiences. Cognitive load theory, for instance, highlights the importance of managing the amount of information presented to avoid overwhelming working memory (Lovell et al., 2020).

Constructivism: Argues that learners build their own understanding of the world based on their experiences and interactions. Knowledge is constructed, not transmitted. The theory, associated with Piaget and Vygotsky, emphasises social interaction, problem-solving, and the importance of context in learning (Miller, 2001).

Connectivism: A more modern theory that views learning as a process of forming networks or connections between individuals, ideas, and resources. It emphasises the role of technology and networks in supporting learning and the ability to continuously acquire knowledge from diverse sources, especially in the digital age (Siemens, 2005).

Communicating the vision and strategy

Effective communication of an institute's vision, strategy, and policies is integral to fostering a shared understanding and commitment among staff, students, and stakeholders. Print and media documents, such as handbooks, newsletters, and websites, play a vital role in this process. Such documents must provide clear and consistent messaging to ensure all parties are aligned with the institution's goals and expectations. Above all, information must be easily accessible, and stakeholders must be aware of its existence to ensure its effective dissemination.

A well-articulated vision and strategy help shape the culture of the institution and guide decision-making at all levels. By integrating both traditional and modern communication channels, educational institutions can ensure their strategic messages resonate widely and deeply with all stakeholders, providing clarity, consistency, and engagement across multiple platforms that address the varying needs and preferences of different audiences.

Printed documents, such as strategic plans and policy handbooks, provide a tangible, permanent resource that can be referred to at any time. These documents are crucial for ensuring that all members of the institution, from senior leaders to administrative staff, have a clear understanding of the institution's goals and how to contribute to their achievement. Policies, when clearly documented, offer a foundation for consistency and transparency, ensuring that everyone is aware of the rules, expectations, and procedures in place. This level of clarity is essential for minimising ambiguity and avoiding miscommunication.

Visual elements, such as infographics and videos, can be highly effective in conveying complex strategies and policies in an engaging manner. Visual aids are particularly helpful when trying to explain abstract concepts such as the institution's vision for student success or future growth (Figure 3.1). These materials can simplify the information and make it more accessible to a diverse audience, from educators to parents.

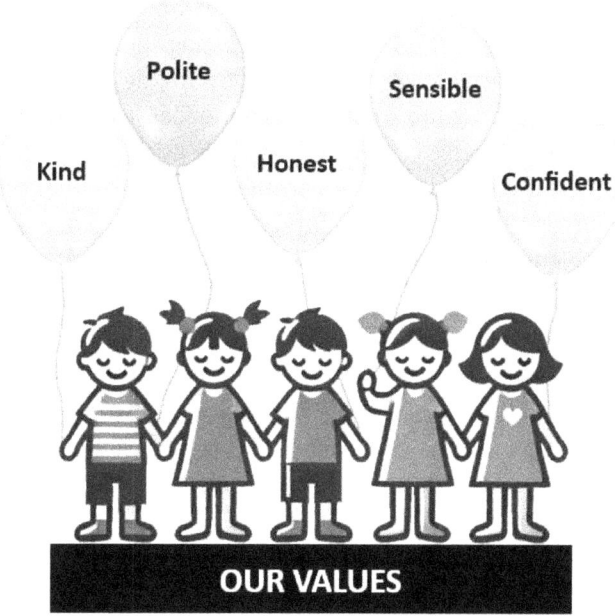

Figure 3.1 - Our values infographic

While printed documents are critical, they must be complemented by digital media, which provides a dynamic and interactive platform for communication. Using digital tools such as institutional websites, social media, and online newsletters helps to extend the reach of the institution's vision and policies to a broader audience, including prospective students and external stakeholders. These tools allow for real-time updates and feedback, making them an essential component of a comprehensive communication strategy.

Pedagogy in strategic planning

Understanding the pedagogical (or andragogical) requirements across age ranges is crucial for leaders when formulating a strategic vision, as effective teaching strategies must address the diverse developmental, cognitive, and emotional needs of learners at different life stages. This involves recognising that children and adults learn in fundamentally different ways and require tailored approaches to instruction. Leaders who incorporate these nuances into their vision ensure that educators can deliver meaningful and engaging learning experiences, fostering growth and achievement across all age groups. Effective education must align with learners' developmental needs, advocating for distinct methodologies for children and adults (Merriam & Bierema, 2013).

For instance, in teaching children, pedagogy often emphasises structure, guided discovery, and scaffolded learning to build foundational knowledge and skills. A primary school science lesson might involve hands-on experiments where students observe plant growth over several weeks, reinforcing the scientific method through a structured and interactive activity. In contrast, andragogy for adult learners focuses on self-direction, relevance to real-life experiences, and problem-solving. For example, an A-Level economics class might involve analysing current market trends and discussing their implications for government policy, enabling students to apply theoretical knowledge to practical scenarios while developing critical thinking and collaborative problem-solving skills.

In a school that caters for a wide age range, here's an example of its vision:

> "Our institution is committed to nurturing lifelong learners by tailoring educational experiences to the developmental needs of all age groups. For younger learners, we aim to build strong foundations in literacy, numeracy, and social skills through engaging, interactive approaches. For mature learners, we prioritise practical, career-focused learning, integrating real-world applications and collaborative problem-solving to enhance personal and professional growth. By equipping teachers with the resources and training necessary to meet these diverse needs, we will create an inclusive and adaptive learning environment that empowers all students to achieve their full potential."

Curriculum design and its alignment with strategic vision

The curriculum design elements of a strategic vision for teaching and learning directly influence how educational goals are translated into practice and how institutions prepare students for both present and future challenges. Effective curriculum design requires leaders to balance theoretical frameworks with practical implementation, ensuring coherence across all levels of learning.

At its core, curriculum design encompasses decisions about content, pedagogy, assessment, and progression, all of which must align with an institution's broader vision and leadership priorities. For instance, Bruner's (1960) spiral curriculum, which advocates revisiting core concepts at increasing levels of complexity, enables learners to build upon their knowledge systematically. This approach fosters deeper understanding and retention, aligning with strategic goals of mastery and lifelong learning. Using theoretical principles, adhering to standards, and promoting inclusivity, leaders can thoughtfully plan and develop curricula that become powerful tools for achieving educational excellence and equity.

Leadership plays a critical role in shaping curriculum design to reflect institutional priorities and societal needs. Leaders must ensure that curricula adhere to national and international standards while retaining flexibility to address local contexts. By doing so, they meet established benchmarks and prepare students for global competencies. For example, aligning a curriculum with frameworks like the *UNESCO Education 2030 Agenda* emphasises skills such as critical thinking, collaboration, and sustainability, which are vital in today's interconnected world (UNESCO, 2015).

Leaders must also navigate the tension between the product model, which focuses on predefined outcomes (Tyler, 2009), and the process model, which prioritises experiential and inquiry-based learning (Stenhouse, 1975). Balancing these models requires a nuanced approach that incorporates both measurable achievements and holistic development.

A strategically designed curriculum also embraces diversity, equity, and inclusion as foundational principles. Cross-cultural teaching approaches enrich curricula by integrating perspectives and content from multiple cultures, fostering inclusivity and global awareness among students. Hargreaves (2003) highlights how such approaches prepare learners to navigate diverse environments, a key strategic priority for institutions aiming to cultivate globally competent graduates. Leaders must champion these efforts, advocating for curricula that reflect varied experiences and address systemic inequities.

Curriculum design is not static but continually evolves in response to emerging trends, societal shifts, and educational challenges. Leaders must foster a culture of innovation, critical reflection, and adaptability within their institutions to stay ahead of change. For example, the integration of digital technologies and hybrid learning models reflects a strategic vision that prioritises 21st-century skills such as collaboration, problem-solving, and digital literacy. As Fullan & Quinn (2015) argue, effective leaders are change agents who guide the alignment of curriculum design with future-focused priorities, ensuring both relevance and resilience in a rapidly changing world.

Teaching and learning beyond the classroom

Effective leaders recognise that the boundaries of teaching and learning extend far beyond traditional classroom settings, necessitating a strategic vision that encompasses private sector training, corporate education, informal learning, and online environments. These alternative contexts demand innovative approaches to curriculum design, pedagogy, and learner engagement, all of which are vital for fostering adaptability and lifelong learning.

In the corporate sector, training focuses on equipping employees with practical skills and real-world applications to meet industry demands. Leadership here involves collaborating with stakeholders to design programmes that align organisational objectives with individual professional growth. For instance, competency-based training models allow for customised learning pathways tailored to employees' roles and career aspirations (Cross, 2011). Leaders must ensure that these training programmes integrate seamlessly into the strategic vision, promoting a culture of continuous improvement and knowledge sharing within organisations.

The rise of *Massive Open Online Courses* (MOOCs), *micro-credentials*, and *independent learning platforms* exemplifies the growing demand for flexible, learner-centred education. MOOCs (offered by universities), and platforms such as *Coursera* or *edX*, democratise access to high-quality learning resources, breaking traditional barriers to education. Leaders in educational institutions must strategically incorporate these tools to complement formal curricula, expanding opportunities for students and professionals alike. Micro-credentials (Appendix 3, Part 4), in particular, highlight the shift toward modular and outcome-focused learning, allowing individuals to acquire specific skills in short, accessible formats (Oliver, 2019).

Informal learning through social media and online communities further emphasises the importance of diverse modalities in modern education. Social media platforms, such as LinkedIn or Twitter, serve as powerful tools for professional networking and knowledge exchange, while YouTube and blogs provide access to expert-driven content on demand. Siemens (2005) underscores the significance of connectivism in these contexts, where learning occurs through networks and shared experiences. Leaders must embrace such technologies to create an ecosystem that integrates formal, informal, and experiential learning opportunities.

Visionary leadership requires bridging the gap between educational institutions and industry by fostering partnerships and aligning academic programmes with market trends. For example, internships, apprenticeships, and work-integrated learning programmes ensure that students develop transferable skills and remain competitive in a global economy. This holistic approach to teaching and learning aligns with a strategic vision that prioritises adaptability, inclusivity, and lifelong learning (Hargreaves & Fullan, 2015).

By extending their vision beyond classrooms, leaders not only prepare learners for evolving career landscapes but also position their institutions as hubs of innovation and community engagement. This requires a commitment to continuous professional development for educators, ensuring they are equipped to navigate and integrate emerging learning modalities into practice.

Building collaborative teaching communities

A collaborative teaching community is a group of educators who work together intentionally and consistently to improve teaching and learning through shared goals, mutual support, and collective responsibility. These communities foster trust, openness, and a commitment to continuous professional growth.

Building collaborative teaching communities enables teachers to share best practices, engage with educational research, and promote interdisciplinary approaches. Leaders play a pivotal role in creating and sustaining these communities, ensuring that collaboration translates into enhanced teaching quality, innovation, and a supportive professional culture. Facilitating professional learning communities (PLCs), promoting team-teaching, engaging with research, and supporting practitioner inquiry are strategies that contribute to this goal. Leadership is critical in providing the vision, resources, and support necessary for collaboration to thrive. As Vangrieken et al. (2015) conclude, collaboration is not just a means to improve teaching but a pathway to transforming educational institutions into dynamic, learning-focused communities. By prioritising collaboration, leaders empower educators to reach their full potential and, ultimately, improve outcomes for students.

The importance of collaboration

Sharing best practices allows teachers to learn from one another's experiences, develop new strategies, and address shared challenges. According to DuFour & DuFour (2013), professional learning communities (PLCs) provide structured opportunities for teachers to reflect on their practices and align them with institutional goals. These communities foster a sense of collective responsibility, where teachers work together to improve student learning outcomes.

Collaboration also helps overcome isolation in teaching. Hargreaves & Fullan (2015) emphasise that collaborative environments encourage teachers to move beyond individualistic approaches, fostering shared accountability and innovation. For example, faculty can co-develop lesson plans, design interdisciplinary projects, or analyse student performance data collectively. Such practices lead to more cohesive teaching strategies and a more supportive professional culture.

Facilitating professional learning communities

Leaders play a crucial role in facilitating PLCs by providing the necessary structures, resources, and support. According to Stoll et al. (2006), successful PLCs require clear goals, time for collaboration, and an atmosphere of trust and openness. Leaders can establish regular meetings where faculty engage in dialogue, share insights, and co-create solutions.

Cross-departmental collaboration is another effective strategy for fostering innovation. For instance, leaders can create interdisciplinary teams to address complex problems or explore shared themes across subjects. Such cross-disciplinary collaboration expands teachers' perspectives and leads to creative pedagogical approaches (Vangrieken et al., 2017).

Peer mentoring programmes also facilitate collaboration, particularly for new or early-career educators. Leaders can pair experienced faculty with novices to provide guidance, share expertise, and build confidence. Mentoring relationships not only benefit mentees but also provide mentors with opportunities to reflect on and refine their own practices (Feiman-Nemser, 2012).

Promoting team-teaching and interdisciplinary approaches

Leaders should encourage team-teaching and interdisciplinary methods. Team-teaching involves two or more teachers working together to plan, deliver, and assess instruction. This approach allows faculty to utilise their diverse expertise, providing students with a richer learning experience. According to Friend & Cook (1992), team-teaching promotes collaboration, improves instructional quality, and enhances student engagement by presenting multiple perspectives.

Interdisciplinary teaching integrates knowledge and methods from different subjects, encouraging students to make connections across disciplines. Leaders can promote this by organising workshops or funding pilot projects that bring together faculty from different departments. For example, a collaboration between science and humanities faculties might explore ethical issues in technology, blending technical knowledge with philosophical inquiry. Senior leaders can support such initiatives by providing time for planning, resources for implementation, and recognition for successful outcomes.

Engaging with educational research

Leaders can encourage faculty to stay abreast of the latest studies and integrate evidence-based strategies into their teaching. Smith (2023) argues that professional development programmes should include opportunities for educators to critically analyse research findings and discuss their practical implications. Providing access to academic journals, organising research seminars, allowing access to conferences, and inviting guest speakers are practical ways to facilitate this engagement. Leaders can also encourage teachers to participate in action research, where they investigate and address specific issues within their classrooms. Action research not only improves teaching practices but also empowers educators to contribute to the broader knowledge base (Carr & Kemmis, 2003).

Empirical research, conducted by teachers within their own settings, is a powerful tool for professional growth and institutional improvement. Cochran-Smith & Lytle (2015) highlight that empirical research allows teachers to examine their practices critically, identify areas for improvement, and test innovative strategies. It bridges the gap between theory and practice, ensuring that research addresses real-world challenges. In schools, empirical research might involve teachers investigating the impact of a new instructional method on student engagement or outcomes. In universities, faculty might explore the effectiveness of different assessment approaches or the integration of technology in teaching. Leaders can support such initiatives by providing funding, and opportunities for dissemination, such as conferences or in-house journals.

Collaboration is integral to practitioner research. By forming research teams, educators can pool their expertise, share findings, and create a culture of inquiry. According to Zeichner (2003), collaborative practitioner research fosters mutual learning and builds professional capital within institutions.

Peer observation of teaching

Peer observation of teaching (POOT) is a practice where teachers observe each other's teaching and provide constructive feedback, promoting professional development and a collaborative culture. This practice enhances teaching quality by fostering reflection, sharing best practices, and improving pedagogical skills. POOT is increasingly recognised in both higher education and schools as an effective tool for teacher growth (MacLeod et al., 2016).

Successful POOT relies on strong institutional support and leadership to create a safe environment for collaboration. Leaders facilitate this process by promoting professional development and ensuring the practice is framed around growth rather than evaluation. POOT is also seen as a valuable alternative to traditional line manager observations, which often focus on compliance, by fostering a more supportive and peer-driven approach to feedback (Bennett et al., 2016).

Ultimately, POOT creates a professional learning community where educators continually refine their practices, engage with new ideas, and contribute to their colleagues' development, resulting in improved outcomes for both teachers and students (Hammersley-Fletcher & Orsmond, 2004). The primary benefit of POOT is its potential to improve teaching practices by encouraging reflective teaching and effective assessment. Observing colleagues provides teachers with the opportunity to assess their own methods in relation to others, often leading to new insights about their practice (Bennett et al., 2016). This process is inherently collaborative, where feedback becomes not only a means of identifying areas of improvement but also a tool for strengthening positive teaching practices (Hammersley-Fletcher & Orsmond, 2004).

Another notable advantage of POOT is its ability to promote inclusivity. As teachers collaborate, they gain a better understanding of diverse teaching styles and strategies. This exposure helps to bridge gaps in pedagogical approaches, enabling educators to adapt their teaching to meet the needs of different learners (MacLeod et al., 2016). In this way, POOT not only enhances individual teaching but also contributes to a more inclusive and equitable learning environment.

Effective leadership plays a crucial role in the successful implementation of POOT programmes. Leaders are responsible for creating an environment that encourages collaboration and ensures that the peer observation process is conducted constructively. Institutional support is vital to embedding POOT into everyday practice. Leaders must promote a culture where peer observation is seen as a valuable tool for growth rather than a form of assessment or surveillance. Leaders can achieve this by ensuring that teachers feel safe to provide and receive feedback, without fear of judgment.

Leadership can facilitate the scheduling and organisation of peer observation sessions. In some institutions, time constraints may be a barrier to effective peer observation and leaders can address this by incorporating peer observation into the professional development framework, allocating sufficient time for teachers to observe each other's classes, and ensuring that the feedback process is manageable and purposeful.

Senior leadership must also promote the integration of peer observation into the institution's overall strategy for teaching and learning. Leadership that supports a vision of collaborative teaching is essential for sustaining POOT. For example, senior leaders can align POOT with institutional goals for enhancing teaching quality, ensuring that it becomes part of the overall approach to improving student outcomes. Leaders can also provide opportunities for teachers to develop the skills necessary to conduct effective peer observations, such as training in feedback techniques and observation methodologies.

Information — While traditionally associated with classroom visits, Peer Observation of Teaching (POOT) does not always require direct, physical observation. It can also take the form of professional dialogue, collaborative planning, or the exchange of teaching strategies and reflections. This flexible approach maintains the core purpose of POOT - mutual learning and development - while allowing educators to engage meaningfully with one another even when in-person observation is not possible.

The practice of POOT offers numerous developmental benefits for teachers. One of the most significant impacts is the opportunity for teachers to reflect on their own practice through the lens of their colleagues' feedback. This reflective process is a cornerstone of professional growth, as it encourages teachers to critically evaluate their methods and make adjustments to improve student engagement and learning outcomes. POOT also helps teachers to stay current with educational trends and innovations. Exposure to different teaching approaches through observation can inspire teachers to incorporate new strategies into their own classrooms, enhancing the learning experience for students. Furthermore, POOT provides an avenue for teachers to develop mentoring and leadership skills. By observing and providing feedback to colleagues, experienced teachers contribute to the professional growth of their peers while refining their own skills in communication, leadership, and pedagogical expertise (O'Leary, 2016).

The collaborative nature of POOT also contributes to teacher retention and job satisfaction. The sense of community created through peer observation programmes can reduce teacher isolation, particularly in large institutions where individual educators may feel disconnected from others. Teachers who engage in POOT are more likely to feel supported in their professional roles, which can enhance their overall satisfaction and commitment to the institution (Bell & Mladenovic, 2008).

Leadership strategies for building collaborative teaching communities

Effective leadership is critical to building and sustaining collaborative teaching communities. Leaders must emphasise the value of collaboration and provide the necessary support to make it a reality. Bryk et al. (2015) suggest that leaders who model collaborative behaviours, such as actively participating in discussions and seeking input from faculty, set a positive tone for the institution. Practical strategies for leaders include:

1. **Providing time and resources:** Ensure that staff have dedicated time for collaboration and access to necessary tools, such as meeting spaces or online platforms.
2. **Recognising and rewarding collaboration:** Celebrate successful collaborations through awards, promotions, or public acknowledgment.
3. **Facilitating communication:** Use technology to connect staff across departments or campuses, enabling broader collaboration.
4. **Investing in professional development:** Offer training on collaboration techniques, such as effective communication or conflict resolution.
5. **Encouraging risk-taking:** Foster an environment where staff feel safe to experiment with new ideas and learn from failures.

Promoting pathways into teaching

A robust and well-supported teaching workforce is essential for ensuring high-quality teaching and learning. Educational institutions must invest in developing pathways that enable aspiring educators to gain the necessary qualifications and experiences.

In schools, one of the most widely recognised pathways into teaching is through obtaining *Qualified Teacher Status* (QTS). This qualification is essential for teaching in maintained schools in many countries, with some exceptions for specific school types. QTS ensures that individuals have met the professional standards for teaching and are equipped to lead learning effectively in the classroom. There are several routes to gaining QTS, including university-led programmes that combine academic study with school placements, school-based pathways like *School Direct* or *Teach First*, and the assessment-only route for experienced, unqualified teachers.

Postgraduate qualifications, such as the *Postgraduate Certificate in Education* (PGCE), and undergraduate routes like the *Bachelor of Education* (BEd) are the most common pathways for those looking to enter teaching. The PGCE combines academic training with practical experience and typically leads to QTS. These programmes offer flexibility through full-time, part-time, or distance learning options, allowing trainees to specialise in particular phases or subjects, such as primary or secondary education, science, or languages. The BEd, an undergraduate qualification, also provides a comprehensive education and practical experience, often leading directly to QTS, and is ideal for those looking to start their teaching career without pursuing postgraduate study. Additionally, both the PGCE and BEd are recognised internationally, making them attractive options for those seeking teaching opportunities abroad. Typically, 50-60% of teachers take the PGCE route and 5-10% the BEd route.

Work-based routes into teaching, such as apprenticeships, are also gaining popularity. These programmes offer salaried, on-the-job training combined with academic study, enabling individuals to earn while they learn and ultimately gain QTS. Similarly, *school-centred initial teacher training* (SCITT) programmes provide practical experience while pursuing academic qualifications, often in collaboration with universities.

Beyond formal teacher qualifications, the role of *Teaching Assistants* (TAs) is also essential in supporting classroom instruction. TAs often work alongside teachers to provide individual or small-group support, making differentiated instruction more feasible. While formal qualifications are not always required for these positions, experience in schools or childcare settings, along with relevant qualifications such as Level 2 or 3 certificates in supporting teaching and learning, can enhance employability.

For more experienced teaching assistants, the role of *Higher Level Teaching Assistant* (HLTA) represents a potential career progression. HLTAs take on greater responsibilities, including planning and delivering lessons, and typically require extensive TA experience, evidence of meeting national standards, and often additional qualifications like a Foundation Degree in Education. This pathway provides opportunities for further career advancement in the education sector.

In further education and higher education settings, the qualifications and routes into teaching vary. In FE colleges, lecturers are often required to hold a Level 5 teaching qualification such as the *Diploma in Education and Training* or a *PGCE in Post-Compulsory Education and Training*, along with a degree in the subject area. In universities, lecturers typically hold a postgraduate qualification, such as a master's degree or a doctorate, in their field, with prior teaching experience and professional recognition often being valued. In vocational or technical fields, significant industry experience may sometimes substitute for traditional academic qualifications.

Teacher leadership

Across all sectors, promoting teacher leadership can further enhance professional growth and improving educational outcomes. When teachers are empowered to take on leadership roles, it fosters a culture of shared responsibility and continuous development.

Teacher leaders contribute to stronger collaboration among staff, help align policies with the needs of students, and bring their classroom expertise into decision-making processes. These leadership opportunities offer a path for teachers to develop new skills and advance their careers. By involving teachers in leadership roles, schools can adopt a shared leadership model that builds resilience and fosters a collective vision for improvement.

However, the promotion of teacher leadership does come with challenges. Teacher leaders often face role ambiguity, balancing teaching responsibilities with leadership duties. This can lead to confusion about their authority and influence, potentially creating tension within teams. The additional workload associated with leadership roles can also contribute to stress and burnout, particularly when teachers are not adequately supported. Furthermore, resistance from colleagues, insufficient training for leadership roles, and the risk of overburdening the same teachers repeatedly can undermine the effectiveness of teacher leadership initiatives.

To mitigate these challenges, educational leaders should ensure that roles and responsibilities for teacher leaders are clearly defined, provide adequate time and support, foster a culture of collaboration, and share leadership opportunities equitably among staff. By addressing these issues proactively, schools, colleges, and universities can maximise the benefits of teacher leadership and create more pathways into teaching that foster a dynamic and well-supported teaching workforce.

Leading inclusive and equitable learning

Leading inclusive and equitable learning emphasises the importance of creating educational environments that cater to the diverse needs of all students. This comprehensive approach to education aims to break down barriers, address systemic inequalities, and provide equal opportunities for success to every learner, regardless of their background or abilities.

Theoretical foundations

The principles of inclusivity and equity in education are rooted in the belief that every student has the right to quality education. Ainscow (2020) argues that inclusive education goes beyond simply placing students with diverse needs in mainstream classrooms; it involves transforming the education system to accommodate the learning requirements of all students. This transformation requires a shift in mindset, policies, and practices at all levels of the educational system.

Historical perspectives on inclusive education reveal a gradual evolution from segregation to integration, and finally to inclusion. Middleton & Kay (2019) conclude that valuing difference and embracing concepts of social justice and equity are fundamental to understanding inclusive education. This shift in perspective has led to a more holistic approach to education that recognises the unique contributions of every individual. Social justice in education plays a crucial role in building equitable systems. According to Terzi (2005), a just distribution of educational opportunities for disabled students and those with special educational needs is essential for achieving educational equality. This emphasises the importance of providing individuals with the necessary resources and opportunities to achieve their full potential.

Strategies for inclusive leadership

Recognising and addressing cultural, linguistic, and socioeconomic diversity is crucial for creating truly inclusive learning environments. Educators must be aware of the various factors that influence student learning and develop strategies to support all learners. This includes supporting students with disabilities in mainstream education, bridging the gender gap in learning outcomes, and addressing systemic biases in education.

Inclusive leadership plays a vital role in creating and sustaining equitable learning environments. The *Supporting Inclusive School Leadership* (SISL) project emphasises the importance of school leaders in addressing inequality, building community, and enabling full participation for all learners, especially those most vulnerable to exclusion (European Agency, 2025). Inclusive school leaders set clear directions, develop human and organisational capacities, and work at the interface between education policies and their implementation in schools.

Developing culturally responsive teaching practices is essential for inclusive education. Gay (2018) defines culturally responsive teaching as using the cultural knowledge, prior experiences, and performance styles of diverse students to make learning more appropriate and effective for them. This approach recognises the importance of students' cultural backgrounds in shaping their learning experiences and outcomes. Implementing *Universal Design for Learning* (UDL) is another key strategy for inclusive education. UDL provides a framework for designing flexible learning environments that can accommodate individual learning differences. Rose & Meyer (2002) argue that UDL principles can help educators create curricula that are accessible to all learners from the outset, rather than making adaptations for specific students after the fact.

Policy and practice

Reviewing and implementing inclusive education policies at the institutional level is crucial for creating lasting change. Hernández-Torrano et al. (2022) highlight the importance of focusing on social justice and democracy when researching and implementing inclusive education policies. This involves not only creating policies that promote inclusivity but also ensuring that these policies are effectively translated into practice.

Creating inclusive and equitable learning environments

Inclusive and equitable learning environments are built through intentional strategies that address systemic inequities and embrace diversity at all levels of education. This involves equipping educators with the necessary knowledge, skills, and strategies to effectively teach in diverse classrooms. Training in cultural competence and addressing implicit biases is essential, and professional development opportunities - such as workshops, seminars, courses, certifications, and online learning platforms - play a crucial role in supporting inclusive practices.

Equity must also be embedded in the curriculum. Designing inclusive curricula involves representing diverse voices and perspectives and integrating social justice throughout teaching and learning. Banks (2015) emphasises the value of multicultural education in helping students see their experiences reflected in the material, thereby enhancing engagement and fostering a sense of belonging.

Creating inclusive classrooms further requires the careful management of *microaggressions* and the promotion of *student agency*. Sue et al. (2019) describe microaggressions as everyday verbal, behavioural, or environmental slights that can marginalise individuals. Addressing such incidents and encouraging students to participate meaningfully in decision-making contribute to safer, more empowering learning environments.

Assessment and evaluation practices must also reflect inclusivity. Culturally responsive assessment, as outlined by Hood (1998), considers students' backgrounds and experiences, ensuring a more equitable and accurate reflection of their learning. This approach helps to redress imbalances often present in standardised testing systems and gives a fuller picture of student potential.

Engaging parents and communities is another critical aspect of inclusive education. Building strong school-family-community partnerships can support student success by addressing barriers to engagement and leveraging external resources. Epstein (2001) highlights how such collaborations can create more responsive and supportive educational settings.

Technology, when used thoughtfully, has the potential to enhance inclusion by increasing accessibility and personalisation in learning. However, the digital divide remains a concern. Facer & Selwyn (2020) caution that if not implemented with equity in mind, educational technology can reinforce existing inequalities. Ensuring that all students benefit from technological advances is essential to achieving inclusive goals.

There are ongoing challenges in the pursuit of inclusive education. These include resistance to inclusive practices and the need to address *intersectionality* in educational leadership. Crenshaw (2013) introduced the concept of intersectionality to show how multiple identities - such as race, gender, and disability - can overlap to create compounded experiences of discrimination. Leaders must understand and address these complexities to develop truly inclusive environments. Looking to the future, emerging technologies like artificial intelligence offer opportunities to personalise learning and better support diverse learners. However, it is critical that these innovations are designed and implemented with equity at their core. Preparing future leaders to address both existing and evolving challenges will be key to ensuring sustained progress toward inclusion and equity in education.

Activity: Enhancing teaching and learning

This activity encourages you to apply the concepts and strategies explored in this chapter to a real or hypothetical educational context. By reflecting on your own experiences and aspirations, you will identify key actions you can take to lead teaching and learning effectively within your institution.

1. **Personal reflection**

Reflect on your current or past teaching context. Consider the following questions:
- How clear is the shared vision for teaching and learning in your institution? How aligned are teaching priorities with the broader institutional goals?
- In what ways have you or your colleagues adopted innovative teaching practices? What technologies or creative approaches have you integrated into your teaching?
- How are collaboration and the exchange of best practices encouraged in your school or organisation?
- What professional development opportunities are available to you and your colleagues? How effective have they been in driving improvements?
- What common challenges (e.g., resistance to change, resource limitations, varying student needs) have you faced, and how have you tackled them?

2. **Identifying a path forward**
   Based on your reflections, choose one of the following focus areas to develop further in your context:
   - *Vision and goals:* How could you help clarify and communicate a shared vision that aligns with institutional goals? Write a brief plan for developing and communicating this vision to colleagues.

- *Innovation and collaboration:* Identify one innovative teaching strategy or technology that you would like to integrate into your practice or encourage within your team. How can you foster collaboration to support its adoption?
- *Inclusive and equitable learning:* Reflect on how you might help create a more inclusive and equitable learning environment for all students. What actions can you take to address disparities and support culturally responsive teaching?
- *Teacher leadership:* If you are in a leadership role, how could you promote teacher leadership within your team? If you are not in a leadership role, how can you take on informal leadership to support change in teaching and learning?

3. **Action plan**

Create a short action plan outlining specific steps you can take to address the area you have chosen. Your plan should include:

- Clear goals for what you want to achieve.
- The resources or support you will need.
- A timeline for implementation.
- Potential challenges and how you might overcome them.

4. **Sharing and feedback**

If you are in a group setting (e.g., a professional development session or course), share your action plan with a peer or colleague. Provide feedback on each other's plans and discuss how you might support one another in achieving your goals.

Reflection

By the end of this activity, you should have a clear strategy for applying the concepts of enhancing teaching and learning within your context, along with practical steps to overcome challenges and drive improvement.

Summary

Successful teaching and learning depend not only on the quality of teachers and the learning experiences they create, but also on effective leaders who prioritise the development of top-rate teachers and communicate a clear, shared vision that aligns teaching priorities with institutional goals, inspiring collective action. They develop strategies to encourage and support educators in adopting innovative teaching practices, integrating new technologies, and fostering creativity. They create inclusive and equitable learning environments, addressing disparities and ensuring success for all students through culturally responsive leadership.

Collaboration is promoted through professional learning communities and peer networks, facilitating the exchange of best practices and resources to enhance teaching. Leaders encourage reflective practices and professional development to drive continuous improvement in teaching and learning. They identify and address common challenges such as resistance to change, resource limitations, and diverse student needs with proactive and adaptive strategies.

Leaders promote pathways into teaching by raising awareness and facilitating various entry routes, such as undergraduate and postgraduate qualifications, to attract diverse and high-quality candidates.

Using teacher leadership as a strategy, leaders empower educators to take on leadership roles within their institutes, guiding instructional practices, mentoring peers, and driving improvements across the school or institution.

4 CULTIVATING FUTURE LEADERS

Ben Hayes

Introduction

Developing leadership capability in education involves more than formal training or positional authority. It is a dynamic, evolving process shaped through purposeful reflection, structured experiences, and strong relational support. This chapter explores how various strategies contribute to the growth of future leaders, with particular emphasis on coaching and mentoring - approaches that are increasingly recognised as pivotal to leadership development in educational settings. It considers how these strategies help to uncover hidden potential, foster professional resilience, and embed leadership values and behaviours within institutional cultures. The discussion also highlights the importance of creating environments where leadership can be cultivated, sustained, and expressed. Alongside coaching and mentoring, attention is given to complementary approaches that promote shared growth and the continual renewal of leadership at all levels within educational organisations.

This chapter:

- Explores a variety of methods for leadership development.
- Discusses the process of identifying and engaging key stakeholders in the development of coaching and mentoring strategies.
- Provides a framework for setting clear objectives and measurable goals for coaching and mentoring programmes.
- Examines different coaching and mentoring models and their suitability for various organisational needs.
- Highlights the importance of training, support, and ongoing professional development for coaches and mentors.
- Outlines how to establish clear roles and responsibilities for all participants in coaching and mentoring programmes.
- Reviews methods for evaluating the success and impact of coaching and mentoring initiatives.
- Offers practical tips on integrating feedback and continuously improving coaching and mentoring programmes within an organisation.

Developing the leaders of tomorrow

Leadership development is a cornerstone of creating effective and sustainable educational practices across schools, colleges, and universities. As the educational landscape evolves, the demand for strong, adaptable leadership intensifies. Leaders must drive improvements, support innovation, and cultivate positive learning environments. The journey to cultivating future leaders in education involves a blend of formal training, hands-on experiences, and continual support, all of which are essential for equipping individuals with the necessary skills to lead effectively.

Central to leadership development is the understanding that leadership capabilities are not inherent but can be developed through a range of methods. From formal Initial Teacher Education (ITE) programmes to internal staff development initiatives and external postgraduate qualifications, numerous pathways exist for individuals to grow as leaders. Whether through mentorship, coaching, shadowing, or on-the-job training, each approach is designed to provide the tools, knowledge, and experiences necessary for aspiring leaders to take on their roles with confidence.

Leadership development extends beyond traditional management skills. It encompasses a broad spectrum of competencies, such as the ability to foster collaboration, engage in reflective practice, uphold ethical leadership, and contribute to institutional improvement. Teachers, for example, are often required to assume leadership roles within classrooms and schools, necessitating the development of skills in classroom management, pedagogical leadership, and teamwork. Similarly, administrators and faculty members are increasingly tasked with leading initiatives and managing change within their institutions.

Practical experience is one of the most effective means of developing leadership capabilities. As such, many organisations provide opportunities for on-the-job learning, job rotation, mentoring, coaching, and shadowing, which immerse individuals in real-world leadership tasks. These methods create supportive environments in which individuals can hone their skills, learning from both their successes and challenges.

Leadership development is not confined to those in formal leadership positions. Many organisations recognise the importance of tapping into the leadership potential of all staff members, empowering them to assume leadership responsibilities in areas such as curriculum development, pedagogical innovation, and project management. By identifying and nurturing existing leadership potential within the workforce, institutions can foster a culture of collaboration, growth, and continuous improvement.

Networking and collaboration also play a pivotal role in leadership growth. Educational institutions benefit from engaging with peers in the field, sharing best practices, and learning from collective experiences. National and international networks, including professional associations, school alliances, and subject-specific groups, provide invaluable opportunities for leaders to connect, exchange ideas, and collaborate on advancing educational improvement.

Formal educational programmes, such as postgraduate degrees and leadership courses, offer structured opportunities for individuals to deepen their understanding of leadership theory and practice. These qualifications equip future leaders with the knowledge to navigate complex educational challenges and prepare them for the responsibilities they will face in their roles.

Formal training and education

Formal training and education are pivotal in cultivating effective leadership within educational settings. Structured programmes such as Initial Teacher Education (ITE), in-house staff development, external postgraduate education, and formal leadership courses provide foundational knowledge and practical skills essential for educational leaders.

Initial Teacher Education (ITE) programmes

ITE programmes serve as the bedrock for developing leadership competencies among prospective educators. Beyond imparting pedagogical skills, these programmes integrate leadership training to prepare teachers for future roles. For instance, the *SUSP ITE* programme emphasises leadership skills aligned with the *Professional Standards for Teaching*, encouraging student teachers to consider leadership roles early in their careers (Harris et al., 2020). A study by Whitfield (2019) highlights the importance of supportive structures within ITE to promote leadership learning among newly qualified teachers.

In-house staff development initiatives

In-house professional development initiatives are instrumental in fostering leadership within educational institutions. These programmes offer tailored training that aligns with the institution's culture and objectives. Vedhathiri (2022) discusses the effectiveness of in-house leadership development programmes in enhancing the capabilities of high-potential faculty members. Such initiatives not only build leadership capacity but also contribute to staff retention and institutional growth.

Formal educational programmes (e.g., postgraduate degrees)

Formal educational programmes, including postgraduate degrees and specialised leadership courses, offer structured learning environments for aspiring leaders. A systematic review by Ueda & Kezar (2024) emphasises the role of formal leadership programmes in developing essential competencies such as strategic planning, communication, and ethical decision-making. These programmes often employ diverse pedagogical approaches, including case studies and simulations, to prepare participants for complex leadership challenges. Pursuing external postgraduate education, such as master's degrees in educational leadership, provides educators with advanced knowledge and a broader perspective on leadership theories and practices. A scoping review by Carson et al. (2023) indicates that master's education significantly contributes to leadership development by enhancing critical thinking and decision-making skills. These programmes often incorporate practical components, allowing educators to apply theoretical concepts to real-world scenarios.

Experiential learning

Experiential learning offers practical, real-world experiences that complement and enhance theoretical knowledge, making it a vital component of effective leadership development. Unlike traditional classroom-based instruction, experiential learning immerses staff in authentic leadership contexts, allowing them to navigate the complexities, uncertainties, and interpersonal dynamics inherent in educational settings. Key methods - such as on-the-job training, job rotation, shadowing experienced leaders, and engaging in practical leadership tasks - provide staff with firsthand insights into decision-making processes, conflict resolution, and strategic planning.

On-the-job training

On-the-job training in education immerses aspiring leaders in authentic environments, enabling them to develop leadership skills through direct, hands-on experience. By taking on real responsibilities - such as coordinating staff meetings, leading curriculum initiatives, or managing school events - educators gain valuable insights into the practical demands of leadership roles. This approach enhances critical capabilities such as decision-making, communication, and adaptability within the context of day-to-day educational operations. Similar to how internships in the business sector have been shown to improve employment prospects and job-related competencies, structured on-the-job leadership experiences in education provide a vital bridge between theory and practice. They offer emerging leaders the opportunities to apply educational leadership concepts in meaningful, situated contexts, thereby fostering professional growth, confidence, and readiness for more formal leadership roles.

Job rotation

Job rotation involves moving staff through various roles within an organisation, exposing them to different functions and challenges. This approach broadens their understanding and enhances problem-solving skills. Research by Jorgensen et al. (2005) highlights that job rotation can lead to increased job satisfaction and performance by providing diverse experiences that develop a well-rounded skill set. By navigating different roles, individuals gain a comprehensive view of organisational operations, which is crucial for effective leadership.

At some research-intensive universities, early- to mid-career academics are offered rotational leadership roles - such as acting Programme Leader, Deputy Head of Department, or Chair of a committee (e.g., Learning & Teaching, Ethics). This exposes staff to leadership responsibilities while under the mentorship of a senior academic. In doing so it builds skills, confidence and readiness for formal leadership posts without full commitment.

Shadowing

Shadowing allows individuals to observe experienced leaders in their daily activities, offering insights into leadership styles and decision-making processes. This method bridges the gap between theory and practice. Nicolini & Korica (2024) discuss structured shadowing as a pedagogy that enables learners to understand the nuances of leadership through close observation. Such experiences can demystify leadership roles and inspire confidence in emerging leaders.

Practical experience in leadership tasks

Engaging in practical leadership tasks, such as leading projects, managing teams, or coordinating initiatives, offers hands-on experience that is essential for developing core leadership competencies. These real-world opportunities allow individuals to apply theoretical knowledge in dynamic settings, confronting challenges and making decisions in real time. Kolb's experiential learning theory underscores the value of concrete experiences in the learning cycle, where reflection, conceptualisation, and experimentation lead to deeper understanding and growth (Kolb, 2014). By taking on authentic leadership roles, individuals not only build confidence but also develop critical thinking, problem-solving, and adaptability - key attributes for effective and responsive leadership in complex educational environments.

Reflective practice

Reflective practice involves the deliberate and structured examination of one's experiences, thoughts, and actions to gain deeper insights and inform future decision-making. In the context of educational leadership, it serves as a vital tool for professional growth, helping leaders to evaluate their strategies, recognise areas for improvement, and refine their practice over time. It promotes self-awareness, emotional intelligence, and a commitment to lifelong learning - key qualities for navigating the complex and dynamic environments of schools and colleges.

Effective leaders use reflective practice to assess the outcomes of their decisions, understand how their leadership style affects others, and identify new approaches to improve performance. This process can take various forms, including journaling, peer discussions, coaching conversations, and structured self-evaluations. Research by HALO Psychology (2025) highlights that reflective learning and expressive writing can assist employees in managing negative emotions, leading to improved well-being and job performance. These reflective techniques are especially useful in high-pressure educational contexts, where leaders must balance strategic responsibilities with relational and emotional demands.

Reflective practice contributes to leadership effectiveness by encouraging critical thinking, flexibility, and responsiveness to change. According to EDIS (2024), leaders who engage regularly in reflection are more likely to adapt their approaches in light of feedback and evolving circumstances, enhancing their ability to lead diverse teams and drive school improvement.

Shared leadership opportunities

Shared leadership opportunities in education foster collaborative environments where responsibilities are distributed among various stakeholders, enhancing institutional effectiveness. This approach encompasses project management roles, teachers assuming leadership within classrooms and schools, and empowering staff to undertake leadership tasks irrespective of formal titles.

Project management roles

Assigning project management responsibilities to educators allows them to lead initiatives, fostering ownership and accountability. Such roles enable teachers to develop strategic planning and organisational skills, contributing to school improvement efforts. Research indicates that shared leadership in project teams enhances team performance and adaptability, as members collectively navigate challenges and share decision-making responsibilities (Zhu et al., 2018). This collaborative approach not only improves project outcomes but also cultivates a culture of mutual respect and shared purpose.

Primary: A teacher leads a *sensory garden project*, coordinating staff and parents, building leadership and planning skills.

Secondary: An English teacher manages a *school literacy strategy*, working across departments to drive school-wide improvement.

Further Education (FE): A lecturer leads a *blended learning redesign*, managing staff training and digital curriculum development, enhancing adaptability and coordination.

Higher Education (HE): A senior lecturer oversees an *international student induction programme*, collaborating across academic and professional teams to improve student support and institutional cohesion.

Teachers as leaders in classrooms and schools

Empowering teachers to take on leadership roles within their classrooms and schools promotes a sense of agency and professional growth. When teachers lead professional development sessions, mentor peers, or spearhead curriculum initiatives, they contribute to a culture of continuous improvement. A study by Wenner & Campbell (2017) emphasises that teacher leadership positively impacts instructional practices and student achievement, as teachers bring classroom insights into leadership decisions. Involving teachers in leadership roles fosters a sense of ownership and commitment to school goals.

Empowering staff beyond formal roles

Encouraging staff members to undertake leadership responsibilities without formal titles democratises leadership and makes use of diverse talents within the community. This approach recognises the potential of all staff members to contribute meaningfully to initiatives. Research by Harris & Jones (2019) highlights that distributed leadership models, where leadership tasks are shared among staff, lead to increased innovation and responsiveness to student needs. By valuing the contributions of all staff, institutes can build a more inclusive and dynamic leadership structure.

Collaborative learning

Collaborative learning has emerged as an effective approach in educational leadership development, emphasising the importance of networking, engagement in professional communities, and the exchange of best practices. This method fosters a culture of shared knowledge and continuous improvement among educators.

Networking and collaboration

Networking and collaboration are fundamental to collaborative learning, enabling educators to connect, share experiences, and develop professionally. Digital platforms have significantly enhanced these interactions, allowing for seamless communication and resource sharing across geographical boundaries. Research indicates that digital literacy plays a crucial role in facilitating effective collaboration and networking, as it empowers educators to engage in online communities and access diverse perspectives.

Engagement in national and international networks

Participation in national and international networks provides educators with opportunities to engage with a broader educational community, fostering the exchange of innovative practices and collaborative problem-solving. Such engagement promotes a global perspective on education, encouraging the adoption of diverse strategies to address common challenges. Studies have shown that involvement in international collaborative learning initiatives enhances educators' capacity to implement effective teaching practices and adapt to various educational contexts.

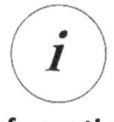

Information

At the national level, membership in organisations such as the *Association for School and College Leaders (ASCL)* in the UK allows educational leaders to share policy updates, engage in professional development, and collaborate on leadership challenges within their own system.

Internationally, networks like the *International Baccalaureate (IB) Educator Network (IBEN)* enable educators across the globe to participate in training, curriculum development, and peer support, fostering a shared commitment to high-quality, globally-minded education.

Participation in professional associations, alliances, and groups

Professional associations, school alliances, and subject-specific groups serve as platforms for educators to collaborate, share resources, and engage in professional development. Organisations like the *Association for Supervision and Curriculum Development* (ASCD) and the *National Education Association* (NEA) offer resources, conferences, and publications that support educators in their professional growth. These groups facilitate the dissemination of best practices and foster a sense of community.

Sharing best practices and learning from others

The exchange of best practices is a cornerstone of collaborative learning, enabling educators to learn from each other's experiences and refine their teaching and assessment strategies. Collaborative environments encourage the sharing of successful approaches, fostering innovation and continuous improvement in educational practices. Research highlights that educators who engage in collaborative practices report higher levels of job satisfaction and self-efficacy, as they benefit from the collective wisdom of their peers.

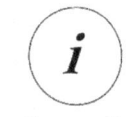
Information
A common approach to exchanging best practice is through Professional Learning Communities (PLCs), where educators meet regularly to share strategies, reflect on practice, and improve student outcomes. PLCs promote collaboration, peer support, and continuous improvement by enabling teachers to co-plan, observe, and give feedback in a structured, trust-based environment.

Coaching and mentoring in leadership development

Leadership development has progressed beyond traditional training to include more personalised, experiential strategies such as coaching and mentoring, both of which play a pivotal role in enhancing individual performance and building organisational resilience and adaptability.

Information
Coaching and mentoring are arguably the most popular and widely endorsed methods of staff development. Coaching is usually more goal-focused and short-term, often used with aspiring or newly appointed leaders. Mentoring is usually more relational and long-term, often offered by experienced leaders guiding less experienced colleagues.

Many leadership frameworks (e.g. NPQ qualifications in the UK) embed coaching and mentoring as key developmental tools.

Definitions and distinctions

Coaching and mentoring are sometimes used interchangeably but serve distinct purposes and operate differently. Coaching is typically goal-focused and short-term, designed to develop specific skills and enhance performance. It involves a structured relationship where the coach facilitates the coachee's reflection, learning, and action planning. In contrast, mentoring is more relational and long-term, offering holistic support that includes career development, emotional encouragement, and role modelling (Ragins & Kram, 2007). In education, coaching often targets specific areas like instructional strategies or leadership behaviours, while mentoring supports broader professional development, especially for early-career educators.

Purpose and focus

Coaching typically involves setting concrete, measurable goals to improve task performance (Passmore, 2015). Coaches do not usually provide solutions; rather, they enable coachees to explore and reflect, fostering self-awareness and problem-solving (Jones et al., 2016). In education, this could mean refining teaching techniques or enhancing leadership capabilities.

Mentoring, by contrast, supports the mentee's growth across multiple dimensions, including identity formation, career navigation, and emotional resilience (Kram, 1988). It is especially effective in helping novices adapt to complex environments, such as new teachers understanding school culture or experienced teachers transitioning into leadership roles.

Scope and structure

Coaching operates within a defined structure, often with a set timeline and specific outcomes. Models like GROW (Goal, Reality, Options, Will) offer a framework for sessions (Whitmore, 2017). Regular meetings, progress reviews, and targeted feedback are typical features.

Mentoring tends to be more informal and adaptive. Relationships develop organically based on the mentee's needs, and objectives may evolve over time. This flexibility allows for a more personalised developmental journey that may extend beyond immediate performance goals.

Relationship dynamics

In coaching, the dynamic is typically collaborative, with the coach acting as a facilitator rather than a director. The focus is on active listening, questioning, and reflection, empowering the coachee to develop their own insights and solutions (Jones et al., 2016). This approach supports self-directed learning and fosters greater ownership of personal and professional development.

Mentoring, on the other hand, often involves a more hierarchical relationship, where the mentor draws on their own experience to provide guidance and support. Mentors share insights, offer advice, and act as role models, helping mentees navigate formal expectations as well as the often-unspoken cultural and organisational norms of a workplace (Ragins & Kram, 2007). While more directive than coaching, mentoring relationships can evolve over time into more reciprocal partnerships as the mentee gains confidence and experience.

Enhancing leadership development

Both coaching and mentoring can significantly contribute to leadership development. Coaching enhances specific competencies such as communication, decision-making, and strategic thinking (Ely et al., 2010). Leaders benefit from structured opportunities to reflect on their actions and refine their approaches.

Mentoring supports long-term growth through shared experiences and contextualised advice. Mentors help leaders understand how to manage complex issues like team dynamics or organisational politics (Kram, 1988), offering a developmental perspective that complements the goal-oriented nature of coaching.

Fostering reflective practice

Reflection is central to leadership growth. Coaching encourages reflection through open-ended questioning and structured feedback, promoting deeper understanding of leadership styles, decision-making, and interpersonal effectiveness. Mentoring supports reflective practice by creating a safe space for dialogue. Mentors encourage mentees to process their experiences and draw lessons, often leading to improved self-awareness, emotional regulation, and resilience (Goleman, 2005).

Developing emotional intelligence

Emotional intelligence (EI) is a cornerstone of effective leadership. Coaching helps leaders develop EI by facilitating awareness of emotional responses and their impact on others. Leaders learn to manage their emotions, build relationships, and lead with empathy. Mentors contribute to EI development by modelling emotional competence and guiding mentees through emotionally challenging situations. Through empathetic listening and shared narratives, mentees learn how to navigate interpersonal dynamics (Goleman, 2005).

Organisational impact

At an organisational level, coaching and mentoring foster a culture of learning and improvement. Leaders who engage in these practices often serve as catalysts for wider cultural change, modelling reflective, adaptive behaviours that benefit the organisation as a whole (Avolio, 2010). Institutions that invest in coaching and mentoring signal a commitment to developing their human capital. These programs contribute to talent retention, succession planning, and enhanced organisational performance.

Leadership styles in coaching and mentoring

The effectiveness of coaching and mentoring is influenced by the leadership style adopted. Leadership styles - such as transformational, transactional, autocratic, democratic, and laissez-faire - shape how leaders engage with others and manage developmental relationships (Northouse, 2021).

Transformational and transactional approaches

Transformational leadership, with its emphasis on vision, empowerment, and innovation, aligns well with coaching. Transformational leaders inspire coachees to pursue long-term growth, self-improvement, and higher-order goals (Bass & Stogdill, 1990).

Transactional leadership, focused on clear expectations, rewards, and performance monitoring, may align more closely with mentoring relationships that require structure and directive support (Bass & Avolio, 1994). This style can be effective for mentees who need clarity and stability.

Leadership flexibility

Effective leaders adapt their style to the developmental needs of those they support - a concept known as *leadership flexibility* (Hersey & Blanchard, 2015). Coaches may need to move between directive and facilitative approaches depending on the coachee's readiness. Similarly, mentors might vary their involvement based on the mentee's experience, offering more hands-on guidance early on and greater autonomy over time.

Coaching and mentoring models and frameworks

Various models and frameworks exist to guide the processes of coaching and mentoring, providing structure and clarity for both coaches and mentors. These models offer a roadmap for facilitating personal and professional development, helping individuals identify strengths, weaknesses, and goals. By utilising established models, coaches and mentors can tailor their approaches to meet the specific needs of their staff, thereby enhancing the effectiveness of these developmental tools.

The GROW model

One of the most widely recognised coaching models is the GROW model - Goal, Reality, Options, and Will. Developed by John Whitmore (2009), this model provides a clear framework for structuring coaching sessions. The model (Figure 4.1) begins with the identification of the coachee's goal, which serves as the focus of the coaching relationship. The coach then helps the coachee assess their current reality - understanding where they are in relation to the goal. The third stage, exploring options, involves considering different ways to achieve the goal, while the final stage focuses on the coachee's commitment to action and follow-through.

The GROW model is particularly effective because of its simplicity and flexibility. It can be applied to a wide range of coaching scenarios, from performance improvement to career development. By systematically addressing these four elements, the GROW model helps coaches and coachees maintain focus, ensuring that coaching sessions are productive and goal-oriented. Research suggests that coaching based on the GROW model leads to improved self-awareness and goal clarity, which in turn enhances performance and personal growth (Passmore, 2015).

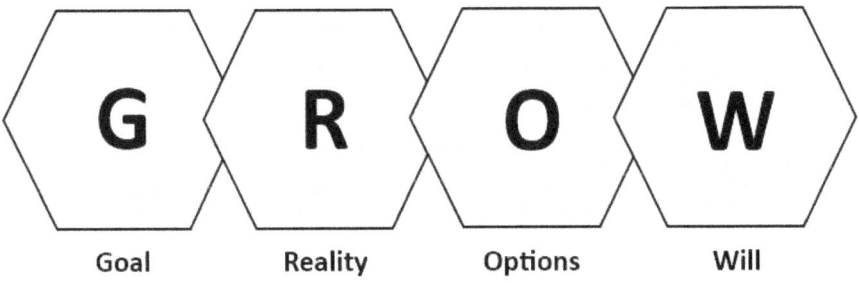

Figure 4.1 - The GROW model

Using the GROW model for a new subject head

A secondary school teacher has just been promoted to Head of Science and is being coached to support her transition into leadership, particularly around leading departmental improvement.

Goal (What does she want to achieve?)
She defines a goal:
"I want to lead the department in improving student outcomes in GCSE Science, particularly for lower-attaining students".

Reality (What's happening now?)
Through reflection, she recognises:
"Our lower-attaining groups are underperforming. Teachers are working hard but there's little consistency in how support strategies are applied. Differentiation is varied, and we don't always use assessment data effectively".

Options (What could she do?)
Together with the coach, she explores strategies:
- Conduct a department audit of current support strategies.
- Lead a CPD session on differentiation and targeted intervention.

> - Develop a shared resource bank for scaffolded activities.
> - Use regular departmental meetings to track progress using data.
> - Arrange paired observations to share good practice.
>
> *"I could start by leading a CPD session on effective differentiation and follow up with some team planning time to implement agreed strategies".*
>
> **Will** (What will she do?)
> She commits to an initial action:
> *"I'll schedule the CPD session for next week's meeting, send out a short survey to gauge current practice, and use that to shape what we cover. I'll also ask one colleague to co-lead the session so we build shared ownership".*

The CLEAR model

The CLEAR model - Contracting, Listening, Exploring, Action, Review, developed by Peter Hawkins (2021), offers another framework for coaching. This model (Figure 4.2) places a strong emphasis on the relationship between coach and coachee, starting with the establishment of clear contracts regarding the goals and scope of the coaching. It then moves through active listening and exploration of the coachee's issues and potential solutions. The action stage focuses on creating a plan for change, while the review stage provides an opportunity to assess progress and reflect on learning.

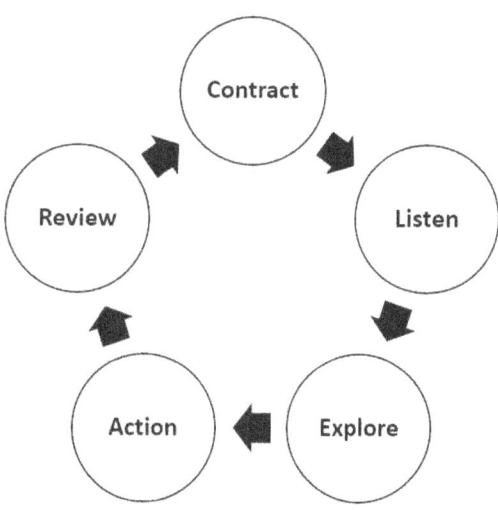

Figure 4.2 - The CLEAR model

The CLEAR model is particularly useful for deepening the coaching relationship. It encourages coaches to listen actively and empathetically, providing space for the coachee to explore their thoughts and feelings. The emphasis on reviewing progress is also beneficial for ensuring that coaching outcomes are achieved. The CLEAR model has been shown to enhance both the coachee's ability to reflect on their learning and their motivation to take action (Hawkins, 2021).

The OSKAR model

Another widely used model is the OSKAR coaching model (Outcome, Scaling, Know-how, Affirm & Action, Review). This model emphasises the importance of setting clear outcomes, identifying current resources and strengths, and reviewing progress toward goals.

While the GROW model is more widely known, OSKAR (Figure 4.3) offers a more explicitly coaching-oriented approach that emphasises behaviours and ways of working, not just actions. It helps individuals move from their current state toward a desired future by drawing on their existing strengths and resources.

Outcome
Clarify the purpose of the session.
How will success look and feel?

Scaling
Uses a 1-10 scale to help the coachee assess their current position and desired progress.

Know-how
Helps coachees understand the skills and resources they require to reach their goals.

Affirm & Action
Helps the coachee to reflect on the current state and actions required to improve it.

Review
Helps the coachee to reflect on their progress, and also to keep them accountable for progressing their actions.

Figure 4.3 - The OSKAR model

Outcome

The coaching conversation begins by clarifying the purpose of the session. The coach supports the coachee in identifying what they want to achieve and how success will look and feel. Key questions:

- What outcome do you want from today's session?
- How will you know the session has been successful?
- What's your main goal?

Scaling

This step introduces a 1-10 scale to help the coachee assess their current position and desired progress. It encourages reflection on how far they've come and how far they want to go. Key questions:

- On a scale of 1-10, where are you now?
- Where do you realistically want to get to?
- What would a '10' look like?

Know-how

The third stage of the OSKAR coaching model is designed to help coachees understand the skills and resources they require to reach their goals. This exploration helps them understand the capabilities they currently have, and those they must acquire. By exploring these topics, the coachee starts to form a loose plan of action to help them achieve their goal. Questions you might want to ask as a coach could include:

- What knowledge do you need to help you achieve your goal?
- Are there more resources you require?
- What do you need to learn?
- Whose support do you need?
- What new skills should you invest in to help you reach your goal?
- Who can provide the resources you need to achieve your goal?
- What else do you need to change to achieve your goal?

Affirm & Action

The fourth stage of the OSKAR coaching model helps the coachee reflect on the current state and actions to improve it. It is specifically designed to help the coachee reflect on things that are working well and that they may wish to continue. As with all models though, it also focuses on drawing out actions that the coachee wants to undertake to help them achieve their objectives. Questions you might want to ask as a coach could include:

- What's working well at the moment?
- What are you already doing that's good?
- Are there things that you would like to continue doing?
- What would you like to change?
- Which actions do you need to take to reach your goal?
- What's your first step?
- What are the first 5 things you need to do?

Review

The last stage of the OSKAR coaching model is the review stage, and this stage actually takes place in a subsequent session. The purpose of this stage is to help the coachee reflect on their progress, but also to keep them accountable for progressing their actions. Questions you might want to ask as a coach in the next follow up session to review what progress has been made could include:

- What progress have you made in relation to your actions?
- Tell me about the things you have done differently since we last spoke.
- What new things are you doing - what old ways have you dropped?
- How do you feel about your progress?

The mentoring cycle

Mentoring, while similar to coaching, tends to be more focused on long-term development and support. The mentoring cycle model provides a structured approach to mentoring relationships, which often span a longer duration than coaching (Kram, 1988). This model (Table 4.1) typically consists of five stages: initiation, building trust, setting goals, developing the relationship, and termination.

In the initiation phase, mentors and mentees establish the scope of their relationship, set expectations, and build rapport. Trust is critical in the next phase, as the mentee must feel comfortable discussing challenges and aspirations with the mentor. Goal setting follows, with the mentor supporting the mentee in identifying both short-term and long-term objectives. As the relationship develops, the mentor provides guidance, feedback, and emotional support. Finally, in the termination phase, the mentee is encouraged to become more self-reliant, with the mentor transitioning out of an active role.

The mentoring cycle emphasises a holistic, ongoing relationship, which differentiates it from the more focused, short-term nature of coaching. Studies show that mentoring relationships foster personal growth, career development, and greater organisational commitment (Allen et al., 2004).

Initiation	The mentoring relationship begins. Initial contact is made and interest is expressed.
Building Trust	Rapport is developed; roles, boundaries, and expectations are clarified.
Setting Goals	Clear, mutually agreed goals and objectives are established for the mentee's development.
Developing the Relationship	Ongoing mentoring activities occur - support, feedback, challenges, and skill-building.
Termination	Formal relationship comes to an end or transitions to a different form (e.g., peer or friendship).

Table 4.1 - The mentoring cycle

The 70:20:10 model

The 70:20:10 model of learning and development, popularised by Johnson et al. (2018), is another valuable framework that can be applied to both coaching and mentoring. This model posits that 70% of learning comes from on-the-job experiences, 20% from feedback and interactions with others, and 10% from formal education. While not a coaching or mentoring model in the strict sense, it is highly relevant to these developmental practices because it highlights the importance of experiential learning and social learning in leadership development.

In coaching and mentoring, the 70:20:10 model encourages leaders to learn through hands-on experience and through dialogue with others, which can be facilitated by coaches and mentors. For instance, mentors may provide advice and feedback based on real-world experiences, while coaches may help coachees reflect on their learning in the workplace. This model underscores the importance of a blended approach to learning that includes both formal and informal learning experiences.

The role of leadership in coaching and mentoring

Leadership is essential to the success of coaching and mentoring initiatives within an organisation. These developmental processes rely heavily on leadership to foster a culture of continuous learning and growth, enhancing both individual capabilities and organisational outcomes.

Establishing a vision for development

Leaders play a critical role in setting the direction for coaching and mentoring by clearly articulating their purpose and aligning them with broader organisational goals. Day (2000) emphasises the importance of visionary leadership in coaching, which sets the tone for growth within the organisation. By integrating coaching and mentoring into strategic objectives, leaders inspire engagement and ensure these practices contribute to long-term success.

Integrating coaching and mentoring into strategic objectives

In a strategic plan, coaching and mentoring would typically appear under a section related to staff development, leadership development, or organisational culture. Here's how it might be framed:

Goal:
To embed coaching and mentoring as core components of professional development, aligned with the institution's long-term vision and values.

Key actions:
- Establish a clear vision and purpose for coaching and mentoring across all departments.
- Align coaching and mentoring programmes with organisational goals, including teaching quality, staff retention, and leadership capacity.
- Communicate this vision consistently through leadership briefings, CPD plans, and performance management frameworks.
- Appoint and train coaching champions or mentors to lead by example and support implementation.
- Monitor and evaluate the impact of coaching on staff wellbeing, performance, and progression.

Success indicators:
- Staff can articulate the purpose of coaching and mentoring in line with the organisation's vision.
- Increased engagement in coaching/mentoring schemes across all levels.
- Evidence of coaching contributing to staff development, innovation, and organisational improvement.

Building trust and psychological safety

Edmondson (1999) highlights that trust and psychological safety, where individuals feel free to share ideas and concerns without fear of retribution, is critical for fostering a learning environment. Leaders establish this safety by modelling transparency, consistency, and confidentiality, ensuring that coaching and mentoring conversations remain focused on development rather than immediate performance outcomes (Kram, 1988).

Providing feedback and accountability

Effective feedback and accountability are crucial in coaching and mentoring processes. Goleman (2005) suggests that leaders who provide feedback while holding individuals accountable foster a sense of ownership and responsibility, which leads to greater engagement and success. Constructive feedback, when delivered thoughtfully, helps individuals recognise their progress and areas for improvement.

Embedding coaching and mentoring in organisational culture

Creating a culture where coaching and mentoring thrive requires intentional leadership, structural integration, and a commitment to ongoing learning. A supportive environment - where feedback is valued and mistakes are viewed as opportunities for growth - is fundamental (Crisp & Alvarado-Young, 2018). Leaders play a critical role by modelling openness, self-reflection, and a dedication to lifelong learning (Senge, 2006), thereby setting the tone for a learning-oriented culture.

Leadership commitment is central to embedding coaching and mentoring. When leaders actively engage in these practices, they demonstrate their value and establish trust. As Day (2000) argues, such role modelling signals that coaching and mentoring are vital to the organisation's success, reinforcing their place within everyday professional practice.

To sustain these efforts, coaching and mentoring must be integrated into organisational structures. This includes the creation of accessible, formal programmes aligned with wider strategic goals. Garvey et al. (2021) recommend embedding these frameworks within HR and leadership development systems to ensure inclusivity and coherence, supporting talent development at all levels. Ultimately, the integration of coaching and mentoring supports the development of a learning organisation - one that prioritises continuous improvement, adaptability, and shared growth. As Senge (1990) notes, these systems enable individuals and teams to learn collectively, with coaching and mentoring acting as key mechanisms for feedback, development, and innovation.

Developing coaching and mentoring skills for leaders

Leaders must develop specific coaching and mentoring skills to effectively support continuous learning and leadership development across the organisation. These skills include active listening, asking powerful questions, giving constructive feedback, and facilitating reflective dialogue. Mastery of these techniques enables leaders to build trusting relationships, support professional growth, and empower others to find their own solutions.

Developing these capabilities also helps leaders model the values of openness, collaboration, and ongoing self-improvement. When leaders coach and mentor others with confidence and authenticity, they not only enhance individual performance but also contribute to a wider culture of trust, knowledge sharing, and distributed leadership. Targeted training, peer coaching, and opportunities to practise these skills in real settings are essential for embedding coaching and mentoring as everyday leadership practices.

The role of emotional intelligence in coaching and mentoring

Emotional intelligence (EI) is the ability to recognise, understand, and manage emotions - both one's own and others' (Goleman, 2005). Leaders with high EI can build strong relationships, empathise with mentees, and offer effective feedback. Salovey & Mayer (1990) assert that EI is essential for managing interpersonal dynamics and resolving conflicts, making it vital for coaching and mentoring.

Active listening as a foundational skill

Active listening is fundamental in coaching and mentoring. Brownell (2015) describes it as the process of fully understanding and responding thoughtfully to another person's perspective. Leaders who listen actively can better identify mentees' needs and offer tailored guidance, enhancing the effectiveness of the relationship and contributing to a learning culture.

Active listening in practice

During a one-to-one meeting, a head of department notices that one of her programme managers seems hesitant when discussing recent curriculum changes. Instead of moving quickly through the agenda, the head pauses and says, *"I noticed you hesitated just now - would you like to share your thoughts on how the changes are affecting your team?"*.

The programme manager explains that staff are feeling overwhelmed by overlapping deadlines and unclear guidance. The head listens without interrupting, nods occasionally, and takes notes. She then paraphrases what she heard: *"So you're saying the team needs more clarity and staggered timelines to manage the changes effectively - is that right?"*.

After confirming, the head invites suggestions and together they agree on a short-term action plan. She follows up with a thank-you email, reaffirming the importance of the manager's insights and contributions.

By listening actively - giving full attention, reflecting back key points, and encouraging dialogue - the head builds trust, addresses concerns meaningfully, and fosters a supportive, learning-focused culture.

Providing constructive feedback

Constructive feedback is another key skill for leaders. Stone & Heen (2014) emphasise that feedback should be specific, actionable, and encouraging. Leaders should offer balanced feedback that acknowledges strengths while identifying areas for improvement, helping mentees take ownership of their development.

Implementing coaching and mentoring programs

A successful coaching and mentoring programme requires careful design and clear goals. McKeen & Bujaki (2007) recommend designing programs that align with organisational goals and culture. Once goals are defined, the program structure, including the type of coaching (one-on-one, group, or peer), duration, and delivery method, should be determined. Resources such as funding, time, and staffing must also be considered.

Selecting coaches and mentors

The selection of coaches and mentors is crucial to programme success. Garvey (2021) highlights the importance of selecting individuals with the right skills and personal qualities. Coaches should be able to listen actively, offer constructive feedback, and help participants develop self-awareness. Mentors, on the other hand, should provide guidance based on their experience and foster long-term development.

Measuring the impact of coaching and mentoring

Evaluating the impact of coaching and mentoring programmes is essential for understanding their effectiveness, refining their design, and demonstrating value to stakeholders. Without a robust evaluation process, it is difficult to determine whether key objectives - such as enhanced leadership skills, improved staff performance, and organisational growth - have been achieved (Passmore, 2020).

Measuring impact supports data-informed decision-making and helps ensure that coaching and mentoring remain aligned with strategic goals. Regular evaluation also enables the identification of areas for improvement and strengthens long-term outcomes like staff retention, career progression, and leadership development (Ely et al., 2010; Fillery-Travis & Lane, 2020).

A balanced evaluation approach should include both quantitative measures - such as engagement metrics, retention rates, and leadership KPIs - and qualitative insights from feedback, interviews, and reflective journals (Bachkirova et al., 2020). These data sources help to build a fuller picture of success and allow organisations to refine coaching and mentoring initiatives over time.

Sustaining coaching and mentoring as embedded organisational practices requires leadership commitment, appropriate policies, and structural support. Barnett & O'Mahony (2009) highlight the importance of making these practices part of daily operations through initiatives such as mentor recognition schemes, scheduled coaching time, and ongoing training. With clear goals and a culture of evaluation, coaching and mentoring can become powerful tools for continuous professional development and institutional improvement.

Methods of measuring impact

1. **Participant feedback**

   Participant feedback is a widely used method for evaluating coaching and mentoring programmes. Surveys, interviews, and questionnaires from coachees, mentees, and their supervisors offer valuable insights into the programme's perceived impact. Feedback typically focuses on goal achievement, relationship quality, and perceived benefits such as increased confidence or job satisfaction (Garvey & Stokes, 2021). Collecting feedback at multiple stages of the programme enables assessment of both formative and summative outcomes.

2. **360-degree feedback**

   360-degree feedback involves gathering input from multiple sources, including peers, direct reports, and supervisors, providing a comprehensive perspective on the mentee's or coachee's development. This tool is particularly useful for assessing leadership competencies, communication skills, and team collaboration - key outcomes of coaching and mentoring programmes.

3. **Behavioural change**

   Behavioural change is a key indicator of a programme's success. Assessing shifts in areas such as decision-making, interpersonal skills, and leadership effectiveness is vital for evaluating meaningful outcomes (Joo, 2005). These changes can be measured through a combination of self-assessments, peer and supervisor feedback, and direct observation. Input from colleagues and line managers offers valuable insight into how participants apply their learning in real-world settings, particularly in terms of enhanced leadership and other critical behaviours.

4. **Organisational outcomes**

   Beyond individual development, coaching and mentoring programmes can be assessed through their wider impact on organisational performance and culture. Key metrics such as staff engagement, retention rates, leadership capacity, and overall team effectiveness offer insight into their success. For example, a leadership-focused mentoring programme might be evaluated by tracking mentee promotions, improved decision-making, or their influence on team outcomes (Joo, 2005). Such programmes often contribute to cultivating a learning-oriented, supportive culture that encourages continuous improvement, knowledge sharing, and collaboration across departments (Passmore, 2020). This cultural shift can enhance organisational resilience and innovation over the long term.

Tools for measuring impact

Organisations can use various tools to assess coaching and mentoring programmes, ranging from informal surveys to formal performance management systems:

- **Surveys and questionnaires:** Custom surveys for participants, mentors, and supervisors can gather feedback using Likert-scale and open-ended questions.
- **Interviews and focus groups:** These qualitative methods offer deeper insights into participants' experiences and the emotional benefits of the programme.
- **Coaching logs and journals:** Logs maintained by coaches and coachees document progress and reflections, providing valuable data on the learning process.
- **Performance management systems:** These systems track employee performance and development, helping evaluate the impact of coaching and mentoring on job performance and career progression.

Ongoing monitoring and continuous improvement

Evaluation is an ongoing process. Organisations should establish regular check-ins, gather participant feedback, and monitor progress to ensure the programme remains effective and aligned with evolving needs. Continuous evaluation helps refine coaching and mentoring programmes, maximising their impact and return on investment.

Developing a coaching and mentoring strategy

A well-developed coaching and mentoring strategy is essential for organisations seeking to use these approaches as effective developmental tools. Such a strategy provides clear goals, structured frameworks, and alignment with broader organisational objectives. It supports individual growth, leadership development, succession planning, and fosters a culture of continuous learning and improvement. By embedding coaching and mentoring into everyday practice, organisations can create supportive environments where talent is nurtured, collaboration is strengthened, and long-term capacity is built.

Identifying key stakeholders

Developing a coaching and mentoring strategy requires identifying key stakeholders involved in the programme's design, implementation, and evaluation. Stakeholders typically include senior leaders, HR professionals, L&D teams, and the mentors and mentees. Early involvement of these stakeholders ensures the programme is tailored to organisational needs and has the necessary support for success. Senior leaders play a crucial role in promoting the programme, while HR and L&D teams help integrate the programme into the broader talent management strategy (Witherspoon et al., 2020).

Defining clear objectives and goals

Clear, specific, measurable, achievable, relevant, and time-bound (SMART) objectives are essential for guiding the programme's direction and assessing its success. For example, a leadership coaching objective might be to improve decision-making abilities by 20% over six months, as measured by pre- and post-programme assessments. Both short-term and long-term goals should address immediate developmental needs and foster sustainable growth.

Selecting the right coaching and mentoring models

Different coaching and mentoring models can be applied depending on organisational needs and resources. Common models include:

1. **One-to-one mentoring:** Pairs a mentor with a mentee for extended support.
2. **Group coaching:** Provides collective learning with individualised feedback. Often used for leadership development.
3. **Peer coaching:** Encourages colleagues to coach one another, promoting knowledge sharing and collaboration.
4. **E-mentoring:** Utilises technology to connect mentors and mentees. Ideal for geographically dispersed teams (Clutterbuck et al., 2016).

Organisations should consider a mix of models to cater to diverse needs and provide a richer learning experience (Garvey et al., 2021).

Providing adequate support and training

Effective training and ongoing support for mentors and coaches are critical. Training should include practical coaching techniques, communication skills, and feedback delivery. Additionally, continuous support, such as regular check-ins and professional development opportunities, enhances program success. Peer coaching networks can also be established to further develop coaches' skills.

Establishing clear roles and responsibilities

Clearly defining the roles and responsibilities of all participants ensures programme structure and clarity. The mentor or coach provides guidance, while the mentee or coachee actively engages in setting goals and working toward them. Defining these roles helps align expectations and ensures accountability throughout the coaching or mentoring relationship.

Evaluating programme success

Once implemented, coaching and mentoring programs should be evaluated using both qualitative and quantitative methods, including feedback surveys, performance assessments, and goal achievement tracking. Evaluation should assess individual outcomes, such as leadership development, as well as organisational outcomes, like improved employee retention. A feedback loop ensures the programme evolves to meet changing needs (Witherspoon et al., 2000).

Activity: Designing a coaching and mentoring strategy

Imagine you have recently been appointed to spearhead a leadership development initiative within your organisation - a role that signals trust in your vision and capability. During your initial meetings with the senior leadership team, there's a shared recognition that nurturing leadership talent at all levels is essential for future success. After thoughtful discussion, the team reaches a clear consensus: a structured coaching and mentoring programme must sit at the heart of this initiative. Using the ideas from this chapter, design a draft proposal for a coaching and/or mentoring programme tailored to your context.

Your proposal should include the following:

1. **Aims and objectives**
   - What are the goals of the programme?
   - How will success be measured?

2. **Stakeholder engagement plan**
   - Who are the key stakeholders, and how will you engage them in the design and delivery of the programme?

3. **Choice of model(s)**
   - Which coaching and/or mentoring models will you use?
   - Justify your selection in relation to organisational needs.

4. **Roles and responsibilities**
   - What roles will mentors, coaches, and participants play?
   - How will accountability be managed?

5. **Support and development**
   - What training or ongoing development will be provided for coaches/mentors?

6. **Evaluation strategy**
   - How will the impact of the programme be reviewed and improved over time?

Present your plan to a peer or colleague and invite feedback. Reflect on how their comments might shape your approach.

Summary

Leadership development takes many forms, and effective strategies often combine multiple approaches. Engaging key stakeholders early in the process ensures buy-in and relevance, especially when designing coaching and mentoring programmes. Clear objectives and measurable goals provide direction and help assess progress.

Coaching and mentoring are particularly effective methods of developing leaders. When aligned with individual and organisational goals, they can be seamlessly integrated into a broader leadership development framework. Drawing on established models and approaches, coaching and mentoring programmes are designed, implemented, and evaluated to ensure meaningful impact.

The selection of coaching and mentoring models depends on organisational needs, with each of a number of models offering its own strengths. Success also relies on well-defined roles, consistent training, and ongoing professional development for all involved. Regular evaluation allows organisations to track impact, while integrating feedback supports continuous improvement and long-term success.

It is particularly important to select the right coaches and mentors, setting clear objectives, and continuously measuring the impact of these initiatives. It is also paramount that coaches and mentors receive the support and training needed for them to foster successful, sustainable development programmes.

5   INSPIRING AND ENGAGING STAFF

David Hall

Introduction

Effective people management in education underscores the idea that leadership is fundamentally a social skill. It calls for a shift from impersonal, process-driven approaches to focusing on the human aspects of relationships, cooperation, and emotional intelligence. In this context, leaders are viewed as enablers, adept at understanding and addressing the motivations, needs, and aspirations of their team members. This approach not only fosters improved performance but also enhances job satisfaction. To achieve this, leaders must develop key emotional and psychological skills, such as empathy, self-control, and active listening. These skills are essential for building trust, promoting collaboration, and creating a shared sense of purpose among staff, which in turn supports a positive and effective working environment.

This chapter:

- Highlights the importance of managing people in education and its impact on classrooms, institutions, and stakeholders.
- Explores the roles, relationships, and interdependencies among teachers, leaders, support staff, students, parents, and the wider community.
- Emphasises self-leadership, focusing on skill development, reputation, resilience, and career growth.
- Discusses building strong relationships with staff through coaching, motivation, conflict management, diversity, inclusion, and professional development.
- Examines fostering teamwork and collaboration through distributed and shared leadership models.
- Addresses organisational challenges, including navigating change, avoiding derailment, and modelling positive leadership behaviour.
- Prioritises staff well-being by promoting stress reduction, work-life balance, and supportive workplace policies.
- Advocates ethical leadership, emphasising trust, empathy, and decision-making that respects people and strengthens organisational culture.

Fostering inspiration and engagement

Managing and leading people is often considered the most challenging task for any manager, regardless of the sector. This complexity stems from the inherent diversity of human behaviour, motivations, and needs. Unlike systems or processes, people bring individuality, emotions, and unpredictability to the workplace, requiring managers to balance organisational objectives with empathy and adaptability (Goleman et al., 2013).

Effective leadership involves navigating interpersonal dynamics, addressing conflicts, fostering collaboration, and inspiring teams to achieve shared goals. These tasks are further complicated in education, where leaders must manage not only staff but also relationships with students, parents, and the wider community (Bush, Bell and Middlewood, 2019). Building trust, maintaining morale, and ensuring clear communication are vital but demanding aspects of leadership.

The rapid pace of change in education - from evolving curricula to advancements in technology - places additional pressure on managers to support their teams through uncertainty while maintaining focus on long-term goals. Leading people requires a nuanced understanding of both individual and collective needs, making it one of the most multifaceted and critical responsibilities of any manager.

The motivation of staff in the educational sector directly influences teaching quality, student outcomes, and institutional success. Educational institutions are fundamentally relational entities, where the interplay between administrators, teachers, support staff, students, and the community shapes the learning environment (Day et al., 2011). Fostering a motivated and well-managed workforce is essential for achieving educational excellence. By understanding the complex interplay of intrinsic and extrinsic motivational factors and implementing supportive management practices, educational leaders can create environments that foster teacher satisfaction, retention, and student success.

Motivation is a complex, multifaceted construct that significantly impacts teachers' performance and job satisfaction. Intrinsic motivation, driven by personal fulfilment and passion for teaching, often leads to higher levels of commitment and effectiveness (Ryan & Deci, 2020). Conversely, extrinsic motivation, influenced by external rewards or pressures, also plays a role but may not sustain long-term engagement. Understanding these motivational dynamics is crucial for educational leaders aiming to enhance staff performance and retention.

Recent studies underscore the importance of motivation in education. Research by Skaalvik & Skaalvik (2011) highlights that intrinsic motivation among teachers significantly influences their satisfaction, commitment, and levels of student engagement. Teachers who are intrinsically motivated tend to remain in the profession longer and exhibit higher levels of engagement and effectiveness. Furthermore, systemic support, including autonomy and opportunities for professional growth, contributes to sustaining teacher motivation (Ingersoll & Strong, 2011).

Leadership that prioritises clear communication, professional development, and supportive supervision fosters a positive work environment. Such an environment enhances teacher motivation and contributes to improved student outcomes (Leithwood et al., 2020). Educational leaders play a pivotal role in creating conditions that support teacher motivation and engagement. By understanding and addressing the factors that influence motivation, leaders can implement strategies that promote a positive and productive work environment.

Building strong relationships, providing opportunities for professional growth, and recognising achievements are strategies that enhance teacher motivation (Fullan, 2023). Team-building activities and creating opportunities for teachers to collaborate contribute to a positive organisational culture. Additionally, innovative practices that encourage teachers to explore creative teaching strategies can boost motivation and satisfaction (Hargreaves & O'Connor, 2018).

External strategies also play a role in motivating teachers. Allowing teachers to implement innovative teaching strategies and fostering collaboration can create a sense of professional autonomy and fulfilment (Creemers & Kyriakides, 2007). Recognition of teachers' efforts and contributions enhances job satisfaction, creating an environment that values and respects educators' work.

Principles of people leadership

Brent & Dent (2013), identified three categories of best-practice principles, designed to enhance leadership and management effectiveness in the 21st century: *self-development*, *building relationships*, and *organisational dynamics* (Table 5.1). While each individual element within the categories holds intrinsic importance, it is the synergistic integration of all elements that generates the most profound and impactful outcomes.

Self-development: Effective leadership begins with self-awareness, self-belief, and self-confidence. These qualities are foundational for success because they enable leaders to navigate challenges, build strong relationships, and inspire trust and motivation in others. Each quality contributes uniquely to a leader's ability to succeed in diverse and complex environments.

A leader's self-development	Building relationships	Organisational dynamics
Skill set Reputation Resilience Career path Development Adaptability Self-reflection Lifelong learning	Coaching and influencing Facilitation Team building Motivation Performance management Conflict management Empathy Networking Collaboration skills	Change Innovation Crisis management Sustainability practices Technology integration Strategic thinking Leading by example

Table 5.1 - Principles for leading and managing people
Adapted from Brent & Dent, 2013

Building relationships: Leading and managing people revolves around skills, attitudes, and interpersonal behaviours. Success in this area depends on a range of competencies and capabilities, which are essential for fostering collaboration and navigating relationships effectively.

Organisational dynamics: Leadership also involves addressing broader organisational issues such as driving change and using positive psychology to achieve better outcomes. These aspects require a strategic approach to management that aligns individual and team goals with institutional objectives.

Understanding the people in educational settings

A leader's ability to successfully guide an educational institution begins with a deep understanding of the multifaceted roles and interdependencies of the individuals within it. Recognising how teachers, support staff, students, parents, and the broader community interact and contribute is essential for creating an environment where students can excel academically, socially, and emotionally. Effective leadership involves not only understanding the distinct contributions of each group but also fostering a culture of collaboration and mutual respect. By valuing these interconnections, a leader can ensure that all stakeholders are aligned toward a common goal of student success, while also supporting a positive and inclusive school culture.

Teachers, leaders, and support staff

In educational institutions, teachers, leaders, and support staff each play distinct yet interconnected roles that collectively contribute to the holistic development of students.

- *Teachers:* Beyond delivering curriculum content, teachers often assume leadership roles such as resource providers, instructional specialists, and mentors. These roles enable them to influence school improvement initiatives and support their peers in enhancing instructional practices (Harris, 2004). Teachers' dual responsibilities of direct instruction and broader leadership roles highlight their critical contribution to institutional effectiveness (Day & Sammons, 2016).
- *Leaders:* School leaders, including principals, senior leaders, and middle managers, are responsible for setting the vision and direction of the institution. Effective leaders recognise the importance of shared responsibility and foster a culture where leadership is distributed among various stakeholders. This collaborative approach enhances decision-making and institutional resilience (Leithwood & Azah, 2016).
- *Support staff:* Support staff, including administrative personnel, counsellors, and para-professionals, play a vital role in the daily operations of educational institutes. Their contributions ensure that teachers and leaders can focus on instructional and strategic responsibilities. The interdependence among these roles is essential; for instance, counsellors support students' emotional well-being, directly impacting their academic performance and classroom behaviour (Roffey, 2017).

The synergy among teachers, leaders, and support staff creates a cohesive educational environment. Distributed leadership and collaborative professional development can further help in sustaining this synergy (Harris & Spillane, 2008).

Engaging students as stakeholders in educational success

Recognising students as active stakeholders in their education is pivotal for fostering engagement and ownership of their learning journey.

- *Student voice:* Involving students in decision-making processes related to their education promotes a sense of agency and responsibility. When students are encouraged to express their opinions and participate in shaping the learning environment, they are more likely to be engaged and motivated (Cook-Sather, 2020).
- *Collaborative learning:* Implementing instructional strategies that promote collaboration among students helps develop critical thinking, communication, and interpersonal skills. Such approaches prepare students for real-world challenges and emphasise the value of teamwork (Vygotsky, 1978).
- *Feedback mechanisms:* Establishing regular channels for students to provide feedback on teaching methods, curriculum relevance, and school policies enables educators to make informed adjustments that enhance the learning experience (Hattie, 2008).

Engaging students as stakeholders necessitates a shift from traditional teacher-centred models to more student-centred approaches, where learners are active participants in their educational journey.

The role of parents and community in educational ecosystems

The involvement of parents and the broader community is integral to the success of educational institutions.

- *Parental engagement:* Active participation of parents in their children's education correlates with improved academic performance, better attendance, and enhanced social skills. Research shows that parental involvement contributes significantly to creating a supportive learning environment (Epstein, 2001).
- *Community partnerships:* Collaborations with local businesses, organisations, and cultural institutions provide students with enriched learning experiences and resources beyond the classroom. Such partnerships can offer mentorship opportunities, internships, and exposure to diverse career paths (Warren, 2005).
- *Cultural relevance:* Engaging with the community ensures that the curriculum and educational activities reflect the cultural and social contexts of the students. This relevance enhances student engagement and fosters a sense of belonging (Gay, 2018).

Effective family and community engagement strategies include regular communication, involvement in school governance, and participation in school events. Overcoming barriers to engagement, such as language differences or scheduling conflicts, is essential for creating inclusive educational environments (Bryk, 2010).

Understanding yourself as a leader

Leadership in any context begins with self-awareness and an understanding of one's own capabilities, limitations, and aspirations.

> "Knowing yourself will give you valuable insights into your aptitude for managing others".
>
> Hunsaker & Hunsaker (2015)

This foundational insight is critical for enabling leaders to influence and inspire others effectively. Before managing or leading others, leaders must first develop a deep and comprehensive understanding of themselves, encompassing their skill set, reputation, resilience, and career aspirations. These interconnected elements lay the foundation for impactful leadership, each contributing to a leader's ability to inspire trust, navigate challenges, and foster growth within their organisations.

The journey of self-awareness is ongoing, requiring continuous reflection, feedback, and a commitment to both personal and professional development. As leadership demands evolve, so must leaders, striving to enhance their capabilities and adapt to new realities. By doing so, they not only achieve personal success but also create environments where others can thrive, ultimately advancing the goals of their organisations and communities.

A leader's skill set

Effective leadership starts with the cultivation of a robust and versatile skill set. Core leadership competencies include communication, decision-making, emotional intelligence, and strategic thinking (Goleman et al., 2013). Communication, in particular, is a fundamental skill that enables leaders to articulate a clear vision, provide constructive feedback, and foster collaboration. Emotional intelligence, encompassing self-awareness, self-regulation, and empathy, is equally essential for understanding the needs and motivations of others (Bradberry & Greaves, 2009).

Problem-solving and adaptability are increasingly important in dynamic environments. Leaders who can analyse complex issues, evaluate multiple perspectives, and implement innovative solutions are better equipped to navigate the challenges of modern organisations (Northouse, 2021). Developing these skills requires a commitment to continuous learning and reflection, as leadership demands evolve with societal and organisational changes.

A leader's reputation

A leader's reputation matters because trust and credibility are key to strong relationships with their teams. It is shaped by actions, decisions, and demonstrated values. Kouzes & Posner (2023) highlight that credibility stems from consistency, transparency, and ethical decision-making. Leaders who act in line with their values are more likely to earn trust and loyalty.

Reputation also depends on showing competence and reliability. Leaders who keep promises and display expertise gain their team's respect and confidence (Carucci, 2014). However, reputation is not fixed - it demands continuous effort. A single breach of trust can damage years of credibility, reinforcing the need for integrity and accountability.

A leader's resilience

Leadership is inherently challenging, requiring individuals to navigate uncertainty, setbacks, and conflict. Resilience is a critical attribute that enables leaders to persevere in the face of adversity and maintain their effectiveness. According to

Luthans et al. (2004), resilience involves the ability to recover from setbacks, adapt to changing circumstances, and remain focused on long-term goals.

Resilient leaders exhibit emotional stability and a growth mindset, viewing challenges as opportunities for learning and development. This perspective not only helps leaders maintain their composure but also inspires confidence among their teams. Developing resilience requires self-care and a support network. Leaders who prioritise their mental and physical well-being are better equipped to handle stress and make sound decisions under pressure. Additionally, seeking mentorship and building relationships with trusted colleagues can provide valuable guidance and encouragement during challenging times.

A leader's career and development

Leadership is not a destination but a journey of continuous growth and self-improvement. Effective leaders are lifelong learners who actively seek opportunities to enhance their knowledge, skills, and perspectives. This commitment to professional development is essential for staying relevant in an ever-changing landscape.

Professional development can take many forms, including formal education, such as pursuing advanced degrees or certifications, and informal learning, such as attending workshops and conferences, reading, and engaging in reflective practice (Kolb, 2014). Mentorship and networking are also valuable tools for career growth, providing leaders with insights and opportunities to expand their horizons.

Career development involves setting clear goals and aligning them with one's values and passions. Leaders who have a strong sense of purpose are more likely to be motivated and fulfilled in their roles, which translates to greater effectiveness and impact (Pink, 2011). This sense of purpose also enables leaders to inspire others, fostering a shared commitment to organisational and societal goals.

The interconnection of self-knowledge and leadership

Understanding oneself is not only a prerequisite for personal effectiveness but also a key to influencing others positively. Self-aware leaders are better equipped to recognise their biases, adapt their leadership style to different situations, and empathise with the experiences of their teams (Ashkanasy & Humphrey, 2011). This self-knowledge fosters authenticity, a quality that has been consistently linked to effective leadership (Avolio & Gardner, 2005).

In educational settings, where the stakes are high, and the challenges are complex, self-awareness enables leaders to make thoughtful decisions that prioritise the needs of students, staff, and the community. For example, leaders who understand their strengths and limitations can delegate tasks effectively, empowering their teams and promoting a culture of collaboration.

Activity: Leadership effectiveness

This activity asks you to consider how your self-awareness impacts your leadership effectiveness and to identify areas for growth. Self-awareness is an ongoing journey that requires continuous reflection and adaptation.

1. What are your top three leadership strengths?
   - Reflect on specific situations where you've demonstrated these strengths.
2. Identify two areas where you need improvement as a leader.
   - How do these areas impact your effectiveness?
3. How would your team members describe your leadership style?
   - Compare this with how you perceive your own style.
4. Recall a recent challenging decision you made.
   - What values guided your decision-making process?
5. How do you typically respond to setbacks or failures?
   - Consider how this impacts your team's perception of you.
6. What is your preferred method of communication with your team?
   - How might this style affect different team members?
7. Describe a situation where you successfully adapted your leadership approach.
   - What prompted this adaptation?
8. What personal biases might influence your leadership decisions?
   - How do you work to mitigate these biases?
9. How do you prioritise your own professional development?
   - List two specific goals for your leadership growth this year.
10. In what ways does your leadership style align with your organisation's culture?
    - Where might there be misalignment?
11. How do you balance empathy with maintaining professional boundaries?
    - Provide an example of when this was challenging.
12. What strategies do you use to maintain resilience in the face of stress?
    - How effective are these strategies?
13. How do you seek and incorporate feedback from others?
    - Describe a time when feedback led to a significant change in your approach.
14. What is your long-term vision for your leadership career?
    - How does this vision align with your personal values?
15. How do you make use of your emotional intelligence in leadership situations?
    - Provide an example of when this was particularly effective.

A leader's relationship with staff

Establishing a good relationship with staff will pay dividends and help to create a positive work environment, enhance staff motivation, and promote professional growth. By focusing on key facets such as influencing, motivating, coaching and mentoring, facilitation, and team building, leaders can create a supportive environment that brings out the best in everyone. Investing in continuous professional development, fair performance management, and conflict resolution ensures that staff feel valued and engaged. In addition, addressing diversity, inclusion, and retention strengthens the educational workforce and enriches the learning environment, ultimately contributing to the success of the organisation.

Influencing others

Influential leaders inspire and guide their staff by articulating a compelling vision and modelling desired behaviours (Northouse, 2021). This ability to influence is rooted in a leader's capacity to clearly define and communicate the organisation's goals, ensuring staff understand their roles and contributions. Effective leaders utilise various communication strategies to convey expectations, provide constructive feedback, and recognise achievements, creating a sense of purpose and belonging among team members.

Northouse (2021) also emphasises the importance of emotional intelligence in influencing others. Leaders who demonstrate empathy and actively listen to their staff can better understand their needs and concerns, allowing them to tailor their approaches to inspire action. For instance, understanding individual motivators and challenges enables leaders to connect personally with team members, fostering stronger relationships built on mutual trust and respect.

Fostering an environment of trust empowers staff to take initiative and innovate without fear of failure, ultimately leading to a more dynamic and productive workplace. Leaders who act with integrity, transparency, and consistency are more likely to earn the confidence and loyalty of their teams.

Effective influencing involves encouraging a collaborative culture. Leaders who empower their teams to participate in decision-making processes and problem-solving initiatives create a shared sense of ownership over organisational objectives. By cultivating such an environment, leaders not only motivate their staff to commit to these objectives but also inspire them to strive for excellence in their roles. Influencing, therefore, is not merely about directing others but about fostering a shared vision that drives collective success.

Motivation

Motivating staff is a vital aspect of effective leadership, requiring an understanding of human needs and tailored strategies to foster engagement and productivity. Leaders can draw on Maslow's 1943 hierarchy of needs (Figure 5.1), which outlines five levels of human motivation.

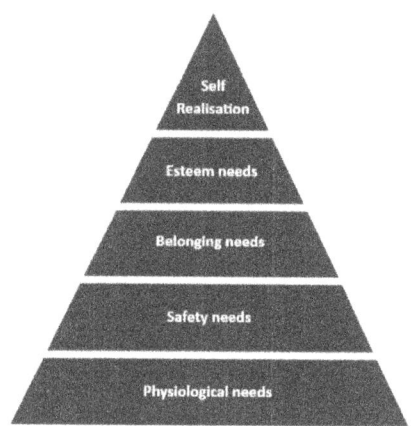

Figure 5.1 - Maslow's hierarchy of needs

By addressing these levels, leaders create an environment where staff feel valued and empowered to contribute their best (Maslow, 2023).

To begin, leaders must ensure that the basic physiological needs of staff are met by providing fair compensation, comfortable working conditions, and reasonable workloads. Herzberg's (1959) two-factor theory underscores the importance of addressing these hygiene factors to eliminate dissatisfaction, forming a foundation for higher levels of motivation.

At the safety level, leaders should prioritise job security, consistent communication, and access to necessary resources. Providing clear goals, transparent decision-making, and stability fosters trust and reduces workplace anxiety (Bass & Riggio, 2006).

A sense of belonging is crucial for maintaining morale and collaboration. Leaders can promote collegiality by encouraging teamwork, fostering inclusive practices, and organising activities that build relationships. Goleman et al. (2013) highlight the value of creating a supportive workplace where individuals feel connected and appreciated.

To address esteem needs, leaders must recognise and celebrate staff achievements, both formally and informally. Providing constructive feedback, celebrating milestones, and offering opportunities to showcase expertise enhances intrinsic motivation (Ryan & Deci, 2000). Public acknowledgment of contributions can significantly boost morale and reinforce positive behaviours.

Supporting self-actualisation involves helping staff reach their full potential. Leaders can achieve this by offering professional development, challenging assignments, and opportunities for creative problem-solving. Kouzes & Posner (2023) emphasise that leaders who inspire their teams to exceed expectations foster a culture of innovation and growth. Aligning organisational goals with personal aspirations allows individuals to find meaning and satisfaction in their work.

Coaching and mentoring

Coaching and mentoring are powerful tools for fostering professional growth and leadership development, offering distinct but complementary approaches to supporting individuals in achieving their potential. According to Van Nieuwerburgh (2019), coaching emphasises the enhancement of specific skills and performance through structured guidance and targeted feedback. This personalised process allows individuals to identify and overcome barriers, set achievable goals, and refine their abilities in a focused manner.

Coaching is often short-term, task-oriented, and designed to improve immediate outcomes. On the other hand, mentoring encompasses a broader spectrum of personal and professional growth, with mentors offering wisdom, advice, and support based on their experience. Mentors help mentees navigate career trajectories, provide long-term perspective, and offer guidance on overcoming personal and professional challenges. While coaching is often more formal and goal-specific, mentoring fosters a deeper, ongoing relationship that encourages broader developmental growth. Both approaches are crucial in cultivating leadership potential and enhancing professional practice.

Coaching and mentoring have both been covered in detail in Chapter 4.

Facilitation

Facilitation fosters collaboration and enables effective problem-solving within teams. Schein (2010) emphasises the role of leaders as facilitators who create an environment where open communication is encouraged, and diverse perspectives are valued. Facilitative leadership involves not just guiding discussions but also actively ensuring that all voices are heard, cultivating an atmosphere of psychological safety where individuals feel empowered to contribute ideas without fear of criticism.

Effective facilitation goes beyond merely managing meetings or discussions; it requires leaders to strategically frame conversations, pose thought-provoking questions, and ensure the team stays focused on objectives. This process includes setting clear expectations, clarifying roles, and mediating conflicts that might hinder collaboration. Leaders who excel in facilitation often act as neutral arbiters, steering discussions constructively while remaining unbiased, thus fostering a spirit of inclusivity and fairness (Schein, 2010). Such practices ensure that diverse viewpoints are considered, leading to more innovative and well-rounded solutions to organisational challenges.

Research by Edmondson (2018) highlights the importance of psychological safety in collaborative settings, noting that teams with a strong sense of safety are more likely to engage in open dialogue and take calculated risks. Leaders who prioritise facilitation actively work to reduce power imbalances within teams, ensuring equitable participation and making space for innovative ideas. This approach not only enhances team cohesion but also boosts morale, as individuals feel their contributions are recognised and valued.

Facilitation also plays a vital role in problem-solving, where leaders act as catalysts for creative and critical thinking. Kaner (2014) notes that skilled facilitators can balance structured processes with flexibility, allowing teams to explore multiple perspectives while maintaining focus on actionable outcomes. Leaders can introduce tools such as idea gathering sessions, SWOT analysis, or design thinking frameworks to encourage collaborative problem-solving. For example, idea gathering sessions provide a platform for diverse input, while design thinking fosters empathy and user-centric approaches to challenges (Brown, 2009).

Leaders as facilitators must be adept at managing group dynamics. This involves identifying and addressing barriers to collaboration, such as interpersonal conflicts or unequal participation, which can derail team efforts. By intervening strategically and diplomatically, leaders can redirect energy toward constructive engagement and problem resolution. For instance, fostering a culture of active listening and mutual respect can mitigate misunderstandings and align team efforts toward shared goals (Covey, 2020).

Facilitation also extends to using technology to enhance collaboration, especially in remote or hybrid work environments. Tools such as virtual whiteboards, collaborative software, and real-time communication platforms enable teams to engage effectively across distances. Leaders must not only implement these tools but also guide their appropriate use to ensure they complement the team's workflow and objectives (Wheatley, 2006).

Team building

Team building focuses on creating cohesive and productive teams that thrive in both routine and challenging environments. It is a multifaceted leadership skill that requires a focus on trust, communication, inclusivity, and resilience. By employing targeted team-building activities, promoting open dialogue, and utilising the strengths of diverse individuals, leaders can cultivate cohesive and productive teams capable of driving organisational success. Team building is not only beneficial for individual teams but also for the broader organisational culture, fostering innovation, collaboration, and adaptability in the face of change.

Lencioni (2010) identifies trust as the foundation of strong teams, emphasising that it is cultivated through transparency, vulnerability, and a commitment to mutual respect. Leaders play a critical role in fostering this trust by modelling integrity, promoting open communication, and addressing conflicts constructively. Without trust, teams are unlikely to function cohesively, as members may hesitate to share ideas or voice concerns, thereby stifling innovation and collaboration.

Effective team building begins with establishing clear roles and expectations. High-performing teams align their efforts toward shared objectives, which requires clarity in responsibilities and a unified vision (Katzenbach & Smith, 2015). Leaders can facilitate this alignment by involving team members in goal-setting processes, ensuring that everyone feels a sense of ownership over the outcomes. This collaborative approach not only clarifies expectations but also enhances motivation and commitment to team goals.

Team-building activities are a practical tool for enhancing cohesion and strengthening interpersonal relationships. These activities range from icebreakers and trust-building exercises to more complex problem-solving challenges that encourage collaboration. For instance, outdoor challenges or escape-room-style games simulate real-world scenarios that require teamwork, communication, and collective problem-solving. By engaging in such activities, team members develop a deeper understanding of each other's strengths and working styles, which can be harnessed in the workplace to improve efficiency and synergy (Levi & Askay, 2020).

Fostering open communication is another pillar of effective team building. Leaders must create an environment where team members feel safe to express their ideas, concerns, and feedback. When individuals feel secure in voicing their opinions, the team is more likely to engage in constructive debates and make well-rounded decisions (Edmondson, 2018). Regular team meetings, one-on-one check-ins, and feedback sessions can facilitate open communication, allowing leaders to address issues promptly and collaboratively.

Inclusive practices are vital for building cohesive teams, particularly in diverse and dynamic work environments. Diverse teams bring varied perspectives and experiences, which can drive innovation and creativity when managed effectively. Leaders must actively promote inclusivity by ensuring equitable participation and recognising the unique contributions of all team members. Research by Shore et al. (2011) highlights that inclusive teams are more likely to be engaged and productive, as individuals feel valued and respected for their differences.

Leaders must also focus on resilience-building as part of team development. Resilient teams can adapt to change, recover from setbacks, and maintain high levels of performance under pressure. Sinek (2009) argues that creating a sense of belonging and purpose within teams is key to fostering resilience. Leaders can achieve this by emphasising the team's mission, celebrating milestones, and supporting members through challenges. Resilience training and workshops can further equip teams with the skills to navigate uncertainty and stress effectively.

Finally, fostering innovation within teams is a critical outcome of effective team building. Amabile & Kramer (2011) highlight that teams with strong internal cohesion are more likely to engage in creative problem-solving and generate innovative ideas. Leaders can encourage innovation by providing the necessary resources, fostering a culture of experimentation, and rewarding creative efforts.

Case Study: Promoting teamwork in a school leadership team

Mr. Thompson, head of a large secondary school, recognised the need to improve teamwork within his leadership team, which was made up of department heads and senior staff. While the team members were highly skilled individually, they struggled with collaboration, which affected the school's overall performance.

Mr. Thompson identified key issues such as a lack of trust, unclear roles, and poor communication. The team members had different working styles, causing friction in decision-making. Some were hesitant to share their ideas due to fear of conflict, and there was a noticeable divide between departments, leading to siloed efforts.

To address these challenges, Mr. Thompson introduced a series of team-building initiatives. First, he facilitated workshops aimed at improving communication and trust. These sessions included opportunities for team members to share personal and professional challenges, which helped to foster empathy. Mr. Thompson led by example, discussing his own challenges to encourage openness.

> Next, he introduced collaborative goal-setting, where team members worked together to define goals. This clarified each person's role and how their work contributed to the school's success. It gave the team a sense of ownership and aligned their efforts.
>
> Mr. Thompson also implemented regular one-on-one check-ins and weekly leadership meetings, creating a space for open dialogue. These sessions allowed team members to raise concerns and provide feedback, promoting a culture of constructive communication.
>
> Recognising the importance of inclusivity, Mr. Thompson made sure that all voices were heard in decision-making. This helped generate diverse ideas and solutions to the school's challenges.
>
> To build resilience, Mr. Thompson offered training to help the leadership team cope with stress and setbacks. He also encouraged the team to celebrate successes, fostering a sense of accomplishment and motivation.
>
> The efforts led to gradual improvements. Trust and communication strengthened, the team aligned around shared goals, and collaboration increased. Once the leadership team became more cohesive, Mr. Thompson encouraged department heads to apply similar strategies within their teams, spreading the culture of teamwork across the school.

Continuous professional development

Continuous professional development (CPD) ensures that staff maintain and enhance their skills to meet the evolving demands of teaching and learning. As Fullan (2023) asserts, leaders who prioritise CPD create a culture of continuous improvement that benefits educators and students alike. CPD enables educators to stay up-to-date with the latest pedagogical strategies, curriculum developments, and technological advancements, equipping them with the tools to deliver high-quality education in dynamic environments. By embedding CPD into the fabric of their institutions, leaders can nurture a culture of lifelong learning, drive innovation, and achieve meaningful improvements in both staff performance and student outcomes.

From a leadership perspective, investing in CPD signals a commitment to staff development and organisational excellence. By offering tailored CPD opportunities, leaders demonstrate their dedication to supporting teachers' professional journeys, enhancing job satisfaction, and retaining talent. Research by Darling-Hammond et al. (2017) indicates that CPD programmes aligned with staff needs and organisational goals improve teacher performance and positively impact student outcomes. CPD serves as a catalyst for collaboration and knowledge sharing. Leaders can design CPD initiatives that encourage staff to work together, exchange best practices, and build professional networks. This collaborative approach not only strengthens individual capabilities but also enhances organisational cohesion and adaptability. Guskey (2002) highlights that effective CPD programmes foster collective efficacy among educators, enabling them to tackle complex issues with confidence and creativity.

Leaders also play a crucial role in integrating CPD into institutional strategies, ensuring that professional learning aligns with organisational objectives and priorities. By linking CPD to broader educational goals, such as equity, inclusion, and technological integration, leaders can drive systemic change and elevate educational standards. For example, integrating training on digital tools and innovative teaching methods allows educators to harness technology effectively, creating more engaging and personalised learning experiences for students (Mishra & Koehler, 2006).

CPD also contributes to the personal and professional well-being of staff. Leaders who prioritise CPD foster a sense of purpose and accomplishment among staff, reducing burnout and promoting long-term commitment to the profession. Research by Skaalvik & Skaalvik (2017) suggests that opportunities for professional growth and development are closely linked to job satisfaction and teacher retention. Leaders who support CPD initiatives create a more resilient and motivated workforce, capable of meeting the challenges of the educational landscape.

Creating pathways for leadership and growth

Bush (2008) underscores the importance of creating clear pathways for leadership and growth with structured opportunities for career advancement which empower staff to take on leadership roles and contribute meaningfully to their institutions. Developing leadership capacity within an organisation is not only essential for individual growth but also critical for ensuring institutional resilience and adaptability in the face of future challenges.

Leadership pathways provide a strategic framework for nurturing talent and preparing staff to transition into leadership positions. This involves offering targeted skill development opportunities, such as workshops, training programmes, and on-the-job leadership experiences. Well-structured leadership pathways increase staff confidence and competence, enabling them to take on greater responsibilities and drive positive organisational change. Leaders who invest in such initiatives ensure that their institutions have a robust pipeline of qualified individuals ready to meet emerging demands.

Providing access to leadership roles through distributed leadership models can also serve as a powerful pathway for growth. Distributed leadership, as highlighted by Harris & Spillane (2008), allows staff to take ownership of specific projects or initiatives, fostering a sense of agency and responsibility. This approach enables individuals to demonstrate and refine their leadership capabilities in a practical context while contributing to the organisation's goals. Leaders who embrace distributed leadership create inclusive environments that encourage staff at all levels to step into leadership roles and develop their potential.

Leaders also play a pivotal role in recognising and rewarding leadership potential within their teams. By identifying individuals with leadership aptitude and providing them with tailored development plans, leaders can cultivate a culture of aspiration and progression. For example, targeted leadership academies or talent identification programmes can be instrumental in preparing staff for senior roles. Transparent and equitable processes for leadership development enhance staff morale and ensure diversity within leadership pipelines.

Creating pathways for leadership and growth involves addressing systemic barriers that may hinder staff progression. This includes providing equitable access to leadership opportunities for underrepresented groups and ensuring that professional development initiatives are inclusive and accessible. As Lumby (2012) emphasises, diversity in leadership is critical for fostering innovation and addressing the multifaceted challenges faced by educational institutions. Leaders must therefore prioritise strategies that support the advancement of diverse talents and perspectives within their teams.

Leadership pathways must be aligned with long-term organisational goals to ensure sustainability and impact. Leaders should actively integrate leadership development into their strategic planning processes, linking individual growth opportunities to broader institutional priorities. This alignment ensures that leadership pathways contribute not only to personal advancement but also to organisational success. Fullan (2023) argues that strategic leadership development strengthens institutional capacity and enhances the ability to navigate complex and rapidly changing educational landscapes.

Performance management

Performance management provides a structured approach to evaluating and enhancing individual and organisational performance. Aguinis (2023) emphasises that fair appraisals and constructive feedback are pivotal in building a high-performing workforce. Through thoughtful and balanced evaluations, leaders can help staff recognise their strengths and identify areas for improvement, fostering professional growth.

Fair appraisals form the foundation of an equitable performance management system. By implementing transparent criteria and standardised processes, leaders can ensure that assessments are perceived as unbiased and reliable. This fairness not only enhances trust but also reinforces a culture of accountability. Research by

Armstrong & Taylor (2020) highlights that appraisal systems grounded in objectivity and clarity increase employee engagement and reduce dissatisfaction, particularly when staff perceive their efforts and contributions are being accurately recognised. Effective leaders prioritise fairness by involving employees in the goal-setting process, providing clarity on expectations, and using evidence-based metrics to assess performance.

Supportive feedback is another essential component of performance management, serving as a catalyst for continuous improvement. Northouse (2021) argues that constructive feedback is most impactful when delivered in a manner that is both empathetic and actionable. Leaders who engage in regular, open dialogue with their team members provide opportunities for reflection and growth, creating an environment where employees feel valued and supported. For instance, adopting a "feed-forward" approach, which focuses on future improvements rather than dwelling on past shortcomings, can help employees stay motivated and solution-focused (Goldsmith, 2010).

The timing and frequency of feedback play a crucial role in its effectiveness. Research by Pulakos & O'Leary (2011) demonstrates that continuous feedback, integrated into day-to-day interactions, is more effective than relying solely on annual appraisals. This approach ensures that staff receive timely insights into their performance, enabling them to make immediate adjustments and improvements. Leaders who adopt a continuous feedback model can foster a sense of ongoing development and adaptability, which is particularly important in dynamic organisational environments.

Salas et al. (2012) underscore the importance of integrating performance management with professional development, noting that this combination drives higher levels of employee satisfaction and retention. Leaders who invest in their team's development signal their commitment to employee growth, creating a positive and engaged workplace culture.

Performance management should be adaptive and responsive to meet the varied and evolving needs of diverse teams. Recognising that staff bring different strengths, learning preferences, cultural backgrounds, and career aspirations, effective leaders must tailor feedback, goal-setting, and professional development strategies accordingly. This creates a more personalised and meaningful performance dialogue that supports growth and motivation. Inclusive performance management practices that acknowledge and address the unique needs, experiences, and contributions of individuals help foster a culture of equity, engagement, and trust. These practices empower all staff to contribute fully and confidently to the organisation's success and long-term sustainability (DeNisi & Murphy, 2017).

Information: Current performance systems rely on self-appraisal. While potentially effective, these can sometimes be too one-sided, as they rely mainly on an individual's perspective, which may be biased or overly optimistic. Without external feedback, key areas for improvement may be overlooked, and strengths may be exaggerated. It is important therefore to balance self-assessment with input from peers, supervisors, or objective data to provide a more well-rounded and accurate evaluation.

Conflict management

Conflict is inevitable in any workplace and unresolved conflicts can harm team dynamics, erode trust, and lower morale, ultimately affecting an organisation's overall performance. Effective conflict resolution ensures that issues are addressed constructively, fostering a positive environment where differences are reconciled, and relationships are strengthened. A proactive approach to conflict management can prevent disputes from escalating. Leaders should foster a culture where conflicts are seen as opportunities for growth rather than threats. For instance, regular team meetings and open forums for discussion can address minor issues before they escalate into larger problems. Providing training in conflict resolution for staff members further empowers them to manage disagreements effectively, reducing the burden on leadership and enhancing the overall workplace climate (Runde & Flanagan, 2012).

Conflict is perhaps best understood through the *Thomas-Kilmann Conflict Model* (Figure 5.2). The model identifies five conflict management styles based on the dimensions of assertiveness (the extent to which an individual attempts to satisfy their own concerns) and cooperativeness (the extent to which an individual attempts to satisfy the concerns of others). The model emphasises choosing an appropriate style depending on the context and desired outcomes.

Research by Alhamali (2019) highlights the importance of a leader's conflict management style. Leaders who adopt integrating, obliging, and compromising styles are shown to have the most significant positive effects on team performance. Integrating involves seeking win-win solutions that address the needs of all parties, while obliging demonstrates a willingness to accommodate others to maintain harmony. Compromising seeks a middle ground, ensuring that each party feels their concerns have been considered. Conversely, avoiding and dominating styles were found to negatively impact team performance, as these approaches often lead to unresolved tensions or feelings of resentment.

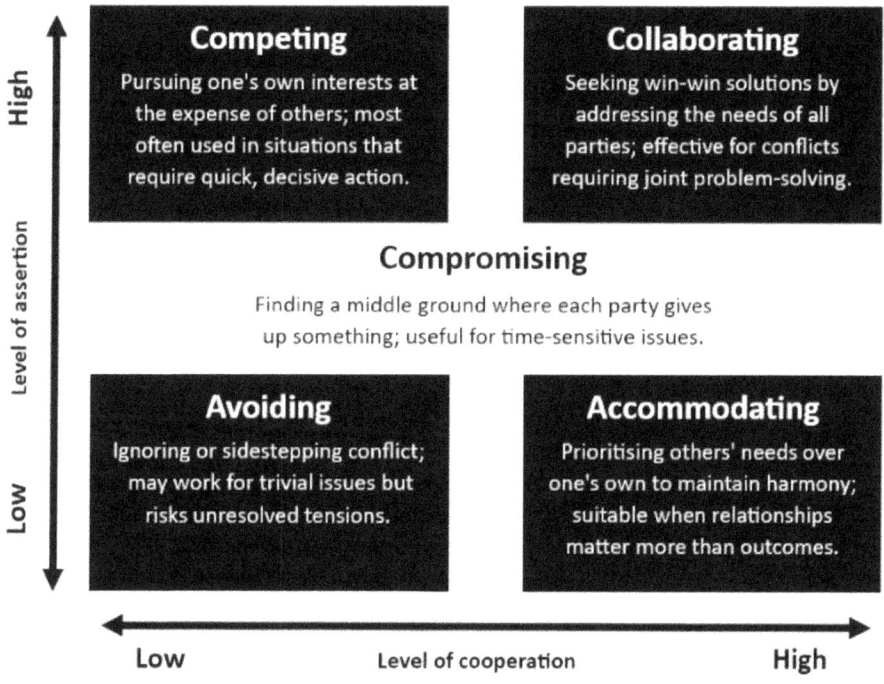

Figure 5.2 - Thomas-Kilmann Conflict Model

Empathy is a cornerstone of effective conflict management. Leaders who actively listen to the concerns of all parties involved create a sense of psychological safety, encouraging open and honest communication. Empathy allows leaders to understand the underlying causes of conflict, such as unmet expectations, miscommunications, or differing values, and to address these root issues rather than merely addressing surface-level disagreements (Goleman et al., 2013). For example, a leader who empathises with a teacher's frustrations about workload may uncover systemic issues requiring broader organisational changes.

Clarity is equally vital in resolving conflicts. Leaders must articulate the issues at hand, set clear expectations for behaviour, and establish a transparent process for resolution. According to Benke (2023), clear communication reduces misunderstandings and ensures that all parties understand their roles in achieving a resolution. Leaders should facilitate structured discussions where conflicting parties can express their perspectives and collaboratively identify solutions. Clarity in communication also involves defining the consequences of unresolved conflicts, ensuring accountability, and emphasising the importance of moving forward collectively.

Promoting emotional intelligence across the organisation plays a significant role in preventing and resolving conflicts. Emotional intelligence equips staff with the ability to manage their emotions and navigate interpersonal challenges, creating a more cohesive and resilient team (Goleman et al., 2013). Leaders who model emotional intelligence in their interactions set a standard for constructive communication and mutual respect.

Conflict management also requires leaders to maintain impartiality and fairness. Addressing conflicts without favouritism ensures that all parties feel heard and valued, which is essential for restoring trust and maintaining team cohesion. Leaders must avoid allowing personal biases to influence their decisions, as doing so can exacerbate tensions and damage workplace relationships (Lencioni, 2010).

Attracting talent

Attracting talented educators is a crucial component of building a high-quality and sustainable teaching workforce. Ingersoll & Merrill (2017) emphasise the importance of strategic recruitment efforts in addressing challenges related to teacher shortages, workforce diversity, and long-term educational improvement. These strategies require a multifaceted approach that includes building partnerships, enhancing working conditions, and developing targeted initiatives to draw skilled professionals into the teaching profession. One of the most effective strategies for attracting talent involves establishing strong partnerships with teacher preparation programmes. Collaborative efforts between schools and universities can help create pipelines for highly qualified educators.

Maintaining attractive working conditions is essential to recruiting and retaining talented educators. A supportive environment, characterised by strong leadership, collaboration, and opportunities for professional growth, makes the teaching profession more appealing. Ingersoll & Merrill (2017) note that leadership plays a pivotal role in shaping these conditions. Leaders who invest in teacher development, provide access to modern resources, and foster an atmosphere of respect and recognition can significantly enhance job satisfaction. For example, schools that offer competitive compensation packages, manageable workloads, and pathways for career progression are better positioned to recruit top-tier talent (Garcia & Weiss, 2019).

Targeted recruitment strategies further enhance the quality and diversity of the teaching workforce. These strategies involve tailoring outreach efforts to specific groups, such as career changers, individuals with STEM expertise, or candidates with multilingual skills. Highlighting the unique opportunities and benefits of teaching, such as making a societal impact or contributing to community development, can attract individuals who may not have previously considered the profession.

Initiatives like alternative certification pathways can also broaden the talent pool by providing accessible entry points for individuals transitioning from other careers. As noted by Podolsky et al. (2016), such programmes are particularly valuable in addressing shortages in high-need subject areas and geographic regions.

Utilising technology and social media platforms can expand the reach of recruitment campaigns. Online job boards, virtual job fairs, and digital marketing strategies enable institutes to connect with prospective teachers across a broader geographic area. Tools such as LinkedIn or education-focused platforms like Teach.org allow schools to showcase their values, achievements, and professional development opportunities, making them more attractive to potential candidates. Darling-Hammond et al. (2017) argue that institutes that effectively communicate their commitment to student success and teacher well-being through these platforms are more likely to capture the interest of high-calibre educators.

Fostering relationships with community stakeholders can also support recruitment efforts. Engaging parents, local businesses, and nonprofit organisations in the recruitment process can build a sense of shared purpose and community investment in education. Community-based recruitment efforts, such as "grow-your-own" programmes, focus on identifying and training local talent who have a vested interest in the success of their schools and neighbourhoods. Research by Gist et al. (2019) demonstrates that such initiatives not only address teacher shortages but also contribute to the stability and cohesion of the teaching workforce.

Case Study: Attracting talented staff at Cranstone College

Cranstone College struggled to attract and retain highly skilled academic staff, particularly in STEM, business, and education. Principal Emily Jordan implemented a more targeted approach to recruitment to address these challenges.

The college began collaborating with nearby universities that provided teacher education programmes, aiming to build pipelines for future educators. While not as smooth as hoped, they set up some joint initiatives like internships and research projects to increase visibility and draw in candidates.

To improve retention, Cranstone introduced a modest professional development programme, funding a limited number of faculty members to attend conferences or pursue further qualifications. They also adjusted work policies to offer more flexible hours and improved career progression opportunities, though this was still a work in progress.

Cranstone's recruitment campaigns targeted specific groups, including career changers and STEM experts, though success was mixed. While the college did attract some candidates with diverse backgrounds, the pool was smaller than expected, especially for hard-to-fill positions.

> The college also made use of social media to promote job openings and faculty experiences, but engagement was lower than anticipated. They hosted virtual job fairs, which drew some interest, but didn't reach as broad an audience as hoped.
>
> An in-house (grow-your-own) programme was introduced, partnering with local schools and businesses to nurture local talent. This programme had limited success, as only a handful of students from the initiative moved into faculty roles, though it provided a pipeline for future recruits.
>
> Ultimately, these efforts led to a 17% increase in faculty applications, with more successful recruitment in STEM and business departments. Retention improved modestly, but challenges remained. Cranstone's approach, with its focus on partnerships and professional growth, helped attract and retain talent but highlighted areas for further development.

Addressing burnout and enhancing well-being

Teacher burnout is a pervasive issue with far-reaching consequences for both educators and the institutions they serve. Skaalvik & Skaalvik (2011) underscore the necessity of addressing burnout to improve teacher retention and foster a sustainable workforce. Burnout, characterised by physical and emotional exhaustion, depersonalisation, and a reduced sense of personal accomplishment, can undermine job satisfaction and effectiveness. Addressing this issue requires a proactive approach that includes fostering a supportive work environment, providing professional development opportunities, and prioritising well-being.

A supportive work environment is foundational in mitigating burnout. Teachers who feel valued and supported by leadership and colleagues are more likely to remain committed to their roles. This includes creating open channels for communication, where teachers can voice concerns and receive constructive feedback. Supportive leadership, as highlighted by Northouse (2021), plays a pivotal role in setting a positive tone and ensuring that educators have the resources they need to succeed. For example, leaders who implement manageable workloads, fair policies, and flexible scheduling can alleviate the pressures that contribute to burnout. Additionally, fostering a culture of collaboration and peer support can help teachers share strategies and build resilience (Taris et al., 2005).

Professional development opportunities that emphasise self-care, time management, and stress reduction can be particularly beneficial too. For instance, mindfulness-based professional development sessions have been shown to reduce stress and improve overall well-being (Jennings et al., 2013). Also, leadership programmes that prepare teachers for career advancement can renew their sense of purpose and commitment to the profession.

Promoting well-being must extend beyond professional development and into the broader organisational culture. Comprehensive well-being initiatives should address physical, mental, and emotional health. This includes providing access to mental health resources, such as counselling services, and creating opportunities for staff to engage in restorative activities. Institutes that prioritise well-being through wellness programmes, fitness initiatives, and social activities contribute to a healthier and more connected staff community (Greenberg et al., 2016). Leaders who model healthy work-life balance and openly support well-being initiatives send a clear message about the value of teacher health and satisfaction.

Diversity and inclusion in the workforce

Diversity and inclusion create equitable, enriching learning environments that reflect society's complexity. Santamaria & Santamaria (2016) highlight that promoting these values enhances both ethics and educational outcomes. A diverse workforce brings varied perspectives that support richer dialogue, innovation, and cultural understanding. Schools can attract and retain diverse talent through targeted recruitment, alternative entry routes into teaching, and inclusive workplace practices.

Standard hiring often overlooks underrepresented groups, but outreach efforts and partnerships with diversity-focused organisations help broaden applicant pools. Initiatives like scholarships and career-change pathways improve access for those facing entry barriers (Ingersoll & May, 2011). Alternative certification routes, such as residencies and fast-track programmes, support non-traditional candidates - bringing fresh skills and life experience into classrooms.

Sustaining diversity requires inclusive cultures where all staff feel respected, supported, and empowered to contribute. Without genuine inclusion, diverse hires may feel marginalised or isolated, leading to disengagement and higher turnover. Inclusion ensures that differences are not only accepted but actively valued as strengths. Leaders play a central role in shaping this environment by modelling equitable behaviours, addressing unconscious bias, offering training in cultural competence, and implementing supportive structures such as mentoring schemes. These actions help create a workplace where diversity is not only present but fully integrated and appreciated, allowing all staff to thrive (Northouse, 2021).

A diverse and inclusive workforce strengthens educational outcomes. Teachers with different backgrounds enrich teaching and relate more closely to diverse learners. Dee (2004) found that students, especially from minority groups, benefit when taught by culturally similar educators - gaining deeper engagement, understanding, and academic success. Exposure to diverse role models also promotes global awareness among all learners.

Activity: Leadership ability

Using the table below, and for each listed aspect, rate your ability as a leader in relation to other staff. *Where: 1 = Needs Improvement, 5 = Excellent.* Provide specific examples to justify your rating.

Aspect	Rating (1-5)	Reflection
Influencing others		How effectively do I inspire trust, communicate vision, and align staff with organisational goals?
Motivation		How well do I recognise and foster intrinsic motivation among team members?
Coaching and mentoring		To what extent do I support staff in achieving their potential through regular coaching and mentoring?
Facilitation		How skilled am I in enabling effective collaboration and removing barriers to progress within the team?
Team building		How successful have I been in creating a cohesive and high-performing team?
Continuous professional development		How committed am I to providing meaningful growth opportunities for my staff?
Creating pathways for leadership and growth		How often do I identify and nurture future leaders within my team?
Performance management		How consistently do I provide constructive feedback and hold staff accountable for their performance?
Conflict management		How effectively do I resolve disputes while maintaining a positive work environment?
Attracting talent		How actively do I contribute to attracting and retaining talented individuals in the organisation?
Addressing burnout / enhancing well-being		How proactive am I in promoting staff well-being and addressing burnout signs promptly?
Diversity and inclusion		How inclusive is my leadership in recognising and celebrating workforce diversity?

Organisational issues in managing people

For people management to be truly effective, leaders require a comprehensive understanding of organisational issues that influence staff behaviour, satisfaction, and performance. These include workplace culture and climate, decision-making processes, technology and innovation in workforce management, change management, derailment, work-life balance, sustainability practices, crisis management, strategic thinking, and positive leadership behaviour.

Workplace culture encompasses the shared values, beliefs, and norms that shape staff behaviour, while climate refers to the collective perceptions of the work environment. A positive culture and climate are crucial for employee engagement and organisational success. Ethical leaders influence the dynamic process of shaping and transforming organisational culture, leading to increased staff satisfaction and reduced turnover. Leading by example is particularly impactful in cultivating trust and alignment with organisational values.

Decision-making processes within an organisation determine how choices are made and who is involved in making them. Participative decision-making, where employees are involved in the process, has been shown to enhance job satisfaction and organisational commitment. Participatory leaders treat workers fairly and involve them in decision-making to reduce work-life balance stress. Inclusive decision-making processes lead to more innovative solutions and improved team performance. Strategic thinking enables leaders to evaluate complex organisational challenges holistically, ensuring decisions align with long-term objectives while fostering adaptability.

The integration of technology in workforce management has transformed how organisations operate, offering tools for recruitment, performance monitoring, and employee engagement. However, the implementation of artificial intelligence (AI) and other technologies presents challenges, including job insecurity and occupational stress. The fear of technological unemployment due to AI can lead to heightened stress levels among staff. However, when effectively implemented, technology can enhance performance and efficiency. Leaders must balance the benefits of technology with sustainability practices to ensure innovations align with organisational values and long-term viability.

Educational institutions must adapt to evolving pedagogical approaches, technologies, and societal expectations, making change management a vital skill for leaders and administrators. Effective change management involves preparing, supporting, and helping individuals and teams navigate organisational change. Transformational leaders are instrumental in guiding organisations through change and often inspire confidence during times of crisis. Leaders who can manage crises effectively demonstrate resilience, quick decision-making, and the ability to maintain team morale under pressure (Hall, 2025).

Leaders often fail to meet the expectations of their role due to interpersonal relationship issues, inability to adapt, or failure to meet business objectives. Understanding the factors that lead to this *derailment* is essential for developing effective leaders. Emotional intelligence and adaptability are key predictors of leadership success and can mitigate the risk of derailment. Mentoring and continuous professional development are effective strategies to prevent it, while integrating innovative approaches ensures leaders stay relevant and forward-thinking.

Achieving work-life balance is essential for staff well-being and productivity. In this respect, positive leadership behaviours and leadership styles, such as transformational and ethical leadership, have profound effects. Transformational leaders inspire and motivate employees to exceed expectations, fostering an environment conducive to innovation and high performance. Ethical leadership contributes to a positive organisational culture, enhancing job satisfaction and reducing turnover. By embedding sustainability practices, leaders can further enhance organisational stability and employee satisfaction, creating a work environment that is both supportive and future-focused.

Activity: Your relationship with your organisation

Answer the following questions, scoring each on a scale of 1 (strongly disagree) to 5 (strongly agree). Be honest in your responses.

Workplace culture and climate
- I actively contribute to fostering a positive workplace culture.
- Employees feel valued and engaged under my leadership.
- I model ethical behaviour that promotes trust and satisfaction among staff.

Decision-making processes
- I involve employees in key decision-making processes.
- My decision-making approach encourages collaboration and fairness.
- Decisions made in my organisation are often innovative and inclusive.

Technology and innovation
- I support staff in adapting to new technologies.
- Technology implementation in my organisation has positively influenced staff engagement and productivity.
- I address concerns about job insecurity and stress related to technology.

Change management
- I provide clear guidance and support during times of change.
- My leadership helps staff adapt to new policies, technologies, or pedagogy.
- I am proactive in preparing my team for organisational changes.

Derailment
- I regularly reflect on and seek to improve my interpersonal and leadership skills.
- I actively pursue professional development opportunities for myself and my staff.
- I seek mentoring or provide mentoring to prevent leadership derailment.

Work-life balance
- I promote a culture that values work-life balance for all staff.
- I address workload concerns that could negatively affect well-being.
- My leadership style helps reduce stress and burnout among team members.

Positive leadership behaviours
- I inspire and motivate staff to achieve their potential.
- I model transformational and ethical leadership practices.
- My leadership style contributes to a positive organisational climate and reduced turnover.

Analysis and reflection
- Review your scores. Identify your strengths (scores of 4–5) and areas for improvement (scores of 1–3).
- Reflect on each area where you scored 3 or below. Ask yourself:
    - What specific actions can I take to address this issue?
    - How can I involve my team in creating solutions?
    - What additional support or training might I need to improve?

Summary

Inspiring and engaging staff in education involves balancing responsibilities with building relationships and fostering a supportive culture. Teachers, leaders, support staff, students, parents, and the wider community all play interlinked roles, and their collaboration is key to success. Effective leadership begins with self-awareness, resilience, and a commitment to growth, forming the basis for guiding others.

Strong relationships are built through coaching, motivation, conflict resolution, and promoting inclusion. Collaborative leadership and team-building support a shared vision and institutional cohesion. Tackling challenges like change management and modelling positive leadership is essential for stability and morale.

Leadership rooted in emotional intelligence, trust, and ethics supports well-being, reduces stress, and enhances job satisfaction. Empowering individuals and cultivating a growth-oriented culture helps everyone thrive.

6 DEVELOPING HUMAN RESOURCES

Sue Ellis

Introduction

Human Resource Management (HRM) plays an important role in the development and support of staff, with direct implications for both organisational performance and student outcomes. Encompassing activities such as recruitment, professional development, performance management, and staff relations, HRM seeks to cultivate a workforce that is motivated, competent, and responsive to change. There is substantive evidence linking effective HRM practices with enhanced student achievement, with the quality of teaching widely acknowledged as the most influential determinant of student success. Beyond these core functions, HRM also contributes to the shaping of a positive organisational culture, advances the principles of diversity and inclusion, and responds to the evolving demands of the education sector. In an era characterised by continual shifts in pedagogical practice, technological advancement, and societal expectation, the role of HRM in sustaining institutional adaptability and resilience cannot be overstated.

This chapter:

- Provides an overview of HRM and its significance in various educational contexts.
- Explains the role of HRM in aligning HR strategies with educational goals.
- Examines the importance of leadership in shaping HR practices.
- Discusses recruitment and selection, focusing on attracting talent for diverse educational settings.
- Highlights staff development, including professional development, mentoring, and training.
- Explores performance management practices, including goal setting and addressing underperformance.
- Addresses staff well-being, work-life balance, and creating a supportive work environment.
- Discusses the role of technology and innovation in modern HR management in education.

Overview of human resource management

Human Resource Management (HRM) constitutes an essential pillar in optimising the effectiveness of organisational workforces and cultivating positive working environments, with particular significance in educational settings where staff performance directly influences the quality of education and, consequently, student outcomes. HRM encompasses a range of core functions, including recruitment and selection, staff development, retention strategies, and the advancement of an organisational culture that aligns with institutional goals (Armstrong & Taylor, 2020). Through the strategic placement of individuals in roles supported by targeted development initiatives and robust performance management systems, HRM seeks to enhance both organisational efficacy and educational achievement.

In educational contexts, HRM practices are necessarily tailored to the distinctive demands of schools, colleges, and universities. Teachers and administrative personnel form the bedrock of the educational process, and effective HRM mechanisms are critical in supporting staff as they navigate the complexities inherent to contemporary education. Recruitment is conceptualised not merely as the selection of technically qualified individuals, but as the identification of candidates whose values and professional dispositions resonate with the mission of the institution, thereby fostering cohesion and motivation within the workforce (Day, 2002).

Recognising the dynamic nature of teaching, HRM positions professional development as a fundamental imperative, encompassing training, mentoring, and opportunities for career progression. Performance management systems, similarly, are expected to function not simply as mechanisms of oversight, but as instruments of constructive, equitable feedback aligned with the strategic ambitions of the institution (Mercer et al., 2010).

The cultivation of a positive organisational culture is a further critical function of HRM. A culture underpinned by collaboration, trust, and a shared sense of purpose is seen as vital in maintaining a work environment conducive to teaching and learning. Strategies that prioritise work-life balance and staff well-being are not peripheral concerns but essential components in preventing burnout and sustaining high levels of staff engagement.

The application of HRM principles varies across educational sectors. In primary and secondary education, the emphasis rests on recruiting and developing teachers capable of managing classrooms, delivering curricula effectively, and addressing the increasingly complex and differentiated needs of learners. In the higher education sector, HRM practices must accommodate the dual responsibilities of faculty as both educators and researchers, with attendant pressures relating to research output and academic development. In further education contexts, HRM strategies are necessarily oriented towards supporting staff working with diverse, often non-traditional student populations, requiring a particular focus on adaptability and inclusivity.

Recent shifts towards diversity and inclusivity within HRM practices mirror broader societal imperatives towards equity, with institutions increasingly recognising the need to construct workforces that reflect the diversity of their student bodies and to ensure equitable opportunities for all (Chugh, 2024). HRM must, therefore, remain strategic, ensuring that recruitment, development, and performance management systems are not only aligned with institutional aims but also responsive to evolving societal expectations, including the integration of technology and the redefinition of educational policy priorities.

Equity, inclusion, and diversity now sit at the forefront of HRM agendas within education. A diverse workforce is not merely an aspirational goal but a vital asset in enriching the educational experience and supporting institutional missions. HRM policies that seek to recruit and retain individuals from underrepresented groups serve as catalysts for transformative change, promoting cultures of inclusivity and equity within educational institutions (Przytuła et al., 2024). In fulfilling these roles, HRM is positioned not only as an operational function but as a strategic partner in ensuring educational institutions remain resilient, responsive, and committed to the improvement of educational outcomes.

Strategic HRM in education

Strategic Human Resource Management (SHRM) in education is fundamental to aligning human resource practices with the strategic aims of educational institutions, with the dual purpose of enhancing student learning outcomes and institutional effectiveness. Through the integration of HR strategies with educational objectives, the exercise of effective leadership, and the balancing of long-term planning with short-term operational needs, SHRM facilitates the development of a competent and motivated workforce that evolves alongside students. In adopting such a strategic orientation, educational institutions are better positioned not merely to meet immediate operational demands but to sustain success within an increasingly complex and dynamic educational landscape (Karman, 2020).

At the core of SHRM in education is the alignment of HR strategies with the overarching goals of the institution. Given that the primary mission of educational organisations is to deliver high-quality learning experiences that promote student success, HR practices must be carefully synchronised with these imperatives. For example, where an institution seeks to integrate greater use of technology into teaching and learning, HR functions must prioritise the recruitment of educators proficient in digital pedagogies, alongside the provision of professional development initiatives aimed at upskilling existing staff. Strategic alignment of this nature ensures that the deployment of human capital actively contributes to and propels the institution's mission (Karman, 2020).

Leadership within educational institutions exerts a critical influence over the shape and execution of HR strategy. Leaders, including headteachers, principals, and deans, are instrumental in establishing organisational culture and strategic priorities. Their active engagement with HR as a strategic partner is essential in attracting, nurturing, and retaining high-calibre staff. Moreover, empirical evidence highlights that leadership styles exert significant effects on the design and implementation of HR practices, with consequential impacts on both teacher performance and student achievement (Vekeman et al., 2016). Effective leadership thus operates as a key enabler of strategic HRM.

A further dimension of strategic HRM involves the balance between long-term workforce planning and the resolution of immediate staffing needs. Long-term HR planning entails forecasting future staffing requirements, informed by trends in student enrolment, curriculum innovation, and technological change. Such foresight is essential in equipping institutions to anticipate and respond to future challenges and opportunities. Nevertheless, the exigencies of day-to-day operations frequently necessitate short-term HR interventions, whether to address unexpected staff turnover or sudden increases in student numbers. Although short-term responsiveness is vital, an over-reliance on reactive decision-making can undermine the coherence of the institution's strategic vision. Sustainable success in educational HRM demands a balanced approach that integrates both forward-looking strategic planning and pragmatic responses to immediate needs (Smith, 2023).

Recruitment and selection

Recruitment and selection are critical functions within educational institutions, directly influencing institutional effectiveness through the quality of appointed staff. These processes must be strategically designed and adapted to the specific demands of diverse educational contexts - including primary and secondary schools, further education (FE) colleges, and higher education (HE) institutions - to ensure the identification, appointment, and retention of talent that aligns with the institution's mission and values.

Recruitment and selection in education present inherent complexities that necessitate a strategic orientation. Institutions must develop approaches that address both immediate staffing needs and longer-term workforce planning. By tailoring recruitment strategies to the requirements of each educational sector, prioritising diversity and inclusion, and employing robust selection methodologies, institutions can attract and appoint a highly skilled and diverse workforce capable of responding to the evolving demands of education. Strategic recruitment efforts serve not only to meet current institutional needs but to build organisational capacity for future success in an increasingly competitive educational landscape (Collings & Mellahi, 2019).

An essential dimension of recruitment and selection lies in the contextual adaptation of hiring practices. In primary and secondary education, for instance, recruitment efforts must prioritise candidates who demonstrate proficiency in classroom management, curriculum delivery across multiple subjects, and the capacity to meet the varied learning needs of students (Torrington et al., 2020). In contrast, HE institutions require academics who are capable of excellence in both teaching and research, often necessitating a strong publication record and engagement with scholarly activities that contribute to the institution's research objectives (Metcalf et al., 2005). Within the FE sector, where students often pursue vocational and professional qualifications, there is an emphasis on recruiting staff with substantial industry experience alongside pedagogical expertise. FE institutions also benefit from staff skilled in adult learning theory and able to support diverse, non-traditional student populations (Hodkinson & Jenkings, 2020). Recruitment strategies must therefore exhibit sufficient flexibility and nuance to address these varying sectoral expectations.

Attracting high-calibre talent across educational sectors requires the deployment of targeted recruitment strategies. In primary and secondary education, institutions must appeal to individuals who not only meet the necessary professional standards but who also embody personal attributes such as empathy, patience, and strong interpersonal communication skills (Rhodes & Brundrett, 2012). Recruitment campaigns should emphasise the broader social impact of teaching, highlighting the opportunity to shape the development of young people.

In the FE sector, attracting staff often involves engaging with professionals outside the traditional educational sphere. FE institutions seek individuals who combine technical expertise with the ability to teach and mentor learners in vocational disciplines. Incentives such as competitive salaries, professional development opportunities, and pathways for industry professionals into teaching can enhance the attractiveness of FE roles.

In the HE sector, the focus is predominantly on academic credentials, research productivity, and pedagogical innovation. Universities must position themselves as environments that support both research excellence and high-quality teaching, using professional networks, academic conferences, and specialist job boards to attract the best candidates (Bohlander & Snell, 2017). Across all sectors, the use of diverse recruitment channels, including digital platforms and social media, can extend the reach to a broader pool of applicants.

Diversity and inclusion are indispensable components of contemporary recruitment and selection practices within education. Institutions committed to reflecting the diversity of their communities must proactively encourage applications from underrepresented groups. Beyond compliance with equality legislation, the strategic promotion of diversity enhances institutional effectiveness by fostering inclusive environments that benefit all learners (Fradella, 2018). Recruitment policies should not only address demographic representation but also embrace the broader dimensions of diversity, including diverse professional experiences, cultural perspectives, and cognitive approaches. Measures such as targeted outreach initiatives and training programmes for selection panels to mitigate unconscious bias are critical to achieving these aims. Nurturing an inclusive organisational culture is essential to retaining diverse talent.

The final stage of the recruitment process - selection - is critical in ensuring that the most suitable candidates are appointed. Effective selection processes are grounded in clear, role-specific criteria and involve multiple stages to provide a comprehensive evaluation of candidates. Initial stages typically involve systematic shortlisting based on applications, CVs, and personal statements, assessed against pre-determined criteria.

Behavioural interviewing techniques, which require candidates to provide evidence of past behaviours and achievements, are particularly effective in evaluating competencies essential to educational roles, such as communication, resilience, and problem-solving. The incorporation of practical assessment components, such as teaching demonstrations or case studies, provides a valuable opportunity to observe candidates' professional practice in action. Additionally, involving multiple assessors in the selection process, particularly potential colleagues, can help reduce individual biases and ensure a more rounded, objective assessment of candidates' suitability.

Staff development and training

Staff development and training are essential for maintaining high standards and meeting the evolving needs of students. As educational contexts and learner profiles change, it is vital for institutions to invest in the continuous development of their staff. A robust staff development strategy enhances the skills and knowledge of educators while fostering a culture of lifelong learning and professional growth. This includes identifying professional development needs, designing tailored training programmes, implementing effective continuing professional development (CPD) across different educational sectors, and integrating mentoring and coaching as key development tools. By prioritising these elements, educational institutions not only strengthen their workforce but also create an environment of continuous improvement that benefits both educators and learners.

Identifying professional development needs

Effective professional development starts with a clear understanding of the specific needs of staff. Identifying these needs is a dynamic process that involves regular assessments, feedback, and alignment with institutional goals. One approach to identifying development needs is through performance appraisals, where staff members receive constructive feedback on their strengths and areas for improvement (Serbati et al., 2020). These appraisals provide valuable insights into the professional growth of individual staff members and can highlight the skills required to enhance teaching effectiveness or meet new educational demands.

Institutions can use self-appraisals, surveys, focus groups, or one-on-one interviews to collect feedback directly from staff about their perceived training needs. These methods ensure that the professional development offered is relevant and meaningful to those who will benefit from it. An important aspect of identifying development needs is considering the changing demands of the educational context, such as the integration of technology in teaching, the need for inclusive teaching practices, and the introduction of new curricula or standards (Carroll et al., 2020).

Professional development needs can also be identified through analysis of student outcomes and feedback. For example, if students are struggling with specific learning outcomes, educators may require further training in those areas. Similarly, emerging educational trends, such as blended learning, may prompt institutions to invest in technology-based training to ensure that staff are equipped to meet the evolving expectations of their role.

Providing targeted training and development opportunities

Once professional development needs are identified, the next step in effective HRM is to ensure access to high-quality training and development opportunities that meet the specific requirements of staff across different educational levels. These opportunities may take the form of bespoke, in-house programmes designed around institutional priorities, or they may be sourced from external providers, consultants, or professional networks offering ready-made or customisable solutions.

The training needs of staff in primary and secondary education often differ markedly from those in further education (FE) or higher education (HE). As such, training provision must be appropriately selected or designed to reflect this diversity.

In primary and secondary settings, key areas for development may include classroom management, differentiated instruction, assessment strategies, and the integration of digital tools into teaching. There is also a strong emphasis on safeguarding, special educational needs (SEN), and promoting pupils' mental health and wellbeing (Morrison et al., 2020). These needs may be met through school-led CPD, local authority initiatives, or independent consultants with relevant expertise.

In FE settings, training and development may prioritise upskilling staff to deliver vocational qualifications, engage adult learners effectively, develop digital literacy, and maintain industry-relevant competencies. External partners - such as awarding bodies, industry experts, and training consultants - can often provide targeted input that aligns closely with curriculum and workplace expectations.

In the HE context, staff often combine teaching with research, requiring access to development that addresses both pedagogical and scholarly needs. Training provision may include workshops on curriculum design, teaching adult learners, research methodology, academic writing, and digital learning strategies. While many universities have dedicated professional development units, partnerships with external CPD providers or participation in national training schemes can also broaden opportunities and perspectives. Flexibility is key to addressing the varying needs of lecturers, researchers, support staff, and academic leaders.

Across all sectors, training opportunities should be guided by clear learning outcomes, use delivery methods appropriate to the context, and include mechanisms for feedback and evaluation. Blended learning approaches - combining online and in-person elements - offer both flexibility and accessibility, particularly for time-pressured staff. Whether developed internally or commissioned externally, aligning training content with sector-specific roles enhances its impact and relevance.

CPD plays an essential role in keeping staff current with pedagogical trends, policy changes, and emerging technologies. A robust CPD strategy should blend formal and informal learning opportunities, such as workshops, seminars, peer observation, mentoring, action research, or self-paced learning through digital platforms. In HE, this might include academic leadership development or integrating research into teaching practice. In FE, dual professionalism and workplace alignment remain central themes. Ultimately, providing effective training and CPD - whether internally crafted or externally sourced - supports a culture of continuous learning, enabling educational institutions to cultivate skilled, agile, and empowered professionals equipped to meet the demands of a rapidly evolving education sector.

Mentoring and coaching as development tools

Mentoring and coaching are powerful development tools that can complement formal training programmes by providing staff with personalised guidance and support.

Mentoring typically involves a more experienced individual providing advice and guidance to a less experienced colleague. In education, mentors can support staff in navigating complex teaching challenges, adapting to new curricula, or developing leadership skills (Serbati et al., 2020). Mentoring is particularly valuable in contexts where staff may be transitioning into new roles, such as new teachers, heads of departments, or those taking on leadership responsibilities.

Coaching, on the other hand, is typically a more structured and goal-oriented process, focused on specific areas of improvement. Coaching involves regular, focused interactions between a coach and a coachee, with the aim of enhancing performance and professional growth. In education, coaching can be particularly effective for teachers looking to improve their instructional practices, develop leadership skills, or address specific challenges in the classroom.

Both mentoring and coaching offer numerous benefits, including the development of confidence, the sharing of expertise, and the building of a supportive professional network. Institutions should integrate these tools into their staff development programmes, ensuring that staff at all levels have access to the guidance and support necessary to achieve their full potential.

Performance management

Effective performance management ensures that staff are clear about expectations, supported in their development, and held accountable for their roles in delivering quality education. It is not merely about evaluating staff performance, but about fostering a system that promotes continuous improvement, professional growth, and alignment with institutional goals. Performance management in education is a dynamic and ongoing process that involves setting clear expectations and goals, conducting objective evaluations, and offering timely and constructive feedback through appraisals. When underperformance occurs, it should be addressed with empathy and a focus on support, ensuring staff have access to the necessary resources to improve and contribute effectively.

Setting clear expectations and goals for staff

Setting clear expectations ensures that staff understand what is expected of them. As a result, they are better equipped to align their efforts with the institution's educational objectives. In educational settings, these expectations typically relate to various dimensions of the role, such as teaching quality, student engagement, research output, and administrative responsibilities (Bach, 2009). Goal setting is integral to performance management, as it provides staff with a clear sense of direction and purpose.

SMART goals (Specific, Measurable, Achievable, Relevant, and Time-bound) are an effective tool for setting performance expectations (Doran, 1981). By ensuring that goals are clear and measurable, educational leaders can track progress over time and provide staff with a sense of achievement as they meet these targets. These goals should be aligned with the broader goals of the institution, such as improving student outcomes, increasing research productivity, or enhancing the institution's reputation. Moreover, these goals should be tailored to the unique needs of different staff members, ensuring that they are relevant to their specific roles and responsibilities.

In a teaching context, goals might focus on aspects such as lesson planning, student progress, or the integration of new pedagogical approaches. For research-focused roles, goals could include the publication of peer-reviewed articles, the securing of research grants, or the supervision of graduate students. By setting clear, individualised goals, institutions can ensure that staff know what success looks like and have a roadmap for achieving it.

Evaluating staff performance effectively

Evaluating staff performance is a necessary component of effective performance management, but it must be conducted in a manner that is fair, transparent, and supportive. A comprehensive evaluation goes beyond merely reviewing outcomes; it should encompass the quality of work, professional conduct, response to challenges, and evidence of ongoing development (Gordon, 2005). A range of evaluation methods - such as student feedback, peer reviews, self-assessments, and direct observations - can offer a holistic view of performance across educational contexts.

In primary and secondary education, while student outcomes and feedback are often central to assessing teacher effectiveness, other important factors include the ability to foster a positive classroom climate, engagement with pupils beyond lessons, and participation in the wider school community (Robinson & Timperley, 2007). In higher education, performance evaluations may consider teaching effectiveness, research outputs, and contributions to departmental or institutional initiatives.

Central to effective performance evaluation is the establishment of clear, consistent, and well-communicated criteria. Transparency in expectations reduces ambiguity and helps staff understand the standards by which they will be assessed. Rather than relying solely on annual reviews, institutions should adopt a continuous approach to performance monitoring, offering regular opportunities for feedback throughout the year. This enables staff to make timely improvements and feel supported in their professional journey.

Feedback plays a pivotal role in this process. Constructive, timely feedback provides staff with actionable insights into their strengths and areas for improvement. Effective feedback should focus on observable behaviours and specific outcomes rather than vague or personal commentary (Hattie & Timperley, 2007). For instance, instead of stating that a teacher needs to improve classroom management, feedback should offer targeted strategies - such as ways to structure lessons more effectively or techniques to boost student engagement.

Constructive appraisals should be grounded in objective data, incorporating multiple sources such as student evaluations, peer observations, and self-reflection. A well-structured appraisal process promotes dialogue between staff and their supervisors, allowing for reflection on achievements, discussion of challenges, and agreement on future goals. When feedback is framed positively and coupled with support for professional development, it not only motivates staff but also reinforces a culture of growth and continuous improvement.

Managing underperformance and providing support

Managing underperformance is an inevitable aspect of performance management. While most staff will perform at a high level, there will always be instances where individual performance does not meet the institution's standards. It is essential that underperformance is addressed promptly and effectively, as it can have a negative impact on student outcomes, the overall institutional success, and, most importantly, on individuals themselves.

When underperformance is identified, it is important for managers to approach the issue with empathy and a problem-solving mindset. Underperformance may be due to a variety of factors, such as lack of resources, personal challenges, or insufficient training. Therefore, it is essential to engage in open conversations with underperforming staff to identify the root causes and offer appropriate support (Bach, 2009). Support may include additional training, mentoring, or adjustments to workload. For example, a teacher struggling with classroom management may benefit from targeted professional development or mentoring from a more experienced colleague. In some cases, it may be necessary to implement a performance improvement plan (PIP), which sets out clear expectations for improvement, provides additional resources or support, and outlines timelines for achieving these goals (Robinson & Timperley, 2007).

In more severe cases, where performance does not improve despite support, institutions may need to consider formal disciplinary actions. However, this should be a last resort, as it is crucial that all efforts are made to support staff before resorting to punitive measures. Effective performance management should focus on providing the necessary tools and guidance for staff to succeed, ensuring that the overall performance of the institution is continually improving.

Staff well-being and work-life balance

In recent years, the importance of staff well-being and work-life balance has gained significant attention in educational settings, driven by the growing recognition that a healthy, engaged workforce is vital to the effective delivery of education. Educators and support staff who are physically and mentally well are more likely to provide high-quality teaching, foster positive learning environments, and contribute meaningfully to the success of their institutions. Addressing key aspects such as mental health, the creation of supportive work environments, work-life balance policies, and strategies to prevent burnout is essential for enhancing job satisfaction and sustaining professional effectiveness. Ensuring that staff have access to the necessary resources, support systems, and recognition enables institutions to cultivate a workforce that is both motivated and resilient. Ultimately, prioritising employee well-being is critical to maintaining high standards of education and enriching the overall educational experience.

Addressing staff mental health and well-being

The mental health and well-being of staff have become central concerns in education, as the demands placed on educators can often lead to stress, anxiety, and burnout. Teachers and educational leaders work in high-pressure environments where the stakes are high, and the emotional toll of supporting students' learning and development can sometimes be overwhelming (Ainscow, 2020). It is therefore essential that institutions recognise the importance of addressing mental health and provide appropriate support for staff.

Supporting staff mental health starts with creating a culture of openness around well-being. Staff should feel comfortable discussing mental health challenges without fear of stigma or discrimination (Leithwood et al., 2010). Institutions can offer various mental health resources, such as counselling services, stress management workshops, and peer support groups, which help to alleviate the mental and emotional burdens that staff may face. In addition, encouraging a work environment that prioritises self-care, regular breaks, and flexibility can have a significant impact on staff well-being. By normalising discussions about mental health and integrating support systems into the organisational culture, educational institutions can help reduce the stigma and barriers that often prevent individuals from seeking help.

Leadership plays a vital role in fostering a supportive environment for staff well-being. Educational leaders must lead by example, prioritising their own mental health and encouraging staff to do the same. When leaders show that they value well-being, it sets the tone for the rest of the institution.

Creating a supportive work environment

Creating a supportive work environment is foundational to improving employee well-being. Such an environment includes not only a physical space that is conducive to work but also a culture that promotes collaboration, trust, and respect. Educational staff who feel supported by their peers and leaders are more likely to experience job satisfaction and have a positive impact on students.

Key elements of a supportive work environment include open communication, recognition of staff contributions, and fostering a sense of belonging within the institution. Staff should feel that their voices are heard, and their contributions to the institution are valued. Regular meetings, feedback sessions, and professional learning communities can facilitate communication, enhance collaboration, and ensure that staff feel supported in their roles.

Leadership is again critical in this regard. Principals, heads of departments, and other leaders must be approachable, empathetic, and willing to provide guidance and support to staff (Skaalvik & Skaalvik, 2020). A supportive environment should also encourage professional development and offer opportunities for growth, which helps staff feel more engaged and invested in their roles.

A positive work environment also encompasses the physical and logistical conditions in which staff operate. Access to appropriate resources, well-maintained facilities, ergonomic workspaces, and dedicated time for planning and collaboration all contribute to a sense of professional dignity and efficiency. When educators have the tools and space needed to perform their roles effectively, they are more likely to feel valued and motivated. Thoughtful attention to the physical environment signals institutional respect for staff well-being, reinforcing a culture of care. In turn, such conditions foster not only greater productivity but also higher morale, job satisfaction, and a stronger commitment to the institution's mission. A well-resourced, thoughtfully designed workplace becomes a foundation for sustained excellence in teaching and learning.

Policies for work-life balance in education

Work-life balance is particularly important in the education sector, where teachers and staff often experience high workloads that can spill over into personal time. Effective policies that promote work-life balance are necessary to ensure that staff do not experience burnout and can maintain a healthy balance between their professional and personal lives.

One of the ways in which institutions can support work-life balance is by offering flexible working arrangements, such as part-time schedules, job-sharing opportunities, or flexible hours. These arrangements can be particularly helpful for staff with caregiving responsibilities or other personal commitments. Additionally, clear expectations around workloads and hours can help to reduce the pressure on staff. For instance, ensuring that teachers have adequate time for lesson planning, grading, and professional development without having to spend long hours outside of work is vital to maintaining their well-being.

Another key aspect of promoting work-life balance is setting boundaries around communication. Institutions should set guidelines for when it is appropriate to contact staff outside of working hours, thereby protecting personal time. Encouraging staff to disengage from work outside of hours can help prevent stress and allow staff to recharge. Policies should also ensure that vacation time is respected and that staff are encouraged to take breaks when needed, rather than feeling pressured to work continuously.

Preventing burnout and enhancing job satisfaction

Burnout is a significant concern in education, particularly given the emotional and mental demands placed on teachers and other staff. Burnout is characterised by physical and emotional exhaustion, reduced performance, and a sense of detachment from work, and it can severely impact both staff well-being and student outcomes (Leiter & Maslach, 2017). Preventing burnout requires proactive strategies that address the root causes of stress and ensure that staff have the resources they need to manage their workloads effectively.

One of the most effective strategies for preventing burnout is ensuring manageable workloads. Staff should be provided with adequate support in managing their tasks, and workloads should be realistic and achievable. It is essential that staff have opportunities for collaboration and sharing of responsibilities, which can alleviate some of the pressure placed on individual staff members.

Recognising and celebrating staff achievements is another key component in enhancing job satisfaction and preventing burnout. Acknowledging staff efforts, both through formal recognition programmes and informal feedback, helps to reinforce their sense of value and contribution to the institution (Skaalvik & Skaalvik, 2020). Institutions should also encourage staff to take time for self-care and mental health breaks, which can help to prevent exhaustion and burnout. Peer support networks, team-building activities, and regular opportunities for professional development and growth can also help staff feel more connected to their work and less isolated in their roles (Ainscow, 2020).

Reward and recognition systems

Reward and recognition systems are desirable for motivating staff, fostering engagement, and cultivating a positive organisational culture within educational institutions. A well-designed system not only acknowledges individual and collective achievements but also aligns with broader institutional goals such as student success and staff development. Such systems play a key role in maintaining morale, enhancing retention, and promoting excellence across the workforce. Effective strategies include both fair and transparent compensation structures and meaningful non-monetary recognition, alongside initiatives that reward innovation and outstanding performance. Ensuring equity and inclusivity in how rewards are distributed is vital to creating a work environment where all staff feel valued.

Developing effective compensation strategies

Compensation strategies are a core component of an institution's reward system and play a significant role in attracting and retaining talent. In educational settings, compensation must be competitive, transparent, and aligned with the responsibilities and expectations of staff roles. This can include both salary and benefits, such as health insurance, pensions, and performance-related bonuses, which should reflect the value placed on staff contributions.

However, in education, compensation extends beyond financial incentives. In many cases, particularly in public-sector institutions, salaries are determined by national or regional pay scales. In these instances, institutions can focus on enhancing non-monetary benefits and ensuring fair distribution of resources. One key consideration is ensuring that compensation reflects the diverse roles within an educational organisation, from teaching staff to administrative and support teams, acknowledging their unique contributions.

Compensation strategies should be flexible enough to accommodate different types of employment contracts, including full-time, part-time, temporary, or contracted roles. By offering a range of compensation options, institutions can better meet the needs of diverse staff members and create a more inclusive environment that values the contributions of all employees.

Non-monetary recognition: Celebrating achievements and milestones

While financial rewards are important, non-monetary recognition often proves to be even more effective in fostering a positive work environment and encouraging continued high performance. Non-monetary recognition can take many forms, such as public acknowledgment, certificates, awards, or opportunities for professional development. Celebrating achievements and milestones helps staff feel valued and appreciated, which in turn promotes a sense of belonging and motivation.

Regular public recognition - such as "Employee of the Month" programmes, staff meetings that highlight individual and team accomplishments, or social media shout-outs - can create a positive atmosphere within the institution. This recognition fosters a sense of accomplishment and pride in one's work, which is particularly important in high-stress environments like education, where staff often put in long hours without immediate external validation.

Information

The 'Lecturer of the Year' award at the University of Derby is a prominent feature of the institution's annual Education Awards, organised by the Union of Students. This award recognises exceptional teaching across various colleges, with winners selected based on student nominations and feedback. Other UK universities also honour teaching excellence through similar awards.

Additionally, celebrating milestones such as work anniversaries or the completion of professional development programmes can have a significant effect on staff morale. These forms of recognition help staff feel connected to the institution's mission and goals, motivating them to continue contributing to the its success. Importantly, recognition should be tailored to the preferences of staff members, as some individuals may appreciate public acknowledgment while others may prefer more private forms of recognition (Delic et al., 2014).

Rewarding innovation and teaching excellence

Rewarding innovation and teaching excellence encourages staff to continuously improve their practice and remain engaged in their professional roles. Educational institutions thrive when educators and staff bring new ideas, creative solutions, and innovative teaching methods to the classroom. Rewarding innovation can motivate staff to take risks, explore new teaching strategies, and incorporate cutting-edge technology into their practice, ultimately benefiting students and the wider educational community.

Rewards should go beyond just teaching and encompass other aspects of staff contributions, including participation in institutional committees, contributions to extracurricular activities, and involvement in community outreach. A broad-based recognition system ensures that all aspects of an individual's work are appreciated and valued, contributing to the overall success of the institution.

Equity and fairness in HR policies

Equity and fairness in HR policies are essential to creating a transparent, just, and effective working environment. Ensuring that all staff members - regardless of their role, background, or tenure - are treated equitably under institutional policies, fosters a culture of inclusion and mutual respect. Fair HR policies provide consistent application of procedures, access to opportunities, and clear mechanisms for addressing concerns or grievances, thereby promoting trust and morale across the workforce.

A key component of equitable HR practice is ensuring pay equity. This involves establishing fair and transparent compensation structures that are based on clearly defined roles, responsibilities, and performance indicators. Institutions must regularly review pay frameworks to identify and address any unjustified disparities, particularly those related to gender, race, or other protected characteristics (Bakker et al., 2014).

Fairness in HR policy also extends to areas such as recruitment, professional development, workload allocation, and performance evaluation. For example, support staff and administrative personnel should be afforded the same access to development opportunities and career progression as teaching or academic staff. Implementing clear, consistent, and transparent criteria across all HR processes ensures that all employees understand how decisions are made and can trust that those decisions are applied impartially.

Legal and ethical considerations in HR

HR within educational institutions operates within a complex framework of legal and ethical guidelines designed to ensure the protection and fair treatment of staff, students, and the wider community. HR professionals must possess a comprehensive understanding of employment law, be attuned to the ethical implications of their practices, and remain vigilant in safeguarding the rights and well-being of all stakeholders (ACAS, 2023; CIPD, 2022). Legal and ethical considerations are central to effective HRM, and by aligning their practices with both statutory frameworks and ethical values, HR teams can foster trust, fairness, and high-quality educational outcomes.

Understanding employment law in education

Employment law governs the relationship between employers and employees, ensuring obligations are met in a legally compliant manner. In education, these laws are particularly important given the complexities of staff roles, safeguarding duties, and contractual frameworks. Educational institutions must comply with national employment legislation covering areas such as equality, working hours, pay, disciplinary procedures, and health and safety (Department for Education [DfE], 2022; ACAS, 2023).

In the UK, the *Equality Act 2010* offers protection against discrimination in recruitment, promotion, and workplace treatment, while the *Employment Rights Act 1996* provides a foundation for employees' statutory rights, including protection from unfair dismissal and entitlement to redundancy pay (Legislation.gov.uk, 2023). In educational contexts, these laws ensure that staff are recruited, managed, and dismissed fairly, and that recruitment procedures are inclusive and lawful (CIPD, 2022).

A vital part of HR practice in education is ensuring reasonable adjustments for disabled employees under the *Equality Act*, such as flexible work arrangements or physical accessibility (EHRC, 2022). Failure to comply may lead to discrimination claims and reputational damage. Similarly, terminations must follow clear disciplinary or capability procedures, with staff given the opportunity to respond and appeal decisions (ACAS, 2023).

Ethical issues in managing staff and HR practices

While legal compliance is essential, ethical HRM involves going beyond minimum requirements to ensure fairness, integrity, and respect for human dignity. Ethical challenges often arise in recruitment, performance evaluation, and confidentiality (CIPD, 2022). Transparent recruitment practices that avoid unconscious bias and promote diversity are essential to fair staffing in educational settings.

HR professionals must also handle sensitive personal data, such as health records or disciplinary outcomes, with strict confidentiality in line with the *UK General Data Protection Regulation* (UK GDPR) and the *Data Protection Act* 2018 (ICO, 2023).

Breaches of confidentiality may not only be unlawful but may also erode trust between staff and institutional leadership.

Ethical HR practice requires that disciplinary or performance-related actions are handled with fairness and proportionality. Staff should be supported through constructive feedback, access to professional development, and the right to representation during formal procedures (ACAS, 2023).

Safeguarding staff and student rights

In education, safeguarding practices protect individuals from harm and promote well-being. Although safeguarding is often associated with student protection, it also applies to staff. For students, safeguarding policies address abuse, neglect, and safe learning environments. Schools and colleges in the UK are legally required to follow statutory guidance such as *Keeping Children Safe in Education* (DfE, 2023).

For staff, safeguarding involves protection from harassment, bullying, and psychological harm at work. Educational employers have a duty of care under the *Health and Safety at Work Act 1974* and must provide a safe working environment (HSE, 2022). This includes addressing workload, stress, and supporting mental health through employee assistance programmes and occupational health services (CIPD, 2022).

Additionally, policies should be in place for reporting grievances, accessing whistleblowing protections, and appealing employment decisions. Clear contracts and well-communicated HR policies help ensure that staff understand their rights and how to access support when needed (ACAS, 2023).

HR leadership in differing educational contexts

Effective HR management must be tailored to the unique challenges and demands of diverse educational contexts - including primary and secondary schools, further education (FE), and higher education (HE) institutions - as well as specialised settings such as special education and alternative provision.

A nuanced approach is essential, as each sector presents distinct HR needs. While common challenges such as recruitment and retention, staff development, and promoting diversity persist across all sectors, HR leaders must adapt their strategies to address the specific conditions of each educational environment.

- **Primary and secondary education**: In primary and secondary schools, HR management is typically focused on recruitment, retention, and professional development of teaching staff. Teachers in these settings must be prepared to handle a wide range of teaching responsibilities and student needs, which requires effective leadership and strong support systems. HR leaders in primary and secondary schools are often involved in the recruitment of new teachers, ensuring that staff are well-trained in the specific curricula, and managing performance appraisals and ongoing professional development. Effective communication and collaboration with teachers, administrators, and unions are also critical for maintaining a harmonious work environment (Smith & Brown, 2019).

- **Further Education (FE)**: FE institutions face a different set of HR challenges. They serve a more diverse student population, including adults returning to education, and often offer vocational and technical courses. HR leaders in FE must focus on recruiting staff with practical expertise in specific vocational fields, as well as ensuring that staff are equipped with pedagogical skills to teach adult learners. In addition to managing recruitment and retention, HR in FE must also address the ongoing development of staff to keep up with industry changes and technological advancements. Professional development in FE often involves upskilling staff in specific trades or industries and developing tailored training programmes for adult learners.

- **Higher Education (HE)**: HR management in HE institutions is often more complex due to the diverse roles within the institution, including academic staff, researchers, and administrative support. HR leaders must navigate the recruitment of highly specialised academic staff, the management of tenure and promotion processes, and the balancing of teaching with research responsibilities. HR practices in HE institutions also need to support faculty autonomy while ensuring alignment with institutional goals and values.

Table 6.1 provides an overview of those tasked with HR leader responsibilities across educational contexts.

Context	Those responsible for HR leadership
Primary and secondary education	**Headteachers (Principals)** - who have overall responsibility for staffing decisions, including recruitment, performance management, and professional development. **Deputy or Assistant Headteachers** - particularly those with responsibility for staff development or operations. **School Business Managers** - often involved in the administrative aspects of HR such as contracts, compliance, and policy implementation. **HR Officers or Advisors** (in larger schools or Multi-Academy Trusts) - who provide specialist HR support and ensure policies and procedures are followed correctly.

	Governing Bodies or Trust Boards - may have strategic oversight of HR functions, especially for senior appointments or disciplinary procedures.
Further Education (FE)	**Principals or College Leaders** - have overall strategic responsibility, including workforce planning and leadership of HR policy. **Vice Principals or Directors (e.g. Director of HR or Director of People Services)** - lead on implementing HR strategy, including recruitment, wellbeing, and development. **HR Managers or HR Business Partners** - handle day-to-day HR operations, manage staff relations, support line managers, and ensure compliance. **Curriculum Managers or Heads of Department** - often have delegated HR responsibilities such as conducting appraisals, managing absence, and overseeing professional development within their teams.
Higher Education (HE)	**Vice-Chancellors / Pro-Vice-Chancellors (especially for People or Operations)** - shape institutional HR strategy at the executive level. **Directors of Human Resources (or People and Culture)** - lead the central HR function, overseeing policy development, workforce planning, equality and diversity, and employee relations. **HR Business Partners and Managers** - work with faculties and departments to support implementation of HR policy and practice. **Deans / Heads of School or Department** - play a key role in localised HR leadership, such as staff recruitment, appraisal, and managing probation or promotion processes. **Academic Line Managers / Principal Investigators (PIs)** - may lead smaller research teams or units and have HR responsibilities for research staff or teaching fellows.

Table 6.1 - HR leaders across educational contexts

The unique HR needs of specialised educational settings

In specialised educational settings, such as special education and alternative provision, HR leadership must adapt to meet the unique needs of students and staff. These settings often serve students with additional needs, requiring a different approach to staff recruitment, training, and support.

- **Special education:** Special education settings provide tailored support to students with disabilities or additional learning needs. HR leadership in these environments must ensure that staff are highly skilled in specialised teaching methods, such as differentiated instruction, behavioural interventions, and individualised education plans (IEPs). Recruiting staff with expertise in special education, including speech therapists, occupational therapists, and special education teachers, is critical. HR leaders must also provide ongoing professional development to help staff stay up-to-date with the latest research and best practices in special education (Lantang et al., 2023).

- **Alternative provision:** Alternative provision schools serve students who have been excluded from mainstream education or who face challenges in traditional school settings. These students often require a more flexible and individualised approach to learning. HR leaders in alternative provision must focus on recruiting staff with strong interpersonal skills, experience in managing challenging behaviour, and the ability to work within non-traditional educational frameworks. Additionally, HR leaders in these settings must foster an environment that supports staff well-being, as working in alternative provision can be emotionally and psychologically demanding.

Technology and HR in education

The integration of technology in HR management is transforming the educational sector, offering innovative solutions to enhance operational efficiency, improve staff experience, and foster better decision-making. The application of technology in HR can streamline administrative tasks, improve recruitment processes, support employee development, and foster an inclusive and data-driven culture.

Utilising technology for HR management

The use of HR software and data analytics has become an essential part of modern HR management in education. By embracing digital tools, HR departments can improve efficiency, reduce human error, and make data-driven decisions that align with institutional goals.

- **HR software**: Human Resource (HR) software has become an essential tool for managing a wide range of HR functions in educational institutions, including recruitment, onboarding, payroll, performance management, absence tracking, and the maintenance of employee records. These systems help streamline administrative tasks, reduce manual processes, and improve overall efficiency.

International platforms such as *SAP SuccessFactors*, *Workday*, and *BambooHR* are widely adopted across the education sector for their scalability and comprehensive features (Papaevangelou et al., 2023). In the UK context, educational institutions also frequently use systems tailored to local regulatory requirements, such as *SIMS Personnel*, *PeopleSoft*, *Every HR*, *EduPeople*, and *iTrent*. These platforms offer functionality designed to meet the specific needs of schools, colleges, and universities, including integration with school information systems, safeguarding compliance, and workforce census reporting.

HR software allows institutions to track employee performance, manage pay and benefits, and ensure compliance with employment legislation more effectively than traditional methods. For larger organisations, centralised and secure databases improve data accessibility and integrity, enabling better-informed decisions and faster responses to workforce needs. By adopting the appropriate HR software, educational institutions can support more strategic and responsive HR management practices.

- **Data analytics**: Data analytics is another critical component in HR management. Educational institutions can use data analytics to improve decision-making in areas such as recruitment, retention, and professional development. By analysing trends in staff turnover, performance appraisals, and training effectiveness, HR leaders can identify areas for improvement and design targeted interventions (Okon et al., 2024). Data analytics can also provide valuable insights into diversity and inclusion efforts, helping institutions track progress toward goals related to staff demographics and retention rates for underrepresented groups. Additionally, predictive analytics can forecast staffing needs, helping HR departments plan for future challenges, such as expected retirements or changes in student enrolment.

Managing remote and hybrid work environments

The COVID-19 pandemic has accelerated the shift toward remote and hybrid work environments in education, creating new challenges and opportunities for HR management. As educational institutions adapt to these new ways of working, HR leaders must find innovative solutions to support staff, maintain engagement, and ensure productivity.

- **Remote work:** Remote work, while initially a necessity during the pandemic, has become a viable and preferred option for many employees in education. HR leaders need to develop policies and guidelines that support remote work while maintaining a strong organisational culture. This includes establishing clear communication channels, providing necessary technology (such as video conferencing tools and collaboration platforms), and ensuring that staff have access to the resources and support they need to work effectively from home. Additionally, HR must consider how to monitor and assess remote employees' performance without compromising autonomy and flexibility.

- **Hybrid work:** The hybrid work model, where employees split their time between in-person and remote work, is becoming increasingly common in education. Hybrid work presents unique challenges in terms of scheduling, communication, and maintaining a cohesive team culture. HR leaders must design flexible work policies that offer staff the autonomy to balance personal and professional commitments while ensuring that the institution's goals are met. Hybrid work also requires robust technology infrastructures, such as cloud-based systems, to facilitate seamless collaboration across various work environments. HR departments need to focus on building a culture of trust and accountability in hybrid teams, where staff are motivated to deliver results regardless of their physical location.

The role of AI and automation in HR processes

Artificial intelligence (AI) and automation are reshaping HR processes in education by streamlining routine tasks, enhancing decision-making, and enabling HR leaders to focus on more strategic initiatives.

- **AI in recruitment:** AI-powered tools are increasingly used to improve recruitment processes in educational settings. AI can help HR departments screen resumes, analyse candidates' qualifications, and match applicants to job roles more efficiently. By automating the initial stages of recruitment, HR professionals can save time and resources, allowing them to focus on more personalised candidate engagement. AI tools such as chatbots can also enhance the candidate experience by providing immediate responses to inquiries and guiding applicants through the application process (Al-Alawi et al., 2021). These tools help HR leaders make more data-driven hiring decisions by analysing a candidate's skills, experience, and personality traits to predict job fit and success.

- **Automation in administrative tasks**: Automation has the potential to revolutionise HR administration in education by reducing manual workloads and minimising errors. Routine tasks such as payroll processing, benefits administration, and leave management can be automated using specialised HR software, allowing HR staff to focus on more strategic responsibilities. For example, automated systems can track employee attendance and time off, generate payroll reports, and manage benefits claims. This not only improves efficiency but also ensures greater accuracy and compliance with regulatory requirements.

- **AI in employee engagement and performance management:** AI is also being utilised to support employee engagement and performance management. AI-driven platforms can analyse employee feedback, track job satisfaction, and identify potential issues before they escalate. These tools can provide real-time insights into employee performance, helping HR leaders to proactively address concerns, offer tailored professional development opportunities, and maintain high levels of employee engagement. AI can also assist with performance appraisals by analysing data from multiple sources, including peer reviews, self-assessments, and goal achievements, allowing HR leaders to make more objective and comprehensive evaluations (Varma et al., 2024).

Activity: HRM in education - Strategic reflection

The objective of this activity is to encourage critical thinking and the practical application of key Human Resource Management (HRM) principles. By engaging with this task, you will develop your ability to assess current HRM practices within your own professional setting, identify areas for development, and propose informed improvements that are aligned with your organisation's strategic goals.

Reflective analysis

Consider the HRM practices in your current or previous educational context (e.g., primary, secondary, FE, HE, or a specialised setting). Reflect on the following questions:

a. How effectively are HR strategies aligned with the educational institution's overall goals?
b. What leadership styles are evident in shaping HR practices, and how do they influence organisational culture and staff performance?
c. In what ways does the recruitment and selection process reflect the institution's commitment to diversity and inclusion?
d. How are staff development and training opportunities tailored to meet both individual needs and organisational priorities?
e. How does the institution manage performance, set expectations, and support underperforming staff?
f. What measures are in place to promote staff well-being and work-life balance?

Scenario application

Imagine that you are a HR manager tasked with improving HRM practices in your institution. Choose one of the following scenarios and develop a brief action plan:

Scenario 1: Recruitment and retention strategy. The institution is experiencing high turnover rates among staff. How would you improve the recruitment and selection process to attract and retain top talent while promoting a diverse and inclusive workforce?

Scenario 2: Staff development and training. The institution's professional development programmes are not meeting staff needs, and there is a lack of mentoring and coaching opportunities. How would you redesign these programmes to foster continuous professional growth and improve staff engagement?

Scenario 3: Performance management and well-being. The institution has struggled with addressing underperformance and staff burnout. How would you implement a more effective performance management system that provides support for struggling staff while promoting staff well-being and work-life balance?

Action plan

Based on your analysis and the scenario you selected, create a 1–2-page action plan that includes:

o Key objectives (What do you want to achieve?).

- Strategies and actions (What steps will you take to address the identified HR issues?).
- Expected outcomes (What changes do you expect to see as a result of your actions?).
- Measurement and evaluation (How will you assess the success of your initiatives?).

Group discussion

If you are participating in a course or group setting, share your action plan with a peer or group. Discuss how each of you approached the scenario and the differences or similarities in your proposed solutions.

Reflection

After completing this activity, reflect on how HRM practices in your institution align with the educational goals and the strategies that could be implemented to enhance HR effectiveness in supporting both staff and students.

Summary

Human Resource Management (HRM) in education has strategic importance in improving both organisational effectiveness and student outcomes. This includes key HR functions such as recruitment, staff development, performance management, and employee well-being.

Strong leadership is required to shape HR strategies, align them with educational goals, and manage change within institutions. Important considerations include diversity, inclusion, legal and ethical issues, and the impact of technology.

Effective HRM helps in building a resilient, adaptable workforce that is essential to the success of educational institutions.

7 EVIDENCE-BASED DECISION MAKING

David Hall

Introduction

Evidence-based decision-making has long been central to educational practice, ensuring that choices about teaching, learning, and institutional management are grounded in research and proven outcomes. In recent years, however, the concept of 'data-driven' decision-making has gained prominence, reflecting a more systematic and analytical approach to using information. While the term may feel somewhat unfamiliar to some educators, it encapsulates the increasing reliance on data analysis to drive improvement, enhance accountability, and inform strategy at all levels.

This chapter explores the evolving role of data in education, illustrating how it supports evidence-based practices and enables institutions to refine their approaches to teaching, learning, and organisational effectiveness. By examining best practices, ethical considerations, and real-world applications, it provides a comprehensive framework for using data effectively and responsibly in educational settings.

This chapter:

- Examines the increasing importance of data in education, from daily classroom decisions to strategic institutional planning.
- Defines qualitative and quantitative data, illustrating their distinct roles in evidence-based decision-making.
- Explains how to analyse educational data using both basic statistical methods of quantitative analysis and qualitative techniques.
- Discusses leadership's role in fostering a culture of data-driven decision-making through training and collaboration.
- Highlights the ethical considerations surrounding data use, including privacy, bias, and over-reliance on statistics.
- Introduces tools and technologies that simplify data collection, analysis, and visualisation, including dashboards and AI.
- Demonstrates how data can drive pedagogical innovation and strategic goal-setting within institutions.
- Identifies common challenges in implementing data-driven practices and offers actionable solutions.

The growing role of data in educational excellence

In recent years, the education sector has witnessed a significant shift towards data-driven decision-making (DDDM) as a means to enhance educational outcomes and institutional effectiveness. This paradigm shift reflects a growing recognition of the power of data to inform and guide decisions at all levels of the educational system, from individual classrooms to entire local education authorities and higher education institutions.

The increasing importance of data in education stems from the need for evidence-based practices and the desire to optimise resource allocation in an increasingly competitive and resource-constrained environment. Marsh et al. (2006) define data-driven decision-making as "the systematic collection, analysis, and application of many forms of data from myriad sources in order to enhance student performance while addressing student learning needs".

This approach has gained traction as educators and administrators seek to move beyond intuition and guesswork towards more informed and strategic decision-making processes.

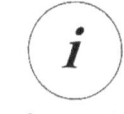

Information — Data-driven decision making is nothing new. Teachers have long used data to identify and address issues. What has changed is not the practice itself but the terminology used and the depth of analysis now expected. If you've been asked to collate and interpret data (rather than relying solely on lengthy narratives), this chapter will provide clarity and guidance on navigating these evolving expectations.

The expanding scope of data in education

The role of data in education has expanded dramatically, encompassing a wide range of applications from classroom-level interventions to strategic institutional planning. At the classroom level, teachers are increasingly using data to tailor instruction, identify struggling students, and monitor progress. According to Dunn et al. (2013), data-driven decision-making (DDDM) at the classroom level involves recognising students' strengths and weaknesses in relation to learning objectives and using this information to inform future lesson planning. This approach facilitates personalised learning and enables more focused interventions.

At the institutional level, data plays a crucial role in strategic planning and resource allocation. Educational leaders use data to identify trends, evaluate programme effectiveness, and make informed decisions about curriculum, staffing, and budgeting. Goldring & Berends (2008) highlight that modern educational leaders heavily rely on data to inform their decision-making, establish and prioritise objectives, and track progress effectively. This macro-level application of data enables institutions to align their strategies with evidence-based best practices and respond proactively to emerging challenges.

Defining data in education

In the context of education, data encompasses a wide range of information types, both *qualitative* and *quantitative*. Quantitative data includes numerical information such as test scores, attendance rates, graduation rates, and demographic statistics. This type of data is often used for statistical analysis and benchmarking. Qualitative data, on the other hand, includes non-numerical information such as student feedback, classroom observations, and teacher evaluations. This type of data provides rich, contextual information that can complement quantitative measures. The integration of both qualitative and quantitative data is essential for a comprehensive understanding of educational processes and outcomes. This requires an understanding of data literacy by teachers and other staff which entails the skill to convert information into practical instructional strategies and knowledge by gathering, analysing, and interpreting various forms of data (Mandinach & Gummer, 2016). This holistic approach to data utilisation allows educators to gain a more nuanced understanding of student performance and institutional effectiveness.

Data as evidence

A fundamental principle of data-driven decision-making is that all improvements must be based on credible evidence. This evidence-based approach ensures that educational interventions and policy decisions are grounded in empirical data rather than assumptions or intuitions. Schildkamp (2019) emphasises that data can drive school improvement when it is transformed into meaningful information and subsequently into actionable knowledge, forming the foundation for decisions aimed at enhancing outcomes. The use of data as evidence serves multiple purposes in the educational context:

1. **Identifying areas for improvement:** By analysing performance data, educators can pinpoint specific areas where students or institutions are struggling and develop targeted interventions.
2. **Evaluating programme effectiveness:** Data allows for the rigorous assessment of educational programmes and initiatives, enabling institutions to allocate resources to the most impactful interventions.

3. **Monitoring progress:** Continuous data collection and analysis enable educators to track progress over time and make real-time adjustments to teaching strategies or institutional policies.
4. **Ensuring accountability:** Data-driven approaches provide transparency and accountability, allowing stakeholders to assess the effectiveness of educational institutions and policies.
5. **Informing policy decisions:** Evidence-based policymaking relies on robust data to inform decisions about educational reforms and resource allocation at local and national levels.

Challenges and considerations

While the benefits of data-driven decision-making are clear, there are also challenges and considerations that must be addressed. Mandinach & Schildkamp (2021) stress that data literacy is a multifaceted concept that necessitates continuous professional development and support. Educators and administrators must be trained in data literacy skills to effectively collect, analyse, and interpret data. There are also ethical considerations surrounding data privacy and security, particularly when dealing with sensitive student information. Institutions must implement robust data governance frameworks to ensure the responsible use and protection of educational data.

Foundations of data-driven decision making

Data-driven decision-making (DDDM) offers a systematic approach to enhancing student outcomes and institutional effectiveness. Its foundations lie in a thorough understanding of both qualitative and quantitative data, a commitment to the cyclical nature of data processes, and proficiency in various analytical techniques. By embracing these principles, educational institutions can harness the power of data to drive continuous improvement and adapt to the ever-evolving educational landscape. As the ability to collect, analyse, and respond to diverse data becomes increasingly essential, building a strong foundation in DDDM enables educators and administrators to meet emerging challenges and provide exceptional learning experiences for students.

Understanding educational data

Educational data encompasses a wide range of information types, broadly categorised into qualitative and quantitative data. Each type offers unique insights into various aspects of the educational process.

Qualitative data

Qualitative data provides rich, descriptive information that captures the nuances of educational experiences. Schildkamp (2019) highlights that qualitative data provides rich context and can uncover the underlying causes behind observed occurrences in educational environments. Common examples of qualitative data include:

1. Surveys with open-ended questions.
2. Student interviews.
3. Classroom observations.
4. Teacher reflective journals.
5. Focus group discussions.

Qualitative data allows for open-ended questioning which encourages deeper thinking, creativity, and critical analysis by allowing respondents to provide detailed, thoughtful answers rather than simple "yes" or "no" responses. It fosters dialogue, uncovers multiple perspectives, and promotes engagement, making it particularly useful in educational and collaborative settings for exploring complex issues and gaining richer insights.

Quantitative data

Quantitative data, on the other hand, provides numerical information that can be statistically analysed. Mandinach & Gummer (2016) underscore the value of quantitative data in enabling accurate measurement and facilitating comparisons across various educational settings. Examples of quantitative data in education include:

1. Standardised test scores.
2. Attendance rates.
3. Enrolment trends.
4. Grade point averages (GPAs).
5. Graduation rates.

The American University School of Education (2024) notes that quantitative research in education generates numerical data, which can be used to validate or challenge a theory, and its results are easily shareable with other schools and districts.

The data cycle

Once educators understand the nature of qualitative and quantitative data, the next step is to apply this knowledge through a systematic, cyclical process, often referred to as the data cycle (Figure 7.1). This iterative approach emphasises the continuous collection, analysis, and application of data to drive informed decision-making and foster ongoing improvements in educational practices. By revisiting each stage of the cycle, this structured yet flexible framework ensures that data is not only utilised effectively but also revisited to assess the impact of decisions and identify opportunities for further enhancement, creating a dynamic system of continuous improvement.

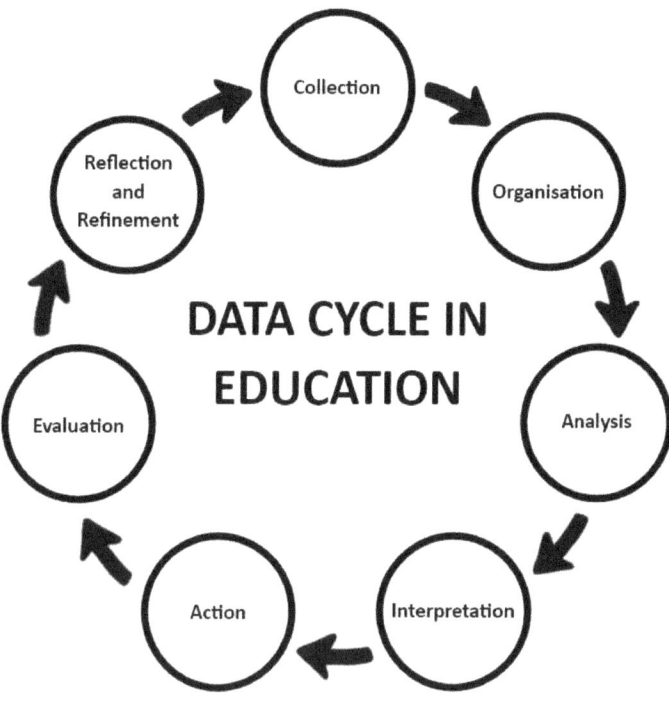

Figure 7.1 - Data cycle in education

Collection
- Data is gathered from diverse sources such as assessments, attendance records, surveys, and classroom observations.
- Both quantitative (e.g., test scores) and qualitative (e.g., student feedback) data is included.

Organisation
- Data is stored and categorised systematically for ease of access and analysis.
- Tools like spreadsheets, databases, or specialised education software are used.

Analysis
- The data is examined using statistical or qualitative methods to identify trends, patterns, and gaps.
- Findings are linked to specific educational goals or challenges.

Interpretation
- The results are contextualised within the educational setting, considering factors such as demographics or curriculum.
- Findings are translated into meaningful insights for decision-making.

Action
- Strategies are developed and implemented to address the identified issues or capitalise on opportunities.
- Changes are monitored and interventions adjusted as required.

Evaluation
- The effectiveness of actions taken is assessed using follow-up data.
- When goals have not been fully achieved, areas for further improvement are identified.

Reflection and refinement
- Reflecting on the entire process improves future data practices.
- Ethical considerations and data integrity are upheld throughout the cycle.

The iterative nature of DDDM is a key aspect of its effectiveness in education. Mandinach & Schildkamp (2021) highlight that utilising data is an ongoing process aimed at continuous improvement rather than a single occurrence. This ongoing cycle allows educators to:

1. Refine instructional strategies based on student performance data.
2. Adjust resource allocation in response to changing needs.
3. Continuously improve curriculum based on learning outcome data.
4. Enhance student support services through regular feedback analysis.

Data analysis techniques in education

The analysis of educational data requires a diverse set of skills and methodologies, tailored to the specific type of data being examined.

Qualitative data analysis

Qualitative data analysis often employs thematic coding techniques. This process involves:

1. Identifying recurring themes in textual or observational data.
2. Categorising data into meaningful groups.
3. Interpreting patterns and relationships between themes.

Holland & Ciachir (2024) emphasise that qualitative insights gathered from sources such as interviews and reflective student journals provide a nuanced understanding of learners' experiences and the contextual factors influencing their education.

Case Study 1: Qualitative data analysis

This case study demonstrates the effective use of qualitative data analysis to enhance classroom engagement at Sunrise Secondary School. The school employed a comprehensive approach to address low engagement among Year 10 science students through the following steps:

1. **Data collection:** The school gathered qualitative data from multiple sources, including student surveys, teacher observations, and focus groups with diverse student participants.

2. **Thematic coding analysis:** The leadership team analysed the data using thematic coding techniques, which involved:
   - Identifying recurring themes such as "lack of hands-on activities" and "unclear instructions".
   - Categorising data into meaningful groups like teaching methods, communication, and curriculum design.
   - Interpreting patterns and relationships between themes, revealing strong links between disengagement and teaching methods.

3. **Intervention design:** Based on the analysis, the school implemented targeted interventions:
   - Incorporating more hands-on experiments and collaborative projects.
   - Providing professional development for teachers to improve instruction clarity.
   - Adjusting the curriculum to balance theoretical and practical components.

4. **Impact assessment:** After three months, the school conducted follow-up surveys and observations, which showed significant improvements in student engagement, including:
   - Increased positive feedback from students.
   - A 40% increase in class discussion / participation.
   - Teachers reporting a more positive classroom environment.

This case study illustrates how qualitative data analysis can be used to develop evidence-based interventions that effectively address educational challenges and improve learning outcomes. By employing thematic coding techniques, Sunrise Secondary School was able to gain deep insights into the factors affecting student engagement and design targeted solutions.

Appendix 4, Part 1 contains more detail on the methods, data collected and subsequent analysis used in the case study.

Quantitative data analysis

Basic statistical methods are widely used to interpret and evaluate quantitative data in educational research. Common approaches include:

1. Descriptive statistics (e.g. mean, median, mode, standard deviation).
2. Inferential statistics (e.g. t-tests, ANOVA, regression analysis).
3. Trend analysis for longitudinal data.

Information

Some data-driven decision-making relies on sophisticated quantitative analysis techniques (Prenger & Schildkamp, 2018). However, teachers should not be expected to master complex statistical methods and, for the majority of their analyses, the use of simple descriptive statistics is sufficient.

Case Study 2: Quantitative data analysis

University students on a MA Education programme achieved the following results in one of their modules:

This year's results (34 students):

42, 45, 48, 52, 53, 54, 55, 55, 56, 57, 57, 58, 58, 59, 60, 60, 60, 61, 61, 62, 63, 63, 63, 64, 65, 65, 66, 66, 67, 68, 68, 68, 68.

Last year's results (28 students):

42, 52, 55, 56, 58, 59, 60, 60, 61, 61, 62, 63, 65, 65, 66, 67, 67, 68, 70, 70, 71, 72, 72, 73, 74, 75, 76, 88.

Quantitative analysis summary:

This year: Mean: 59.74, Range: 26, Standard deviation: 6.91, Pass rate: 91.18%, Failure rate: 8.82%.

Last year: Mean: 63.5, Range: 46, Standard deviation: 8.63, Pass rate: 96.43%, Failure rate: 3.57%.

Comparison between years:

- *Mean*: Decreased by 3.76 points (59.74 vs. 63.50).
- *Range*: Decreased by 20 (26 vs. 46).
- *Standard deviation*: Decreased by 1.72 (6.91 vs. 8.63).
- *Pass rate*: Decreased by 5.25% (91.18% vs. 96.43%).
- *Failure rate*: Increased by 5.25% (8.82% vs. 3.57%).

Key observations:

- *Lower mean:* Reflecting a drop in overall performance.
- *Smaller range:* Indicating fewer outliers and a more compressed distribution of scores.
- *Lower variability:* The standard deviation suggests less variation in results.
- *Increased failure rate:* More students failed this year, though most still passed.
- *Clustering around modes:* Performance concentrated in the middle and upper-middle ranges.

Conclusion:

- *Decline in performance:* A slight drop in average performance and an increase in failure rates warrants attention.
- *Smaller range and variability:* While scores are more uniform, fewer high achievers may indicate a lack of outlier success (i.e. fewer higher achievers).
- *Focus areas:* Investigate potential causes for the decline, offer targeted support to underperforming students, and address any cohort-specific challenges.

Appendix 4, Part 2 contains more detail on the analysis and subsequent action taken by the university.

Integrating qualitative and quantitative approaches

While qualitative and quantitative methods each offer distinct advantages, an increasing number of researchers advocate for the use of mixed-methods approaches in educational research. Poole (2013) highlights that many scholars have moved beyond the traditional 'either/or' debate between qualitative and quantitative paradigms, recognising that integrating both can yield more comprehensive and meaningful insights. As a result, mixed-methods designs have become widely adopted in educational inquiry, enabling researchers to draw on the strengths of both approaches. A mixed-methods approach allows educators to:

1. Triangulate findings from different data sources.
2. Provide context to quantitative trends through qualitative insights.
3. Generate hypotheses through qualitative exploration and test them quantitatively.

Information

If you have studied the detail of the quantitative analysis (Appendix 4, Part 2), you will have noted that, in order to investigate the concerns highlighted by the quantitative analysis, subsequent qualitative analysis was required.

Data sources and technology in education

The role of data sources and technology in education has grown significantly in recent years. Key data sources such as Student Information Systems (SIS), Learning Management Systems (LMS), assessment data, and qualitative inputs like surveys all play vital roles in creating a data-driven approach to educational improvement. By integrating these systems and utilising advanced technologies like predictive analytics, real-time dashboards, and AI-driven tools, educational institutions can make better-informed decisions that lead to improved student outcomes, enhanced operational efficiency, and effective pedagogical strategies. However, challenges related to technical expertise, data privacy, and system integration must be addressed to fully realise the benefits. With the right strategies in place, data can be a powerful tool for advancing educational practices and ensuring that all students succeed.

Student Information Systems and Learning Management Systems

Student Information Systems (SIS) serve as the backbone of administrative data management in educational institutions, acting as centralised databases for storing and managing essential student information such as enrolment, registration, grades, attendance, transcripts, and billing. These systems handle class scheduling, academic advising, student records, and financial management, allowing administrators and educators to access real-time data on student progress. The comprehensive nature of SIS enables efficient tracking of student performance throughout their academic journey and ensures that essential information is readily available for operational tasks, advising, and reporting. Student Information Systems often include communication tools that facilitate interaction between teachers, parents, and students, keeping all stakeholders informed about important updates and progress.

Student Information Systems are complemented with Learning Management Systems (LMS). While SIS focuses on administrative tasks, such as managing student records, grades, attendance, and financial data, an LMS is designed to facilitate online teaching and learning by providing tools for instructors to create, manage, and deliver course content. LMS platforms, like *Moodle*, *Blackboard*, or *Canvas*, enable instructors to assess student learning through assignments, quizzes, and discussions, while allowing students to access materials, submit assignments, and communicate with peers and instructors.

When integrated, SIS and LMS create a holistic environment that supports students throughout their academic journey. The integration allows for comprehensive reporting and analytics, combining student performance data from the LMS with administrative information from the SIS. This provides educators with valuable insights into student progress, engagement, and learning outcomes, offering a more complete and accurate view of student performance.

Appendix 4, Part 3 provides examples of SIS and LMS systems.

Assessment and attendance data

Assessment data, both formative and summative, are fundamental in understanding student progress. Formative assessments, such as observations, quizzes, peer reviews, and class activities, provide immediate feedback on student understanding, allowing teachers to adjust instruction in real time. Summative assessments, including final exams and projects, offer a snapshot of students' overall academic performance. These assessments help identify gaps in knowledge and areas where further support may be needed.

Attendance data, often housed within SIS, is another important data point. Frequent absenteeism can negatively affect academic achievement, and tracking attendance can help institutions identify at-risk students. Combined with assessment data, attendance information provides valuable insights into the factors affecting student performance, enabling schools to create targeted interventions. For instance, students who frequently miss class but perform well on assessments might require additional support with engagement or organisation, while students who have high absentee rates and struggle academically may need more intensive interventions.

Surveys and external benchmarking data

In addition to quantitative data, qualitative data from surveys can provide a deeper understanding of the student experience. Surveys conducted among students, parents, and staff can gauge perceptions of teaching quality, curriculum design, and overall satisfaction with the educational environment. These insights help institutions assess areas for improvement in a way that traditional assessments cannot. For example, student surveys can highlight issues related to instructional delivery, engagement, or school climate, which may not be immediately apparent from academic data alone.

External benchmarking data, such as the results from national assessments or international studies like *PISA* (Programme for International Student Assessment) and *TIMSS* (Trends in International Mathematics and Science Study), provide valuable context for evaluating educational performance. By comparing local or regional results against national or international standards, institutions can assess their strengths and identify areas where they may be falling short. Benchmarking against high-performing schools or systems allows for the identification of best practices and the adoption of strategies that have proven successful in other contexts.

Technology and AI in data collection and analysis

The evolution of technology has dramatically transformed the way educational data is collected, analysed, and utilised. Advances in artificial intelligence (AI), machine learning, and big data analytics have enabled institutions to process vast amounts of data more efficiently and generate actionable insights that were previously difficult to achieve. AI-powered tools can analyse patterns in student behaviour, engagement, and performance to provide real-time feedback and predictive analytics.

For example, machine learning algorithms can analyse historical student data to predict future academic success or identify students at risk of falling behind. These predictive models allow educators to intervene early, providing support to students before they experience significant academic difficulties. The ability to predict future performance is a powerful tool for personalised learning, as it helps tailor interventions to individual students' needs.

Data collection tools like surveys, online assessments, and digital portfolios provide a wealth of information that can be analysed to uncover trends and insights about student behaviour, academic progress, and overall well-being. For example, online assessments allow for immediate feedback to students and teachers, providing insights into knowledge gaps while simultaneously making data collection more efficient. Tools such as *Google Forms* or *SurveyMonkey* can collect survey data, while platforms like *Turnitin* and *Kahoot* offer opportunities for assessment and feedback in real-time.

Predictive analytics and real-time dashboards

One of the most significant advances in the use of data in education is the development of predictive analytics. By using historical data and sophisticated algorithms, predictive analytics allows institutions to forecast student outcomes with a high degree of accuracy. For instance, predictive models can identify students at risk of underperforming on future assessments, enabling educators to implement proactive strategies to support these students.

Predictive analytics can be applied to various aspects of education, from academic performance to behavioural issues, and it helps educational leaders make data-driven decisions about resource allocation, curriculum development, and support services. By identifying potential risks and opportunities, predictive analytics ensures that interventions are timely and targeted, thereby improving student outcomes and institutional effectiveness.

Real-time dashboards are another key tool in data-driven decision-making. These dashboards aggregate data from various sources into a user-friendly interface, allowing educators, administrators, and stakeholders to view critical information at a glance. For instance, dashboards might display data on student performance across different subjects, attendance rates, or behavioural trends. Customisable dashboards allow users to focus on specific data points and track progress over time.

Here are a few examples of real-time dashboard systems that are commonly used in schools, colleges, and universities to support data-driven decision-making:

1. **SIMS (Schools Information Management System)**:
- *Used by:* Many UK schools.
- *Features:* SIMS offers a customisable dashboard (Figure 7.2) that aggregates data on attendance, student performance, behaviour, and other key metrics. The dashboard allows school administrators and educators to monitor student progress in real time and make informed decisions to improve outcomes.

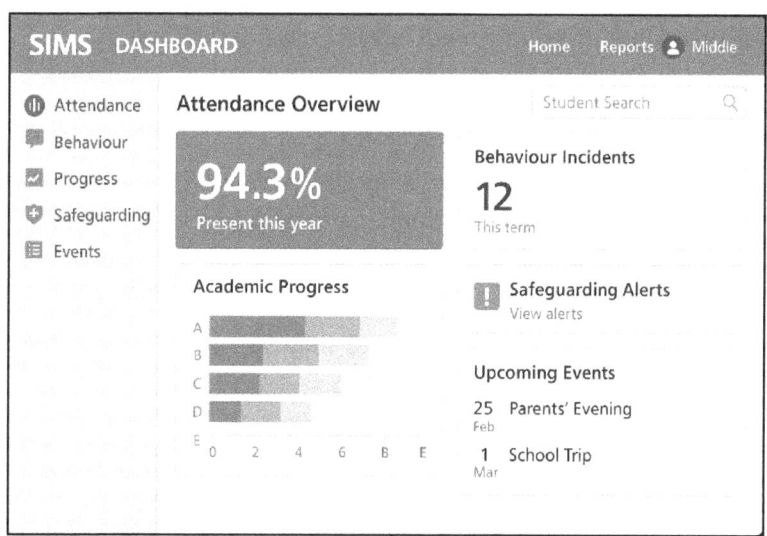

Figure 7.2 - School Management Information System (SIMS)

2. **Power BI (Business Intelligence):**
- *Used by:* Various UK universities and colleges.
- *Features:* Power BI is often used by higher education institutions in the UK to create customised real-time dashboards. It pulls data from various sources, including student information systems and learning management systems, and presents it in a visually accessible format. This tool helps administrators track academic performance, student engagement, and institutional performance metrics.

3. **Canvas LMS (Learning Management System):**
- *Used by:* Many universities in the UK.
- *Features:* Canvas offers real-time dashboards for both instructors and students. Educators can track individual student performance, assignment completion rates, and overall class progress, while students can monitor their grades, course activity, and upcoming deadlines. This integration helps create a complete view of student engagement and performance.

4. **Fronter (Learning Platform):**
- *Used by:* Some schools and universities in the UK.
- *Features:* Fronter provides real-time dashboards that aggregate data from different sources, allowing educators to track attendance, performance, and other key indicators. The system allows teachers to adjust their teaching strategies based on real-time feedback from the dashboard.

Challenges and implementation strategies

While the benefits of data-driven decision-making in education are clear, there are several challenges to overcome in implementing these strategies effectively. One significant barrier is the need for technical expertise to manage complex data systems and analyse large datasets. Many educators and administrators may not have the technical background required to fully harness the power of predictive analytics or machine learning algorithms. To address this, educational institutions should invest in professional development to build data literacy among faculty and staff. Training programmes should focus on equipping educators with the skills needed to interpret and apply data in their teaching practices. In addition, institutions should consider collaborating with technology experts or data scientists to develop customised data solutions that align with their unique needs.

Another challenge is ensuring that data privacy and security are maintained. In order to protect students' personal information, educational institutions must adhere to regulations such as *Family Educational Rights and Privacy Act* (FERPA) in the USA and the *UK Data Protection Act 2018* (DPA), which is aligned with the *General Data Protection Regulation* (GDPR) of the European Union. Ensuring compliance with privacy laws, while still utilising data for educational improvement, requires a careful balance of security protocols and transparency.

While the integration of various data sources can yield powerful insights, it also presents logistical challenges. Institutions need to develop strategies for integrating data from disparate sources, such as SIS, LMS, and external tools, into a cohesive system that allows for seamless data sharing and analysis. This may involve adopting interoperable systems and data standards to ensure that different tools can communicate effectively.

Using data to drive pedagogical innovation

The integration of data-driven decision-making has reshaped teaching methods, curriculum design, and personalised learning. By utilising student performance data and adaptive technologies, educators can create more engaging and equitable learning experiences. As technologies like artificial intelligence and machine learning advance, it is crucial for institutions to remain informed and critically evaluate their impact, unlocking significant potential to meet diverse learner needs and improve outcomes.

Data-driven methods allow educators to refine their practices by analysing student performance, identifying challenges, and adjusting instructional strategies accordingly. The integration of Learning Management Systems (LMS) with Student Information Systems (SIS) enhances this process, providing insights into student progress, engagement, and learning outcomes. Formative assessments offer real-time feedback for immediate adjustments, while summative assessments provide longer-term insights to identify gaps and inform curricular improvements.

Personalised learning experiences are increasingly achievable through the power of data analysis, which allows educators to address the unique needs, strengths, and interests of each student. By closely examining a range of performance metrics, engagement data, and learning preferences, educators gain valuable insights into how students learn best. This data-driven approach enables the creation of tailored learning paths that not only foster deeper engagement but also enhance academic outcomes. By offering customised support, educators can ensure that students receive the precise guidance they need at critical junctures in their educational journey. Ultimately, this personalised approach promotes a more inclusive and effective learning environment, where every student has the opportunity to thrive according to their own pace and potential.

>  **Case Study 3: Personalised learning**
> In a secondary school mathematics department, teachers use *HegartyMaths*, an adaptive learning platform, integrated with *Canvas*, the school's Learning Management System. *HegartyMaths* tracks student progress in topics such as algebra and geometry, gathering data on quiz performance, engagement with video tutorials, and the completion of homework tasks.
>
> The platform identifies that Alex excels in algebra but struggles with geometry, particularly understanding the properties of triangles. *HegartyMaths* flags these areas as requiring improvement and recommends targeted video tutorials and practice exercises. The teacher reviews these insights through the *HegartyMaths* dashboard, accessible via *Canvas*, and assigns Alex additional support sessions during class time to address the challenges.
>
> Meanwhile, the platform highlights that Mia, another student, is completing tasks at an advanced pace but shows signs of disengagement, such as skipping video tutorials and spending less time on problem-solving activities. Using *Canvas*, the teacher tracks Mia's overall activity and arranges a conversation to explore her interests. Upon discovering that Mia enjoys practical applications of mathematics, the teacher incorporates real-world problems, such as designing a budget for a school trip, into her tasks.
>
> By using *HegartyMaths* for actionable insights and using *Canvas* for seamless integration and communication, the teacher provides Alex with specific support to improve his geometry skills and tailors Mia's learning experience to her interests. This data-driven approach helps improve both engagement and academic outcomes for both students.

Adaptive learning technologies, powered by AI, dynamically adjust content based on student performance. Platforms such as *Knewton*, *ScootPad*, and *DreamBox Learning* use real-time data to personalise instruction, significantly improving student engagement. These tools also empower educators with actionable insights, enabling more effective teaching strategies and better allocation of resources. These innovations enhance teaching and learning by providing personalised content that boosts engagement and outcomes. Educators benefit from analytics that reveal learning patterns, support timely interventions, and inform strategic adjustments. This data-driven approach allows for improved progress tracking and evaluation of the effectiveness of interventions.

However, challenges remain. Safeguarding data privacy, training educators to interpret and use data effectively, balancing data-driven insights with professional judgment, and addressing biases in data analysis are all critical considerations.

Overcoming these hurdles is essential to fully realise the potential of data-driven pedagogical innovation.

The role of leadership in data-driven cultures

Leadership plays a crucial role in fostering a data-driven culture within educational institutions, where strategic goals and long-term planning hinge on the effective use of data. For educational leaders, the task is not only about ensuring data is collected and analysed but also about empowering faculty and staff to use this data in ways that align with the institution's broader objectives. This responsibility involves both technical and cultural leadership. Leaders must provide comprehensive training on data literacy, foster a culture of collaboration, and prioritise the ethical use of data to ensure that decisions are based on empirical evidence rather than intuition or guesswork.

A critical component of fostering a data-driven culture is ensuring that faculty members are equipped with the necessary skills to analyse and apply data effectively. This requires leadership to invest in professional development programmes that focus on data literacy and analysis. By clearly communicating the value of data-informed decision-making, leaders send a message throughout the institution that data should drive educational practices, rather than subjective impressions. A culture where data is valued is also one where leaders model its use in decision-making, reward data-informed practices, and integrate data discussions into faculty meetings and evaluations. These actions create an environment in which data is seen as a tool for improvement and innovation.

Question — Do you work for one of the many educational institutions where leaders expect data-driven improvements yet fail to provide staff with adequate training? This is likely due to insufficient resources or a lack of prioritisation and, without this foundational support, staff may struggle to effectively use data in their teaching practices and administrative duties.

In addition to training, educational leaders must create systems of ongoing support to ensure that faculty and staff can continually enhance their data skills. This can involve setting up data teams, appointing data coaches, and providing regular workshops to refresh and deepen knowledge of data analysis techniques. Leaders must also prioritise creating an ethical framework for data use within their institutions. This means developing clear data governance policies that address data privacy, ethical considerations, and transparency in how data is used and shared. The Hechinger Report (2021) highlights the need for leaders to consider the ethical implications of data use, noting that even well-intentioned programmes can fail without proper ethical foresight. By fostering a transparent and accountable data culture, leaders ensure that data-driven practices align with the institution's values and respect student privacy.

Equally important is the alignment of data with the institution's strategic goals. Leaders must ensure that data collection and analysis are directly tied to long-term planning, improvement efforts, and institutional priorities. The use of data in decision-making enables leaders to target areas for improvement, allocate resources more effectively, and make evidence-based decisions that are responsive to changing needs. For instance, data can be used to track progress toward school improvement plans and accountability measures, helping to refine strategies and monitor their effectiveness. Institutions should also consider metrics beyond traditional academic achievement, such as social-emotional learning (SEL), teacher satisfaction, and community engagement. These metrics provide a fuller picture of student success and institutional effectiveness, guiding decisions that support both academic and holistic development.

To implement a comprehensive data strategy, institutions must invest in robust data systems that integrate data from various sources and make it accessible to all stakeholders. Leaders should also prioritise data literacy training for staff and faculty to ensure that they can interpret and act upon data insights. In addition, data visualisation tools such as *dashboards* can help make complex data more understandable and actionable, allowing faculty and leaders to make decisions quickly and efficiently. The quality of education is influenced by factors such as teacher engagement and well-being, which can be tracked through data on teacher satisfaction (Shibiti, 2020). Similarly, tracking community engagement can reveal how well the institution is meeting its broader goals and fostering positive relationships with parents, alumni, and the local community.

Ultimately, creating a culture where data is central to decision-making requires a collaborative approach that breaks down silos and promotes cross-departmental communication. Leaders should encourage data-sharing initiatives and create opportunities for interdepartmental collaboration on data projects. This can involve organising data summits or cross-functional meetings that bring together staff from different departments to analyse and interpret data collectively.

Challenges in implementing data-driven decision making

The implementation of data-driven decision making (DDDM) promises significant benefits but is not without its challenges. These stem from resource limitations, lack of staff training, and resistance to change. However, these challenges can be overcome through targeted strategies such as comprehensive professional development initiatives and effective leadership communication and advocacy.

Barriers to data-driven decision-making

Lack of resources and staff training

One of the primary challenges in implementing DDDM is the lack of adequate resources and staff training. Gummer & Mandinach (2015) point out that the ability of organisations to effectively teach data-driven decision-making is not yet widely developed. This lack of capacity often manifests in several ways:

1. *Insufficient infrastructure:* Many educational institutions, especially smaller ones, may lack the necessary technology and infrastructure to effectively collect, store, and analyse data.
2. *Limited data literacy:* Educators and administrators often lack the skills required to interpret and use data effectively. A principal in a study conducted by Reeves & Burt (2006) stressed the importance of training for teachers and leaders because, while some people are on board with the benefits of data analysis, they are uncertain about how to implement it.
3. *Time constraints:* Educators often struggle to find time for meaningful data analysis amidst their daily responsibilities. Estrellado (2024) notes that educators cannot fully take advantage of DDDM without adequate resources and dedicated time for planning.

Resistance to change among staff or stakeholders

Another significant barrier to DDDM implementation is resistance to change among faculty and other stakeholders. This resistance can stem from various factors:

1. *Fear of evaluation:* Some educators may view data-driven approaches as a threat to their professional autonomy or as a means of excessive evaluation.
2. *Lack of trust in data:* There may be scepticism about the reliability and relevance of data, especially if past experiences with data use have been negative or unproductive.
3. *Cultural shift:* DDDM often requires a significant shift in organisational culture, which can be met with resistance from those comfortable with traditional decision-making processes.
4. *Overwhelming data volume:* Principals in Reeves & Burt's (2006) study expressed frustration with the excessive amount of raw data, stating that it was "overwhelming" and "really hard to choose which data is reliable for what your intended purposes are".

Strategies for overcoming the challenges

Professional development initiatives

To address the lack of data literacy and skills among staff, comprehensive professional development initiatives are crucial. These initiatives should focus on:

1. *Building data literacy:* Ologbosere (2023) suggests creating a well-rounded training programme that incorporates both theoretical and practical components, customised to meet the specific needs of the organisation.
2. *Hands-on training:* Provide practical, hands-on experiences with data analysis tools and techniques. As noted by Kubicle (2024), this could involve providing additional resources or offering one-on-one sessions with experts in the field.
3. *Continuous learning:* Implement ongoing professional development opportunities to keep staff updated on evolving data practices and technologies.
4. *Role-specific training:* Tailor training programmes to different roles within the institution.

Leadership communication and advocacy

Effective leadership is crucial in overcoming resistance to DDDM implementation. Leaders must articulate how DDDM aligns with and supports the institution's overall goals and values. They should focus on:

1. *Clear vision communication:* Develop a clear and shared vision to align data goals with the institutional mission.
2. *Modelling data use:* Modelling the use of data in their own decision-making processes, demonstrating its value and practicality.
3. *Creating a supportive culture:* Fostering a culture that values data-informed practices. This includes recognising and rewarding data-driven initiatives and successes.
4. *Addressing concerns:* Proactively addressing concerns about data use, particularly regarding privacy and ethical considerations. Estrellado (2024) suggests the establishment of a data governance and management system to define roles and responsibilities and set standards and policies.
5. *Facilitating collaboration:* Encouraging cross-departmental collaboration in data analysis and interpretation. As Estrellado (2024) suggests, participating in data discussions and collaboration will facilitate data sharing and enhance learning.

Ethical considerations in data use

The growing reliance on data-driven decision-making in education brings with it a range of ethical considerations that demand careful attention. These include critical issues such as privacy and data security, biases in data collection and interpretation, and the risks of over-reliance on quantitative metrics. By implementing robust measures to safeguard privacy, actively addressing biases, and maintaining a balanced approach, educational institutions can harness the power of data responsibly while upholding ethical standards and prioritising student well-being.

Privacy and data security - protecting sensitive information

As educational institutions collect and utilise more student and staff data, ensuring privacy and data security has become paramount. Strict data governance policies must be in place to protect student privacy (LessonBud, 2023). This involves limiting data collection to only what is necessary and handling it securely. Key considerations in protecting sensitive information include:

1. *Confidentiality:* Educational institutions must ensure robust data security controls are in place to protect student data from unauthorised access or disclosure.
2. *Informed consent:* The extent of the data collected, and how it will be used, must be clearly communicated to those providing the data. This transparency is crucial for building trust in data practices.
3. *Data stewardship:* Teachers and administrators should act as responsible data stewards, ensuring the ethical usage of student data for educational purposes. Decisions about data use should balance educational benefits with ethical considerations around privacy, consent, and inclusion.

Addressing biases in data collection and interpretation

Bias in data collection and interpretation can significantly impact the validity and fairness of data-driven decisions in education. The Data School (2024) defines bias in data collection as "the systematic error that can be introduced into a data set as a result of how the data was collected." Several types of bias can affect educational data:

1. *Selection bias:* This occurs when the method used to select the sample does not result in a representative sample of the population.

    Example: A school decides to evaluate the effectiveness of a new after-school tutoring programme by surveying participants' grades. However, the programme is voluntary, and only high-achieving students or those with highly motivated parents enrol. This leads to an overestimation of the programme's effectiveness, as the sample is not representative of the broader student population.
2. *Measurement bias:* This arises when the way data is collected introduces errors or inaccuracies.

Example: A college administers a satisfaction survey to students but designs the questions in a way that leads to skewed responses. For example, asking, "How excellent do you think our campus facilities are?" presupposes a positive evaluation, which may result in artificially high satisfaction ratings due to the leading nature of the question.

3. *Reporting bias:* This happens when the way data is reported or recorded introduces errors or inaccuracies.

   Example: A university collects data on student attendance through manual registers maintained by tutors. Some tutors may record attendance inconsistently, or students who arrive late may not be marked as present. This results in inaccurate attendance data, which could misrepresent student engagement levels when the data is analysed.

To address these biases, careful consideration must be given to the design, and administration of data collection instruments and the subsequent analysis of data collected.

Risks of over-reliance on data

While data can provide valuable insights, an over-reliance on quantitative metrics in education can lead to significant ethical concerns. One of the primary risks of over-reliance on data is the potential to reduce students to mere statistics, overlooking their individual needs and circumstances This overreliance can manifest in several ways:

1. *Neglecting qualitative factors:* An excessive focus on quantifiable metrics may lead to neglecting important qualitative factors that contribute to a student's overall development and well-being.
2. *Standardisation at the expense of individuality:* Data-driven approaches might push towards standardisation, potentially overlooking the unique strengths and challenges of individual students.
3. *Narrowing of educational goals:* There is a risk of educational priorities becoming distorted, with an obsessive focus on improving measurable outcomes at the expense of broader educational objectives.

Perpetuating biases and inequalities

Unaddressed biases in data collection and interpretation can lead to perpetuating or exacerbating existing inequalities in education. Pragmatic Institute (2024) provides an example of how confirmation bias might manifest in classrooms: "If a teacher believes that boys are naturally better than girls at math and science, that teacher may be more likely to call on boys to answer questions about those topics. This creates a self-fulfilling prophecy, supporting the teacher's belief that girls are not as naturally talented at STEM subjects". To mitigate these risks, educational institutions should:

1. *Maintain a balanced approach:* While using data for insights, educators should also rely on their professional judgment and qualitative observations.
2. *Promote critical thinking:* Encourage students and educators to critically evaluate data and its interpretations, rather than accepting them at face value.
3. *Conduct regular audits:* Regular audits of data collection and analysis processes will help identify and address potential biases.

Stakeholder engagement with data

As data continues to play an increasingly important role in education, the ability to effectively communicate data-driven insights to diverse stakeholders will become equally vital. According to the American Academy of Business (2023), data-driven decision-making promotes transparency and fosters meaningful engagement with various stakeholders. By focusing on stakeholder needs, simplifying complex information, utilising effective visualisations, and crafting compelling data narratives, educators and administrators can ensure that all stakeholders have a full understanding of the data itself and are equipped to contribute meaningfully to data-driven decision-making processes.

Engaging parents with data

Parents are critical stakeholders in education, and engaging them with data can lead to improved student outcomes. By sharing relevant data with parents, schools can:

1. Provide insights into their child's academic progress.
2. Highlight areas where parental support can be most effective.
3. Demonstrate the impact of school initiatives on student achievement.

To effectively engage parents, schools should consider:

- Regular data-driven progress reports.
- Parent-teacher conferences that incorporate data discussions.
- Online portals that provide real-time access to student data.

Engaging school boards with data

School boards are essential in shaping educational policies and managing resource allocation. Providing them with data can support more informed decision-making. Using data allows leaders to pinpoint areas needing improvement, track progress, allocate resources effectively, enhance instruction, and involve stakeholders. Key strategies for effectively engaging school boards with data include:

- Presenting regular data-driven reports on key performance indicators.
- Using data visualisations to illustrate trends and patterns.
- Providing context and interpretation alongside raw data to facilitate understanding.

Engaging community partners with data

Community partners, such as local businesses, non-profit organisations, and government agencies, can provide valuable support to educational institutions. Engaging these stakeholders with data can help align community resources with educational needs. Strategies for engaging community partners include:

- Sharing data on workforce readiness and skill gaps.
- Demonstrating the impact of community partnerships on student outcomes.
- Using data to identify areas where community support can be most effective.

Effective ways to present data to non-experts

Presenting complex educational data to non-expert stakeholders requires careful consideration of audience needs and data visualisation techniques. The goal is to make the data accessible, understandable, and actionable for all stakeholders.

Know your audience

Before presenting data, it is essential to consider the audience's background, interests, and level of data literacy. Understanding whether your audience is familiar with the data or new to it helps determine how to present the information effectively. Knowing whether your audience has experience or not is key to deciding how to present the data. This approach ensures that everyone feels supported and engaged, fostering a collaborative atmosphere where data can be understood and utilised effectively.

Simplify and focus

When presenting data to non-experts, it is crucial to simplify complex information and highlight key insights. This involves breaking down intricate data and providing a clear, high-level summary in straightforward language. Effective strategies for simplification include:

- Focusing on a few key metrics or findings.
- Using clear, jargon-free language.
- Providing context and real-world examples to illustrate data points.

Utilise effective data visualisation

Using visual representations of data can greatly improve understanding for non-expert audiences. Presenting data visually helps convey messages more clearly, capture attention, and evoke emotions. Effective techniques for data visualisation include:

- Choosing appropriate chart types for different data sets.
- Using colour strategically to highlight key information.
- Ensuring consistency in design across multiple visualisations.

Tell a story with data

Crafting a narrative around data can make it more engaging and memorable for non-expert audiences. This approach involves:

- Starting with a compelling question or problem.
- Using data to illustrate key points in the narrative.
- Concluding with actionable insights or recommendations.

Anticipate questions and provide context

When presenting data to non-experts, it is important to anticipate potential questions and provide necessary context.

Case Study 4: Data-driven stakeholder engagement

Brookfield Academy, a medium-sized secondary school, has implemented a comprehensive strategy to engage diverse stakeholders with data. By tailoring their approach to the unique needs of each group, the school has fostered meaningful collaboration and improved decision-making across the board.

Engaging parents with data

To keep parents informed and involved, the Academy introduced several initiatives:

- *Data-driven progress reports*: Parents receive monthly reports that highlight their child's academic progress, attendance, and engagement metrics. These reports focus on key insights, such as areas where students excel or need additional support.
- *Parent-teacher conferences with data discussions*: Teachers use visual aids, such as bar graphs and pie charts, to present students' performance trends during conferences. They also provide actionable recommendations on how parents can support their children at home.
- *Online portal*: Brookfield launched a user-friendly portal that gives parents real-time access to their child's grades, homework submissions, and teacher feedback. This transparency has strengthened trust and improved parent-school communication.

Engaging the school board with data

The Academy developed a robust system for presenting data to their school board:

- *Performance dashboards*: During monthly board meetings, administrators present interactive dashboards that display trends in attendance, test scores, and teacher performance. These dashboards use line graphs and heatmaps to simplify complex data.
- *Contextual analysis*: Each data set is accompanied by a narrative explaining its implications. For instance, when discussing declining math scores, the school paired the data with a proposed intervention plan and budget allocation.
- *Quarterly reports*: These reports focus on high-priority goals, such as resource allocation and curriculum effectiveness. Clear visualisations and concise summaries ensure that board members can make informed decisions efficiently.

Engaging community partners with data

The Academy has strengthened its relationship with local businesses, organisations, and institutions of further and higher education by utilising data:

- *Workforce readiness and career pathways reports*: The school shares data on student readiness for local job markets, emphasising skill gaps and aligning with community workforce needs. For students aiming for further or higher education, the school presents data on university acceptance rates, scholarship successes, and subject-specific achievements to highlight academic preparation.
- *Post-secondary success tracking*: Brookfield collaborates with local colleges and universities to track alumni performance, including retention and graduation rates. This data is shared with stakeholders to demonstrate how well-prepared students are for higher education and to identify areas where additional support is needed.
- *College and career readiness events*: Data is used to tailor events such as college fairs, career days, and apprenticeship workshops. For example, information on student interests and performance in STEM subjects helps identify relevant local industries and higher education programmes to invite.
- *Impact analysis of community-sponsored programmes*: Brookfield measures the outcomes of initiatives, such as mentorship programmes or university partnerships, using metrics like student enrolment in advanced courses, successful college applications, and access to bursaries or scholarships.
- *Collaborative planning with universities and colleges*: The school works closely with higher education institutions to align its curriculum and extracurricular activities with admission requirements and the skills needed for success. This collaboration is informed by data on student performance trends and future academic aspirations.

Effective data presentation for non-experts

Brookfield has adopted best practices to ensure all stakeholders can understand and act on the data:

- *Knowing the audience*: Staff assess stakeholders' data literacy levels before presentations, adjusting the complexity of the information accordingly. For example, teachers receive more detailed analyses, while parents and community members are provided with simplified summaries.
- *Simplification and focus*: Presentations are streamlined to emphasise three key metrics at a time, avoiding jargon and using relatable examples to explain trends.
- *Data visualisations*: Brookfield uses color-coded charts, infographics, and icons to make data visually engaging and easy to interpret. For instance, a bar graph comparing graduation rates over five years is paired with a callout box summarising the key takeaway.
- *Storytelling*: Each presentation begins with a compelling question, such as, "How can we improve student engagement?" Data is used to answer the question, followed by actionable recommendations that resonate with the audience.

Outcomes

Brookfield Academy's data-driven approach has yielded measurable benefits:

- *Improved parent involvement*: Parent-teacher conference attendance increased by 25%, and surveys show 90% of parents feel better informed about their child's progress.
- *Enhanced decision-making*: School board members report greater confidence in allocating resources, resulting in the approval of a new literacy programme.
- *Stronger community partnerships*: Local businesses have pledged additional funding for STEM initiatives, citing the clarity and relevance of the data shared by the school.

Brookfield Academy demonstrates how a thoughtful, stakeholder-focused approach to data can drive collaboration and positive change across an educational community.

Appendix 4, Part 4 provides further detail of effective data presentation.

Other statistical tests used in education

As suggested earlier in this chapter, teachers should not be expected to master complex statistical methods and, for the majority of their analyses, the use of simple descriptive statistics is sufficient. However, for completeness, Appendix 4, Part 5 outlines some other statistical tests that may warrant further exploration.

Activity: Exploring data-driven decision making

The aim of this activity is to encourage you to reflect thoughtfully on the role and importance of data within your own educational setting. You will then develop a practical action plan for incorporating data-driven decision-making into your daily professional practice. This approach ensures that your decisions are not only well-informed by relevant evidence but also carefully aligned with both the immediate short-term objectives and the broader long-term strategies of your institution.

1. Identify key data sources:
- Reflect on your current role (e.g., teacher, leader, administrator). List at least three key data sources that are currently available to you in your setting (e.g., student performance data, assessment results, attendance records, surveys, etc.).
- Briefly describe how these data sources are currently used in your decision-making process.

2. Qualitative vs. quantitative data:
- Consider a recent decision you made in your educational practice. Was the decision based on qualitative data, quantitative data, or both? Explain how the data influenced your decision.
- Reflect on how you could incorporate both types of data more effectively in future decision-making.

3. Data analysis and interpretation:
- Choose one of the data sources you listed in step 1. Discuss how you could analyse this data (e.g., using basic statistical methods, identifying trends, or gathering insights through qualitative analysis).
- How would you interpret the findings and use them to inform teaching, learning, or policy changes?

4. Leadership and data culture:
- If you hold a leadership role, or plan to in the future, think about how you could foster a culture of data-driven decision-making in your team or institution. What strategies could you implement to encourage staff to engage with data and make evidence-based decisions?

5. Ethical considerations:
- Reflect on potential ethical issues related to data use in your setting. Are there any concerns about privacy, bias, or over-reliance on data? How could these concerns be addressed?

6. Action plan:
- Based on your reflections, create a simple action plan for incorporating more data-driven decision-making into your practice over the next three months. Consider:
  - What data will you collect and how will you gather it?
  - How will you analyse and interpret this data?
  - How will you share findings with others (e.g., colleagues, leaders, students)?
  - What steps will you take to ensure ethical and effective use of data?

> **7. Reflection questions:**
> - How might your approach to teaching or leadership change if you integrated more data into your daily decisions?
> - What challenges do you anticipate in using data effectively, and how can you overcome them?

Summary

Improvements in educational processes, including teaching practices, curriculum design, assessment strategies, and institutional planning, must be grounded in the analysis of sound evidence. Data, both qualitative and quantitative, serves as the cornerstone of these improvements, providing objective insights that inform decision-making at all levels. This evidence should be gathered using diverse and reliable evaluation methods, such as surveys, interviews, standardised assessments, classroom observations, and digital tracking systems, ensuring a comprehensive understanding of the factors influencing educational outcomes.

By drawing from multiple credible sources, educational leaders can avoid biased interpretations and gain a holistic view of the strengths and areas for development within their institutions. Sound data analysis enables stakeholders to identify trends, uncover root causes of challenges, and design targeted interventions that lead to measurable improvements. Ultimately, evidence-based approaches ensure that efforts to enhance educational practices are both effective and sustainable, fostering an environment where data-driven insights pave the way for excellence.

8 HARNESSING E-LEADERSHIP AND AI

Nicholas Bowskill

Introduction

In an era where technology is reshaping many aspects of our professional lives, leadership must adapt to the digital age. E-leadership, the practice of leading in a virtual, technology-driven environment, now integrates with artificial intelligence (AI) to further expand the horizons of leadership development. This chapter focuses on how leaders can harness the power of generative AI tools, such as ChatGPT, to enhance decision-making, problem-solving, and personal growth. It explores the use of ready-made prompts to guide AI in leadership development, examining the opportunities and challenges posed by AI integration. It reflects on the evolving role of leadership in navigating AI in organisations, emphasising how leaders can use these technologies to create more efficient, informed, and forward-thinking environments.

This chapter:

- Discusses the concept of e-leadership and its relevance in the digital age.
- Explores how ready-made prompts for generative AI (such as ChatGPT) can be used to facilitate leadership development.
- Examines the advantages and challenges of integrating AI tools into leadership practices.
- Analyses the role of leadership in guiding organisations through AI adoption, ensuring that human values and ethical considerations are maintained.
- Highlights examples of AI-driven leadership development programmes that effectively incorporate ready-made prompts for practical leadership growth.

Introducing E-Leadership and AI

The integration of artificial intelligence into leadership and management practice is no longer a futuristic concept - it is a present-day reality reshaping how leaders operate, learn, and influence. Central to this shift is the increasing use of engagement with generative AI tools such as ChatGPT, which act as gateways to powerful outputs that can support strategic thinking, communication, learning, and personal growth. This chapter is organised into two key thematic areas that reflect the evolving synergy between leadership and AI.

The first area explores the concept of AI and the role of ready-made prompts as practical and pedagogical tools in educational leadership. It looks at the foundational role prompts play in AI interaction, and how pre-designed, purposeful prompts can be integrated into course design, adaptive learning systems, and professional development initiatives. Prompts are more than just inputs - they represent micro-interventions that can trigger deep thinking, simulate dialogue, and personalise leadership training within digital environments.

The second area explores how AI-generated prompts can enhance leadership and management practice more broadly. From improving strategic decision-making to streamlining routine administrative processes, AI tools are increasingly being used to support leaders in responding to complex challenges. Through this lens, the chapter examines how generative AI can assist in communication, reflection, learning design, coaching, and the automation of policy interpretation and guidance. It also considers how AI can support differentiated leadership training, allowing development pathways to be tailored to individuals' evolving needs and contexts.

Together, these sections provide a rich foundation for understanding how leaders can meaningfully harness AI - not just as a technical tool, but as a catalyst for deeper, more adaptive and responsive leadership in a digital age.

Using ready-made prompts as pedagogical tools

Educators are increasingly moving beyond early apprehensions about artificial intelligence (AI) - such as fears of academic dishonesty and the potential replacement of human roles - to actively explore its pedagogical potential in educational settings. While these concerns are still valid, and likely to persist as AI continues to evolve, focusing exclusively on them risks narrowing the broader conversation about the significance of AI in education (Luckin, 2022).

Educational leaders, in particular, must cultivate a nuanced understanding of how AI may influence teaching, learning, and institutional operations. This includes recognising how AI might reshape their own leadership roles, affect team dynamics, and present new opportunities for enhancing strategic effectiveness. Leaders need to know how to collaborate with AI technologies to improve their performance and guide their institutions through informed, data-driven decision-making. At the same time, they must support staff and students in adopting AI responsibly - ensuring its use is ethical, safe, and pedagogically sound - while remaining agile in response to the rapid and ongoing developments in the field (Yang et al., 2024).

There is an urgent need to move beyond superficial or instrumental understandings of artificial intelligence (AI) in education. While early discussions often centred on fears of cheating or the replacement of human roles, the conversation must now elevate to a more critical and pedagogically informed level. Educators, leaders, and learning designers must begin to consider the broader significance, potential, and implications of AI technologies in relation to educational theories, models, and practice - not just their media capabilities or novelty. This requires an understanding of AI not only as a tool but as a transformative force that can shape educational workflows, roles, and strategies. Key stakeholders are rightly concerned with how AI aligns with, challenges, or complements existing educational theories. This is not to discard existing research but to test and enrich it, just as education previously adapted to the arrival of the internet and mobile technologies. Empirical studies and theoretical models continue to offer valid lenses through which to examine the integration of AI - until proven otherwise.

AI technologies now exist in various forms, from algorithmic systems to more advanced generative models. Of particular relevance are generative AI systems, which can produce human-like responses to prompts in text, voice, or image formats. These systems are capable of transforming one form of input into another - such as converting text into images or images into videos - and are becoming increasingly integrated into tools that support teaching, learning, and the broader management of education.

While current discourse largely centres on chat interfaces, the field is rapidly evolving toward AI *agents* and *workflows*. These agents serve as digital assistants that handle repetitive or complex tasks - summarising content, conducting searches, transforming formats - within a workflow of sequenced, goal-oriented actions. Future developments will likely include voice-activated AI, immersive applications within augmented or virtual reality, and adaptive agents operating seamlessly across various educational processes.

Against this evolving backdrop, this chapter focuses on one key element: the *prompt*, and more specifically, the *readymade prompt*. These prompts represent a widely accessible and highly flexible point of interaction between educators and generative AI systems.

To explore their pedagogical value, this chapter examines three distinct applications of readymade prompts:
1. The readymade prompt as a learning resource.
2. The readymade prompt in course design.
3. The readymade prompt as part of an adaptive learning system.

Each application has its own strengths, limitations, and alignment with established educational models such as direct instruction, inquiry-based learning, and collaborative approaches. Readymade prompts are not merely functional tools, but pedagogical agents - purposeful elements of educational design that support repeated instructional activities within AI-enhanced workflows. This framing invites a more sophisticated and educationally grounded understanding of AI, moving past the narrow boundaries of technological hype to explore how these systems can serve real pedagogical ends. Ultimately, the goal is to help educational leaders and practitioners recognise how readymade prompts - and generative AI more broadly - can be harnessed strategically to support learning, leadership, and organisational effectiveness.

Prompts as the basic unit of AI in education

Currently, the basic unit of interaction is largely focused on the *prompt*. An AI prompt is a text-based input or instruction given to an artificial intelligence system to generate a specific response. Prompts can be questions, commands, or context-setting statements that guide the AI in producing relevant and meaningful output. The quality and clarity of a prompt directly influence the accuracy, relevance, and usefulness of the AI-generated response (Khan, 2024).

Here is an example of one of the many prompts that might be used by a primary school teacher, together with the response generated by the AI system - in this case, chatGPT.

Prompt:
"Give me a list of common types of assessment in primary schools and how I might use them as a Year 2 teacher".

AI Response:
Here's a summary of common assessment types used in Year 2 teaching:
- *Formative assessment:* Ongoing checks like whiteboard answers, exit tickets, or class discussions to guide daily teaching.
- *Summative assessment:* End-of-unit tests or projects to evaluate learning outcomes.
- *Diagnostic assessment:* Tools like phonics checks or pre-topic quizzes to identify gaps before teaching.
- *Observational assessment:* Watching pupils during activities to assess skills and understanding in real time.
- *Peer and self-assessment:* Helping children reflect using simple tools like traffic lights or "two stars and a wish".

Each type supports different teaching goals and helps build a well-rounded understanding of pupils' progress.

The example uses a simple, short prompt. However, prompts have now evolved, through increased awareness and experimentation, into thoughtfully crafted entries shaped by the principles of *prompt engineering*.

Information

It is important to recognise that AI technologies are evolving rapidly. Although the focus here is on text-based readymade prompts, the concept of prompts is already expanding to encompass a range of media for both input and output. Prompts are also increasingly used within systems to drive the development of agents and automate workflows. While these advancements are acknowledged, the emphasis on text-based input remains relevant, offering a meaningful foundation for understanding the broader educational implications of AI from a strategic and conceptual perspective.

Readymade prompts

A *readymade prompt* is a pre-written instruction or input designed for use with an AI tool (like ChatGPT), created by someone other than the end-user. Rather than expecting learners or leaders to come up with their own queries from scratch, a readymade prompt provides a structured, purposeful starting point for engaging with AI. It can:

- Guide a learner's thinking or exploration.
- Serve a specific instructional goal.
- Reduce cognitive load by offering clear direction.
- Support personalised learning when adapted to a context.
- Provide a re-usable prompt that can be shared within and across institutes.

Example

In order to teach Year 2 pupils about the water cycle, the class teacher creates the following readymade prompt for use with chatGPT:

"You are helping a Year 2 student learn about the water cycle. When prompted with 'Teach me the water cycle' take them through three steps to build understanding. In each step:

Explain the idea in simple terms, using child-friendly examples.

Ask the pupil a question to check their understanding.

Wait for their response before moving on".

For full details of a pupil-chatGPT exchange, see Appendix 5.

This readymade prompt can be used by all Year 2 teachers within the school, and in other schools too.

Information

AI itself can be used to generate a readymade prompt. A number of prompt generator tools are available including Originality, Bard, Claude, Perplexity, and ChatGPT.

The readymade prompt as a learning resource

Using AI in education requires balancing open-ended exploration with structured guidance. While tools like ChatGPT are celebrated for their capacity to personalise responses based on individual needs, their effectiveness is maximised when usage is informed by thoughtful pedagogy. Concepts such as *learning styles*, *universal design for learning*, and *situated learning* all emphasise the importance of context and individual learner needs.

At first glance, readymade prompts might appear to limit personalisation. However, they can offer essential structure and direction, especially when learners are unfamiliar with how to begin or what to ask. Crafting meaningful queries often depends on prior knowledge, and in this way, readymade prompts can act as scaffolds to support more productive and focused interactions with AI.

Readymade prompts can be adapted to serve different educational aims. For learners, they help ease the initial uncertainty of engaging with AI, guiding them in how to phrase and frame their queries. For educators, they offer a versatile tool that can complement or even substitute other instructional strategies. Table 8.1 below outlines some examples and potential uses of readymade prompts across different learning contexts.

Type	Description and purpose	Basic example
Readymade statement.	Pre-written assertions, used to define terms, or to set the scene.	"Let's discuss the application of [this technology] to support [this leadership model]".
Readymade question.	A pre-written question to organise an inquiry for the learner or to initiate reflective thinking on a given topic.	"What are the pros and cons of using [this leadership model] when supporting institutional change?".

Readymade self-assessment.	Prompts designed to help the learner check and evaluate their own understanding.	"Assess this paragraph given as my response to the leadership challenge set for [this situation]. Give me three ways I might improve it at Level 5".
Readymade scenario.	Prompts to initiate a situation for context-setting or role play for perspective-taking.	"You are [this role] in [this situation]. What are the first actions you would take to gain support for [this change project]?".

Table 8.1 - A prototype taxonomy of readymade prompts

The prototype taxonomy in Table 8.1 is of course limited. For example, the prompts shown are little more than a single line of text. It is more effective to provide detail to the AI by explaining what kind of response is wanted and unwanted. It may also include the format the output should take, such as a table or even an image.

There are more types of readymade prompt possible. They may potentially correspond to the many pedagogical activities used in practice. For example:

- A readymade reflection prompt could be developed to support a review.
- A readymade prompt could make a comparison between concepts or theories.
- Readymade prompts could make predictions.

There are clearly many possibilities beyond a simple taxonomy.

From the perspective of the learner, a readymade prompt provides the learner with a digital object, the pre-constructed text, which then functions as an instructional agent helping the learner to explore the given topic. When used, the prompt organises a form of engagement which supports the learner to achieve an educational goal.

In terms of learning design, and from the perspective of educational models, the readymade prompt can be understood as a form of direct instruction. The readymade prompt serves as a surrogate teacher. This provides a framework for teaching in the absence of the teacher. The prompt thereby embodies the teacher's educational goal.

The readymade prompts in Table 8.1 are designed to support specific instructional goals. For instance, a teacher might use a self-assessment prompt to help learners check their understanding in relation to course assessment criteria. In doing so, the prompt - together with the AI - helps guide focused, purposeful revision.

Similarly, the readymade scenario prompt can be deployed by the teacher to immerse the learner into the application of the key principles discussed in the course. The generated scenario requires that the learner engages with the skills and knowledge required in a course. The context and the nature of the activity is designed into the phrasing of the prompt defined by the teacher. In both these examples - the readymade self-assessment prompt and the readymade scenario prompt - they are part of the learning design process.

The resulting prompts are intentionally designed to produce a known outcome or a predictable learning experience. In this sense, these readymade prompts function as *pedagogical agents*. While AI agents are typically understood as tools that perform repetitive tasks, in education, these tasks often involve setting targeted activities to engage learners. Teachers can design and share such prompts to consistently perform these functions. Although some variation may occur across different chatbots or individual interactions, the core instructional purpose of these pedagogical agents remains the same.

The readymade prompt in course design

The previous section explored the readymade prompt as a standalone tool. While this helped to explain its general purpose, it is also important to understand how it fits within a structured programme of learning. To do this, the prompt needs to be considered alongside other key elements of course delivery such as: course content; tutor input; peer interaction (collaborative learning); and independent learning.

The following model is taken from an online postgraduate module at the University of Derby. The Innovative 21st Century Teaching module comprises 10 units of learning, typically paced at one unit per week. The readymade prompt(s) is embedded within the module's wider system of resources and activities. This system includes several distinct online spaces, each with a specific purpose. The core elements include:

- Study materials.
- Online webinars.
- A dedicated collaborative learning space for using the readymade prompt(s).

Together, these form an integrated learning environment.

Open learning and study materials

In this module, the study materials follow an open learning format. This means that while the materials are structured and interconnected (e.g., as a sequence of 10 study units), they are all available at the outset of the module. Students are therefore free to explore the content in sequential order or choose their own path based on interest or need.

Each unit of study introduces three core ideas or 'threshold concepts' (Land, 2004). These may be theories or models which are central to understanding the subject matter. However, online learners in this module are practicing teachers balancing work, life, and study. Juggling multiple responsibilities can impact continuity of study making it easy to miss or struggle with these important ideas.

Using readymade prompts to support learning

To support learners on this module, a readymade prompt is provided at the start of each unit. It focuses specifically on the threshold concepts and is shared in a dedicated area of the course platform. Students are encouraged to copy and paste the prompt into an AI tool of their choice. Students are then required to share a link to their discussion threads in the forum.

Students can engage with the AI in their own time, at their own pace. They are free to explore the AI's responses based on their own interests and prior knowledge. This activity is meant to supplement the study materials and help reinforce understanding.

As mentioned, AI tools like ChatGPT allow students to share their conversation threads via a link. This is valuable in two ways: it enables peers to see how others approached the challenge and how they discussed the topic. At the same time, it gives tutors insights into the way students think about the topic, and it reveals the level of engagement for each student.

Students are invited to share links to their AI interactions, along with brief reflections on what they learned and how useful the AI was in helping them understand the key concepts. They are also invited to review at least two peers' threads and give constructive feedback. This process follows a *think-pair-share* learning strategy: students first explore the topic independently, then read and respond to the thinking of others, and finally contribute to a shared class discussion archive.

The role of webinars

At the end of each unit, a live online webinar brings everything together. The webinar begins by revisiting key concepts from the previous unit, helping students make connections and build on prior knowledge. It then focuses on deepening understanding of the current unit's content, including the study materials and the AI-supported activity.

Interestingly, these webinars use a more didactic (teacher-led) style. While modern teaching often encourages student-centred approaches, the webinar is deliberately used to provide authoritative guidance. It helps consolidate student learning, clarify misunderstandings, and validates the work done through independent and collaborative tasks.

The tutor's role here is essential - not only as a teacher but as a guide who reassures, evaluates, and validates student efforts. In this sense, even a didactic session can be student-centred, as it is designed to meet learners where they are and move them forward.

A triangulated approach to learning key concepts

Based on the above, we can conceptualise learning design as multimodal. The overall design described in this section, incorporates different learning approaches as follows:

- **Open learning** (via the structured study materials).
- **Independent learning** (through self-paced AI activities).
- **Collaborative learning** (by sharing and reviewing AI discussions).
- **Tutor-led input** (in the webinar).

This triangulated approach seeks to increase engagement and improve understanding of key concepts. Doing so, intentionally organises interdependence and interaction amongst the different modes as part of the learning design process. It reflects principles of *Universal Design for Learning* (Burgstahler & Cory, 2008), providing multiple ways for students to access, engage with, and reflect on the material. Over time, an archive of student and tutor contributions - including multimedia responses - emerges, offering a rich resource for revisiting and reinforcing learning.

The readymade prompt in an adaptive learning system

Since the arrival of the personal computer there has been interest in multimedia training material as a solution for independent learning and situations where teaching resources are limited or unavailable (Ambron & Hooper, 1988). These are freestanding interactive learning experiences which provide structure and content delivery to be accompanied by feedback and self-assessment.

The arrival of the internet, and more specifically internet browsers, saw an interest in these materials being provided online. These early efforts to deliver *Computer Based Training* (CBT) online came to full fruition with the arrival of *Massive Open Online Courses* (MOOCs). These MOOCs were supported with collaborative spaces on third party platforms, and this form of interactive self-study material has become popular both for access to free online learning and as a means of marketing courses from universities.

The downside of CBT-type material is the structure which, despite offering a path through the content, can also be restrictive. There is a sense amongst some critics that this form of provision solves scalability but tends towards universalism in the way it offers a fixed level of provision. For all it seems student-centred in terms of access and engagement, the content is set, and the level of complexity and engagement is fixed. For learners interested in this topic, the challenge remains the age-old issue of finding content that matches their level, personal needs, and specific context.

One solution to these challenges comes from the arrival of generative AI. A learner can engage directly with tools and platforms such as ChatGPT and cover the same topics in an online course by interacting with ChatGPT and, over a series of iterations, they can explore these topics in a personalised manner by asking the questions they have about these topics. In that sense, the need for passworded MOOC platforms may be reduced with the ChatGPT space being easier to access and with less 'noise' for the learner. There is no need to click through various screens to start or to find out where you left the previous session.

The downside of the ChatGPT approach is that learners have different expectations about how to interact with these technologies and the level of engagement needed to achieve an effective learning experience. Some learners may interact with single prompts or with simplistic prompts thereby missing the opportunities and knowledge which might exist within such environments. The lack of structure may cause learners to wander away off-topic or to miss important aspects by interacting within what might become narrow channels of discussion.

An obvious solution to this might be a mixture of CBT and ChatGPT-like environments. By creating a structure and then allowing the learner to have extended conversations within different parts of the new hybrid environment, it is possible to have scaffolded learning, to personalise learning, and to do so at scale. There is however still a risk of ineffective use of the AI technologies within such an environment.

The readymade prompt provides a solution to the risks associated with learner-generated prompts if combined with an established pedagogical structure. Such a structure might be an explanation, the provision of an example, and a self-test option. Each part of the structure would then have its own readymade prompt. This can allow the flexibility and personalisation and initial orientation in each part of the CBT structure providing both direction and personalisation at scale.

There are examples of these ideas being developed (Abolnejadian et al., 2024) providing empirical evidence of the value of this approach in a classroom setting. The pedagogical framework used in Abolnejadian's study included three elements: *Explanation*, *Example*, and *Exercise* (Figure 8.1). Their CBT-style application provided a drop-down menu of available topics. The selection of a given topic from that menu then generated the framework along with the appropriate accompanying prompt. Computing science students using their adaptive learning tool outperformed those in a control group in what was an early intervention study. Based upon which element was clicked, the user would then experience the 'injection' of a readymade prompt into the chatbot interface. The resulting output and subsequent interaction scaffolds the learner to explore the topic in a more focused manner.

```
# Prompts from function section

## Explanation Prompt
Explain the concept of functions to me and
describe their usages. Also, explain the
structure of functions in Python and explain
functions with and without arguments.
## Example Prompt
Give me a real-world example of using functions.
## Exercise Prompt
Give me an exercise of working with functions in
Python.
```

Figure 8.1 - The readymade prompts within the pedagogical framework
(Abolnejadian et al., 2024)

Based upon that early work, a similar pedagogical framework has been developed elsewhere (see below) creating a platform for any subject area and any topic. This tool builds on the earlier work from computing science and provides a shell potentially allowing anyone to edit the content for their audience or discipline. In this latest case, the user would click on *Explain*, *Example*, or *Exam* (Figure 8.2).

Clicking on the *Explain* button displays the injected prompt and the consequent output. This provides an initial shape for user engagement which is also open-ended. Similarly, clicking on *Example* provides an illustration of the concept in practice. Clicking on *Exam* provides a self-assessment test, allowing the learner to check their understanding. Again, this can be extended either by modification of the readymade prompt or through interaction by the learner.

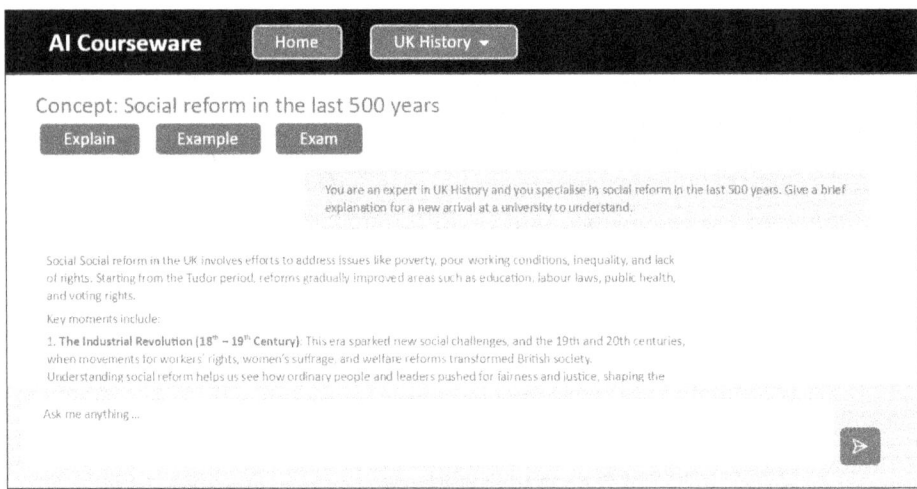

Figure 8.2 - The PromptFrame shell showing an application for UK History
(http://PromptFrame.co.uk, 2005)

This approach allows all stakeholders to adapt the shell including educators, departments or institutions. Any part of the above can be reformatted either in terms of the interface and colour-scheme etc. or in terms of content. Topics can be changed and likewise the readymade prompt can be edited, extended, or changed.

From these examples, it can be seen how the original idea of CBT has evolved to take account of AI tools such as ChatGPT. It is feasible to combine the pedagogical structure of conventional CBT offers of this kind with the engagement and personalisation of the AI technologies. The challenge of rigid structure or a fixed level of provision in previous forms of CBT is addressed by the flexibility of the chatbot and the orientation provided by the readymade prompt.

Enhancing leadership and management with AI prompts

In addition to the applications discussed in previous sections, artificial intelligence (AI) is transforming educational leadership and management by providing tools that enhance strategic decision-making, communication, and administrative efficiency (Igbokwe, 2024). The AI-generated prompts, in particular, serve as catalysts for innovation and personalised professional development within educational institutions. By integrating AI-driven learning design, coaching, and tailored leadership training, educational leaders can improve their effectiveness in driving institutional success. As AI continues to evolve, its role in shaping leadership development in education will expand, offering innovative solutions to address the complexities of modern educational environments. While AI presents new opportunities for educational leadership, it also introduces a range of ethical, moral, and practical challenges that must be carefully navigated (Fullan et al., 2023).

A well-crafted, ready-made prompt is a valuable tool in leadership and management, as its reusability enhances efficiency, supports strategic thinking, and streamlines recurring decision-making processes (Ahmad & Ruslan, 2024). As such, ready-made prompts are highly effective for recurring leadership and management tasks. They support strategic planning, decision-making, and change management by helping structure goals, assess risks, and implement strategies. In team and performance management, they assist with motivation, delegation, feedback, and appraisals. They also enhance leadership development, crisis management, and organisational culture by aiding training, contingency planning, and engagement initiatives.

AI generated prompts in establishing an institute's vision

If a senior leader wants AI to create a prompt that generates a vision statement, it might enter the following into the *Originality.ai* generator:

> *"Purpose of prompt: To articulate my school's vision statement"*.

The generator's output would be a pre-formulated prompt, such as:

> *"You are an expert in educational leadership and vision development. Your task is to articulate a compelling vision statement for a school that reflects its core values, mission, and aspirations. When prompted with 'Create my school vision statement', you should pose questions to help inform your output, which will be a vision statement in 1-3 sentences"*.

The pre-formulated prompt can then be used to create a vision statement.

Activity: Creating a prompt for a school vision statement
1. Copy and paste the prompt "To articulate my school's vision statement" into the *Originality.ai* prompt generator (https://originality.ai/blog/ai-prompt-generator).
2. Copy and paste the output from *Originality.ai* into *chatGPT* (https://chatgpt.com).

> Now type 'Create my school vision statement' into *chatGPT* and examine the output. If the output (vision statement) does not align with expectations, you can modify the original input to *Originality.ai* and repeat the process.

AI generated prompts in strategic decision-making

Ready-made prompts can streamline educational processes by drawing upon the model's vast knowledge base to generate structured, context-aware suggestions, reducing cognitive load and ensuring consistency in repetitive tasks. These prompts are increasingly becoming a valuable asset in strategic decision-making, providing leaders with structured guidance and actionable insights (Guo et al., 2024). They can play a crucial role in clarifying objectives, exploring alternative strategies, and anticipating potential outcomes. With effective use of AI, leaders can access data-driven recommendations that enhance the quality of their decisions. For instance, AI tools can analyse educational trends and generate prompts that help school and university leaders develop data-driven strategies to enhance student outcomes and institutional effectiveness.

A study by Dennis et al. (2023) has found that AI agents are now being recognised as valid members of leadership teams and, as a result, have improved team efficiency and decision-making processes. Indeed, empirical research by Csaszar et al. (2024) has indicated that AI agents can generate and assess strategies at a level comparable to entrepreneurs and investors.

The integration of AI-generated prompts into strategic decision-making offers several advantages. They help leaders identify strengths and opportunities for growth by evaluating current leadership traits and suggesting key areas to utilise or develop. For example, an AI prompt might be: "Evaluate current leadership traits, identifying strengths to capitalise on and possible areas for growth". This approach enables leaders to target specific weaknesses, ensuring development efforts are focused and measurable (Stratpilot, 2024).

AI-generated prompts can also assist in analysing personal performance reviews and identify key areas for leadership improvement over a specified period. For instance, a prompt such as: "Analyse personal performance reviews to identify three key areas for leadership improvement over the next quarter" allows leaders to focus on areas such as communication skills, decision-making under pressure, and team motivation.

After conducting faculty evaluations and reviewing student success metrics, an AI tool was used by a college to generate the following prompt:

"Analyse recent faculty feedback and student achievement data to identify three key areas where college leadership can enhance teaching support, curriculum development, and student engagement for the next academic year".

The resulting output from AI was:

1. **Enhancing faculty collaboration** - Implement structured forums for faculty to share best practices and interdisciplinary teaching strategies.
2. **Strengthening curriculum alignment** - Use AI-driven insights to adjust course offerings based on student performance trends and labour market demands.
3. **Improving student engagement and retention** - Use AI tools to personalise student support services and early intervention programmes.

Acting on these AI-driven insights, the college leaders were better able to make informed decisions that supported faculty development, improved curriculum effectiveness, and enhanced student success.

In educational leadership, AI-generated prompts provide structured guidance that supports institutional planning and policy development. These prompts help clarify objectives, explore alternative strategies, and anticipate potential outcomes. Educational leaders can use AI to access data-driven recommendations that enhance the quality of their decisions. For example, AI tools can analyse enrolment trends, student performance data, and emerging pedagogical methods to generate prompts that guide educational institutions in adapting their curriculum to meet evolving needs. According to Dwivedi et al. (2021), AI-driven decision-making is part of a broader technological transformation, enabled by breakthroughs in algorithmic machine learning and autonomous decision-making and has the potential to augment or replace human tasks across various industries, enabling administrators to make proactive, evidence-based choices.

AI tools also facilitate comprehensive institutional benchmarking by analysing educational trends, student performance data, and institutional effectiveness metrics. This enables the development of predictive models that provide insights into potential strategies, future policy decisions, and institutional positioning. For instance, AI can assess enrolment patterns, curriculum effectiveness, student engagement on digital platforms, and public sentiment toward competing institutions. Educational leaders can use these insights to make data-driven decisions to enhance their institution's competitiveness, improve student outcomes, and adapt to emerging trends in the education sector (Sembly, 2025). In addition, AI can benchmark academic performance metrics, faculty research output, and institutional policies, allowing institutions to make strategic curriculum adjustments (Fu et al., 2024).

Enhancing communication through AI generated prompts

Effective communication and strategic decision-making are foundational to successful educational leadership. The impact of AI on communication processes can be transformative, streamlining message delivery and positively affecting employee behaviour, ultimately boosting productivity and organisational effectiveness (Gonzalez-Mohino et al., 2024). AI enhances writing by detecting and correcting errors, refining grammar and style, and improving overall readability. It also aids in citation management (though its ability to locate real citations remains limited), and supports proofreading, document formatting, and plagiarism detection, ultimately saving time and ensuring clarity and accuracy in academic and professional writing (Esplugas, 2023).

Beyond writing, AI-generated prompts can assist educational leaders in crafting clear, impactful messages and making informed, data-driven decisions. These prompts help streamline communication with stakeholders, align messaging with institutional goals, and foster inclusivity in diverse educational settings. For instance, AI can generate tailored prompts for delivering constructive feedback to educators or articulating an institute's vision statement.

This example relates to the 'vision' activity earlier in the chapter.

The Senior Management Team (SMT) of a primary school utilises an AI Prompt Generator to craft a specialised prompt for ChatGPT, transforming it into an expert in educational leadership and vision development. ChatGPT then gathers key details, including core values, mission, aspirations, and inclusivity, while also considering the preferred style - whether formal, inspirational, forward-thinking, or community-centred. Based on this input, the following vision statement is created:

"Rooted in honesty, respect, and inclusivity, our school empowers every pupil to achieve their full potential. With a commitment to excellence, we inspire a love for learning, nurturing confident and capable individuals who make a difference. Our goal is to be the primary school of choice, where every child thrives in an inclusive, supportive, and high-achieving environment".

AI also plays a critical role in promoting inclusivity within educational leadership and AI assistive technologies make communication more accessible for students with disabilities. Tools such as AI-driven chatbots and word prediction software support students with learning difficulties, such as dyslexia, enabling them to engage more effectively with educational content.

Streamlining administrative efficiency with AI

Administrative tasks often consume a significant portion of a leader's time, limiting their ability to focus on strategic priorities. AI-generated prompts can automate routine communications, schedule reminders, and generate reports, allowing leaders to direct their attention to more impactful initiatives. By reducing the administrative burden, AI enables leaders to allocate their time more effectively. For instance, AI can prompt leaders with daily summaries of key performance indicators, upcoming deadlines, or student performance reports, enhancing overall organisational efficiency.

As highlighted by Lin et al. (2025), AI-based personalised systems, such as virtual tutors, can streamline learning processes, and similar AI-driven solutions can be adapted to support administrative tasks in educational settings. AI can also automate data entry and tracking, reducing human error and increasing efficiency in administrative functions such as scheduling, reporting, and compliance tracking. This allows leaders to dedicate more time to fostering a positive school culture, driving educational improvements, and creating an environment where both leadership and learning can thrive (University of Iowa, 2024).

AI driven learning design for critical decision making

By analysing a leader's past decisions and performance, AI can generate prompts that challenge assumptions, encourage exploration of alternative perspectives, and simulate complex decision-making scenarios. This personalised approach enhances the leader's ability to navigate multifaceted challenges, improving both adaptability and problem-solving skills. AI-driven platforms also integrate real-time feedback mechanisms, allowing leaders to reflect on their choices and refine their decision-making processes continuously. AI-powered simulations and case studies further enable leaders to apply theoretical knowledge to real-world scenarios, enhancing their ability to assess risks and opportunities effectively.

AI driven coaching and leadership reflection

Continuous self-improvement is essential for effective leadership. AI-driven coaching systems utilise prompts to guide leaders through reflection exercises, helping them assess their strengths, identify areas for development, and set actionable goals. These systems can simulate challenging scenarios, allowing leaders to practice responses and refine their approaches in a risk-free environment. Employing AI tools in leadership development offers a strategic advantage by providing personalised coaching experiences (Kaplan, 2025).

Recent advancements in AI have led to the development of sophisticated coaching platforms that enhance leadership growth. One example is *Coaching Copilot*, a blended system combining a large language model (LLM) powered chatbot with human coaching (Arakawa & Yakura, 2024). This approach provides real-time, interactive coaching conversations tailored to individual leaders, thereby augmenting the self-reflective process. Similarly, AI-powered coaching tools such as *Valence's AI Leadership Coach* offer personalised guidance to support leadership growth and business transformation (Valence, 2025).

These AI-driven coaching systems not only provide personalised feedback but also offer scalable solutions, making high-quality coaching accessible to a broader range of leaders within an organisation. By integrating AI into leadership development programmes, educational institutions and businesses alike can foster a culture of continuous learning and adaptability - essential traits for navigating the complexities of modern leadership.

Automated policy guidance through AI

Navigating organisational policies and compliance requirements is a complex endeavour for leaders. Artificial Intelligence (AI) has emerged as a valuable tool in this domain, offering real-time guidance on policy adherence, ethical considerations, and regulatory compliance. By inputting specific scenarios into AI systems, leaders can receive prompts that outline relevant policies and suggest appropriate courses of action, thereby reducing the risk of non-compliance and promoting ethical decision-making. For example, AI can provide leaders with best practices for data privacy when implementing new technologies, ensuring alignment with legal and ethical standards.

A school principal is implementing a new AI-driven student assessment tool and wants to ensure compliance with data protection regulations, such as the UK's GDPR or the US's FERPA. The principal inputs the following prompt into an AI compliance tool:

"Our school is adopting an AI-powered student assessment platform that collects and analyses student performance data. How can we ensure compliance with UK data protection regulations while maintaining ethical use of student data?"

In response, the AI system provides guidance on:
- Ensuring informed parental consent for data collection.
- Implementing data minimisation strategies to collect only necessary student information.
- Encrypting stored data and restricting access to authorised personnel.
- Conducting regular audits to ensure continued compliance.
- Aligning AI use with ethical guidelines for educational technology.

This real-time AI-generated policy guidance helps the principal navigate legal and ethical considerations while making informed decisions.

Integrating AI into policy guidance offers several advantages, particularly in identifying potential ethical dilemmas before they escalate. AI systems can process vast amounts of data to implement proactive compliance measures. By using machine learning algorithms, organisations can ensure their teams consistently adhere to the highest standards of integrity. However, as Choung et al. (2024) highlight, the challenge is to create an institutional framework that promotes the beneficial uses of AI while minimising its potential for abuse, thus preventing the automated production of injustice.

AI can also assist in the development and implementation of organisational policies. For instance, AI tools can generate policy templates tailored to an organisation's specific needs, streamlining the policy creation process (Yar et al., 2024).

ChatGPT is prompted to 'Generate a list of sample prompts that an educational institution could use to develop organisational policies. Focus on areas such as data protection, AI usage, remote work, safeguarding, and inclusion. The prompts should guide leaders in drafting policies that are not only effective in achieving their intended outcomes but also grounded in ethical principles and professional responsibility.

Here are a number of resulting examples of *sample prompts* that chatGPT has generated:

1. **For a data protection policy:**
   "What measures should our institution implement to ensure compliance with GDPR when handling student and staff data?"

2. **For an AI usage policy in education:**
   "What guidelines should be in place to regulate the ethical use of AI tools in teaching, assessment, and administrative tasks?"

> 3. **For a remote work policy:**
>   *"What key considerations should be included in a policy that governs remote teaching for faculty members?"*
> 4. **For a safeguarding policy:**
>   *"What steps should be outlined in a policy to ensure student safety when using online learning platforms and social media?"*
> 5. **For an inclusion and diversity policy:**
>   *"How can our institution develop a policy that promotes inclusive leadership and equitable opportunities for all staff and students?"*
>
> These sample prompts guide organisations in structuring policies that align with legal, ethical, and operational standards while addressing specific institutional needs.

The adoption of AI in policy guidance does, however, necessitate careful consideration of ethical implications. AI systems must be designed to prioritise fairness, transparency, and accountability to prevent unintended harm, particularly in decisions that affect individuals or communities. Implementing robust data governance strategies is crucial not only to protect individual privacy and corporate intellectual assets but also to maintain public trust in the use of such technologies. As applications of artificial intelligence in the public sector continue to grow, early experiments around the world demonstrate both the potential and the risks associated with AI-driven policy tools (Martinho-Truswell, 2018). Ensuring that these technologies are used responsibly requires continuous oversight, stakeholder engagement, and the establishment of ethical frameworks that evolve alongside technological advances.

Personalising leadership training with AI

AI enables the customisation of leadership development programmes to address the unique needs, goals, and contexts of individual leaders. By analysing a wide range of performance data, behavioural patterns, and preferred learning styles, AI systems can generate tailored prompts that recommend highly relevant training modules, suggest curated reading materials or interactive resources, and provide real-time feedback while tracking progress over time.

This personalised approach ensures that leaders are not presented with one-size-fits-all content, but instead receive targeted development aligned with their current capabilities and future aspirations. For instance, an AI platform might identify a leader's need to strengthen strategic thinking and prompt engagement with case studies, simulations, or scenario-based exercises directly relevant to that focus area.

Additionally, AI can adapt the learning path dynamically based on ongoing input and progress, allowing for continuous refinement of the development plan. By doing so, it supports sustained skill acquisition, improves knowledge retention, and boosts overall leadership effectiveness. In a fast-evolving organisational landscape, AI-driven personalisation offers a powerful, data-informed strategy to develop confident, competent, and agile leaders.

Case Study: AI-powered leadership development

Emma, a newly appointed department head at a university, wants to improve her strategic decision-making and team management skills. She enrols in an AI-powered leadership development programme that adapts to her learning style and goals.

1. **Assessment & goal setting:**
   - Emma completes an initial self-assessment and provides insights into her leadership experience.
   - AI analyses her responses and identifies areas for improvement, such as conflict resolution and data-driven decision-making.
2. **Tailored learning pathways:**
   - The AI system recommends a series of microlearning modules, including case studies of effective academic leadership.
   - It suggests articles, videos, and research papers based on her preferred learning format.
3. **Real-time AI-generated prompts:**
   - Before her next team meeting, AI prompts Emma with a case study on managing faculty disputes.
   - She receives scenario-based quizzes that challenge her to apply different conflict resolution techniques.
4. **Progress tracking & feedback:**
   - AI provides Emma with performance analytics, showing her strengths and areas that need further focus.
   - It recommends a mentorship opportunity by connecting her with experienced academic leaders.
5. **Continuous adaptation:**
   - As Emma progresses, AI refines her learning path, introducing more advanced topics and leadership simulations.

Using this AI-driven personalisation, Emma receives a customised leadership training experience that enhances her skills efficiently, aligning with her career aspirations and institutional needs.

>  **Activity: Exploring data-driven decision making**
>
> Reflect on your current leadership practices and identify areas where AI could be utilised to enhance your decision-making and development. Consider the following:
>
> - Select a specific leadership task or challenge and create a ready-made prompt for ChatGPT (or a similar AI tool) to help address that challenge.
> - How can AI assist you in refining your leadership strategies?
> - What ethical considerations must be kept in mind when using AI in leadership development?

Summary

The intersection of e-leadership and AI represents a dynamic and evolving space where technology meets human insight. Generative AI tools - particularly ready-made prompts - are increasingly being used by leaders to enhance decision-making, communication, and strategic vision across both virtual and traditional educational settings. These tools offer structured insights that support leadership development, institutional planning, and skill refinement. As AI becomes more embedded in organisational life, it offers innovative solutions to complex problems while simultaneously presenting ethical, moral, and practical challenges.

Leaders must navigate concerns about reduced human interaction and the risk of overreliance on technology, emphasising the need for comprehensive training and the inclusion of diverse perspectives in AI design and implementation. Ethical considerations - such as data privacy, algorithmic bias, and the transparency of AI-generated recommendations - are paramount.

Ultimately, AI should act as a complement to human judgment, not a replacement. Leadership remains the guiding force in shaping inclusive, ethical, and future-oriented cultures that draw on the strengths of both human and artificial intelligence.

9 RAISING STANDARDS

David Hall

Introduction

The pursuit of quality management in education has evolved into a central concern, influencing outcomes at the level of both student achievement and institutional reputation. Historically, the focus has shifted from the rudimentary goal of broadening access to education towards the more complex task of maintaining consistent, high standards of teaching, learning, and support across increasingly diverse contexts. Quality, in this regard, emerges as a multifaceted construct, rooted in historical developments and operationalised through mechanisms of quality assurance and continuous improvement. Whether manifest in a primary school's aspiration to achieve excellence in literacy, or in a university's endeavour to attain accreditation and enhance its position in global rankings, the drive towards quality must be understood not only as a strategic necessity but also as an ethical commitment.

This chapter:

- Traces the historical evolution of quality management in education, highlighting key milestones and frameworks.
- Differentiates between quality control and assurance, and explores their roles in maintaining and improving standards.
- Examines continuous improvement models, including reflective practices and iterative methodologies.
- Analyses the use of data in driving quality improvements across educational contexts.
- Engages with stakeholder perspectives, understanding how feedback informs quality management.
- Addresses sector-specific challenges, applying tailored strategies for quality management in primary, secondary, further and higher education.

The importance of quality in education

Quality in education has long been a critical focus of educational leadership and policy. It encompasses many dimensions, from ensuring equitable access to fostering excellence in outcomes. Debates around educational quality are central to reforms and initiatives designed to enhance teaching, learning, and institutional performance. Defining, managing, and measuring quality in education is essential yet complex. It demands a cautious and subtle approach based around a thorough understanding of stakeholder needs and contextual differences. As institutes continue to adapt their educational frameworks, maintaining a balance between access and excellence will remain central to ensuring equitable and impactful education for all.

Defining quality in educational contexts

The concept of quality in education is often context-dependent. Harvey & Green (1993) proposed a framework identifying five conceptions of quality: as exceptional (exceeding standards), as perfection (flawless delivery), as fitness for purpose (meeting goals), as value for money, and as transformation (impact on learners). These conceptions underline that quality may be viewed differently depending on priorities, such as access, equity, or excellence.

In the UK, the *Education Inspection Framework* introduced by Ofsted places emphasis on the quality of education through a focus on curriculum intent, implementation, and impact (Ofsted, 2023). Access to high-quality education is also a critical aspect of social justice, as noted by Ball (2021), who highlights the persistent inequalities affecting disadvantaged communities. Quality, therefore, requires not only the delivery of excellent educational experiences but also addressing systemic barriers to access.

The importance of managing quality for stakeholders

Quality management in education holds immense importance for a diverse range of stakeholders. For students, high-quality education fosters personal and academic growth, equipping them with the skills necessary for lifelong learning and employment (Hargreaves & Fullan, 2015). Parents rely on quality assurance mechanisms to ensure that schools meet their expectations for the welfare and development of their children. Employers also have a vested interest in educational quality. As noted by Tomlinson (2021), the alignment between educational outcomes and labour market needs is crucial in addressing skills gaps in an evolving economy. Society also benefits broadly from high-quality education through the cultivation of informed citizens, reduced inequality, and economic growth.

Given these varying interests, managing quality requires transparent and participatory processes, involving all stakeholders in setting standards, evaluating outcomes, and implementing improvements. Quality assurance frameworks, such as the UK's *Quality Code for Higher Education* (QAA, 2018), serve as benchmarks to guide institutions in maintaining accountability and consistency.

Challenges in measuring and ensuring quality across diverse contexts

Measuring and ensuring quality in education is an inherently complex task, particularly across the increasingly diverse landscape of educational provision. Education systems operate across a wide range of contexts, encompassing state-maintained schools, independent and private institutions, further education colleges, adult and community learning centres, and higher education establishments. Each of these settings serves different learner populations, operates under different regulatory frameworks, and often pursues distinct educational aims. For example, while schools are often measured by student attainment and progress in core subjects, universities are judged by research excellence, graduate outcomes, and metrics such as student satisfaction and employability.

One enduring challenge is the tendency toward standardised metrics, particularly high-stakes testing regimes, as dominant indicators of quality. Ball (2021) critiques this overreliance on standardised assessments for reducing the richness of the curriculum and sidelining broader educational aims such as the development of creativity, critical thinking, and emotional intelligence. Such approaches risk promoting surface-level accountability while neglecting the deeper, more holistic purposes of education.

Socio-economic disparities across and within regions significantly complicate efforts to assess and assure quality equitably. Institutions serving disadvantaged communities may face resource constraints, staffing challenges, and complex learner needs, which are not easily captured in standard quality indicators. These contextual variables demand more nuanced and responsive quality assurance frameworks that go beyond one-size-fits-all solutions.

The growing internationalisation of education adds further layers of complexity. Institutions are increasingly expected to align with both national quality standards and global benchmarks, as they compete for international students, collaborate across borders, and participate in global rankings. Altbach & Knight (2007) highlight the tensions that arise when institutions attempt to balance responsiveness to local community needs with the pressures of international competitiveness. Ensuring quality in this context requires not only robust internal processes and external regulation, but also culturally sensitive and context-aware approaches to evaluation.

Finally, the rapid pace of technological change and the rise of new modes of learning - including online, hybrid, and micro-credential-based education - are challenging traditional definitions and measures of quality. These developments call for continuous innovation in quality assurance systems that are flexible, inclusive, and future-oriented.

Historical perspectives on quality in education

Quality in education has evolved as a dynamic concept, reflecting societal, economic, and cultural priorities over time. From the industrial era's focus on standardisation and workforce preparation to the 21st century's emphasis on equity, lifelong learning, and adaptability, educational quality remains central to development.

The evolution of quality concepts in education

The industrial era marked the onset of mass education, driven by the need for a literate and skilled workforce. During this period, quality was often equated with uniformity and standardisation, reflecting industrial values of efficiency and productivity (Labaree, 2010). The curriculum prioritised basic literacy, numeracy, and vocational skills, with little attention to critical thinking or creativity. Quality mechanisms during this time were rudimentary, focusing on compliance with prescribed curricula and standardised assessments.

The mid-20th century saw a gradual shift as nations recognised the role of education in fostering social mobility and democracy. Dewey (1938) critiqued the mechanistic approach to education, advocating for experiential learning and the development of the whole child. In the UK, the *Butler Education Act* of 1944 introduced the tripartite system, which aimed to balance access and quality through grammar schools, secondary modern schools, and technical institutions. However, inequalities in access persisted, leading to debates over educational equity and the comprehensive school movement of the 1960s and 1970s.

The late 20th century witnessed a global transition towards outcome-based education. Governments began to emphasise accountability, driven by concerns over international competitiveness in a globalised economy. In the UK, the introduction of the National Curriculum in 1988 and Ofsted's establishment in 1992 signalled a more structured approach to quality. These measures sought to balance standardisation with the growing need for diverse and inclusive educational practices.

Milestones in global education quality initiatives

Global initiatives have significantly influenced the conceptualisation and measurement of quality in education. UNESCO's *Education for All* (EFA) campaign, launched in 1990, marked a global commitment to universal access to basic education. However, as enrolment rates increased, attention shifted to ensuring that access translated into meaningful learning experiences. UNESCO's *Global Education Monitoring Report* (2024) highlights the persistent challenge of improving learning outcomes because the education that many children receive is not always up to standard.

The Organisation for Economic Co-operation and Development (OECD) has played a pivotal role in redefining quality through its *Programme for International Student Assessment* (PISA). Introduced in 2000, PISA assesses 15-year-olds' abilities in reading, mathematics, and science, providing comparative data on educational performance across countries. The focus on critical thinking and problem-solving has encouraged nations, including the UK, to re-evaluate their curricula and teaching methods (OECD, 2023).

These global frameworks have not only provided benchmarks for assessing quality but also catalysed educational reforms. For example, PISA results have prompted UK policymakers to prioritise areas such as teacher development and curriculum coherence. The *Sustainable Development Goals* (SDG4), adopted in 2015, further reinforce the global commitment to equitable, inclusive, and high-quality education for all.

The shift from quantity (access) to quality (learning outcomes)

Historically, the expansion of educational access was a primary goal, particularly in the post-war era. In the UK, initiatives such as the expansion of comprehensive schooling and the introduction of free higher education sought to democratise education. By the late 20th century, however, it became evident that access alone was insufficient. Studies revealed that disparities in learning outcomes persisted, even among students with similar access to educational resources (Ball, 2021).

The focus on quality emerged as a response to these disparities. Quality in education now encompasses not only academic achievement but also broader competencies, including social skills, digital literacy, and adaptability. In the UK, this shift is reflected in the *Education Inspection Framework* introduced by Ofsted in 2019, which emphasises curriculum intent, implementation, and impact over simple attainment metrics (Ofsted, 2023).

Internationally, the transition from access to quality is also evident. For instance, the World Bank's *Learning Poverty* initiative (2022) highlights that while enrolment rates have improved globally, many children lack basic literacy skills by age 10. This focus on learning outcomes aligns with a broader understanding of education as a tool for personal and societal development.

Quality control - ensuring consistency

Quality control plays a significant role in education for maintaining high standards and ensuring that institutions meet the needs of students, parents, employers, and society. Originating in industrial practices, the concept of quality control has been adapted to the education sector, evolving to encompass various methods aimed at ensuring consistency, accountability, and excellence.

Origins and definitions of quality control in education

Quality control, as a concept, emerged from the industrial sector in the early 20th century, driven by the need to standardise processes and outputs. Pioneers like W. Edwards Deming and Joseph Juran established principles that have since been applied in various sectors, including education. It is a systematic process used to ensure that products, services, or operations meet established standards and requirements (Deming et al., 2018). It involves monitoring, testing, and inspecting various components of a process to identify and address defects or inconsistencies. In education, quality control refers to the mechanisms, such as assessments, inspections, and audits, used to ensure that teaching, learning, and administrative practices adhere to set benchmarks, ultimately aiming to deliver consistent and high-quality outcomes (Ishikawa, 1985; Mukhopadhyay, 2020).

Information

Educators often find the concept of *quality processes* challenging because these processes can feel abstract and disconnected from the immediate, student-focused outcomes they prioritise. Many view quality as inherently tied to teaching and learning rather than as a systematic, measurable framework.

The adaptation of quality control principles in education was formalised with the rise of *outcome-based education* (OBE) in the late 20th century. This approach emphasised measurable standards and performance indicators, ensuring that institutions delivered on their objectives. Ofsted (Office for Standards in Education), established in 1992, and the Quality Assurance Agency for Higher Education (QAA), established in 1997, are two examples of UK agencies that exemplify the operationalisation of quality control in education.

Practical applications in schools and universities

Inspections remain one of the most prominent methods of quality control in UK schools. Ofsted inspections evaluate schools based on their curriculum, teaching quality, leadership, and student outcomes. Inspections provide detailed reports that inform stakeholders about an institute's strengths and areas for improvement (Ofsted, 2023). While inspections aim to ensure consistency and encourage best practices, they also place significant pressure on institutes to perform well within specific frameworks.

Audits

Audits are widely used across the education sector as a tool for quality and accountability. In schools, further education, and higher education alike, audits involve systematic reviews of institutional processes to ensure that standards are being met and maintained. These reviews may be conducted by external bodies - such as Ofsted for schools and further education providers, or the Quality Assurance Agency (QAA) for higher education institutions - as well as through internally driven mechanisms.

External audits often assess areas such as curriculum planning, teaching and learning quality, assessment practices, learner progress, and the effectiveness of leadership and management. For example, Ofsted inspections in schools consider not only academic outcomes but also factors such as safeguarding, personal development, and the wider curriculum. Similarly, in higher education, QAA reviews evaluate whether institutions meet national expectations for academic standards and the quality of the student experience (QAA, 2018).

Internal audits and reviews are also crucial, helping institutions to monitor their own practices and implement continuous improvement. These typically involve self-assessment reports, peer reviews, programme evaluations, and stakeholder feedback mechanisms. Regardless of the setting, effective audit processes rely on transparency, evidence-based evaluation, and a commitment to reflective practice.

Audits play a vital role in promoting accountability, identifying areas for development, and maintaining public trust in educational provision. However, critics caution against overly bureaucratic or compliance-driven approaches, warning that these can lead to a tick-box culture that stifles innovation and professional autonomy.

Accreditation

Accreditation is another critical application of quality control. Accrediting bodies evaluate institutions and specific programmes to certify that they meet established standards. In the UK, organisations like the British Accreditation Council (BAC) and subject-specific accrediting bodies (e.g., the General Medical Council) play key roles in maintaining quality. Accreditation serves as a hallmark of credibility and ensures that qualifications are recognised both nationally and internationally.

Performance metrics and league tables

Performance metrics, often published in league tables, are a modern extension of quality control. By comparing institutions based on measurable indicators like exam results, student satisfaction, and employability rates, these tables aim to guide stakeholders and foster competition. While controversial, they have become a significant factor influencing institutional priorities and public perception (Ball, 2021).

Strengths of traditional quality control methods

Standardisation and accountability

Traditional quality control methods ensure that schools, colleges and universities adhere to national standards, promoting consistency and equity. Standardised inspections and audits provide clear benchmarks, enabling comparisons across institutions (Harvey, 2002).

Transparency for stakeholders

Tools like Ofsted reports and QAA reviews offer transparency to students, parents, and employers, empowering them to make informed decisions. This fosters trust in the education system and holds institutions accountable for their performance.

Continuous improvement

By identifying areas for development, inspections, and audits encourage schools and universities to adopt best practices. Regular reviews provide institutions with actionable feedback, fostering a culture of continuous improvement (Ofsted, 2023).

Global recognition

Accreditation enhances the international credibility of UK qualifications, facilitating student mobility and employability in global markets.

Limitations of quality control

Overemphasis on measurable outcomes

Traditional quality control methods often prioritise easily measurable outcomes, such as exam results or graduate employment rates, over holistic educational goals. Critics argue that this focus narrows the curriculum and undermines creativity, critical thinking, and broader personal development (Biesta, 2015).

Pressure and compliance culture

Inspections and audits can create a compliance-driven culture, where institutions prioritise meeting criteria over genuine innovation. High-stakes inspections, in particular, have been associated with stress among teachers and school leaders (Wilkins, 2015).

One-size-fits-all approaches

Standardised frameworks may fail to account for the unique contexts and challenges of different institutions. For example, schools serving disadvantaged communities may struggle to meet benchmarks despite implementing effective practices tailored to their students' needs (Ball, 2021).

Resource intensiveness

Quality control processes can be resource-intensive, requiring significant time and funding. Smaller institutions or those with limited budgets may find it challenging to implement and sustain these processes effectively.

Potential for gaming the system

Metrics-based evaluations can incentivise institutions to focus on superficial improvements rather than substantive change. For example, universities may prioritise improving league table rankings over addressing systemic issues in teaching and learning (Grosemans et al., 2020).

After-the-event

Quality control is inherently reactive, addressing issues only after they arise, which limits its ability to prevent problems and proactively drive improvement.

Evolving approaches to quality control

Recognising the limitations of traditional methods, the UK education sector is increasingly exploring alternative approaches to quality control. Collaborative models, such as peer reviews and participatory evaluations, are gaining traction. These methods emphasise professional development and shared accountability, fostering a more inclusive and supportive approach to quality assurance (Hargreaves & Fullan, 2015).

The integration of technology also offers new possibilities. Learning analytics, for instance, enable institutions to monitor student progress in real-time, identifying areas for intervention and improvement. Digital platforms like the *Teaching Excellence and Student Outcomes Framework* (TEF) also provide more nuanced insights into teaching quality and student experience (Office for Students, 2023).

Quality assurance - a proactive approach

Quality assurance (QA) offers a stark contrast to quality control (QC). Whereas QC is a reactive process involving inspections and audits, QA emphasises proactive measures to build robust processes that prevent defects or deviations from quality standards. Ideally, it serves to prevent problems from arising in the first place. QA integrates systematic planning, monitoring, and continuous improvement within educational institutions. It promotes a culture of accountability and shared responsibility among staff and stakeholders, prioritising processes over outcomes. According to Harvey & Green (1993), QA redefines quality as a dynamic and evolving concept, moving beyond compliance to focus on improvement and innovation.

QA policies and frameworks in practice

ISO standards and EFQM

International frameworks, such as the *ISO 21001:2018 standard for Educational Organisations*, provide a universal model for QA in education. This standard emphasises learner satisfaction, stakeholder engagement, and effective management systems.

The *European Foundation for Quality Management* (EFQM) framework further advances QA by promoting a holistic approach to organisational excellence. It integrates leadership, strategy, and stakeholder engagement with performance metrics. Studies highlight how EFQM encourages educational institutions to adopt transformative practices that benefit learners and society.

Accreditation and monitoring bodies

Accreditation bodies like Ofsted (UK) and TEQSA (Australia) play pivotal roles in QA. Ofsted's school inspection framework, updated in 2019, focuses on the quality of education, personal development, and leadership (Ofsted, 2023). It shifts attention from exam outcomes to curriculum design and delivery, a hallmark of QA-oriented practices. Meanwhile, TEQSA exemplifies QA in higher education, mandating evidence-based reporting and institutional self-assessment.

Globally, the *Programme for International Student Assessment* (PISA) administered by the OECD serves as a QA tool, benchmarking educational systems worldwide. PISA's focus on critical thinking and problem-solving underscores the shift from rote learning to competency-based education.

Embedding quality assurance into institutional culture

Embedding QA into an institution's culture requires leadership commitment, staff collaboration, and stakeholder involvement. Senge's concept of the "learning organisation" is particularly relevant, as it advocates for adaptability, shared vision, and team learning (Senge, 2006). Educational leaders must create environments where QA is seen as integral to daily operations rather than an external imposition.

Leadership and governance

Effective leadership is the cornerstone of QA. Leaders must articulate a clear vision for quality, fostering an ethos of trust and transparency. According to Fullan (2020), change leadership in education necessitates aligning QA initiatives with institutional goals, ensuring that all staff understand and support quality objectives.

Governance structures, including quality committees and advisory boards, provide platforms for collaborative decision-making. Regular training and professional development help staff internalise QA principles, enabling them to align their practices with institutional standards.

Stakeholder engagement

Engaging stakeholders, including students, parents, and employers, is crucial for sustaining QA. Mechanisms like feedback surveys and focus groups empower stakeholders to contribute to quality enhancement. For instance, universities that integrate alumni and employer feedback into curriculum development demonstrate a commitment to continuous improvement.

Monitoring and continuous improvement

QA thrives on a cyclical process of planning, implementation, evaluation, and refinement. Institutions must establish key performance indicators (KPIs) aligned with their mission and strategic objectives. Regular audits and self-assessments enable organisations to track progress and identify areas for improvement.

Technology also plays a vital role. Learning management systems (LMS) and data analytics provide real-time insights into student engagement and performance, facilitating evidence-based decision-making. For example, the use of predictive analytics in QA enables institutions to identify at-risk students and intervene proactively.

Strengths and limitations of quality assurance

QA offers several advantages over QC, including fostering a culture of continuous improvement and addressing issues before they escalate. It aligns institutional goals with broader societal needs, ensuring education remains relevant and responsive.

However, QA is not without challenges. Implementing QA frameworks requires significant resources, including time, funding, and expertise. Resistance to change among staff can also hinder QA adoption. The subjective nature of "quality" in education further complicates the development of universal standards, as highlighted by Biesta (2015).

Despite these limitations, the proactive nature of QA positions it as a superior approach to ensuring educational excellence. By embedding QA into institutional culture, educational organisations can build resilience and adaptability in an ever-changing landscape.

Continuous improvement in education

Continuous improvement in education refers to an ongoing effort to enhance the quality of educational processes, outcomes, and overall institutional performance. This model is grounded in systematic and iterative methodologies aimed at fostering positive change through feedback and data-driven decision-making.

The approach is cyclical, focusing on small, manageable changes that can collectively lead to significant advancements over time. This continuous improvement process encourages iterative progress rather than sudden, large-scale changes that may be difficult to sustain. For instance, in primary schools, a teacher might implement weekly formative assessments, using these insights to adjust their teaching strategies and address pupils' evolving needs. This approach ensures that learning is always aligned with the current understanding and capabilities of students. In secondary schools, a more data-driven approach could be adopted, where student feedback, performance metrics, and learning outcomes are regularly reviewed to refine curriculum content and teaching methods. This ongoing process of evaluation and adaptation fosters a dynamic learning environment that evolves in response to both student progress and emerging educational trends.

The role of continuous improvement models

Continuous improvement models provide structured frameworks for managing change and enhancing institutional practices.

The Plan-Do-Check-Act (PDCA) Cycle

One of the most widely used models in education is the Plan-Do-Check-Act (PDCA) cycle, also known as the Deming Cycle after W. Edwards Deming (Deming et al., 2018). This cyclical process consists of four stages: planning, implementing, checking or evaluating, and acting to refine practices (Figure 9.1).

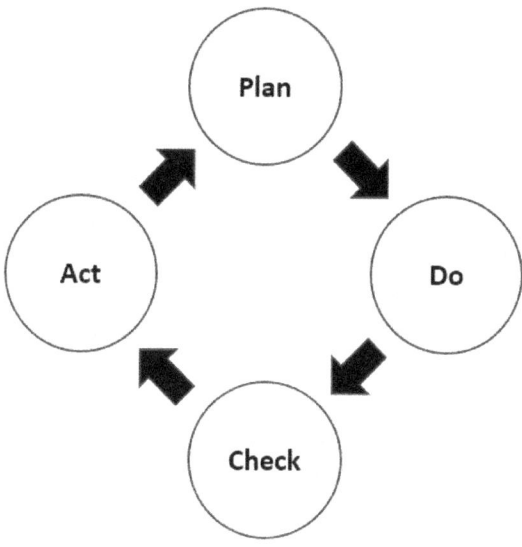

Figure 9.1 - The Plan-Do-Check-Act cycle

The PDCA cycle is adaptable to various educational settings, allowing schools and universities to systematically assess their processes and implement improvements based on reflective evaluation.

1. **Plan**: In the planning phase, institutions identify specific areas for improvement, set measurable objectives, and define strategies. This involves gathering data from stakeholders, including students, staff, and parents, to inform decisions. Planning is not just about setting goals; it requires aligning these goals with broader institutional and educational priorities.

2. **Do**: The "Do" phase focuses on implementing the planned actions. This phase requires stakeholders' active participation and effective communication to ensure that strategies are executed properly. It is also essential to monitor the process closely during this phase to address any challenges or unexpected issues promptly.

3. **Check**: This phase involves evaluating the effectiveness of the implemented changes. Evaluation can be done through qualitative or quantitative data, such as student feedback, academic results, or teacher performance assessments. Regular assessments help identify whether the changes have achieved the desired improvements.

4. **Act**: Finally, the "Act" phase involves refining processes and strategies based on the evaluation findings. This may include adjustments to improve effectiveness or scaling successful changes across the institution. The process then restarts, fostering a continuous cycle of improvement.

The PDCA model encourages a culture of reflection, data analysis, and iterative changes that ensure schools and universities remain responsive to the evolving needs of their students and communities.

The Kaizen model

Kaizen, a Japanese term meaning "continuous improvement" (step-by-step), is centred on incremental changes that result in long-term gains. In educational settings, Kaizen encourages small, manageable changes that accumulate over time, leading to significant improvements.

Kaizen can be mistaken for a tick-box exercise if its principles are misunderstood or poorly implemented. When organisations adopt Kaizen superficially, they may reduce it to a series of checklist tasks aimed at compliance or meeting short-term goals, rather than fostering a genuine culture of continuous improvement. This misapplication often happens when leaders fail to engage employees meaningfully, overlook the importance of incremental and sustainable change, or focus solely on meeting external standards rather than internalising the philosophy of improvement.

True Kaizen involves active participation, problem-solving, and collaboration across all organisational levels, aiming to embed improvement into daily practices. Misinterpreting it as a procedural requirement undermines its effectiveness and can lead to frustration among staff, who may perceive initiatives as burdensome rather than beneficial. Studies on organisational behaviour have highlighted that the success of Kaizen relies heavily on leadership commitment, employee empowerment, and a clear understanding of its long-term value, rather than treating it as a one-off activity (Imai, 1986; Liker, 2004).

An example of Kaizen in education can be seen in the approach taken by several UK schools that implement continuous improvements in teaching methods. By focusing on gradual enhancements, such as introducing new teaching strategies one lesson at a time or adapting classroom management practices incrementally, teachers and leaders have fostered a more collaborative and effective learning environment. Kaizen allows for ongoing monitoring and reflection, ensuring that improvements are sustainable.

Case Study: Improving literacy in a primary school

In a UK primary school, the implementation of Kaizen principles significantly improved literacy outcomes by introducing small, incremental changes in teaching practices. Teachers focused on evidence-based strategies such as peer assessments, where pupils reviewed each other's work, and regular feedback sessions that provided constructive guidance. These strategies allowed pupils to reflect on their progress and areas for improvement in a low-pressure environment. Over time, the cumulative effect of these small adjustments led to a noticeable rise in literacy achievement. The case exemplifies how Kaizen's focus on continual, manageable improvements can lead to sustainable success in education. This approach also fostered a culture of collaboration among teachers and pupils, reinforcing a shared commitment to growth and development.

Building a culture of improvement

For continuous improvement to be successful, it must be embedded within the institutional culture. This requires a strong commitment from leadership, effective staff training, and the promotion of reflective practice across all levels of the institution.

Staff training

Staff training is central to continuous improvement, as educators must be equipped with the skills and knowledge to engage in reflective practice and to implement improvement strategies effectively. Research by Hargreaves (2003) highlights the importance of professional development programmes that promote collaboration among teachers and encourage the sharing of best practices. Training should not only focus on technical skills but also foster a growth mindset, where staff view challenges as opportunities to learn and improve.

Training should align with the institutional vision and strategic goals. For example, if an institution is focusing on improving student engagement or outcomes in specific subject areas, training should target those needs, providing educators with the tools and methodologies necessary to achieve those goals. The success of training initiatives depends on clear objectives, ongoing support, and the active involvement of all stakeholders in the improvement process.

Reflective practice

Reflective practice, a concept popularised by Schön (2008), is another key component in building a culture of continuous improvement. This approach encourages educators to critically assess their teaching practices, identify areas of strength, and recognise opportunities for growth. Teachers who engage in reflective practice are more likely to adapt their approaches based on student needs, resulting in more effective and personalised teaching strategies.

Reflection can take many forms, from formalised peer reviews and collaborative teaching sessions to informal self-assessments. Reflection fosters professional growth, increases job satisfaction, and directly contributes to better educational outcomes for students.

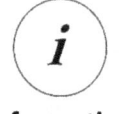

One common method of reflection is a reflective journal where teachers regularly document their thoughts, experiences, challenges, and successes related to their teaching practice. By writing about specific lessons, student interactions, or classroom dynamics, teachers can critically analyse what worked well and what could be improved.

Innovation

Fostering a culture of innovation is equally important for driving continuous improvement. Innovation involves adopting new ideas, technologies, and approaches to enhance educational processes and outcomes. Schools, colleges and universities that prioritise innovation are better equipped to respond to the challenges of a rapidly changing educational landscape, including the rise of digital learning tools, the increasing diversity of student populations, and the need for flexible and adaptive curricula.

Leadership plays a crucial role in encouraging innovation by creating a supportive environment where staff are encouraged to experiment with new methods and learn from their successes and failures. Embracing a "fail-forward" mentality can inspire creativity and motivate staff to take risks that ultimately lead to positive changes.

Fail-forward is a mindset where failure is viewed not as a setback, but as a learning opportunity that drives progress. It treats mistakes as steps toward growth, innovation, and improvement - encouraging quick adaptation and resilience.

In leadership and education, this approach empowers staff to take creative risks without fear of blame, knowing that even unsuccessful attempts contribute to shared learning and future success.

Data-driven improvement

Data-driven improvement refers to the practice of using quantitative and qualitative data to make informed decisions that enhance teaching, learning, and administrative processes in educational institutions. In the UK, the increased availability of digital tools and platforms has made it easier to collect and analyse data, allowing institutes to use evidence to improve student outcomes, refine curricula, and enhance operational efficiency. This approach emphasises the importance of continuous assessment, real-time feedback, and targeted interventions to ensure that educational strategies are not only effective but also adaptable to changing needs.

Using data analytics to improve practice

Data analytics plays a central role in transforming education by providing insights that inform instructional practices and organisational strategies. By analysing student achievement data, teachers and school leaders can identify patterns in student performance, uncover gaps in learning, and assess the effectiveness of teaching methodologies. This allows for the implementation of targeted interventions aimed at supporting struggling students or extending the learning of high-achieving individuals. For instance, a school may analyse standardised test results alongside classroom assessments to identify specific areas where students are struggling, such as reading comprehension or mathematical problem-solving.

At the administrative level, data-driven approaches can optimise resource allocation and improve decision-making processes. By tracking attendance, dropout rates, and retention patterns, educational leaders can identify issues such as low student engagement or barriers to retention, implementing corrective measures to address these challenges. Data analytics can also be used to assess the effectiveness of teaching staff, enabling the identification of professional development opportunities and areas where further support is needed. This data-based approach helps to ensure that decisions are grounded in evidence rather than assumptions, fostering a culture of accountability and continuous improvement (Schildkamp et al., 2012).

Gathering and analysing data

Effective quality assurance relies on a combination of tools and methods tailored to the unique needs of educational institutions. Balancing quantitative and qualitative approaches ensures a holistic understanding of quality dynamics, enabling evidence-based improvements.

In addition to conventional, paper-based approaches, here are a number of commonly used methods for gathering quality assurance data:

1. Surveys and questionnaires.
2. Focus groups and interviews.
3. Observation checklists.
4. Learning analytics from digital platforms.
5. Benchmarking.
6. Feedback forms.
7. Audits and inspections.
8. Student performance metrics.
9. Peer reviews.
10. Ethnographic and case studies.

Appendix 6 outlines the tools associated with each method, and how the data might be analysed.

Other tools

Cause-and-effect diagram

The cause-and-effect diagram (Figure 9.2), also known as a fishbone or Ishikawa diagram, is a powerful visual tool used in quality management to identify, organise, and analyse the potential causes of a specific problem or effect. Developed by Japanese professor Kaoru Ishikawa in the 1960s, it has become a widely adopted method in various industries, including education, healthcare, manufacturing, and service sectors. The diagram's structure resembles a fishbone, with the "head" representing the problem or effect being studied and the "bones" representing the different categories of potential causes. By systematically categorising the possible causes, such as people, processes, equipment, materials, and environment, the diagram helps teams visually organise complex issues and trace the root causes. In education, for instance, it can be used to diagnose challenges such as low student performance, ineffective teaching methods, or operational inefficiencies. The diagram promotes thorough analysis, encouraging teams to think critically about contributing factors and supporting the development of effective solutions.

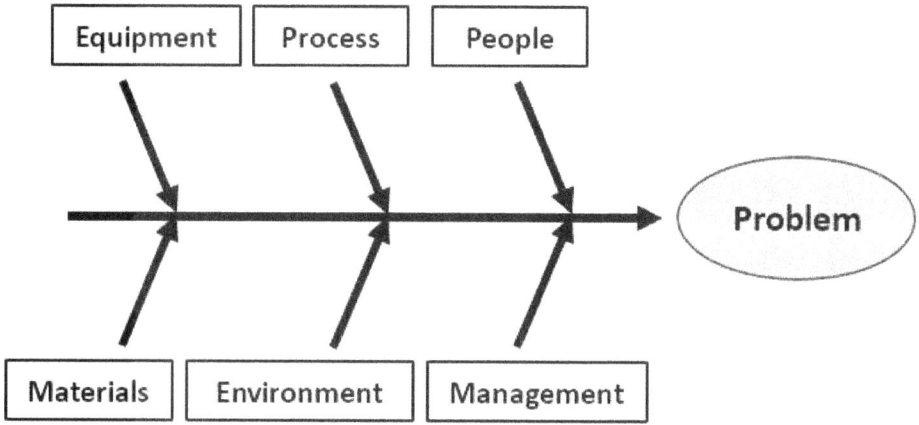

Figure 9.2 - Cause-and-effect diagram

 A secondary school looks to remedy the issue of low student engagement in a number of lessons. It uses a cause-and-effect approach to identify potential causes.

1. Equipment
- Old interactive whiteboards that don't function properly.
- Insufficient laptops for group work.
- Slow internet affecting use of online tools.

2. Process
- Over-reliance on teacher-led instruction.
- Lack of variety in lesson activities.
- Inconsistent use of formative assessment to guide teaching.

3. People
- Teachers not confident using digital tools.
- Students lacking motivation or confidence.
- Teaching assistants not always effectively deployed.

4. Materials
- Textbooks not aligned with student interests.

- Outdated resources lacking relevance to real-life contexts.
- Worksheets not differentiated for different ability levels.

5. Environment
- Overcrowded classrooms.
- Disruptive noise levels from nearby rooms.
- Limited access to stimulating displays or subject-specific environments.

6. Management
- Lack of CPD focused on engaging teaching strategies.
- No clear expectations around lesson planning or student participation.
- Limited student voice in curriculum and lesson design.

Once the causes are mapped out, the leadership team or department heads can identify priority areas for action - such as investing in updated equipment, offering training in active learning strategies, or creating a student-led curriculum review panel.

In the above example, a Pareto analysis might be used to decide which areas should be given the highest priority for action.

Pareto analysis

Pareto analysis is a decision-making tool that helps identify the most significant factors contributing to a problem or achieving an outcome. Rooted in the Pareto Principle (also known as the 80/20 rule), it suggests that roughly 80% of results come from 20% of causes. This principle, introduced by economist Vilfredo Pareto, was later adapted for quality management by Joseph M. Juran.

The analysis involves categorising and prioritising issues to focus on the few key causes that will yield the greatest impact when addressed. It is commonly represented using a Pareto Chart (bar graph) showing frequency or impact ordered from highest to lowest.

In an educational context, Pareto Analysis can be applied to:

- *Student performance*: Identifying which 20% of teaching methods or curriculum issues lead to 80% of learning difficulties.
- *Resource allocation*: Focusing budgets or professional development on areas with the highest impact on outcomes.
- *Administrative issues*: Addressing the most frequent complaints or bottlenecks in processes like admissions or assessment.

Figure 9.3 shows an example of a Pareto Chart displaying the causes of low scores in a secondary school history test.

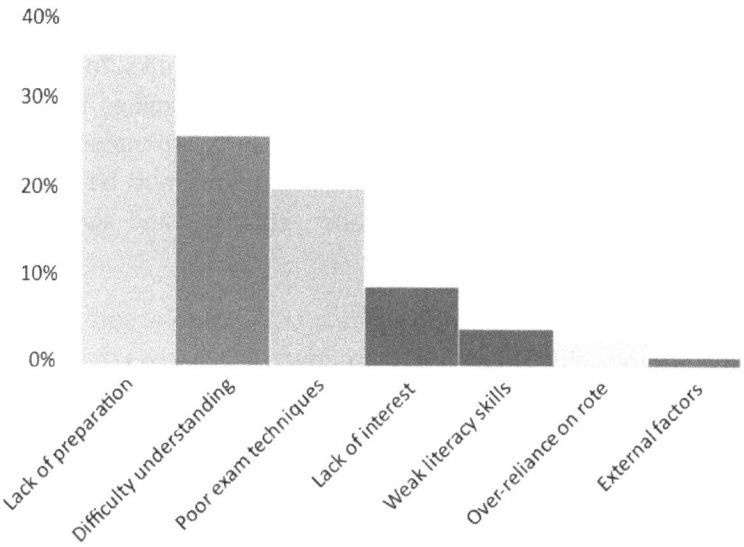

Figure 9.3 - Pareto chart for a history test

The top three causes - lack of preparation, difficulty understanding the topic, and poor exam techniques - together represent 83% of the problem. Focussing attention on remedying these three causes will therefore provide the most efficient remedy.

Information — The 80/20 rule also shows that attempting to resolve the top causes may take only 20% of the time taken to address all issues. Focussing on lesser causes may therefore be extremely inefficient and not a worthwhile investment.

Ethical considerations in data use

While data-driven improvement offers significant benefits, it also raises several ethical considerations that must be carefully addressed to ensure that data is used responsibly and equitably. One of the primary concerns is privacy. Educational data, particularly when it pertains to students, is often sensitive and must be handled in compliance with regulations such as the *General Data Protection Regulation* (GDPR) in the UK. Schools and universities must ensure that student data is anonymised and protected from unauthorised access, with clear policies on how data is collected, stored, and used. Additionally, students and parents should be informed about how their data will be used, and consent should be obtained where necessary.

Equity is another critical ethical consideration. When using data to drive improvements, it is essential to ensure that the interventions and strategies developed do not inadvertently exacerbate existing inequalities. For example, if data shows that certain demographic groups are underperforming, it is important to ensure that the solutions implemented do not disproportionately benefit certain students while neglecting others. Educational institutions must be mindful of issues such as socio-economic background, gender, ethnicity, and special educational needs when analysing and acting on data.

Inclusion must be prioritised when using data analytics to ensure that all students have an equal opportunity to succeed. Data-driven approaches should not reinforce stereotypes or biases but should instead support the development of inclusive practices that accommodate diverse learning needs. For instance, when identifying students at risk of falling behind, schools should consider factors such as language barriers, learning disabilities, and mental health challenges to ensure that interventions are appropriately tailored to support each student's unique circumstances (Bishop & Larsen, 2020).

Total Quality Management

Total Quality Management (TQM) builds on the foundational principles of quality control (QC) and quality assurance (QA) by expanding its focus from merely ensuring compliance with standards to creating a culture of holistic, continuous improvement throughout an organisation. Unlike traditional quality control, which tends to focus on identifying and correcting defects, TQM emphasises a proactive, all-encompassing approach to enhancing quality at every level of the organisation. It encourages active engagement from all stakeholders - staff, leadership, students and others - in the ongoing pursuit of quality, recognising that every individual's contribution is crucial to overall success.

TQM integrates key QA principles with proactive strategies such as staff empowerment, customer-centricity, and process optimisation, making quality improvement an integral part of day-to-day operations rather than a separate or reactive function. By promoting open communication, teamwork, and shared responsibility, TQM fosters an environment where continuous learning and improvement are at the core of organisational culture. This approach goes beyond simply meeting regulatory or compliance standards, encouraging a long-term commitment to excellence that drives sustained organisational growth and innovation. Through TQM, organisations strive not only to meet stakeholder expectations but to exceed them, building a competitive advantage and achieving lasting success.

Key components of TQM

The key components of TQM include:

Customer focus

TQM emphasises identifying and exceeding customer expectations as central to organisational success. In education, "customers" might include students, parents, employers, and society, all of whom demand high-quality learning outcomes. Understanding their needs and feedback ensures that services align with expectations.

Information: Educators often struggle with the notion of treating students and other stakeholders as *customers* due to the unique nature of education as a transformative process rather than a transactional service. This perspective can clash with the customer-centric approach common in business, as it risks oversimplifying education into a commodity, undermining intrinsic values such as intellectual growth and ethical development. Educators may feel that focusing too heavily on customer satisfaction could detract from academic rigor, institutional autonomy, and the long-term societal goals of education. Balancing these concerns remains a challenge in education policy and practice.

Staff involvement

Engaging all employees in quality efforts fosters a sense of ownership and accountability. TQM encourages staff at every level to participate in decision-making, quality measurement, and improvement activities, leading to empowered and motivated teams.

This requires a change in management emphasis which flips the traditional organisational structure and places staff at the top of the hierarchy, with managers and leaders positioned as facilitators and supporters who serve the staff (Figure 9.4). This model underscores the importance of front-line staff, who are often closest to the issues and opportunities within an organisation, as key drivers of success (Oakland et al., 2020).

Figure 9.4 - The flipped TQM structure

Process-centred

Efficient processes are the backbone of TQM. By mapping workflows and identifying inefficiencies, organisations ensure consistent and predictable outcomes. In schools, colleges or universities, this might involve refining assessment procedures or administrative systems.

Strategic and systematic approach

Aligning quality objectives with overall organisational goals ensures that improvement initiatives contribute directly to long-term success. This includes integrating quality measures into strategic planning and maintaining a systematic approach to evaluating their progress.

Continuous improvement

TQM commits to ongoing refinement of processes and outcomes. This principle recognises that quality is not a static goal but requires adaptive and iterative efforts, often using methodologies such as PDCA (Plan-Do-Check-Act). Continuous improvement in TQM (Figure 9.5) operates on the principle that significant advancements are achieved through a series of small, incremental steps rather than drastic overhauls. This approach, often exemplified by the Japanese concept of *Kaizen*, emphasises sustained progress by engaging all staff in identifying and implementing minor changes that collectively lead to substantial improvements over time.

Figure 9.5 - Continuous improvement

By focusing on small-scale, actionable initiatives, organisations can avoid the disruption associated with large-scale change, ensuring improvements are manageable, measurable, and continuous. Such a method fosters a culture of innovation, collaboration, and accountability, where staff actively participate in refining processes and addressing challenges.

Communication

Open, transparent communication within and outside the organisation is essential to TQM. Internally, it ensures that employees understand and align with goals; externally, it fosters trust with stakeholders by showcasing accountability and responsiveness.

Fact-based decision-making

Data-driven strategies underpin effective quality management. TQM encourages using metrics, analytics, and feedback to guide decisions rather than relying on intuition, ensuring that improvements are evidence-based and measurable.

Adoption of TQM in education

In the UK, TQM principles have been integrated into some quality assurance frameworks and initiatives such as Ofsted inspections. Self-evaluation systems reflect elements of TQM by encouraging continuous improvement and accountability. However, full adoption of TQM in education has been limited due to challenges such as bureaucratic constraints, management structures, cultural attitudes, resource availability, and resistance to change (Sallis, 2014).

In higher education, universities apply quality principles to improve student experience, enhance research output, and achieve global competitiveness. This aligns with the UK's *Teaching Excellence Framework* (TEF) by linking funding to measurable quality outcomes. However, one should not mistake the effective use of quality assurance with the notion that such quality is 'total'.

Question — Does your institute practice TQM? Are you sure? Some organisations may believe they are practicing TQM when they are not genuinely adhering to all its principles. This misinterpretation often occurs when organisations focus narrowly on isolated quality initiatives, such as meeting compliance standards or conducting periodic audits, without embedding all the necessary key elements of TQM.

Challenges in applying TQM to education

TQM in education, despite its potential, faces significant challenges. The complexity of educational outcomes, encompassing academic excellence, social equity, and employability, often leads to conflicting objectives. Resistance to change is a major barrier, as implementing TQM demands substantial cultural and structural shifts that educators and administrators may oppose. Additionally, resource limitations hinder its success, as effective TQM requires considerable investment in training, technology, and infrastructure, which are often restricted by tight budgets (Mukhopadhyay, 2020).

Six Sigma

Introduction to Six Sigma

Six Sigma is a rigorous quality management methodology that originated in the manufacturing sector and is designed to reduce defects and optimise performance. Developed by Motorola in the 1980s, Six Sigma aspires to achieve near-perfect outcomes, setting a statistical benchmark of no more than 3.4 defects per million opportunities (DPMO). Rooted in data-driven analysis, it employs a suite of structured tools and techniques to identify inefficiencies, eliminate waste, and streamline processes.

Although traditionally associated with industrial and corporate environments, the core principles of Six Sigma have found growing relevance in the field of education. In the UK and beyond, educational institutions are increasingly applying Six Sigma methodologies to improve administrative operations, enhance teaching quality, and drive better student outcomes (Cudney et al., 2018). This cross-sector application demonstrates Six Sigma's versatility and its potential to foster a culture of continuous improvement in diverse professional settings.

The core principles of Six Sigma

Six Sigma is grounded in the *DMAIC framework* (Define, Measure, Analyse, Improve, Control), which offers a structured approach to problem-solving:

Define: Identify goals, stakeholders, and desired outcomes.

Measure: Gather data to understand current performance.

Analyse: Identify root causes of problems using tools like Pareto analysis or Ishikawa diagrams.

Improve: Implement solutions to address root causes.

Control: Sustain improvements through monitoring and feedback loops.

Six Sigma in educational contexts

Applying Six Sigma to education requires adapting its tools and methodologies to academic and administrative settings. Its application can span across primary, secondary, further and higher education.

Administrative efficiency

In UK institutes, Six Sigma has been used to streamline administrative processes such as admissions, timetabling, and resource allocation. For instance, by analysing bottlenecks in the admissions process, institutions can reduce processing times, enhance communication with applicants, and improve overall satisfaction.

Teaching and learning

Six Sigma principles help educators design interventions that target specific learning outcomes. For example, measuring student performance data can highlight inconsistencies in teaching methods, allowing institutions to develop targeted professional development programmes for staff. By addressing variability in teaching quality, schools can achieve more consistent student outcomes.

Student support services

Universities in the UK have employed Six Sigma to enhance student retention and well-being services. By analysing patterns of student dropouts, institutions can identify early warning signs and implement proactive measures, such as mentoring programmes or academic support sessions.

Challenges of adopting Six Sigma in education

Despite its potential benefits, implementing Six Sigma in education faces unique challenges:

Cultural resistance: Educators may resist adopting a methodology perceived as industrial or corporate in nature, viewing it as incompatible with the holistic mission of education.

Complexity of outcomes: Unlike manufacturing, where outputs are tangible and measurable, education involves nuanced and multifaceted outcomes such as personal development, social skills, and academic knowledge.

Resource constraints: Effective Six Sigma implementation requires expertise, training, and technology, which may strain budgets, particularly in underfunded schools.

Success stories in UK education

A notable case of Six Sigma's application in UK education involved a higher education institution addressing delays in feedback on student assignments. By using the DMAIC process, the university analysed root causes, such as inefficient workflows and unclear marking criteria. Implementing standardised marking rubrics and automating administrative tasks resulted in a 40% reduction in turnaround time, enhancing student satisfaction.

Future prospects

The increasing availability of educational data and digital tools, such as learning management systems and AI-driven analytics, positions Six Sigma as a valuable approach for quality management in education. As the UK education system continues to face pressure to enhance outcomes amidst funding challenges, Six Sigma provides a pathway for achieving efficiency and effectiveness.

Future directions in quality management

As education systems around the world continue to evolve, the future of quality management is being shaped by technological advancements, globalisation, and changing expectations of stakeholders. The integration of artificial intelligence (AI), big data, and digital learning platforms is transforming how quality is assessed and enhanced, while globalisation presents both challenges and opportunities for maintaining high educational standards internationally. As the expectations of students and other stakeholders grow, there is a clear trend towards deeper engagement in quality improvement processes.

The impact of technology

Technology has already had a profound effect on education, and its role in quality management is becoming increasingly significant. Artificial intelligence (AI) and big data are reshaping how educational institutions assess and improve the quality of teaching, learning, and administrative functions. AI, for instance, can be used to personalise learning experiences, offering tailored content and feedback that is aligned with students' individual needs and learning styles. This personalised approach is not only improving student engagement but also supporting better learning outcomes, which can be integrated into broader quality assurance frameworks.

In addition to AI, big data is playing a central role in quality management by providing schools and universities with a wealth of information on student performance, attendance, engagement, and even mental health. By harnessing this data, institutions can identify patterns and potential issues early on, enabling proactive interventions and more effective resource allocation (Siemens, 2020). Digital learning platforms, such as learning management systems (LMS), are facilitating continuous feedback and assessment, enabling both students and teachers to monitor progress and identify areas for improvement in real time.

Information

Big data refers to the vast amounts of digital information that educational institutions collect and store about various aspects of their operations - especially student-related data. This includes: Performance data (e.g. grades, assessments, test scores); Attendance records; Engagement metrics (e.g. participation in online platforms); and Wellbeing indicators, such as patterns that may signal mental health concerns (e.g. sudden drops in engagement or attendance).

What makes it "big" is not just the volume of data, but also its variety, velocity (how fast it's generated), and complexity.

Globalisation and quality management in international education

As education becomes more globalised, the demand for consistent and high-quality education across borders is growing. International students now represent a significant proportion of university enrolments, and institutions are increasingly held to international standards of quality management. However, this expansion of international education brings about challenges related to maintaining consistent quality across different cultural, social, and economic contexts. Globalisation requires educational institutions to be adaptable and responsive to diverse student needs while ensuring that they meet national and international accreditation standards (Hénard & Roseveare, 2012).

To address these challenges, many institutions are turning to international quality frameworks and benchmarks, such as those provided by the European Higher Education Area (EHEA) and the Organisation for Economic Co-operation and Development (OECD). These frameworks encourage educational institutions to adopt practices that ensure comparability and credibility of qualifications across borders, facilitating student mobility and recognition of qualifications (OECD, 2020). Globalisation calls for educational institutions to embrace international collaboration and cross-cultural competencies in their teaching and quality management strategies to accommodate diverse student populations.

Trends in student and stakeholder engagement

A significant trend in the future of quality management is the increasing engagement of students and other stakeholders, such as parents, employers, and industry leaders, in the quality improvement process. In the past, quality management was often a top-down process led by administrators and external bodies. Today, however, there is a growing emphasis on stakeholder-driven approaches, where the perspectives and feedback of students, faculty, and external partners are seen as critical to ensuring the relevance and effectiveness of educational programmes.

Student engagement in particular is becoming a key factor in improving quality. Research suggests that when students are actively involved in the design and evaluation of their educational experience, they are more likely to succeed and feel satisfied with their learning outcomes (Serrano et al., 2024). Initiatives such as student satisfaction surveys, course evaluations, and focus groups are now standard practices in many institutions, allowing students to have a voice in shaping the quality of their education.

Similarly, engagement with employers and industry leaders is increasingly seen as vital to ensuring that educational programmes meet the demands of the job market. Institutions are increasingly working with businesses to align curricula with industry needs, ensuring that students graduate with the skills and competencies that are most valued by employers (Knight & Yorke, 2003). This collaborative approach not only enhances the quality of education but also improves employability outcomes for students.

Quality in action - bridging theory and practice

The theoretical principles of quality assurance (QA) often provide a framework for guiding excellence in teaching, learning, and institutional management. However, the true impact of quality lies in the ability to translate these principles into practical, repeatable, and documented procedures. It is important therefore to move beyond abstract concepts of quality to the creation of practical systems that can be monitored, refined, and shared.

For processes that recur every semester or academic year - such as curriculum delivery, student assessment, and staff appraisals - it is essential to establish clear, actionable, standardised procedures that not only ensure consistency, but also embed a culture of continuous improvement within the institution. For instance, the annual review of student assessments or the periodic observation of teaching should follow a structured approach, with detailed protocols outlining steps, roles, and timelines.

Documented procedures serve as a repository of institutional knowledge, ensuring that even as staff change, the organisation maintains its standards. Such procedures enable transparency and accountability, as they provide a clear record of actions and decisions.

 **Case Study: Examples of quality processes**

1. Higher Education: Course validation

Stage 1: Proposal submission

A course team submits a detailed proposal for a new course. The proposal, based on an approved template, includes, learning outcomes, objectives, curriculum content, assessment methods, and resource requirements.

Stage 2: Scrutiny by validation panel

A panel of internal and external experts reviews the proposal, evaluates its relevance, feasibility, and alignment with institutional and national standards.

Stage 3: Feedback and revision

The panel provides detailed feedback, and the course team makes revisions.

Stage 4: Final approval

Once the revised proposal is approved, the course is scheduled for periodic review after 3-5 years.

2. Assessment moderation in GCSE exams

Stage 1: Sampling: A senior examiner reviews a random sample of marked scripts from each teacher to ensure marking consistency.

Stage 2: Double marking: For borderline grades, two assessors independently review scripts.

Stage 3: Standardisation meetings: Teachers attend pre-assessment meetings to review marking schemes and discuss ambiguous cases.

Stage 4: Appeals: Students can appeal grades, prompting a re-marking process.

3. Lesson planning and peer observation in a primary school

Stage 1: Lesson planning submission: Teachers submit weekly lesson plans to senior leaders for review, ensuring alignment with curriculum objectives and differentiation for diverse learner needs.

Stage 2: Peer observation schedule: A termly observation schedule pairs teachers, allowing them to observe each other's lessons. This process focuses on specific areas such as behaviour management, use of questioning, and differentiation strategies.

Stage 3: Observation framework: Observers use a standardised observation form with pre-defined criteria to evaluate lesson delivery (e.g., clarity of objectives, pupil engagement, resource use).

Stage 4: Post-observation discussion: Observers provide feedback during a debrief session, highlighting strengths and areas for improvement, and suggesting actionable strategies.

Stage 5: Action points and follow-up: Teachers set action points based on feedback and may request further observations to track their progress.

Stage 6: Sharing best practices: Effective strategies observed during lessons are shared at staff meetings or included in a best-practice repository.

Standardised documentation used:
- Reviewed lesson plans.
- Observation forms with feedback.
- Meeting notes from post-observation discussions.
- Best-practice examples shared during training sessions.

Managing quality in education

Effective quality management in education relies on clear standards, robust processes, and the engagement of all stakeholders. While primary and secondary sectors focus on measurable outcomes aligned with national goals, FE and HE adopt more complex, stakeholder-driven approaches. Across all levels, the integration of reflective practices and a focus on enhancement rather than mere compliance can drive sustainable improvements.

Primary and secondary education

In primary and secondary schools, quality management primarily involves adherence to national standards set by regulatory bodies such as Ofsted. Schools focus on curriculum delivery, teaching effectiveness, and student outcomes, often evaluated through inspections and performance metrics like standard attainment tests (Sats) and examination results. QA processes here are tightly linked to leadership practices, including setting strategic goals, staff development, and stakeholder engagement.

Schools often establish internal systems for monitoring progress, such as tracking student performance against benchmarks and implementing intervention strategies where necessary. Leadership in these sectors, often the preserve of the senior management team (SMT), must also account for diverse student needs and community contexts, making QA both operationally and socially responsive.

Further education (FE)

In FE, quality management involves balancing vocational and academic offerings while meeting regulatory standards such as those outlined by the Education and Skills Funding Agency (ESFA). FE institutions often engage with stakeholders such as employers to ensure their programmes align with workforce needs. The dual focus on academic outcomes and employability requires tailored QA processes that evaluate both pedagogical quality and practical relevance (FE News, 2022).

The Quality Department in FE institutions typically oversees these efforts, ensuring compliance with frameworks like the *Common Inspection Framework* while driving internal reviews and quality enhancement initiatives. Student feedback plays a significant role in shaping QA strategies, reflecting the sector's commitment to inclusivity and responsiveness.

Higher Education (HE)

HE institutions operate within a highly regulated yet autonomous environment. QA in HE is guided by frameworks like the *UK Quality Code for Higher Education*, developed by the Quality Assurance Agency (QAA). This framework sets expectations for academic standards and student experiences while encouraging innovation and institutional distinctiveness (QAA, 2024).

The QA processes in HE include programme validation, periodic review, and external peer assessment, emphasising academic rigour and the employability of graduates. Institutions often have dedicated Quality Departments tasked with aligning their practices to regulatory requirements and fostering a culture of continuous improvement. The integration of student voices and external referencing, such as through external examiners, ensures that QA is both rigorous and inclusive.

Activity: Quality in practice

This activity aims to reinforce the theoretical knowledge presented in the chapter and also encourages practical application and critical thinking about quality management in education.

Consider the following scenarios (or a scenario that presents itself in your own organisation):

1. **Primary education:** A primary school struggles with inconsistent teaching quality across year groups, leading to varying pupil outcomes.
2. **Secondary education:** A secondary school introduces new technology to improve teaching and learning but faces resistance from staff and uneven implementation.
3. **Higher education:** A university department seeks to balance academic freedom with adherence to accreditation requirements while addressing declining student satisfaction scores.

Select one scenario and design a quality management intervention plan addressing the challenges posed. Your plan should include the following elements:

- **Objective:** What specific quality issue is being addressed?
- **Tools and methods:** What tools (e.g., surveys, data analytics, feedback mechanisms) will you use to gather, present and analyse data?
- **Stakeholder engagement:** How will you involve students, staff, and other stakeholders in the process?
- **Implementation strategy:** Outline steps to implement the intervention, using quality management principles from the chapter.

Points to consider:

- How do quality assurance and quality control differ in your proposed intervention?
- What role does continuous improvement play in addressing the case study challenges?
- How can feedback loops be incorporated to ensure ongoing refinement of the intervention?

  Can you make use of any existing quality procedures used by your organisation?

Summary

Quality in education is dynamic and multifaceted, requiring thoughtful integration of frameworks, tools, and stakeholder perspectives to achieve meaningful and sustained impact.

Quality management has evolved from early accountability-focused models to more sophisticated frameworks that integrate reflective practices, continuous improvement, and data-driven decision-making. Today's quality systems are based around the reactive approach of *Quality Control* - focused on maintaining consistency – and *Quality Assurance*, which emphasises proactive measures to foster institutional growth and adaptability.

Key concepts such as continuous improvement models (e.g., iterative cycles like Plan-Do-Check-Act) can enhance teaching, learning, and administration. Data analytics are critical in driving informed decisions while also acknowledging the ethical considerations surrounding its use, particularly regarding privacy and equity.

Total Quality Management (TQM) and *Six Sigma*, originally developed for business contexts, have found applications in pockets of education, particularly in enhancing institutional processes and improving outcomes. While these frameworks align naturally with business priorities like efficiency and customer satisfaction, educational institutions have adapted some of their principles to address challenges such as enhancing teaching quality, streamlining administrative processes, and promoting student success. Their emphasis on continuous improvement and data-driven decision-making resonates with efforts to create effective and accountable educational environments (Mukhopadhyay, 2020; Antony, 2019).

In recent times, stakeholder engagement has emerged as a cornerstone of quality management, with feedback from students, staff, and external bodies providing valuable insights for refining practices.

10 BRINGING IT ALL TOGETHER - TOM'S STORY

David Hall

Introduction

In this final chapter, we meet Tom, an accomplished educational leader whose story brings to life the key institutional functions explored throughout this volume. Drawing on his extensive experience as a teacher, middle leader, and curriculum strategist in secondary education, Tom offers a grounded and reflective account of what it means to lead with clarity, purpose, and integrity. His narrative highlights how effective leadership in areas such as curriculum design, assessment, staff development, and quality assurance is not merely about systems and structures - but about people, values, and informed decision-making. Through his journey, Tom illustrates how the principles and strategies discussed in this book come together in practice, providing a compelling example of leadership that is strategic, evidence-informed, and deeply human.

Meet Tom Bennett

Tom Bennett's professional journey spans over two decades and reflects a deep-rooted commitment to improving teaching, learning, and leadership in secondary education. Currently Head of Subject for Humanities at a large comprehensive in the North West of England, Tom has steadily progressed through various leadership roles, each shaped by his passion for curriculum innovation, staff development, and inclusive teaching.

Tom began his career as a history teacher in a diverse urban secondary known for its inclusive ethos and strong community ties. Early in his teaching, Tom displayed a knack for bringing history alive through creative pedagogy and enquiry-based learning. His lessons often blended traditional narratives with contemporary themes, encouraging critical thinking and deeper engagement. Within a few years, he was appointed Key Stage 3 Coordinator for History, where he led the development of a thematic curriculum that was both knowledge-rich and responsive to students' lived experiences.

It was during this period that Tom became interested in the broader structures shaping learning. He took on a cross-departmental role as Teaching and Learning Champion, working with colleagues across subjects to implement evidence-informed strategies. His initiatives included peer coaching, lesson study cycles, and a programme of short, focused CPD sessions that soon became embedded in the school's professional development culture. Encouraged by the impact of his work, Tom undertook a Master's degree in Leadership and Management in Education, focusing on strategies for building high-trust, collaborative staff teams.

Tom's next move brought him to his current position where he is able to focus on his true passion - developing curriculum and teaching within the humanities. As Head of Subject, he leads a large team of teachers delivering history, geography, and RE. He is known for building high-functioning teams through coaching, mentoring, and distributive leadership practices. Under his guidance, the department has embedded curriculum maps that prioritise disciplinary thinking, cultural literacy, and the development of transferable skills. Tom is also a key member of the school's Teaching and Learning Strategy Group and has contributed to whole-school initiatives on metacognition, literacy, and student voice.

An advocate for continuous learning, Tom regularly contributes to regional networks for subject leaders and has presented at education conferences on topics such as curriculum leadership and staff motivation. He is currently part of a local authority working party exploring the use of artificial intelligence to support personalised learning in Key Stage 4. Tom remains committed to growing others, and many of his team have progressed to middle and senior leadership roles under his mentorship.

What sets Tom apart is his blend of strategic thinking, moral purpose, and hands-on leadership. Grounded in classroom practice but always looking to the bigger picture, he exemplifies the kind of leadership that bridges policy and pedagogy. His story offers a powerful example of how leaders can shape institutional functions - from curriculum and assessment to staff development and innovation - while staying rooted in the day-to-day reality of the school.

Shaping the curriculum

Throughout his career, Tom has developed a deep understanding of how curriculum shapes the educational experience - not just for learners but for staff, too. His approach to curriculum has evolved from focusing on content delivery to leading more holistic and collaborative curriculum development processes.

Early in his career, Tom was given responsibility for refreshing the Key Stage 3 curriculum in his subject area, at a time when the school was undergoing a major reorganisation. With limited guidance but a great deal of enthusiasm, he concentrated on aligning content with national standards and assessments. However, he later came to realise that what he had designed was largely a collection of disconnected units. It was only after attending professional development sessions on curriculum theory that he began to appreciate curriculum as a *lived experience* and not just a product.

When he later became Head of Subject, Tom led a full curriculum review that was more strategically grounded. Drawing on the principles of the curriculum design cycle, he facilitated planning meetings that involved both early-career and experienced teachers, ensuring that curriculum intentions, implementation methods, and impact measures were clearly articulated. He began incorporating student voice, linking curriculum design to learner feedback, local context, and progression routes beyond GCSE. This shift toward shared curriculum leadership allowed his team to feel ownership of the process and contributed to a more cohesive curriculum model.

Tom also worked closely with senior leaders to align departmental plans with whole-school priorities. He valued the principal's role in giving curriculum leaders autonomy while providing clear accountability measures. This balance allowed Tom to take calculated risks, such as trialling interdisciplinary projects and introducing more flexible schemes of learning that supported cross-curricular links - especially in literacy and personal development.

More recently, Tom has begun mentoring new middle leaders across the school on curriculum planning, drawing attention to the importance of sequencing, cognitive load, and assessment for learning. He advocates for embedding curriculum conversations into routine departmental meetings, rather than treating them as annual or ad-hoc exercises.

Tom's comments

"Curriculum used to be something I wrote alone in the summer term. Now, it's a shared and ongoing conversation. I see curriculum as an evolving ecosystem that connects intent, practice, and learner outcomes. My best curriculum decisions have come not from working in isolation, but from listening carefully - to my team, to students, and to leaders across the school. I now start every new planning cycle with three simple questions: What's the purpose? Who's it for? And how will we know it's working?".

Effective assessment strategies

Tom has made steady progress in developing his assessment practice, although he recognises that this remains a growth area. Early in his teaching career, assessment was largely about compliance: inputting grades, ticking boxes, and meeting deadlines. Over time, he began to appreciate the importance of aligning assessments with learning outcomes, particularly after attending a cross-school professional development session on assessment for learning. This prompted him to rework some of his department's schemes of learning, ensuring that tasks genuinely assessed the skills and knowledge they were designed to develop.

As Head of Subject, Tom has introduced more structured internal moderation and peer review to promote consistency across the team. He has also encouraged the use of shared success criteria and common assessment frameworks, aiming to align more closely with national standards. Despite this, he still finds grading consistency challenging, especially in extended written work, where subjectivity sometimes creeps in. Managing the balance between formative and summative assessment also continues to stretch him - he's aware that some of his team default to 'marking everything' rather than using assessing more strategically.

Tom is beginning to experiment with technology-enhanced assessment, including the use of interactive quizzes and digital rubrics. However, uptake across his department is uneven, and he admits that more could be done to embed assessment tools that support both learning and efficiency.

Tom's comments

"I used to think assessment was about giving students a grade. Now I realise it's really about giving them direction. I'm getting better at building that into our systems, but we're not there yet. Some of the tech looks promising, and I've seen how it can streamline feedback, but change takes time - especially when everyone's already stretched. I've learned that making assessment meaningful is as much about culture as it is about tools. That's my next focus".

Harnessing E-Leadership and AI

Tom's school is only just beginning to explore the implications of e-leadership and artificial intelligence, and the terrain still feels uncertain. As a middle leader, Tom has started to see how digital platforms can streamline aspects of school leadership - from automated tracking of student progress to using analytics to identify gaps in attainment. He's also dabbled with AI-powered tools like adaptive learning apps and AI-generated feedback, although uptake across the department remains cautious.

In meetings with senior leadership, there's increasing talk about AI's potential for workload reduction, particularly in areas like report writing and intervention planning. Tom sees the potential but is wary. He's conscious that not all staff feel confident with the pace of technological change, and he worries that some of the solutions being trialled may create new issues - such as over-reliance on predictive grading or reduced professional judgment in assessment. He is also concerned about the possible abuse of AI leading to student plagiarism.

On the e-leadership front, Tom has embraced some aspects of digital collaboration. He now runs weekly planning meetings via Microsoft Teams, and uses cloud-based tools to monitor curriculum coverage and resource development. These changes have improved communication and allowed for greater flexibility, but he's mindful of digital fatigue and the risk of replacing meaningful dialogue with screen-based updates.

Ultimately, Tom recognises that both e-leadership and AI bring promise, but he believes a cautious, critically reflective approach is essential.

Tom's comments

"AI and e-leadership feel like the new frontier. There's definitely some potential - especially when it comes to reducing admin and improving insight - but there's also a real danger of rushing in without understanding the long-term impact. I've seen staff switch off when things get too tech-heavy, and I get it. The human side of leadership matters just as much. For now, I'd say we're exploring, learning, and trying to keep our eyes wide open".

Cultivating future leaders

Leadership development is not yet a formalised strand of Tom's school strategy, but coaching and mentoring are present in other guises. New teachers are routinely assigned mentors, and there is an established programme of peer observations and developmental conversations across departments. However, the use of coaching and mentoring to *specifically grow future leaders* remains underdeveloped.

Tom himself benefited from an informal mentoring relationship early in his leadership journey, but there was no structure or follow-up beyond the initial transition into post. He has since tried to replicate that support for junior colleagues, offering feedback and encouragement in a more ad-hoc way. Some of these interactions take on a coaching tone, particularly when helping others reflect on their aspirations and strengths - but these moments tend to be spontaneous rather than strategic.

The school does have a professional development policy that highlights pathways to leadership roles, but there is currently no embedded framework or model for coaching aspiring leaders. Conversations about leadership styles, career progression, or leadership-specific mentoring are rare, and there is little evaluation of how current mentoring practices impact readiness for leadership roles.

While there is goodwill and a general openness to supporting colleagues, Tom recognises that a more strategic and structured approach would be needed to grow and retain leadership talent across the school.

Tom's comments

"We've got some great mentoring going on, especially for new staff - and I'd say there's a definite culture of support. But when it comes to actually developing future leaders, I don't think we've joined the dots yet. If someone's got potential, they tend to be noticed and encouraged, but there's no programme or model behind it. Coaching could really help us unlock that next level - we just haven't made that shift yet".

Managing professional development

Professional development is a real strength of Tom's school, where CPD is seen not just as an operational necessity but as a core value. The school maintains a clear and structured approach to CPD, ensuring that opportunities are available to all staff, not just teachers. There is a strong emphasis on continuous learning, with regular INSET days, external training courses, and collaborative CPD across departments.

Tom's own journey illustrates this commitment. He was fully sponsored by the school to undertake a master's degree in education, with leadership as a key strand. He recalls how the senior team actively encouraged staff to pursue higher-level qualifications, professional accreditations, and specialist courses. This encouragement extended beyond financial support and included time allocation, peer discussion groups, and regular check-ins to share progress and challenges.

The school also promotes internal CPD through communities of practice, twilight sessions, and a culture of sharing. Staff often lead workshops or action research projects, and outcomes are disseminated across the school to maximise impact. There's an expectation that CPD will not only support individual growth but also feed back into team and whole-school improvement.

While the school has not yet formalised succession planning or leadership pipelines, its investment in high-quality CPD means that staff feel valued and equipped to take on new responsibilities. For Tom, this strong foundation in professional development provided the springboard for his transition into leadership.

Tom's comments

"I've always felt fortunate to be in a school that takes CPD seriously. When I started my masters, the support was incredible - not just financially, but in terms of time, interest, and encouragement. CPD isn't just a tick-box here; it's embedded in how we grow as a staff. It really shaped my confidence to step up into leadership".

Quality and standards

Tom's school is well-regarded in the community and performs reasonably well in inspections, but its approach to quality and standards is largely reactive. Rather than embedding a culture of continuous quality assurance and improvement, much of the effort tends to be cyclical, prompted by external inspections or accreditation visits. When inspectors highlight areas for improvement, the school is quick to act, but there is limited follow-through or systematic embedding of quality principles between visits.

There's an awareness among senior leaders that a more proactive quality assurance model would benefit the school, but competing priorities and a lack of dedicated structures for quality management mean that consistent, data-driven improvement is not yet the norm. While teachers like Tom contribute to internal moderation and some reflective practices, there's little sense of a unified or strategic quality framework in place. Approaches such as Total Quality Management (TQM) or Six Sigma are not part of the school's discourse.

Tom observes that while individual departments sometimes engage in improvement planning, these efforts are fragmented and often disconnected from a wider institutional vision of quality. In practice, bridging the gap between inspection-led compliance and sustained improvement remains an ongoing challenge.

Tom's comments

"If I'm honest, our focus on quality really ramps up when inspections are on the horizon - then we're all over it. Between inspections, it's not a major part of our day-to-day thinking. We don't have a clear system for quality assurance or ongoing improvement. There's potential there, definitely, but we're a long way off perfecting it".

Enhancing teaching and learning

Tom speaks with confidence about the school's commitment to high-quality teaching and learning, which he sees as one of its greatest strengths. There is a clear strategic vision in place, consistently communicated by senior leaders, that emphasises inclusive practice, high expectations, and continuous improvement. This vision is backed by a culture that actively supports collaborative working across departments and year groups, with frequent opportunities for teachers to share practice, observe one another, and trial new approaches.

There's also strong encouragement for teacher leadership. Many staff members take responsibility for subject areas, projects, or pedagogical initiatives, contributing to a sense of ownership over teaching and learning. CPD sessions often focus on evidence-informed strategies and inclusive classroom practice, and there is a healthy culture of experimentation and reflection. In particular, the school's focus on equitable learning experiences for all students, regardless of background or ability, has been championed by both middle and senior leaders.

Tom's comments

"I like to believe this is one of our major strengths. We're not perfect, but our teachers really care about their craft, and about each other. There's a shared commitment to getting better, together. We support one another, challenge one another, and celebrate the wins in the classroom, no matter how small. Teaching and learning *is* the heartbeat of our school".

Inspiring and engaging staff

As Head of Subject, Tom sees staff leadership as both a responsibility and a privilege. He understands that managing and motivating a team requires not only a grasp of the school's wider vision but also a strong sense of emotional intelligence and relational leadership. He places high value on knowing his team - their strengths, interests, pressures, and professional goals - and works to balance the needs of the department with the wellbeing and development of individual colleagues.

Tom describes himself as approachable, consistent, and supportive, and his colleagues often turn to him for advice and encouragement. He recognises the importance of clear communication and shared leadership, making space for team members to contribute ideas and lead initiatives. While he admits he's still learning, particularly when it comes to handling difficult conversations or challenging underperformance, he feels increasingly confident in his role. He is also aware of how his own motivation, values, and behaviours influence the team culture.

Although broader organisational HR systems and processes (such as recruitment, absence management or union relations) sit outside his remit, Tom remains mindful of how these systems impact morale and cohesion. Within his sphere of influence, he works hard to create an atmosphere of trust, shared purpose, and professional growth.

Tom's comments

"As a head of subject, I think I'm reasonably adept at leading and managing my staff. I try to keep things human. I check in regularly, I share the load, and I hope I inspire them by showing that I still care deeply about the classroom. I don't always get it right, but I do try to lead in a way that's honest, empathetic, and encouraging".

Evidence-based decision making

Tom's school values feedback and professional dialogue, and there is a strong culture of gathering qualitative data from both staff and students. Surveys, learning walks, student voice panels, and reflective meetings are common features of the school's approach to improvement. As a subject leader, Tom actively engages in these processes and appreciates the rich insights that emerge from qualitative conversations.

However, while qualitative data is plentiful, its interpretation and integration into decision-making is inconsistent. Often, valuable insights are noted but not systematically analysed or followed up. Tom sees room for more structured approaches to turning qualitative input into clear action plans, with follow-through and accountability.

When it comes to quantitative data, the school tends to focus narrowly on student grades and headline achievement measures. There is little use of wider data sets or deeper analysis techniques. Most staff, Tom admits, wouldn't feel confident analysing trends, applying statistical tools, or using data dashboards to inform planning. There is also limited professional development in this area, and few opportunities to learn how data can drive innovation in pedagogy or leadership.

Tom sees potential in building a stronger, more data-literate culture - but also recognises the need for training, time, and support to make that a reality.

Tom's comments

"We're quite good at collecting qualitative data. We ask the right questions, and people are usually willing to share their views. But we don't always take the next step. As for quantitative data, aside from student grades, it's almost non-existent. To be honest, most staff wouldn't know what to do with it! If we're serious about evidence-based practice, that's something we need to tackle".

Developing human resources

Tom plays an active role in human resource management within his subject area, working closely with senior leaders to ensure his team is well-supported, professionally developed, and equipped to thrive. The school has a strong track record in recruiting capable and committed staff, and Tom feels that new staff are well-matched to both the ethos of the school and the specific needs of the department.

Once staff are in post, Tom leads on mentoring, especially for early career teachers, and supports them through both formal and informal processes. He also leads appraisals for his team, identifying training needs and discussing career aspirations. CPD opportunities are often tailored based on these discussions, and Tom works to ensure workload is managed fairly and realistically within the team.

Staff well-being is taken seriously in the school, and Tom sees it as a personal responsibility to model balance, maintain open communication, and foster a collaborative and respectful culture. While broader HR systems are handled by senior leaders and the central office, Tom's local leadership has been key to building a stable and motivated team.

Tom's comments

"I think we do well when it comes to recruiting the right people. I've always been involved in selecting and mentoring staff in my department, and I lead on appraisals too. It's a part of the job I take seriously, making sure people feel valued, supported, and not overwhelmed. If our staff are thriving, so are the students and this is demonstrable in their attitude and performance".

Activity: Leadership and management self-audit

Reflecting on the themes presented through Tom's experiences, and the content of this book as a whole, complete the self-audit below to evaluate how effectively each area is developed in your own institution or context. Be honest and use this as a starting point for discussion or action planning.

Instructions:

For each leadership and management area below, rate your setting using the following scale: 1 = Not developed at all; 2 = Early stages of development; 3 = Developing, but inconsistent; 4 = Consistently effective in most areas; 5 = Strong and embedded practice across the setting.

Leadership/management area:

1. Shaping the curriculum.
2. Effective assessment strategies.
3. Enhancing teaching and learning.
4. Cultivating future leaders.
5. Inspiring and engaging staff.
6. Developing human resources.
7. Evidence-based decision making.
8. Harnessing E-leadership and AI.
9. Raising standards.

Reflection questions:

Which areas scored the highest, and why do you think that is?

Which areas scored the lowest? What are the barriers to progress in those areas?

Choose one low-scoring area. What would a small, achievable improvement look like in the near future?

How can you use your own role to influence change or improvement in one or more of these areas?

Summary

Tom's professional journey offers a grounded and insightful account of leadership and management in today's schools. As a head of subject in a busy secondary setting, he has encountered a wide spectrum of challenges and successes that reflect the everyday reality of educational leadership. His story reveals a strong commitment to staff development, teaching and learning, and student success, underpinned by a pragmatic and reflective approach.

Tom's department is particularly strong in areas like staff recruitment, professional development, and fostering a positive learning culture. He takes pride in mentoring new staff, leading appraisals, and managing workloads in a way that promotes well-being and motivation. Teaching and learning are other clear strengths, with a collaborative ethos and an inclusive vision that ensures all students have the chance to thrive.

While areas like coaching and mentoring for leadership, strategic quality management, and evidence-based decision-making are less developed across the school, Tom is aware of their importance and open about the need for growth. In particular, he identifies the potential of data and digital tools, though he notes that staff confidence and skills in these areas vary widely. He's also candid about the school's reactive stance on quality, typically responding to inspections rather than embedding a culture of continuous improvement.

Through his reflections, Tom demonstrates a thoughtful balance between realism and aspiration. He acknowledges where his school excels and where it needs to grow, and he remains committed to contributing to that growth. His story serves as a valuable reminder that leadership isn't just about grand visions. It's about getting the basics right, supporting others, and constantly learning from experience.

APPENDIX 1
ESTABLISHING LEARNING OBJECTIVES AND LEARNER NEEDS

Objectives, learning outcomes and standards

Learners pursue specific goals, such as acquiring knowledge and skills, meeting defined standards, and obtaining certification. Various terms are commonly used, often interchangeably, to denote the achievement of these goals in whole or in part. The most prominent terms include *objectives*, *outcomes*, and *standards*.

Learning outcomes

Learning outcomes describe the desired knowledge, skills, behaviours, or attitudes that learners are expected to achieve. As the term suggests, outcomes generally refer to the end results - or outputs - of a learning activity or course, and they are typically stated in broad terms. Spady (1993, p.10) summarises this as "the clearly defined outcomes we want all students to demonstrate when they leave school". In other words, outcomes refer to the tangible capabilities that students can apply in *real life* as a result of the learning process.

Here is a sample set of learning outcomes from a course on *Materials, Energy and Environment*:

By the end of the course, you should be able to:

- differentiate between material and product lifecycles and be able to discuss these in relation to the environment;
- explain limits and constraints to material selection and use, and the effect on the environment;
- rank common materials by production energy requirements and environmental impact;
- evaluate the influence and environmental impact that social and personal choices have on energy and material;
- interpret trends in energy and material use over time.

Learning outcomes are described using appropriate 'action' verbs (see Annex A). The complexity of the verb usually indicates the level of expertise required in achieving the outcome, as gauged by an appropriate learning taxonomy such as Bloom's Taxonomy (see Annex B).

Learning objectives

Learning objectives break down the steps required to achieve the intended learning outcomes. They are more explicit than outcomes and they place emphasis on the skills and competencies that need to be achieved. By way of example, the statutory framework for the early years foundation stage refers to them as 'stepping stones', and technician training courses often refer to them as 'enabling objectives'. They are sometimes called 'teacher inputs'. Objectives are usually recorded in documents such as course specifications and statements of objectives. The level of detail can vary considerably.

Objectives greatly assist the planning process for course planners and teachers, and help to focus on what will be evaluated. Marsh & Willis (2003, p.131) imply that "the foundation for well-planned teaching is, unquestionably, clearly stated objectives". However, learning objectives are considered by some to be too subjective (the end result of a value judgement on someone's part), too prescriptive (spontaneity withers and initiative is stifled) and too limiting (objectives may address specific areas but don't provide for a balanced, rounded education).

Objectives are often formulated as behavioural or instructional.

Behavioural objectives

Behavioural objectives focus on observable and measurable changes in student behaviour. They include three criteria: evidence of achievement, conditions of performance and acceptable levels of performance.

Evidence of achievement
Performance is stated in observable terms such as state, list, spell, describe, estimate, multiply and explain.
- Example: Multiply 2.32 by 4.25.

Conditions of performance
Any essential conditions of performance are stated.
- Example: Find the product of multiplying 2.32 x 4.25 to two decimal places, without the use of a calculator.

Acceptable levels of performance
Students can be deemed successful if they meet a minimum level of performance.
- Example: Correctly solve 8 out of 10 multiplication problems involving decimals stated to two decimal places.

Combining the three criteria then results in a detailed behavioural objective.

- Example: Correctly solve 8 out of 10 multiplication problems to two decimal places, without the use of a calculator.

Instructional objectives

Instructional objectives provide a clear pathway through a learning activity and specify distinctive, step changes in behaviour. They should be unambiguous and convey the minimum detail required to achieve the step. If such objectives have not already been compiled by a course designer, teachers might use them to expand on learning outcomes or higher-level objectives that have not been fully developed. They will also provide the basis for formative assessment and should therefore each be measurable.

Consider the learning outcome/objective: 'Students will be able to write a complete sentence'. Breaking this outcome down into more detailed steps might produce the following instructional objectives:

- Students are able to distinguish parts of speech.
- Students are able to distinguish subject and predicate.
- Students are able to distinguish a complete thought.
- Students are able to distinguish a clause.
- Students are able to distinguish a subordinate clause.
- Students are able to distinguish a phrase from a clause.

Classifying objectives (taxonomies)

Objectives are typically classified in terms of specific behaviours:
a. *Cognitive:* Intellectual processes such as perception, memory, judgement and reasoning.
b. *Affective:* Feeling, emotion, appreciation and valuing.
c. *Psychomotor:* Body movement associated with mental activity.

Standards

Learning that focuses on outcomes has been termed *Outcome Based Education* (OBE). OBE has attracted criticism for its over-emphasis on outcomes rather than processes, and some prefer a standards-based approach to ensure consistency in delivery and outcomes, particularly at national level. A recent example in the UK is the *National Standards for Literacy and Numeracy*, introduced in the first decade of the 21st century. Supporters of standards argue that they provide a common focus, clarify understanding and promote collective purpose. Opponents, however, suggest that standards are often too vague in content and, therefore, are not enduring.

Establishing learner needs

In order to design a curriculum, it is first necessary to establish the needs of the learner in terms of:

- the profile of the learners;
- what learners need to know (and what they already know).

A learning needs analysis is therefore a research project that determines the desired outcomes of a learning programme, and how best to match it to the characteristics of the intended learners. Like a research project, it will collect data using a range of survey instruments including:

- Interviews.
- Focus groups - a small group is selected to represent the interests of the larger group and a group interview is then conducted.
- Questionnaires.
- Observation.
- Inspection of documents (e.g. procedures for accomplishing tasks).
- Referral to subject matter experts.
- Action research (e.g. by school teachers).

Once analysed, the information gathered will generate a set of objectives, the accomplishment of which should achieve the desired learning outcomes.

Learner profile

Curriculum design must consider the profile of the learners for whom the curriculum is intended. It is important to know who your learners are, both as individuals and as a group. Knowledge of the learner will help to create conditions and environments that are conducive to learning. There are many factors that affect how a person learns from a particular learning environment.

Such factors may include ability levels and range, previous experiences, entry behaviours, academic motivation, personal learning styles, attitude toward the institute, interaction with the learning environment and group characteristics. This may seem like a lot of information to collect about learners, but it can aid immensely in providing more meaningful learning experiences for them. Some of it will already be known, but much of it will be elicited from learners, instructors and managers, and by visiting classrooms, training facilities and the learners' actual workplace. Other helpful methods include surveys, questionnaires and observation.

What learners need to know

Analysis of what learners need to know varies from the simple to the complex, depending on the context. For example, if you were asked to design a training programme to prepare staff in your organisation to undertake a new role, you would examine the requirements of that role in terms of the tasks that staff members would be expected to undertake. A task analysis would then reveal the knowledge and skills required.

If, however, you were asked to design a computing curriculum for primary school children you might find the prospect tricky. Even if you have a knowledge of computing yourself, you still need to decide what it is that the pupils themselves need to know. In this case, you would most likely refer to an established curriculum framework, i.e. the *National Curriculum for Computing*. Nevertheless, you may well ask yourself how the Computing curriculum was devised in the first place.

What learners need to know does, of course, depend on what they already know. Candidate learners may need to satisfy entry requirements or be subject to baseline testing.

Annex A - Action verbs for learning objectives

Abstract	Collect	Develop	Implement
Activate	Combine	Differentiate	Improve
Acquire	Compare	Direct	Increase
Adjust	Compute	Discuss	Infer
Analyse	Contrast	Discover	Integrate
Appraise	Complete	Discriminate	Interpret
Arrange	Compose	Distinguish	Introduce
Articulate	Compute	Draw	Investigate
Assemble	Conduct	Dramatise	Judge
Assess	Construct	Employ	Limit
Assist	Convert	Establish	List
Associate	Coordinate	Estimate	Locate
Breakdown	Count	Evaluate	Maintain
Build	Criticise	Examine	Manage
Calculate	Critique	Explain	Modify
Carry out	Debate	Explore	Name
Catalogue	Decrease	Express	Observe
Categorise	Define	Extrapolate	Operate
Change	Demonstrate	Formulate	Order
Check	Describe	Generalise	Organise
Cite	Design	Identify	Perform
Classify	Detect	Illustrate	Plan

Point	Reflect	Separate	Trace
Predict	Relate	Sequence	Track
Prepare	Remove	Sing	Train
Prescribe	Reorganise	Sketch	Transfer
Produce	Repair	Simplify	Translate
Propose	Repeat	Skim	Update
Question	Replace	Solve	Use
Rank	Report	Specify	Utilise
Rate	Reproduce	State	Verbalise
Read	Research	Structure	Verify
Recall	Restate	Summarise	Visualise
Recommend	Restructure	Supervise	Write
Recognise	Revise	Survey	
Reconstruct	Rewrite	Systematise	
Record	Schedule	Tabulate	
Recruit	Score	Test	
Reduce	Select	Theorise	

Annex B - Bloom's taxonomy of educational objectives

One of the most widely used ways of organising levels of expertise is according to *Bloom's Taxonomy of Educational Objectives*. Bloom's Taxonomy (Tables 1-3) uses a multi-tiered scale to express the level of expertise required to achieve each measurable student outcome. Organising measurable student outcomes in this way allows for the selection of appropriate classroom assessment techniques for a course.

There are three taxonomies. Which of the three to use for a given measurable student outcome depends upon the original goal to which the outcome is connected. There are knowledge-based goals, skills-based goals, and affective goals (values, attitudes, and interests); accordingly, there is a taxonomy for each. Within each taxonomy, levels of expertise are listed in order of increasing complexity. Measurable student outcomes that require the higher levels of expertise will require more sophisticated assessment techniques.

A knowledge-based goal requires that students learn certain facts and concepts. A skills-based goal requires that the students learn how to do something. An affective goal requires that the students' values, attitudes, or interests are affected by the course.

LEVEL OF EXPERTISE	DESCRIPTION OF LEVEL / EXAMPLE OF MEASURABLE STUDENT OUTCOME
1. Knowledge	Recall/recognition of terms, ideas, procedure, theories, etc. *Example: When is the first day of Spring?*
2. Comprehension	Explain, translate, interpret, extrapolate, … *Example: What does the summer solstice represent?*
3. Application	Apply abstractions, general principles, or methods to specific concrete situations. *Example: What would Earth's seasons be like if its orbit was perfectly circular?*
4. Analysis	Separation of a complex idea into its constituent parts and an understanding of organisation and relationship between the parts. Includes realising the distinction between hypothesis and fact as well as between relevant and extraneous variables. *Example: Why are seasons reversed in the southern hemisphere?*
5. Synthesis	Creative, mental construction of ideas and concepts from multiple sources to form complex ideas into a new, integrated, and meaningful pattern subject to given constraints. *Example: If the longest day of the year is in June, why is the northern hemisphere hottest in August?*
6. Evaluation	To make a judgment of ideas or methods using external evidence or self-selected criteria substantiated by observations or informed rationalisations. *Example: What would be the important variables for predicting seasons on a newly discovered planet?*

Table 1: Bloom's taxonomy of educational objectives for knowledge-based goals

LEVEL OF EXPERTISE	DESCRIPTION OF LEVEL / EXAMPLE OF MEASURABLE STUDENT OUTCOME
Perception	Uses sensory cues to guide actions. *Example: Some of the coloured samples you see will need dilution before you take their spectra. Using only observation, how will you decide which solutions might need to be diluted?*
Set	Demonstrates a readiness to take action to perform the task or objective. *Example: Describe how you would go about taking the absorbance spectra of a sample of pigments?*

LEVEL OF EXPERTISE	DESCRIPTION OF LEVEL / EXAMPLE OF MEASURABLE STUDENT OUTCOME
Guided response	Knows steps required to complete the task or objective. *Example: Determine the density of a group of sample metals with regular and irregular shapes.*
Mechanism	Performs the task with developing confidence and proficiency, demonstrating correct technique with some consistency but occasional reliance on external guidance. *Example: Follow the given procedure to determine the quantity of copper in your ore sample. Ensure accurate measurement and basic data reporting, including the calculation of mean and standard deviation.*
Complex overt response	Performs the task with confidence and mastery, demonstrating fluency, independence, and consistency. Adapts techniques as needed to accommodate challenges. *Example: Independently design and conduct a titration to determine the Ka of an unknown weak acid, adjusting your approach as necessary to ensure accurate results.*
Adaptation	Performs task or objective as above, but can also modify actions to account for new or problematic situations. *Example: You are performing titrations on a series of unknown acids and find a variety of problems with the resulting curves, e.g., only 3.0 ml of base is required for one acid while 75.0 ml is required in another. What can you do to get valid data for all the unknown acids?*
Organisation	Creates new tasks or objectives incorporating learned ones. *Example: Recall your plating and etching experiences with an aluminium substrate. Choose a different metal substrate and design a process to plate, mask, and etch so that a pattern of 4 different metals is created.*

Table 2: Bloom's taxonomy of educational objectives for skills-based goals

LEVEL OF EXPERTISE	DESCRIPTION OF LEVEL / EXAMPLE OF MEASURABLE STUDENT OUTCOME
Receiving	Demonstrates a willingness to participate in the activity. *Example: When I'm in class I am attentive to the instructor, take notes, etc. I do not read the newspaper instead.*
Responding	Shows interest in the objects, phenomena, or activity by seeking it out or pursuing it for pleasure. *Example: I complete my homework and participate in class discussions.*

LEVEL OF EXPERTISE	DESCRIPTION OF LEVEL / EXAMPLE OF MEASURABLE STUDENT OUTCOME
Valuing	Internalises an appreciation for (values) the objectives, phenomena, or activity. *Example: I seek out information in popular media related to my class.*
Organisation	Begins to compare different values, and resolves conflicts between them to form an internally consistent system of values. *Example: Some of the ideas I've learned in my class differ from my previous beliefs. How do I resolve this?*
Characterisation by a value or value complex	Adopts a long-term value system that is "pervasive, consistent, and predictable". *Example: I've decided to take my family on a vacation to visit some of the places I learned about in my class.*

Table 3: Bloom's taxonomy of educational objectives for affective goals

To determine the level of expertise required for each measurable student outcome, first decide which of these three broad categories (knowledge-based, skills-based, and affective) the corresponding course goal belongs to. Then, using the appropriate Bloom's Taxonomy, look over the descriptions of the various levels of expertise.

Determine which description most closely matches that measurable student outcome. As can be seen from the examples given in the three tables, there are different ways of representing measurable student outcomes, e.g., as statements about students, as questions to be asked of students, or as statements from the student's perspective.

Bloom's Taxonomy is a convenient way to describe the degree to which students are expected to understand and use concepts, to demonstrate particular skills, and to have their values, attitudes, and interests affected. It is critical that the levels of expertise that students are expected to achieve are determined because this will determine which classroom assessment techniques are most appropriate for the course. Though the most common form of assessment used in introductory college courses - multiple choice tests - might be quite adequate for assessing knowledge and comprehension, this type of assessment often falls short when we want to assess our student's knowledge at the higher levels of synthesis and evaluation.

Multiple-choice tests also rarely provide information about achievement of skills-based goals. Similarly, traditional course evaluations, a technique commonly used for affective assessment, do not generally provide useful information about changes in student values, attitudes, and interests. Thus, commonly used assessment techniques, while perhaps providing a means for assigning grades, often do not provide useful feedback for determining whether students are attaining course goals. Usually, this is due to a combination of not having formalised goals to begin with, not having translated those goals into outcomes that are measurable, and not using assessment techniques capable of measuring expected student outcomes given the levels of expertise required to achieve them.

Thus, Bloom's Taxonomy can be used in an iterative fashion to first state and then refine course goals. Bloom's Taxonomy can finally be used to identify which classroom assessment techniques are most appropriate for measuring these goals.

APPENDIX 2
THE ASSESSMENT CYCLE

The assessment cycle is a versatile framework applicable in various learning environments, fostering continuous improvement and meaningful evaluation. While its implementation may differ in schools, higher education, or professional training, its foundational principles remain consistent and impactful.

Primary Schools

In primary education, the assessment cycle supports holistic development, early identification of learning needs, and the shaping of daily teaching practices. For example:

- **Baseline:** Initial reading or phonics checks, numeracy tasks, or observational assessments establish starting points.
- **Formative:** Ongoing teacher observations, verbal feedback, class discussions, and self-assessments help tailor support.
- **Summative:** End-of-term tests, moderated writing samples, or national assessments provide insight into attainment and curriculum coverage.

Secondary Schools

In secondary settings, the assessment cycle aligns curriculum delivery with academic targets and examination preparation. For example:

- **Baseline:** Transition assessments in Year 7 or subject-specific pre-tests identify prior knowledge.
- **Formative:** Homework tasks, low-stakes quizzes, and in-class questioning provide timely feedback for progression.
- **Summative:** Formal tests, mock exams, and coursework submissions contribute to tracking attainment and reporting.

Further and higher education

In universities and colleges, the assessment cycle supports the design of courses and evaluation of student progress. For example:

- **Baseline**: Diagnostic tests in introductory courses assess students' preparedness.
- **Formative**: Regular quizzes, peer reviews, and draft submissions guide ongoing learning.
- **Summative**: Final exams, projects, or dissertations evaluate cumulative understanding.

Professional training

Organisations and industries use the cycle to structure employee development programmes:

- **Baseline**: Skills audits or entry-level tests identify training needs.
- **Formative**: Regular feedback, role-play scenarios, or interim reports monitor progress.
- **Summative**: Certification exams or performance evaluations assess overall competency.

Corporate settings

In corporate training, assessment cycles ensure employees acquire and apply skills effectively:

- **Baseline**: Assessing knowledge gaps before initiating a learning module.
- **Formative**: Continuous feedback during workshops or training sessions.
- **Summative**: Post-training evaluations or assessments to measure skill application.

Health and social care training

Healthcare institutions implement assessment cycles in training programmes for practitioners:

- **Baseline**: Initial skills evaluations identify gaps in knowledge or practice.
- **Formative**: Feedback during clinical simulations or peer learning sessions.
- **Summative**: Certification exams or competency tests ensure readiness for practice.

Military and aviation training

These fields rely on rigorous assessment cycles to ensure readiness and compliance:

- **Baseline**: Aptitude tests and entry-level assessments.
- **Formative**: Simulation exercises with immediate feedback.
- **Summative**: Evaluations post-mission or at the end of training phases.

Flexibility across contexts

The principles of the assessment cycle make it highly adaptable:

- **Baseline** assessments establish starting points, whether for students, trainees, or employees.
- **Formative** assessments provide continuous insight, allowing for adjustment and improvement.
- **Summative** assessments offer conclusive evaluations, valuable for certification, grading, or performance reviews.

APPENDIX 3
TEACHING AND LEARNING

Part 1: Commonly used models of instruction

Schools, colleges and universities often draw on a variety of instructional models, depending on their philosophy, priorities, and student needs. Some commonly used models are shown in the table below.

Model	Outline
Direct instruction	This didactic approach represents teacher-centred instruction where the teacher takes a central role as the primary source of knowledge and authority in the classroom, often delivering content through lectures or direct instruction. The focus is on the teacher imparting information to students, with minimal interaction or student autonomy. *Examples:* Traditional lectures, demonstrations, or structured teaching where the teacher leads the lesson, and students passively receive information. This method is often referred to as the *sage on the stage*.
Student-centred instruction	The teacher acts as a facilitator or mentor, supporting students as they explore and construct their own understanding of the material. The focus is on active learning, collaboration, and critical thinking, with students taking a more active role in the learning process. *Examples:* Project-based learning, inquiry-based learning, group discussions, or activities where the teacher provides guidance and resources but encourages student initiative. This method is often referred to as the *guide on the side*.
Inquiry and project based learning	Encourages students to ask questions, investigate, and develop solutions, fostering critical thinking and curiosity. This model is a type of cognitivist teaching model that focuses on how learners process and organise information, emphasising understanding, mental structures, and the use of prior knowledge.
Collaborative learning	Promotes group work and peer interaction to develop teamwork and communication skills.
Experiential learning	Students learn through real-world experiences, such as fieldwork, projects, or role-playing activities.

Play-based learning	Used in early education, where structured and unstructured play fosters learning and development.
Mastery learning	Focuses on ensuring all students achieve a high level of understanding before progressing to the next topic.
Flipped classroom	Students learn at home with content placed online. They use classroom time for application and discussion.
Socio-constructivist approaches	Draws from the theories of Piaget and Vygotsky, emphasising learning as a social process supported by scaffolding from teachers or peers.

Table 1: Commonly used models of instruction

Advantages of implementing a consistent model

- *Alignment with vision:* A clear model provides coherence and ensures all teachers work within the same pedagogical framework.

- *Clarity for students:* Consistent strategies can help students know what to expect, reducing confusion and improving engagement.

- *Ease of professional development:* Training and development can be tailored to a specific model, ensuring all staff are equipped to implement it effectively.

- *Monitoring and evaluation:* A unified approach makes it easier to assess teaching quality and student progress against shared benchmarks.

Weaknesses and risks of mandating a model

- *Restricts teacher autonomy:* Teachers bring unique styles and strengths to the classroom, and strict models may stifle creativity and flexibility.

- *Inappropriate for diverse needs:* Different students, subjects, and contexts may require varied approaches, which a rigid model cannot accommodate.

- *Resistance to change:* Imposing a model can lead to push-back from teachers who feel their expertise is undermined.

- *Limits innovation:* A single model may overlook emerging practices or technologies that could enhance learning.

Part 2: Relating vision and strategy to teaching and learning

Further practical examples that illustrate the relationship between vision & strategy and teaching & learning:

Example 1. Engaging stakeholders

A headteacher holds regular parent-teacher forums to ensure families are aware of and invested in the school's vision. These forums encourage parents to support initiatives, such as improving student attendance or participation in extracurricular activities, which contribute to shared objectives.

Example 2. Developing core values and mission statements

Leaders collaborate with teachers and students to create a set of core values - such as respect, innovation, and inclusivity - that guide everyday decisions. For instance, a focus on inclusivity translates into adopting teaching strategies that accommodate different learning styles.

Example 3. Building a culture of reflection and feedback

A head of department implements a structured feedback system, where teachers reflect on their practice during peer reviews or coaching sessions. This aligns daily teaching practices with the institution's commitment to continuous improvement and the overarching vision of excellence in education.

Example 4. Showcasing success stories

A programme leader shares stories of students who have achieved significant milestones - such as securing scholarships or excelling in extracurricular activities - illustrating how the school's vision translates into real-world success.

Example 5. Using data-driven insights

Leaders introduce data dashboards to track student performance and provide actionable insights for teachers. A dashboard is a visual tool that provides a consolidated, real-time overview of data and key performance indicators (KPIs) relevant to a specific goal or process. For example, if the vision focuses on personalised learning, the data can help teachers tailor their approaches to individual student needs, ensuring alignment with institutional goals.

Example 6. Aligning assessment strategies with the vision

A school leader implements formative assessments across all subjects to monitor ongoing student progress. These assessments, which may include observations, quizzes, written reflections, or project-based evaluations, align with the institution's vision of continuous learning and mastery, helping to ensure that students are consistently moving toward their academic goals.

Example 7. Promoting inclusive teaching practices

A college leader initiates a focus on *Universal Design for Learning* (UDL) principles to ensure that teaching methods and materials are accessible to all students, regardless of ability. This strategy aligns with the institution's commitment to inclusivity and equity, providing equal opportunities for success in learning.

Example 8. Creating a digital learning strategy

In alignment with the school's vision of preparing students for a digital future, a leader develops a comprehensive digital learning strategy. This includes the introduction of online learning modules, flipped classrooms, and virtual collaboration tools to enhance the learning experience and foster digital literacy.

Example 9. Developing a mentoring programme

To align with the school's vision of student support and success, a leader introduces a mentoring programme where senior students or alumni mentor new students. This initiative fosters a sense of community, provides academic and social support, and strengthens students' connection to the institution's mission of academic and personal development.

Example 10. Encouraging project-based and real-world learning

A leader ensures that all departments incorporate project-based learning (PBL) into their curriculum, allowing students to work on real-world problems. This aligns with the institution's vision of preparing students for future careers by developing practical, problem-solving, and teamwork skills in a dynamic, real-world context.

Example 11. Supporting student autonomy through choice

A school leader empowers students by offering more choices in their learning pathways, such as elective subjects or self-directed projects. This strategy supports the school's vision of fostering student agency and developing lifelong learners who can pursue their passions and interests.

Example 12. Encouraging interdisciplinary teaching

A school leader creates opportunities for teachers across subject areas to design interdisciplinary lessons that combine skills from multiple disciplines. For example, a history and geography collaborative project investigates the environmental effects of historical events, supporting the institution's vision of providing a holistic and interconnected educational experience.

Example 13. Promoting environmental sustainability in curriculum

A school leader integrates environmental education into the curriculum as part of the school's commitment to sustainability. This involves teaching students about climate change, sustainable practices, and the role of individuals and communities in protecting the environment, directly aligning with the school's vision of producing responsible, globally-conscious citizens.

Example 14. Hosting industry partnership events

A school leader partners with local businesses and industry leaders to host career exploration events or internships, providing students with opportunities to engage directly with professionals in their intended fields. This supports the school's vision of connecting education to career readiness and equipping students with the skills needed for the workforce.

Example 15. Supporting mental health and wellbeing

A leader introduces initiatives focused on student mental health, such as mindfulness programmes, stress management workshops, and access to counselling services. This strategy supports the school's vision of fostering a safe, supportive, and nurturing environment for all students, prioritising their emotional and psychological wellbeing alongside their academic success.

Part 3: Strategic plan for teaching and learning

The following extract from a strategic plan links to the teaching and learning vision of a school (chapter 3). It outlines clear responsibilities for each action and includes deadlines for action steps, ensuring that the vision is implemented in a timely and effective manner.

PART OF AN INSTITUTE'S STRATEGIC PLAN

GOAL 1
Fostering an inclusive, student-centred learning environment.

Objective 1.1: Ensure that all teaching materials and activities are accessible and inclusive for students including those with a diverse range of needs (e.g., special educational needs, language barriers).

Action Steps:
- Conduct audits of teaching resources and adapt materials where necessary to ensure accessibility for all learners. *(Lead: Curriculum Development Coordinator, Deadline: June 2025).*

- Provide training for staff on inclusive teaching practices, such as differentiated instruction and universal design for learning. *(Lead: Head of Professional Development, Deadline: September 2025).*
- Promote peer support programmes to help students from diverse backgrounds feel integrated and supported. *(Lead: Student Support Manager, Deadline: Ongoing).*

KPIs: Improved student satisfaction scores related to inclusivity, as measured by annual surveys.

Objective 1.2: Provide personalised learning pathways for all students, particularly in vocational and academic tracks, to meet their individual goals.

Action Steps:
- Develop tailored learning plans for each student in consultation with course tutors. *(Lead: Head of Student Success, Deadline: July 2025).*
- Offer a range of elective modules that allow students to specialise in their areas of interest. *(Lead: Head of Curriculum, Deadline: September 2025).*
- Establish mentorship programmes where students are paired with staff or senior students for guidance. *(Lead: Head of Student Engagement, Deadline: Ongoing).*

KPIs: Increased completion rates of personalised learning pathways, as measured by student progression data.

GOAL 2
Encouraging active participation and collaborative teaching.

Objective 2.1: Foster a culture of high expectations by setting clear learning outcomes and encouraging active student participation in all courses.

Action Steps:
- Align course objectives with high standards, ensuring that expectations are clearly communicated at the start of each term. *(Lead: Academic Leaders, Deadline: Ongoing).*
- Use formative assessments, peer review activities, and collaborative group projects to engage students actively. *(Lead: Subject Coordinators, Deadline: Ongoing).*
- Promote a flipped classroom model where students engage with content before class, allowing for deeper discussions during face-to-face sessions. *(Lead: Teaching Staff, Deadline: September 2025).*

KPIs: Higher engagement rates, as reflected in increased participation in class activities and improved assessment outcomes.

Objective 2.2: Enhance collaborative teaching practices by encouraging inter-departmental projects and cross-disciplinary learning opportunities.

Action Steps:
- Create opportunities for joint modules where students from different courses (e.g., A Level maths and physics) collaborate on problem-solving tasks. *(Lead: Head of Curriculum, Deadline: December 2025).*

- Encourage staff to share best practices and co-plan lessons that integrate knowledge from different subject areas. *(Lead: Head of Professional Development, Deadline: Ongoing).*
- Implement regular peer observation sessions to allow teachers to observe and learn from one another. *(Lead: Teaching Staff, Deadline: March 2025).*

KPIs: Increased cross-departmental collaborations, as measured by the number of interdisciplinary projects and teacher feedback.

GOAL 3
Integrating modern technologies in teaching and learning.

Objective 3.1: Incorporate modern digital tools and technologies to enhance student learning and engagement.

Action Steps:
- Invest in digital platforms (e.g., virtual learning environments, video conferencing) to provide flexible learning options and foster student engagement beyond the classroom. *(Lead: IT Department, Deadline: June 2025).*
- Provide staff with ongoing professional development in the use of emerging educational technologies, such as augmented reality (AR), virtual simulations, and interactive e-books. *(Lead: Head of Professional Development, Deadline: Ongoing).*
- Integrate technologies in both academic and vocational courses to allow students to apply modern tools relevant to their future careers. *(Lead: Curriculum Development Team, Deadline: September 2025).*

KPIs: High levels of student satisfaction with digital resources, as indicated in end-of-term surveys, and greater engagement with online platforms.

Objective 3.2: Ensure that all students are digitally literate and equipped with the technological skills they need for future education and employment.

Action Steps:
- Integrate digital literacy modules into the curriculum, ensuring that students can confidently use a variety of digital tools. *(Lead: Head of Curriculum, Deadline: July 2025).*
- Offer workshops on specific software or platforms commonly used in professional environments, such as Microsoft Office, coding languages, or industry-specific software. *(Lead: IT Department, Deadline: Ongoing).*
- Encourage the use of digital portfolios where students can showcase their work and track their progress. *(Lead: Teaching Staff, Deadline: September 2025).*

KPIs: Increased digital competency among students, as measured by digital literacy assessments and employer feedback.

GOAL 4
Continuous professional development for staff.

Objective 4.1: Provide continuous professional development (CPD) opportunities for all staff to enhance their teaching practices and subject knowledge.

Action Steps:
- Organise regular CPD sessions that focus on both pedagogy (e.g., active learning, formative assessment) and subject-specific knowledge. *(Lead: Head of Professional Development, Deadline: Ongoing).*
- Create a mentorship scheme where experienced staff can support newer teachers with best practices. *(Lead: HR Manager, Deadline: September 2025).*
- Encourage staff to attend external conferences and participate in online learning communities to stay updated with educational trends. *(Lead: Head of Professional Development, Deadline: Ongoing).*

KPIs: High staff satisfaction with CPD opportunities, as measured through annual feedback surveys.

Objective 4.2: Ensure that staff are equipped to use emerging technologies effectively to support student learning.

Action Steps:
- Provide targeted training on using technologies for teaching and assessment, such as learning management systems, video creation tools, and interactive whiteboards. *(Lead: Head of Professional Development, Deadline: Ongoing).*
- Set up internal 'tech champions' who are experts in different technologies and can support their colleagues in integrating these tools into their lessons. *(Lead: IT Department, Deadline: December 2025).*

KPIs: Increased use of technology in teaching, as measured by lesson observations and staff surveys.

GOAL 5
Preparing students for success in future careers and further education.

Objective 5.1: Align teaching and learning activities with real-world applications to prepare students for success in their chosen fields.

Action Steps:
- Invite industry professionals to lead workshops, provide guest lectures, and offer real-world case studies for students to work on. *(Lead: Careers and Employability Team, Deadline: Ongoing).*
- Establish strong relationships with local employers and further education institutions to create clear pathways for students after graduation. *(Lead: Head of Careers and Employability, Deadline: December 2025).*
- Offer work placements, internships, or project-based learning experiences where students can apply their learning in a professional context. *(Lead: Placement Coordinator, Deadline: Ongoing).*

KPIs: Increased student placements and higher rates of employment or further study within six months of graduation.

Part 4: Micro-credentials: An overview

Micro-credentials are a form of certification that validate specific skills, knowledge, or competencies in a targeted area. Unlike traditional degrees, which require years of study and cover broad academic content, micro-credentials are typically short, focused, and designed to meet specific industry or professional needs. They are increasingly popular in education, corporate training, and professional development due to their flexibility and relevance in today's fast-changing job market.

Key features of micro-credentials

Focused and modular: Micro-credentials are modular in nature, allowing learners to build specific skills step by step. For instance, a teacher might complete a micro-credential in digital assessment strategies, while an IT professional might focus on cloud computing fundamentals.

Flexible and accessible: Many micro-credential programmes are offered online, enabling learners to study at their own pace. This flexibility is especially valuable for working professionals and students balancing education with other commitments.

Recognition and portability: They often come with digital badges or certificates that can be shared on professional networks like LinkedIn, providing evidence of achievement. When linked to standards or frameworks, they can be recognised across organisations and sectors.

Alignment with industry needs: Micro-credentials are often developed in collaboration with industry partners to ensure relevance. For example, a micro-credential in data visualisation might align directly with the tools and techniques used in business analytics.

Benefits of micro-credentials

For learners: They offer a faster, more affordable way to gain new skills. They enable learners to remain competitive in a rapidly changing job market. They encourage lifelong learning by providing opportunities for continuous skill development.

For employers: Employers can identify candidates with specific skills validated by micro-credentials. They can use micro-credentialing programmes to upskill or reskill their workforce efficiently.

For educational institutions: Universities and colleges can expand their offerings to include stackable micro-credentials that lead to full qualifications, attracting non-traditional learners.

Examples of micro-credentials in action

Education: Teachers can earn micro-credentials in classroom management, digital teaching tools, or differentiated instruction, enhancing their professional practice.

Technology: Tech companies often partner with platforms like Coursera or edX to offer micro-credentials in fields like AI, cybersecurity, or programming languages.

Leadership implications: For leaders in education and training, integrating micro-credentials into strategic planning offers opportunities to:

- Enhance employability: By aligning micro-credentials with industry standards, institutions ensure their learners are workforce-ready.
- Support lifelong learning: Leaders can create pathways for learners to build and update their skills throughout their careers.
- Foster partnerships: Collaboration with industries ensures the relevance and recognition of micro-credentials.

Micro-credentials are reshaping the education and training landscape, offering a more personalised, flexible, and industry-responsive approach to learning. Leaders who embrace this trend are better positioned to meet the demands of today's learners and tomorrow's workforce.

APPENDIX 4
DATA-DRIVEN DECISION MAKING

Part 1: Qualitative data analysis

This part of the appendix provides further detail of the methods, data collected and subsequent analysis used for Case Study 1 in chapter 7.

Methods of data collection

Student survey (Collected via open-ended survey questions)

Sample questions (4 of 10):

1. What do you find most challenging about your science lessons?
2. Which part of the lessons do you enjoy the most and why?
3. How do you think science lessons could be improved?
4. Do you feel supported by the teacher when you find something difficult? Why or why not?

Teacher observations (Collected during lessons using an observation rubric)

> *Part of rubric (6 observation points from 15):*
>
> To evaluate classroom activities based on specific dimensions using a Likert scale for consistent measurement.
>
> 1 = Strongly Disagree, 2 = Disagree, 3 = Neutral, 4 = Agree, 5 = Strongly Agree.
>
> - **Clarity of instruction:** Instructions were clear and easy to follow throughout the lesson.
> - **Student engagement:** Students were actively engaged and participated enthusiastically in the lesson.
> - **Use of hands-on activities:** Hands-on activities were effectively designed and supported learning objectives.
> - **Classroom management:** The teacher maintained a well-managed classroom with minimal disruptions.
> - **Use of technology/multimedia:** Technology or multimedia resources were appropriately used to enhance learning.
> - **Collaboration and group work:** Group work was well-structured, with students collaborating effectively.

Focus groups (With small groups of students of various performance levels)

Sample questions (4 of 10):

1. How do you feel about the way science is taught in your class?
2. What would make science lessons more interesting for you?
3. How do group activities affect your learning experience?
4. Do you think technology can enhance your understanding of science? If so, how?

Answers / findings

From student feedback

Sample answers (8 of 150):

- "I don't understand the explanations in class; they're too complicated".
- "We don't get to do enough experiments. It's mostly reading and writing".
- "The teacher talks a lot, but it's hard to keep up".
- "I like the practicals because they're fun and make things easier to understand".
- "Sometimes, I don't know what we're supposed to be doing during group work".
- "I feel like there are too many topics in one lesson, and we move too fast".
- "I like when we watch videos because they help me understand concepts better".
- "The teacher is nice, but sometimes it's hard to ask questions because the lesson is too rushed".

From teacher observations

Sample observations (7 of 75):

- "During lectures, many students appeared disengaged, with minimal note-taking or questions".
- "When conducting experiments, students were highly engaged, asking questions and collaborating actively".
- "Several students struggled to follow multi-step instructions, leading to frequent interruptions to clarify tasks".
- "Behavioural issues often arise during lengthy theoretical sessions but are almost non-existent during practical activities".
- "Students responded well to lessons that incorporated multimedia, with increased participation during video-assisted instruction".
- "Group work dynamics varied; some groups collaborated effectively, while others required teacher intervention to stay on task".

- "Students showed heightened interest when lessons connected science concepts to real-life applications".

From focus groups

Sample answers (8 of 110):

- "I enjoy the subject, but I think there could be more hands-on learning. Experiments make everything clearer".
- "Sometimes the lessons are too fast, especially when it's theory. I prefer when we work in groups for experiments".
- "I don't get most of the stuff in class. But the practicals are cool-they help me understand things better".
- "More experiments and projects where we can work with others".
- "Explain things step by step and give examples that we can relate to".
- "Maybe show us videos or let us use computers to learn more interactively"
- "It's easier to understand when the teacher links the topic to something we see every day"
- "Group work is fun, but sometimes it's hard when others don't do their part"

Analysis of collected data

The analysis of the data from student feedback, teacher observations, and focus groups was conducted using thematic coding techniques. This process involved identifying recurring themes, categorising data into meaningful groups, and interpreting the patterns and relationships between these themes.

Step 1: Identifying recurring themes

The raw data from each source were reviewed to pinpoint commonalities and repeated ideas. Examples of recurring themes include:

- **Engagement**: Practical activities and multimedia lessons generated higher engagement.
- **Clarity**: Students struggled with unclear instructions and fast-paced lessons.
- **Learning preferences**: Strong preference for hands-on activities, relatable examples, and the use of technology.
- **Pacing**: Students found the pace of theoretical content overwhelming.
- **Support**: Students appreciated teacher support but felt hesitant to ask questions during rushed lessons.

Step 2: Categorising data into meaningful groups

The initial codes were grouped into broader categories to provide a structured view of the data. Examples include:

- **Teaching methods:** Effectiveness of hands-on activities and multimedia-assisted learning.
- **Communication:** Challenges with unclear instructions and pacing.
- **Curriculum design:** Need for balanced theoretical and practical content.
- **Classroom dynamics:** Variability in group work success and its impact on learning.
- **Student support:** Accessibility of teacher support during lessons.

Step 3: Interpreting patterns and relationships

The relationships between themes revealed actionable insights:

- **Practical activities and engagement:** There was a direct correlation between hands-on experiments and higher student interest and collaboration.
- **Clarity of instruction and understanding:** Unclear or rushed instructions led to frustration and disengagement, particularly in theoretical lessons.
- **Theoretical challenges and learning preferences:** Students who struggled with abstract concepts preferred relatable, real-world examples and practical applications.
- **Pacing and content overload:** Overly fast-paced lessons made it difficult for students to keep up, especially with theoretical content.
- **Support and confidence:** Students were more likely to seek help when the teacher created a supportive and unhurried classroom environment.

Conclusion of analysis

The thematic analysis provided valuable insights into the challenges and opportunities for improving science lessons. Key findings included:

- A strong preference for practical, hands-on activities that enhance understanding and engagement.
- The need for clearer, step-by-step instructions to improve student comprehension and reduce frustration.
- The importance of integrating multimedia and real-life applications to make theoretical concepts more relatable.

- Adjusting the pace of lessons to allow for deeper exploration and student questions.
- Strengthening group work dynamics through clearer guidelines and teacher support.

These insights informed specific recommendations, such as increasing the frequency of experiments, improving instructional clarity, incorporating technology, and adjusting lesson pacing to align with student needs. By addressing these areas, the school aims to foster a more engaging and effective learning environment for all students.

Part 2: Quantitative data analysis

This part of the appendix provides further detail of the data collected and subsequent analysis used for Case Study 2 in chapter 7.

1. This year's results (34 students):

% Scores: 42, 45, 48, 52, 53, 54, 55, 55, 56, 57, 57, 58, 58, 59, 60, 60, 60, 61, 61, 62, 63, 63, 63, 64, 65, 65, 66, 66, 67, 68, 68, 68, 68.

Mean score (Average): $\frac{\text{Sum of Scores}}{\text{Number of Students}} = \frac{2031}{34} = 59.74$

Range: 68 - 42 = 26

Standard deviation: $\sigma = \sqrt{\frac{\sum(x_i - \mu)^2}{N}} = \sqrt{\frac{\sum(x_i - 59.74)^2}{34}} = 6.91$

σ = Standard deviation
x_i = Each student score
N = Number of students
μ = Mean score

Number of passes: 31/34 = 91.18%

Number of failures: 3/34 = 8.82%

2. Last year's results (28 students):

% Scores: 42, 52, 55, 56, 58, 59, 60, 60, 61, 61, 62, 63, 65, 65, 66, 67, 67, 68, 70, 70, 71, 72, 72, 73, 74, 75, 76, 88.

Mean score (Average): $\frac{\text{Sum of Scores}}{\text{Number of Students}} = \frac{1778}{28} = 63.5$

Range: 88 - 42 = 46

Standard deviation: $\sigma = \sqrt{\frac{\sum(x_i - \mu)^2}{N}} = \sqrt{\frac{\sum(x_i - 63.5)^2}{28}} = 8.63$

Number of passes: 27/28 = 96.43%

Number of failures: 1/28 = 3.57%

3. Comparison between years

Metric	This year	Last year	Difference
Mean	59.74	63.50	-3.76
Range	26	46	-20
Standard deviation	6.91	8.63	-1.72
Pass rate (%)	91.18	96.43	-5.25
Failure rate (%)	8.82	3.57	+5.25

4. Key observations

Lower mean and median: This year's mean score is 3.76 points lower than last year, and the median dropped by 4 points, reflecting a noticeable dip in performance.

Smaller range of scores: The range has decreased significantly (from 46 last year to 26 this year), suggesting a more compressed distribution of scores with fewer outliers.

Lower variability: The standard deviation has decreased (from 8.63 to 6.91), indicating less variation in the results.

Increased failure rate: The failure rate has risen from 3.57% last year to 8.82% this year, though most students still passed.

Clustering around modes: The most common scores this year (60, 63, and 68) indicate performance concentrated near the middle and upper-middle ranges.

5. Conclusion

Decline in average performance: The drop in the mean and median, alongside the increased failure rate, suggests some cause for concern about overall student achievement.

Smaller range and lower variability: While the range and standard deviation have decreased, this reflects more uniformity in scores but may also indicate fewer high-achieving outliers.

Areas for focus:

- Investigate whether curriculum changes, instructional strategies, or external factors may have contributed to the slight decline.
- Provide targeted support for students scoring below 60 to improve average performance and reduce the failure rate.
- Identify and address challenges faced by this cohort compared to previous years.

6. Action taken

While this year's results show a slight dip, there is no immediate cause for concern. However, the module leader took proactive measures to help reverse the trend. He investigated the results by performing further, qualitative analysis. This included student feedback (from the end of module survey) and faculty input. He found that several factors contributed to the decline in student performance. The two main issues were:

- A newly introduced assignment format, intended to improve clarity, was deemed overcomplicated, causing confusion and adding stress.
- The curriculum had been updated to include recent changes to national policy but the module activities did not adequately reflect the changes.

Further modifications were made to both.

To support underperforming students, the university offered targeted tutoring, flexible office hours and a peer mentoring programme. They also organised briefing sessions to clarify the new assignment format.

Part 3: Examples of SIS and LMS systems

SIS systems

Here are some widely used examples of Student Information Systems (SIS):

PowerSchool: A comprehensive SIS widely used in schools for attendance tracking, gradebook management, and parent-student communication.

Infinite Campus: Provides tools for managing student enrolment, grades, attendance, and special education needs, along with reporting and analytics.

Skyward: Offers features such as gradebook management, scheduling, and financial tracking for schools and districts.

Blackbaud Education Management Solutions: Includes a suite of tools for private schools, covering admissions, academic records, and student lifecycle management.

RenWeb: Designed for private and faith-based schools, it integrates student data management with financial and administrative tools.

CampusVue: Commonly used in higher education institutions for enrolment management, academic tracking, and financial aid administration.

Arbor: A UK-based SIS for primary and secondary schools, offering features like behaviour tracking, reporting, and attendance management.

iSAMS: Popular with international and independent schools, providing modules for academic records, extracurricular management, and communication.

Jenzabar: A higher education SIS offering tools for admissions, academic management, and alumni relations.

Synergy SIS: Focuses on K-12 education with features like student scheduling, grade reporting, and communication tools for parents and teachers.

Each system offers varying degrees of customisation and integration with other tools, enabling institutions to meet specific administrative and academic needs.

LMS systems

Here are some widely used examples of Learning Management Systems (LMS):

SIMS: Popular in primary schools. An all-in-one solution combining school management (SMS) and learning management (LMS), crafted for the digital age. Simplifies administrative processes, supports teachers in delivering exceptional education, and fosters stronger connections with parents and students.

Canvas: Popular in higher education and K-12 settings, it offers robust tools for course management, grading, collaboration, and integration with third-party apps.

Moodle: An open-source LMS that allows institutions to customise learning environments with tools for assignments, quizzes, forums, and more.

Blackboard Ultra: A versatile platform used in higher education and K-12, known for its virtual classroom tools, grading systems, and analytics.

Google Classroom: A lightweight, user-friendly platform integrated with Google Workspace, commonly used for assignment management and collaboration.

Schoology: Offers tools for creating and sharing content, tracking grades, and facilitating discussions.

Docebo: A scalable LMS used for corporate training, offering AI-driven learning paths, gamification, and analytics.

TalentLMS: Focused on business training, it includes features for creating courses, tracking progress, and certification.

Absorb LMS: A corporate LMS with a focus on user experience, offering integrations with HR software and analytics tools.

SAP Litmos: An LMS for enterprise training, with tools for creating content, monitoring performance, and compliance management.

Edmodo: Combines classroom learning with collaboration tools, widely used in schools for teacher-student interactions and assignments.

Kahoot! EDU: An engaging platform for creating quizzes and interactive learning experiences, used in classrooms and training sessions.

EdApp: A microlearning-focused LMS for corporate environments, emphasising short, engaging lessons.

Thinkific: Designed for course creators and entrepreneurs, it allows users to create and sell online courses.

Teachable: A platform for individual educators to design and monetise online courses with minimal technical expertise.

D2L Brightspace: Used in education and corporate training, offering tools for adaptive learning, analytics, and multimedia content delivery.

Each LMS caters to different educational or training needs, providing tools for course creation, delivery, and tracking progress. Institutions and organisations choose LMS platforms based on scalability, user experience, and integration capabilities.

Part 4: Effective data presentation for non-experts

This part of the appendix provides further detail of effective data presentation for non-experts covered in Case Study 4, chapter 7.

Scenario: Presenting student literacy progress to parents

The leadership team at Levensworth Primary aimed to communicate the impact of a new phonics-based literacy programme to parents, highlighting how it had improved their children's reading skills and providing actionable steps for home support. They took the following steps:

1. Understanding parents' concerns and interests:

Levensworth identified parents' concerns about their children's reading progress through various methods: surveys, parent-teacher conferences, feedback from Parent Advisory Groups, focus groups, informal conversations, and data from past communications. Parents wanted to know:

- Is my child making progress in reading?
- How does my child compare to their peers?
- What can I do at home to help?

To address these concerns, the school designed a presentation that focused on individual progress, grade-level achievements, and practical support strategies.

2. Simplifying and focusing on key insights:

- The presentation highlighted only the most relevant metrics, such as the percentage of pupils reading at or above grade level and how much progress pupils had made in six months.
- Clear, jargon-free language was used to explain the literacy programme and its impact, avoiding complex educational terminology.

3. Using effective data visualisation:

- *Personalised progress reports:* Each parent received a simple, one-page report showing their child's reading progress, including a comparison to grade-level expectations.
- *Bar graphs:* Bar graphs showed the reading level of each pupil against the national average reading level for year groups 1 to 6.
- *Pie charts:* Pie charts showed the percentage of students in each reading level and for each year group.
- *Infographics and tables:* Key points were visually summarised, such as:
  - "85% of students improved by at least one reading level".
  - "40% of students now read above grade level".

4. Telling a story with data:

The presentation began with a relatable story of a student who struggled with reading but, after engaging with the programme, gained confidence and started reading aloud at home.

- Parents were shown how the programme was structured, from daily phonics lessons to personalised reading assignments.
- Testimonials from teachers and parents were included to illustrate the programme's broader impact.

5. Providing context and anticipating questions:

- A brief comparison to national literacy rates showed how Levensworth pupils were excelling.
- Common parental concerns, such as "What if my child is still struggling? " and "How are students with additional needs supported? " were addressed with specific examples and reassurances.

6. Sharing actionable insights for parents:

The presentation ended with practical, easy-to-implement tips for supporting literacy at home:

- *Shared reading time:* Encouraging parents to read with their child for 20 minutes daily.
- *Book recommendations:* A curated list of age-appropriate books was shared.
- *Interactive tools:* Parents were introduced to a new online portal where they could track their child's reading progress in real time and access additional resources, such as phonics games.

Outcome:

Parents left the session feeling informed, confident, and equipped to play an active role in their children's literacy journey. Many expressed appreciation for the clarity of the data and the personalised support provided. This strengthened the school's partnership with parents and increased engagement in home-based learning, contributing to further student success.

Sample parent report:

Here is an example of a report for the Year 4 pupil, Emily Butterworth.

Levensworth Primary - Reading Progress Report

Pupil name: Emily Butterworth   **Year group:** Year 4   **Age:** 8 years old

Dear Mr and Mrs Butterworth,

We are pleased to share Emily's reading progress and celebrate her achievements this term. Below is a summary of her progress and performance compared to her peers and national expectations.

Emily's reading level

- *Current reading Level:* Level 5
- *Year 4 expectation:* Level 4
- *National average for age 8:* Level 4

Emily is currently reading at Level 5, which is above the expected level for her year group (Figure 1). This indicates that she is developing as a confident and fluent reader, able to engage with texts that are more complex and diverse than those typical for her age.

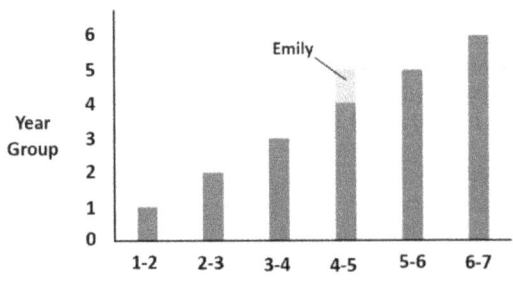

National reading level averages for year groups 1 to 6

Figure 1 - Emily's reading compared with national averages

Progress highlights

- Emily has improved by *one full level* this term.
- She demonstrates strong comprehension skills and excellent vocabulary usage.

- She actively participates in group reading sessions and shows a genuine interest in exploring new books.

Comparison with peers

Emily is performing *above the national average* for her age, as well as exceeding the expectations set for Year 4. She is among the *top 25%* of readers in her class (Figure 2).

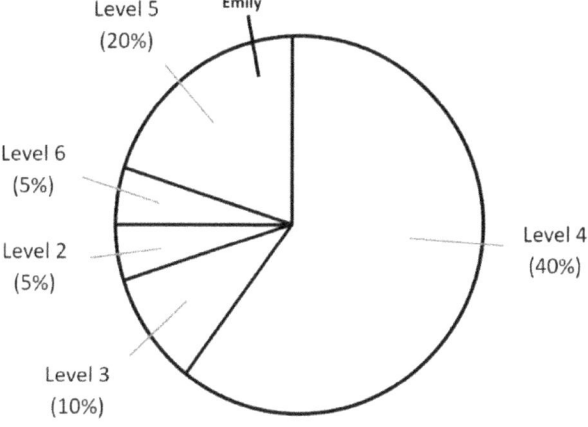

Figure 2 - Emily's reading compared with other pupils in same class

Key points

Improvement: Emily is one of the *85%* of students who improved by at least one reading level.

Reading level: Emily is one of the *40%* of students now reading above grade level.

Fluency and accuracy: Emily's reading fluency has increased by *15 words per minute* this term, bringing her performance in line with advanced readers for her age group.

Vocabulary growth: Emily's vocabulary test results show a *10% increase in understanding complex words,* which has enriched her ability to interpret more challenging texts.

Comprehension success: Emily scored *92%* on her last comprehension assessment, significantly above the class average of *78%,* reflecting her ability to engage deeply with texts and extract meaning.

What this means for Emily

Emily's progress positions her as a strong and confident reader who enjoys exploring books above her age level. Her success lays an excellent foundation for continued achievement across all areas of learning.

Next steps for Emily

To further support Emily's reading development, we recommend:

1. Encouraging her to read a variety of genres, such as historical fiction or poetry, to broaden her literary exposure.
2. Continuing to discuss the books she reads at home to enhance her critical thinking and comprehension.
3. Participating in local library challenges or reading events to keep her motivated.

How you can help at home

- Spend 15-20 minutes daily listening to Emily read aloud, focusing on her pronunciation and fluency.
- Ask her open-ended questions about the characters, themes, or plot to deepen her understanding.
- Introduce her to books by authors like Michael Morpurgo (e.g., War horse, The butterfly lion, Kensuke's kingdom, and Running wild) or Cressida Cowell (e.g., How to train your dragon, The wizards of once, and Emily Brown and the thing), which align with her current level and interests.

Celebrating success

We are incredibly proud of Emily's progress and enthusiasm for reading. Her hard work and dedication to improving her skills are a testament to her bright future as a lifelong learner.

If you have any questions or would like to discuss Emily's progress further, please do not hesitate to reach out.

Best regards,
Mrs. Jane Carter
Year 4 Class Teacher

Part 5: Other statistical tests used in education

This final section provides a brief outline of some other statistical tests that might be used in education and may warrant further exploration.

1. T-test / Z-test (independent samples)

Use: Compare average scores between two different groups.
Example: Compare the average scores of students: male vs. female; white vs. ethnic minority; disabled vs. non-disabled.

2. T-test / Z-test (paired samples)

Use: Compare scores from the same students at two time points.
Example: Compare students' pre-test and post-test scores after a teaching intervention.

* T-tests are used with sample data. Z-tests are used with the entire population.

3. One-way ANOVA

Use: Compare average scores across more than two groups.
Example: Compare test results of students taught by three different methods.

4. Two-way ANOVA

Use: Examine effects of two factors on performance.
Example: Explore how both teaching method and gender affect test scores.

5. Chi-square test of independence

Use: Check if two categorical variables are related.
Example: Is there a relationship between gender and choice of subject?

6. Chi-square goodness-of-fit test

Use: Compare observed vs. expected frequencies.
Example: Do the number of students choosing different exam options match expected trends?

7. Pearson correlation

Use: Measure strength of linear relationship between two continuous variables.
Example: Is there a relationship between time spent studying and exam scores?

8. Spearman's rank correlation

Use: Measure relationship between two ranked or ordinal variables.
Example: Correlate students' rank in maths with their rank in science.

9. Mann-Whitney U test

Use: Compare two groups when data isn't normally distributed.
Example: Compare boys' and girls' scores on an open-ended task with non-normal distribution.

10. Wilcoxon signed-rank test

Use: Compare two related samples when data isn't normally distributed.
Example: Compare pre- and post-intervention reading scores for the same students using a non-parametric test.

11. Kruskal-Wallis test

Use: Compare more than two groups with non-normal data.
Example: Compare test scores across three classrooms with small sample sizes.

12. Friedman test

Use: Compare repeated measures across more than two conditions.
Example: Compare student scores across three assessment types (quiz, essay, presentation) for the same group.

13. Linear regression

Use: Predict one variable from another.
Example: Predict final exam score based on homework completion rate.

14. Multiple regression

Use: Predict a variable using two or more predictors.
Example: Predict final grade from attendance, homework scores, and participation.

15. Shapiro-Wilk test (normality)

Use: Test if data is normally distributed.
Example: Check whether test scores follow a normal distribution before doing a t-test or z-test.

16. Levene's test (equality of variances)

Use: Check if two groups have equal variances.
Example: Before comparing boys and girls, confirm that their score variances are similar.

17. Kolmogorov-Smirnov test

Use: Test if sample distribution differs from a reference distribution.
Example: Assess whether students' scores follow a normal distribution.

18. ANCOVA

Use: Compare groups while controlling for other variables.
Example: Compare teaching methods while adjusting for students' starting ability.

19. Logistic regression

Use: Predict a yes/no outcome.
Example: Predict whether a student will pass or fail based on attendance and homework completion.

20. Factor analysis

Use: Identify underlying patterns or traits in data.
Example: Group related items on a student attitude questionnaire into key themes (e.g., motivation, anxiety).

21. Item analysis

Use: Evaluate effectiveness of test questions.
Example: Identify which multiple-choice questions were too hard or poorly discriminated between high and low performers.

22. Reliability analysis (e.g., Cronbach's alpha)

Use: Assess consistency of a questionnaire or test.
Example: Check whether items on a self-esteem survey are reliably measuring the same thing.

23. Cluster analysis

Use: Group students based on similar characteristics.
Example: Group students by similar learning preferences or study habits.

24. Trend analysis (time-series)

Use: Examine changes over time.
Example: Track average reading scores over five terms to see if there's improvement.

APPENDIX 5
READYMADE PROMPTS

This appendix provides further detail of the Water Cycle example in chapter 8.

The prompt

In order to teach Year 2 pupils about the water cycle, the class teacher creates the following readymade prompt for use with chatGPT:

> "You are helping a Year 2 student learn about the water cycle. When prompted with 'Teach me the water cycle' take them through three steps to build understanding. In each step:
>
> Explain the idea in simple terms, using child-friendly examples.
>
> Ask the student a question to check their understanding.
>
> Wait for their response before moving on".

The response

A pupil enters the prompt into chatGPT and here are the subsequent exchanges.

> **chatGPT:** Let's learn about the water cycle together. We'll go through it in three steps, nice and easy. Here's the first one:
> *Step 1: Evaporation - Water Goes Up* ○ ● ⬆
> When the sun shines on water in rivers, lakes, or puddles, it makes the water warm. The warm water turns into invisible water vapour and floats up into the sky. That's called *evaporation*. It's kind of like when you spill water on the floor and after a while, it's gone - the sun helped it evaporate!
> 🧠 Your turn: Can you tell me something that gets dry after being wet in the sunshine? *(I'll wait for your answer before we go to Step 2!)*
>
> **Pupil:** Clothes
>
> **ChatGPT:** Great answer! Yes - clothes dry in the sunshine because the water in them evaporates and goes into the air. 😊 🎩

chatGPT: *Step 2: Condensation - Clouds Are Made* ☁

When the water vapour floats high up into the sky, it gets cooler. The cool air turns the water vapour back into tiny water drops, and these drops stick together to make clouds. This part is called condensation. It's a bit like when you breathe on a cold window and see mist appear - that's condensation too!

🎨 Your turn: Have you ever seen steam from a kettle turn into little water drops on a window? Or can you tell me where you've seen mist or clouds form?
(I'll wait for your answer before we go to Step 3!)

Pupil: In my shower.

ChatGPT: Exactly! When you take a shower, the warm steam condenses on the bathroom mirror or window, turning into little water drops - just like clouds forming in the sky. 💧☁

---

chatGPT: *Step 3: Precipitation - Rain Comes Down* 🌧

After clouds get full of tiny water drops, they can't hold it anymore. So, the water falls back down to Earth as rain, snow, or hail. This is called precipitation.
It's like when the clouds get so full of water that it starts to rain!

🎨 Your turn: Have you ever seen rain or snow fall from the sky? What happens when it rains? *(I'll wait for your answer before we wrap up!)*

Pupil: I get wet.

ChatGPT: Yes, exactly! When it rains, we get wet because the water falls from the clouds - that's precipitation. 🌧

ChatGPT: And that's the water cycle in three simple steps:
1. *Evaporation* - Water goes up into the sky.
2. *Condensation* - Clouds are made.
3. *Precipitation* - Water comes down as rain, snow, or hail!

It keeps going over and over, like a big, never-ending circle. 😊

Thanks for learning with me! Would you like to learn more about something else?

APPENDIX 6
GATHERING QUALITY ASSURANCE DATA

This appendix expands on the methods of data collection presented in chapter 9 and also includes the tools associated with each method, and how the data might be analysed.

1. Surveys and questionnaires

Tools

- *Collection*: Google Forms, Microsoft Forms, SurveyMonkey, Typeform.
- *Storage*: Google Drive, Microsoft SharePoint, dedicated database systems (e.g., SQL databases).
- *Display*: Data visualisation platforms such as Tableau, Excel, or Power BI.

Analysis

- Quantitative data can be analysed using statistical software like SPSS, MS Excel or R to identify trends, averages, and correlations.
- Qualitative data from open-ended responses may be coded and thematically analysed using NVivo or MAXQDA.
- *Example*: Analysing student satisfaction levels to measure the effectiveness of teaching methodologies.

2. Focus groups and interviews

Tools

- *Collection*: Zoom, Microsoft Teams (for virtual focus groups), audio recorders, and transcription services (e.g., Otter.ai or Sonix).
- *Storage*: Cloud platforms (Google Drive, OneDrive) or transcription software databases.
- *Display*: Summaries and insights visualised using concept maps or thematic charts.

Analysis

- Thematic analysis to identify recurring themes or concerns.
- Tools like NVivo support text analysis and help uncover patterns in participant feedback.
- *Example*: Using feedback from parents to refine extracurricular programme offerings.

3. Observation checklists

Tools

- *Collection*: Digital forms (e.g., JotForm), mobile apps (e.g., ClassDojo, iObserve), or paper-based checklists / tally charts.
- *Storage*: Cloud storage systems or school management systems like SIMS or iSAMS.
- *Display*: Graphical representation of trends via Excel or Google Sheets.

Analysis

- Trends and outliers in observed behaviours can be analysed through frequency counts and cross-tabulations.
- *Example*: Monitoring teaching practices to ensure consistency with school quality frameworks.

4. Learning analytics from digital platforms

Tools

- *Collection*: Learning Management Systems (LMS) like Moodle, Blackboard, or Canvas.
- *Storage*: Integrated LMS databases or cloud-based analytics dashboards.
- *Display*: Heat maps, dashboards, or trend graphs generated within the LMS or external platforms like Tableau.

Analysis

- Engagement metrics (e.g., logins, time spent on tasks) are analysed to identify participation patterns.
- Machine learning models may predict at-risk students based on usage behaviour.
- *Example*: Analysing time-on-task data to improve course design.

5. Benchmarking

Tools

- *Collection*: External databases like National Student Survey (NSS), government reports (e.g., Ofsted), or PISA datasets.
- *Storage*: Institutional databases or benchmarking software like i-graduate.
- *Display*: Comparative graphs and tables using Excel, SPSS, or Power BI.

Analysis

- Descriptive statistics and visual comparisons to identify where performance lags behind peers.
- *Example*: Using National Student Survey results to compare student satisfaction across departments.

6. Feedback forms

Tools

- *Collection*: Online forms (e.g., Microsoft Forms, LimeSurvey), mobile apps, or paper feedback forms.
- *Storage*: Centralised school or university database systems.
- *Display*: Word clouds for open-ended questions, bar graphs for quantitative ratings.

Analysis

- Quantitative ratings are analysed for mean scores and variability.
- Qualitative feedback is thematically analysed to identify common concerns or suggestions.
- *Example*: Collecting feedback on new courses to determine areas for improvement.

7. Audits and inspections

Tools

- *Collection*: Inspection frameworks and tools like Ofsted's digital evaluation systems or bespoke audit checklists.
- *Storage*: Institutional databases or cloud systems.
- *Display*: Dashboards or inspection reports summarising compliance levels.

Analysis

- Compliance data is reviewed against pre-defined standards to identify gaps.
- Trend analysis for recurring issues across audits.
- *Example*: Auditing curriculum delivery to ensure alignment with national standards.

8. Student performance metrics

Tools

- *Collection*: Student Information Systems (SIS) such as Arbor or SIMS, and assessment platforms like Turnitin or Gradescope.

- *Storage*: Integrated SIS databases or external servers.
- *Display*: Progress tracking through dashboards, scatter plots, or trend charts.

Analysis

- Statistical models to explore correlations between teaching methods and student outcomes.
- Predictive analytics to identify underperforming groups.
- *Example*: Analysing standardised test results to evaluate curriculum effectiveness.

9. Peer reviews

Tools

- *Collection*: Google Forms or dedicated review platforms like Peergrade or EduSourced.
- *Storage*: Shared drives or institutional repositories.
- *Display*: Aggregated feedback summaries or comparative charts.

Analysis

- Peer feedback is categorised and aggregated to identify strengths and areas for improvement.
- *Example*: Using peer reviews for teaching staff evaluations and professional development.

10. Ethnographic and case studies

Tools

- *Collection*: Field notes, audio recorders, and video recordings.
- *Storage*: Secure digital archives or qualitative analysis software.
- *Display*: Narrative accounts or thematic visualisations (e.g., flowcharts).

Analysis

- Detailed qualitative analysis to gain insights into lived experiences or institutional dynamics.
- *Example*: Understanding challenges faced by marginalised student groups through case studies.

REFERENCES

9ine (2024) AI in education: What are the risks and challenges? (online). Available at https://www.9ine.com/newsblog/ai-in-education-what-are-the-risks-and-challenges (Accessed: 4/1/24).

Abolnejadian, M., Alipour, S. and Taeb, k. (2024) Leveraging ChatGPT for Adaptive Learning through Personalized Prompt-based Instruction: A CS1 Education Case Study. In Extended Abstracts of the CHI Conference on Human Factors in Computing Systems (CHI EA '24), Association for Computing Machinery, New York, NY, USA, Article 521, 1–8.

ACAS (2023) Advice for employers and employees (online). Available at: https://www.acas.org.uk (Accessed: 11/4/25).

Adapt IT Education (2024). Student information system vs learning management system (online). Available at https://education.adaptit.tech/blog/student-information-system-vs-learning-management-system (Accessed: 3/1/24).

Advance HE (2024) Athena Swan FAQs: Benchmarking (online). Available at https://www.advance-he.ac.uk/equality-charters/athena-swan-charter/FAQs/benchmarking (Accessed: 2/1/24).

Aguinis, H. (2023) Performance management, Sage Publications.

Ahmad, N. & Ruslan, S. (2024) Crafting Effective Prompts: A Guideline for Successful Image Generation, in 2024 14th International Conference on System Engineering and Technology (ICSET) (pp. 84-89). IEEE.

Ainscow, M. (2020) Inclusion and equity in education: Making sense of global challenges, Prospects, 49(3), pp.123-134.

Ainscow, M. (2020) Promoting inclusion and equity in education: Lessons from international experiences, Nordic Journal of Studies in Educational Policy, 6(1), 7-16.

Ainscow, M. (2024) Developing Inclusive Schools: Pathways to Success, Routledge.

Al-Alawi, A., Naureen, M., AlAlawi, E. and Al-Hadad, A. (2021) The role of artificial intelligence in recruitment process decision-making, in 2021 International Conference on Decision Aid Sciences and Application (DASA) (pp. 197-203). IEEE.

Alhamali, R. (2019) Impact of conflict management styles on team performance on supervisors of teams in universities, Global Journal of Management and Business Research, 1-6. 10.34257/GJMBRAVOL19IS3PG1.

Allen, T., Eby, L., Poteet, M., Lentz, E. and Lima, L. (2004) Career benefits associated with mentoring for mentors: A meta-analysis, Journal of Applied Psychology, 89(1), 127–136.

Altbach, P. & Knight, J. (2007) The internationalization of higher education: Motivations and realities, Journal of Studies in International Education, 11(3-4), 290-305.

Amabile, T. & Kramer, S. (2011) The progress principle: Using small wins to ignite joy, engagement, and creativity at work, Harvard Business Review Press.

Ambron, S. & Hooper, K. (1988) Interactive Multimedia: Visions of Multimedia for Developers, Educators, and Information Providers, Redmond, WA: Microsoft Press.

American Academy of Business (2023) The role of data-driven decision-making in effective educational leadership (online). Available at www.abacademies.org/articles/the-role-of-datadriven-decisionmaking-in-effective-educational-leadership-15998.html (Accessed: 2/1/24).

American School Counselor Leadership Association [ASCL] (2015) Accountability measures (online). Available at https://www.ascl.org.uk/ASCL/media/ASCL/Our%20view/Policy%20Papers/policy_paper_accountability_measures_may_2015_final.pdf (Accessed: 2/1/24).

American University School of Education Online (2024) Qualitative vs. quantitative research: Comparing the methods and applications in education (online). Available at https://soeonline.american.edu/blog/qualitative-vs-quantitative/ (Accessed: 3/1/24).

Anderson, L. (2000) A Taxonomy for Learning, Teaching, and Assessing: A Revision of Bloom's Taxonomy of Educational Objectives, Pearson.

Anderson, L. & Krathwohl, D. (2001) A taxonomy for learning, teaching, and assessing: A revision of Bloom's Taxonomy of educational objectives, Longman.

Antony, J. (2020) Lean Six Sigma in Higher Education: A Practical Guide for Continuous Improvement Professionals in Higher Education, Routledge.

Apple, M. (2018) Ideology and Curriculum, Routledge.

Arakawa, R. & Yakura, H. (2024) Coaching Copilot: Blended form of an LLM-Powered Chatbot and a Human Coach to effectively support self-reflection for leadership growth, in ACM Conversational User Interfaces 2024 (pp. 1-14). ACM.

Armstrong, M. & Taylor, S. (2020) Armstrong's Handbook of Human Resource Management Practice, Kogan Page.

ASCD (2025) Teaching Associations (online). Available at https://relay.libguides.com/teaching-associationsrelay.libguides.com (Accessed: 16/4/25).

Ashbee, R. (2021) Curriculum: Theory, culture and the subject specialisms, Routledge.

Ashkanasy, N. & Humphrey, R. (2011) Current emotion research in organizational behavior, Emotion Review, 3(2), 214–224.

Association of Colleges (2023) Protecting vocational education: Why BTECs matter (online). Available at https://www.aoc.co.uk/services/news-insights/the-fe-curriculum-beyond-2023-implications-of-qualification-reform (Accessed: 25/12/24).

Avolio, B. & Bass, B. (2004) Multifactor Leadership Questionnaire, Mind Garden.

Avolio, B. & Gardner, W. (2005) Authentic leadership development: Getting to the root of positive forms of leadership, The Leadership Quarterly, 16(3), 315–338.

Avolio, B. (2010) Full range leadership development: Pathways for people, profit, and performance, Sage Publications.

Avramidis, E. & Norwich, B. (2002) Teachers' attitudes towards integration/inclusion: A review of the literature, European Journal of Special Needs Education, 17(2), 129-147.

Bach, S. [ed] (2009) Managing human resources: personnel management in transition, John Wiley & Sons.

Bachkirova, T., Arthur, L. and Reading, E. (2020) Evaluating a coaching and mentoring program: Challenges and solutions, Coaching researched: A coaching psychology reader, pp.361-378.

Bachkirova, T., Jackson, P. and Clutterbuck, D. (2021) Coaching and Mentoring Supervision: Theory and Practice, McGraw-Hill Education (UK).

Bakker, A., Demerouti, E. and Sanz-Vergel, A. (2014) Burnout and work engagement: The JD-R approach, Annual review of organizational psychology and organizational behavior, 1(2014), pp.389-411.

Ball, S. (2003) The teacher's soul and the terrors of performativity, Journal of Education Policy, 18(2), 215-228.

Ball, S. (2021) The Education Debate, Policy Press.

Banks, J. (2015) Cultural diversity and education: Foundations, curriculum, and teaching (6th ed.), Routledge.

Barnett, R. & Coate, K. (2005) Engaging the curriculum in Higher Education, Maidenhead: Open University Press.

Barnett, B. & O'Mahony, G. (2009) Mentoring and coaching programs for the professional development of school leaders, In International handbook on the preparation and development of school leaders (pp. 232-262). Routledge.

Bass, B. & Stogdill, R. (1990) *Bass & Stogdill's handbook of leadership: Theory, research, and managerial applications,* Simon and Schuster.

Bass, B. & Avolio, B. (1994) Improving organizational effectiveness through transformational leadership, Sage Publications.

Bass, B. & Riggio, R. (2006) Transformational leadership (2nd ed.), Lawrence Erlbaum Associates.

Bauer, G., Hämmig, O., Schaufeli, W. and Taris, T. (2014) A critical review of the job demands-resources model: Implications for improving work and health, Bridging occupational, organizational and public health: A transdisciplinary approach, pp.43-68.

Bearman, M., Dawson, P., Boud, D., Hall, M., Bennett, S., Molloy, E. and Joughin, G. (2014) Guide to the assessment design decisions framework (online). Available at https://www.assessmentdecisions.org/wp-content/uploads/2014/09/Guide-to-the-Assessment-Design-Decisions-Framework.pdf (Accessed: 22/12/24).

Bell, A. & Mladenovic, R. (2008) The benefits of peer observation of teaching for tutor development, *Higher Education,* 55, 735–752.

Benke, M. (2023) How to solve conflict situations better with the model of Thomas Kilmann, Economic and Social Development: Book of Proceedings, pp.229-238.

Bennett, R. (2011) Formative assessment: A critical review, Assessment in Education: Principles, Policy & Practice, 26(1), 4-30.

Biesta, G. (2015) Good education in an age of measurement: On the need to reconnect with the question of purpose in education. Educational Assessment, Evaluation and Accountability, 21(1), 33–46.

Biggs, J. & Tang, C. (2022) Teaching for quality learning at university. McGraw-Hill Education.

Black, P. & Wiliam, D. (1998) Assessment and classroom learning, Assessment in Education: Principles, Policy & Practice, 5(1), 7–74.

Black, P. & Wiliam, D. (2009) Developing the theory of formative assessment, Educational Assessment, Evaluation and Accountability, 21(1), 5-31.

Blackmore, P. & Kandiko, C. (2012) Strategic curriculum change in universities: Global trends, Abingdon: Routledge.

Bloxham, S. & Boyd, P. (2007) Developing effective assessment in higher education: A practical guide. McGraw-Hill Education.

Bohlander, G. & Snell, S. (2017) Principles of Human Resource Management, Cengage Learning.

Booth, T. & Ainscow, M. (2002) Index for Inclusion: Developing learning and participation in schools, Centre for Studies on Inclusive Education.

Boud, D. & Falchikov, N. (2007) Rethinking Assessment in Higher Education: Learning for the Longer Term, Routledge.

Boud, D., Lawson, R., & Thompson, D. G. (2021). The calibration of student judgement through self-assessment: Disruptive effects of assessment patterns. Assessment & Evaluation in Higher Education, 46(1), 23-35.

Bozer, G. & Jones, R. (2018) Understanding the factors that determine workplace coaching effectiveness: A systematic literature review, European Journal of Work and Organizational Psychology, 27(3), pp.342-361.

Bradberry, T. & Greaves, J. (2009) Emotional Intelligence 2.0, TalentSmart.

Bradbury, A. (2018) The impact of the Phonics Screening Check on grouping by ability: A 'necessary evil' amid the policy storm, British Educational Research Journal. 44. 10.1002/berj.3449.

Brent, M. & Dent, F. (2013) The leader's guide to managing people, FT Publishing International.

BrightCall AI (2023). The power of real-time dashboards: Enhancing data visualization and decision-making (online). Available at https://brightcall.ai/blog/the-power-of-real-time-dashboards-enhancing-data-visualization-and-decision-making (Accessed: 2/1/24).

Bromley, M. (2023) Intent Implementation Impact: How to design and deliver an ambitious school curriculum Paperback, Independently published.

Brookhart, S. (2013) How to create and use rubrics for formative assessment and grading, ASCD.

Brown, T. (2009) Change by design: How design thinking creates new alternatives for business and society, Collins Business.

Brown, M., Mhichil, M., Beirne, E. and Mac Lochlainn, C. (2021) The global micro-credential landscape: Charting a new credential ecology for lifelong learning, Journal of Learning for Development, 8(2), 228-254.

Brownell, J. (2015) Listening: Attitudes, Principles, and Skills, Routledge.

Bruner, J. (1960) The Process of Education, Harvard University Press.

Bryk, A. (2010) Organizing schools for improvement, Phi delta kappan, 91(7), pp.23-30.

Bryk, A., Gomez, L., Grunow, A. and LeMahieu, P. (2015) Learning to improve: How America's schools can get better at getting better, Harvard Education Press.

Bush, T. & Glover, D. (2003) School Leadership: Concepts and Evidence, London: SAGE Publications.

Bush, T. (2008) Leadership and management development in education, London: Sage.

Bush, T., Bell, L. and Middlewood, D. (2019) Principles of educational leadership & management (3rd ed.), SAGE publications.

Bush, T. (2020) Theories of educational leadership and management, SAGE Publications.

CAA (2024) Safety training and promotion (online). Available at caa.co.uk/safety-initiatives-and-resources/how-we-regulate/state-safety-programme/safety-promotion/safety-training-and-promotion (Accessed: 23/12/24).

Carless, D. (2020) Feedback loops and the longer-term: Towards feedback spirals, Assessment & Evaluation in Higher Education, 45(6), 885-895.

Carr, W. & Kemmis, S. (2003) Becoming critical: Education, knowledge and action research, Routledge.

Carson, O., McAloon, T., Brown, D. and McIlfatrick, S. (2023) Exploring the contribution and impact of master's education for leadership development in adult general nursing: a scoping review, Nurse Education in Practice, 71, p.103697.

Carucci, R. (2014) Rising to Power: The Journey of Exceptional Executives, Greenleaf Book Group.

Center for Transformative Learning (2023). The Importance of Instructional Vision in School Improvement (online). Available at https://ctlonline.org/the-importance-of-instructional-vision-in-school-improvement (Accessed: 31/12/24).

Chapman, C. & Muijs, D. (2022). School effectiveness and improvement research, policy and practice, Routledge.

Chartered College of Teaching (2023) Professional learning networks and curriculum development (online. Available at https://chartered.college (Accessed: 8/12/24).

Chiriac, E. (2014) Group work as an incentive for learning - Students' experiences of group work, Frontiers in Psychology, 11, 534.

Choung, H., David, P. and Seberger, J. (2024) A multilevel framework for AI governance, in The Routledge Handbook of Global and Digital Governance Crossroads (pp. 310-323), Routledge India.

Chugh, U. (2024) Diversity and inclusion in human resource management, Journal of Advanced Management Studies. 1. 16-20.

CIPD (2022) Ethical practice in HR (online). Available at: https://www.cipd.org (Accessed: 11/4/25).

CIPD (2024) Professional Standards Framework (online). Available at www.cipd.org/uk/membership/professional-standards (Accessed: 23/12/24).

City & Guilds (2023) Qualifications in Health and Social Care (online). Available at https://www.cityandguilds.com/qualifications-and-apprenticeships/health-and-social-care#fil=uk (Accessed: 23/12/24).

City & Guilds (2024) The impact of T Levels: Benefits for learners and industry (online). Available at www.cityandguilds.com/news/november-2024/the-impact-of-t-levels (Accessed: 23/12/240.

Clutterbuck, D. (2014) Everyone needs a mentor. Kogan Page Publishers.

Clutterbuck, D., Whitaker, C. and Lucas, M. (2016) Coaching supervision: A practical guide for supervisees, Routledge.

Cochran-Smith, M. & Lytle, S. (2015) Inquiry as stance: Practitioner research for the next generation, Teachers College Press.

Cohen, E. (1994) Designing Groupwork: Strategies for the Heterogeneous Classroom, Teachers College Press.

Compunnel (2024). Boost decision-making with data visualization in education (online). Available at https://www.compunnel.com/blogs/boosting-decision-making-with-data-visualization-in-education/ (Accessed: 2/1/24).

Computeam (2023) The power of data-driven decision making in education (online). Available at https://www.computeam.co.uk/videos-and-blog/article/the-power-of-data-driven-decision-making-in-education (Accessed: 2/1/24).

Cook-Sather, A. (2020) Student voice across contexts: Fostering student agency in today's schools, Theory into practice, 59(2), pp.182-191.

Covey, S. (2020) The 7 habits of highly effective people, Simon & Schuster.

Crawford, J., Butler-Henderson, K., Rudolph, J., Malkawi, B., Glowatz, M., Burton, R., Magni, P. and Lam, S. (2020) COVID-19: 20 countries' higher education intra-period digital pedagogy responses, Journal of Applied Learning & Teaching, 3(1), 1-20.

Creemers, B. & Kyriakides, L. (2007) The dynamics of educational effectiveness, Routledge.

Crenshaw, K. (2013) Demarginalizing the intersection of race and sex: A black feminist critique of antidiscrimination doctrine, feminist theory and antiracist politics, *Feminist legal theories* (pp. 23-51). Routledge.

Crisp G. & Alvarado-Young, K. (2018) The role of mentoring in leadership development, New directions for student leadership, (158), 37-47.

Cross, J. (2011) Informal Learning: Rediscovering the Natural Pathways That Inspire Innovation and Performance, John Wiley & Sons.

Cudney, E., Venuthurumilli, S., Materla, T. and Antony, J. (2018) Systematic review of Lean and Six Sigma approaches in higher education, Total Quality Management & Business Excellence, 31(3–4), 231–244.

Cumming, T. & Miller, M. (2017) Enhancing assessment in Higher Education: Putting psychometrics to work, Routledge.

Darling-Hammond, L., Hyler, M. and Gardner, M. (2017) Effective teacher professional development, Learning Policy Institute.

DataVersity (2024) Developing a data literacy program for your organization (online). Available at https://www.dataversity.net/developing-a-data-literacy-program-for-your-organization/ (Accessed: 4/1/24).

Day, D. (2000) Leadership development: A review in context, The Leadership Quarterly, 11(4), 581-613.

Day, C. (2002) Developing Teachers, Routledge.

Day, C., Sammons, P., Leithwood, K., Hopkins, D., Gu, Q., Brown, E. and Ahtaridou, E. (2011) Successful school leadership: Linking with learning and achievement, Open University Press.

Day, C., Sammons, P. and Gorgen, K. (2016) Successful school leadership. Education development trust, Reading Berkshire, England RG1 4RU.

De Boer, A., Pijl, S. and Minnaert, A. (2011) Regular primary schoolteachers' attitudes towards inclusive education: A review of the literature, International Journal of Inclusive Education, 15(3), 331-353.

Dee, T. (2004) Teachers, race, and student achievement in a randomized experiment, The Review of Economics and Statistics, 86(1), 195-210.

Delic, A., Kozarevic, E., Peric, A. and Civic, B. (2014) The monetary and non-monetary incentives impact on job satisfaction: Evidence from Bosnia and Herzegovina banking sector, In Annual Paris Business and Social Science Research Conference.

Deming, W. E., Cahill, K. and Allan, K (2018) Out of the Crisis, MIT Press.

DeNisi, A. & Murphy, K. (2017) Performance appraisal and performance management: 100 years of progress?, Journal of Applied Psychology, 102(3), 421–433.

Dennis, A., Lakhiwal, A. and Sachdeva, A. (2023) AI agents as team members: Effects on satisfaction, conflict, trustworthiness, and willingness to work with, Journal of Management Information Systems, 40(2), pp.307-337.

Department for Education (DfE) (2022) Working together to safeguard children (online). Available at: https://www.gov.uk/government/publications/working-together-to-safeguard-children--2 (Accessed: 11/4/25).

Department for Education (DfE) (2023) Keeping children safe in education: Statutory guidance for schools and colleges (online). Available at: https://www.gov.uk/government/publications/keeping-children-safe-in-education--2 (Accessed: 11/4/25).

Department for Education (2023) National Curriculum Framework (online). Available at https://assets.publishing.service.gov.uk/media/5a81a9abe5274a2e8ab55319/PRIMARY_national_curriculum.pdf (Accessed: 7/12/14).

Department for Education (2024) National conversation on curriculum begins, GOV.UK (online). Available at gov.uk/government/news/national-conversation-on-curriculum-begins (Accessed: 2/1/25).

Dewey, J. (1986) Experience and Education, Macmillan.

DfE (2021) Skills for Jobs: Lifelong Learning for Opportunity and Growth (online). Available at https://www.gov.uk/government/publications/skills-for-jobs-lifelong-learning-for-opportunity-and-growth (Accessed: 23/12/24).

Digital Learning Institute (2024) AI-driven evolution in learning analytics for digital education (online). Available at https://www.digitallearninginstitute.com/blog/ai-driven-evolution-in-learning-analytics-for-digital-education (Accessed: 2/1/24).

Dion Leadership (2023) Leadership coaching effectiveness research study (online). Available at: https://dionleadership.com/leadership-coaching-effectiveness-research-study/Dion Leadership (Accessed: 16/4/25).

Doll, R. (1992) Curriculum Improvement: Decision Making, Allyn and Bacon.

Donley, J., Detrich, R., States, J. and Keyworth, R.. (2020). Distributed Leadership (Wing Institute Original Paper). 10.6084/m9.figshare.14272685.

DuFour, R. & DuFour, R. (2013) Learning by doing: A handbook for professional learning communities at work, Solution Tree Press.

Dunn, K., Airola, D., Lo, W. and Garrison, M. (2013) What teachers think about what they can do with data: Development and validation of the data driven decision-making efficacy and anxiety inventory, Contemporary Educational Psychology, 38(1), 87-98.

Duterte, J. (2024) Technology-enhanced learning environments: Improving engagement and learning, IJRISS, 8(10), pp.1305-1131.

Dweck, C. (2006). Mindset: The New Psychology of success, Random House.

Dwivedi, Y., Hughes, L., Ismagilova, E., Aarts, G., Coombs, C., Crick, T., Duan, Y., Dwivedi, R., Edwards, J., Eirug, A. and Galanos, V. (2021) Artificial Intelligence (AI): Multidisciplinary perspectives on emerging challenges, opportunities, and agenda for research, practice and policy, International journal of information management, 57, p.101994.

EASA (2024) Aviation Training at EASA. (online). Available at https://www.easa.europa.eu/en/domains/safety-management/aviation-training-easa (Accessed: 23/12/24).

EDIS (2024) The use of reflection as an effective leadership practice (online). Available at: https://edis.ifas.ufl.edu/publication/WC473Ask (Accessed: 16/4/25).

Edmondson, A. (1999) Psychological safety and learning behavior in work teams, Administrative Science Quarterly, 44(2), 350-383.

Edmondson, A. (2018) The fearless organization: Creating psychological safety in the workplace for learning, innovation, and growth, Wiley.

Education Policy Institute (2023) Education in England: Annual Report 2023 (online). Available at https://epi.org.uk/publications-and-research/annual-report-2023 (Accessed: 15/1/25).

Education Elements (2024) How bias affects our perceptions of data: 3 ways to guard against unconscious bias (online). Available at www.edelements.com/

blog/how-bias-affects-our-perception-of-data-3-ways-to-guard-against-unconscious-bias (Accessed: 4/1/24).

Education Endowment Foundation (EEF) (2023) Leadership approaches: A rapid evidence assessment (online). Available at educationendowmentfoundation.org.uk/education-evidence/evidence-reviews/leadership-approaches (Accessed: 8/12/24).

Education Horizons (2024) Understanding learning management systems: A comprehensive guide for schools (online). Available at educationhorizons.com/blog/understanding-learning-management-systems-a-comprehensive-guide-for-schools (Accessed: 2/1/24).

EHRC (2022) Your rights to reasonable adjustments (online). Equality and Human Rights Commission. Available at: https://www.equalityhumanrights.com (Accessed: 11/4/25).

Ellucian (2024) The importance of data-driven decision making in higher education (online). Available at https://www.ellucian.com/emea-ap/blog/importance-data-driven-decision-making-higher-education (Accessed: 2/1/24).

Ely, K., Boyce, L., Nelson, J., Zaccaro, S., Hernez-Broome, G. and Whyman, W. (2010) Evaluating leadership coaching: A review and integrated framework, The Leadership Quarterly, 21(4), 585-599.

Epstein, J. (2001) School, family, and community partnerships: Preparing educators and improving schools, Westview Press.

ESFA (2023) Apprenticeships Funding Rules (online). Available at https://www.gov.uk/government/collections/apprenticeship-funding-rules (Accessed: 23/12/24).

ESFA (2024) What we do (online). Available at www.gov.uk/government/organisations/education-and-skills-funding-agency/about (Accessed: 23/12/24).

Esplugas M. (2023) The use of artificial intelligence (AI) to enhance academic communication, education and research: a balanced approach, Journal of Hand Surgery (European Volume). 2023;48(8):819-822.

Estrellado, R. (2024) Data-driven decision making in education: Benefits and challenges (online). Available at https://www.linkedin.com/advice/0/what-benefits-challenges-using-data-driven-3e (Accessed: 4/1/24).

European Agency (2025) Supporting inclusive school leadership (online). Available at www.european-agency.org/activities/supporting-inclusive-school-leadership (Accessed: 2/1/25).

Facer, K. & Selwyn, N. (2021) Digital technology and the futures of education: Towards 'Non-Stupid' optimism, Futures of Education initiative, UNESCO.

Farrell, P. (2000) The impact of research on developments in inclusive education, International Journal of Inclusive Education, 4(2), 153-162.

FE News (2022) What does quality mean in UK Higher Education today? (online). Available at www.fenews.co.uk (Accessed: 22/11/24).

FE News (2024) Building a data-driven culture in higher education institutions (online). Available at https://www.fenews.co.uk/exclusive/building-a-data-driven-culture-in-higher-education-institutions/ (Accessed: 2/1/24).

Feiman-Nemser, S. (2012) Teachers as Learners, Harvard Education Press.

Fillery-Travis, A. & Lane, D. (2020) Does coaching work or are we asking the wrong question?, Coaching researched: A coaching psychology reader, pp.47-63.

Fradella, H. (2018) Supporting strategies for equity, diversity, and inclusion in higher education faculty hiring, Diversity and inclusion in higher education and societal contexts: International and interdisciplinary approaches, pp.119-151.

Fu, Y., Weng, Z. and Wang, J (2024) Examining AI Use in Educational Contexts: A Scoping Meta-Review and Bibliometric Analysis, *International Journal of Artificial Intelligence in Education* (2024).

Fullan, M. & Quinn, J. (2015) Coherence: The Right Drivers in Action for Schools, Districts, and Systems, Corwin.

Fullan, M. (2015) The New Meaning of Educational Change, Teachers college press.

Fullan, M. (2020) Leading in a Culture of Change, Jossey-Bass.

Fullan, M. (2023). The principal: Three keys to maximizing impact, Wiley.

Fullan, M., Azorín, C., Harris, A. and Jones, M. (2023) Artificial intelligence and school leadership: challenges, opportunities and implications,. School Leadership & Management, 44(4), 339–346.

Friend, M. & Cook, L. (1992) Interactions: Collaboration skills for school professionals, Longman Publishing Group.

Gao, R., Merzdorf, H., Anwar, S., Hipwell, M. and Srinivasa, A. (2024) Automatic assessment of text-based responses in post-secondary education: A systematic review, Computers and Education: Artificial Intelligence, p.100206.

Garcia, E. & Weiss, E. (2019) The teacher shortage is real, large, and growing, and worse than we thought, Economic Policy Institute.

Garvey, R. & Stokes, P. (2021) Coaching and mentoring: Theory and practice, Sage Publications.

Gay, G. (2018) Culturally responsive teaching: Theory, research, and practice, Teachers college press.

Gee, J. (2007) What video games have to teach us about learning and literacy, Palgrave.

Gershon, M. (2015) How to use Bloom's Taxonomy in the classroom: The complete guide: Vol 8, CreateSpace.

Gillard, D. (2011) Education in England: a history, Education in England (online). Available at: www.educationengland.org.uk/history (Accessed: 10/1/25).

Gist, C., Bianco, M. and Lynn, M. (2019). Examining grow your own programs across the teacher development continuum: Mining research on teachers of color and nontraditional educator pipelines, Journal of Teacher Education, 70(1), pp.13-25.

Goldring, E. & Berends, M. (2008) Leading with data: Pathways to improve your school, Thousand Oaks, CA: Corwin Press.

Goldsmith, M. (2010) What got you here won't get you there: How successful people become even more successful, Profile books.

Goleman, D. (2005) Emotional intelligence: Why it can matter more than IQ, Bantam.

Goleman, D., Boyatzis, R. and McKee, A. (2013) Primal Leadership: Unleashing the Power of Emotional Intelligence, Harvard Business Review Press.

Gonzalez-Mohino, D., et al. (2024) The Impact of Artificial Intelligence on Communication Dynamics and Performance in Organizational Leadership, Administrative Sciences, 15(2), 33.

Göransson, K. & Nilholm, C. (2014) Conceptual diversities and empirical shortcomings - a critical analysis of research on inclusive education, European Journal of Special Needs Education, 29(3), 265-280.

Gordon, S. (2005) Teacher evaluation and professional development, Evaluating teaching: A guide to current thinking and best practice, p.268.

GMC (2024) Standards, guidance and curricula (online). Available at https://www.gmc-uk.org/education/standards-guidance-and-curricula (Accessed: 23/12/24).

Greenberg, M., Brown, J. and Abenavoli, R. (2016) Teacher stress and health: Effects on teachers, students, and schools, Edna Bennett Pierce Prevention Research Center, Pennsylvania State University.

Grosemans, I., Hannes, K., Neyens, J. and Kyndt, E. (2020) Emerging adults embarking on their careers: Job and identity explorations in the transition to work, Youth & Society, 52(5), 795-819.

Gummer, E. & Mandinach, E. (2015) Building a conceptual framework for data literacy, Teachers College Record, 117(4), 1-22.

Gund, S. & Swaroop, D. (2024) A study on diversity and inclusion: HR perspective, International Journal of Engineering and Management Research, 14(1), pp.127-135.

Guo, X., Huang, K., Liu, J., Fan, W., Vélez, N., Wu, Q., Wang, H., Griffiths, T. and Wang, M. (2024) Embodied LLM Agents Learn to Cooperate in Organized Teams, arXiv:2403.12482v2.

Guskey, T. (2002) Professional development and teacher change, Teachers and Teaching: Theory and Practice, 8(3/4), 381-391.

Guskey, T. & Bailey, J. (2010) Developing Standards-Based Report Cards, Corwin Press.

Hall, D. (2025) Leading Change in Education: Adaptation, Innovation and transformation, DHP.

HALO Psychology (2025) Why leaders should engage in reflective practice (online). Available at: https://halopsychology.com/2025/03/10/why-leaders-should-engage-in-reflective-practice (Accessed: 16/4/25).

Hargreaves, A. (2003) Teaching in the Knowledge Society: Education in the Age of Insecurity, Teachers College Press.

Hargreaves, A. & Fullan, M. (2015) Professional Capital: Transforming Teaching in Every School, Routledge.

Hargreaves, A. & O'Connor, M. (2018) Collaborative professionalism: When teaching together means learning for all, Corwin.

Harris, A. (2004) Distributed leadership and school improvement: Leading or misleading?, Educational management administration & leadership, 32(1), pp.11-24.

Harris, A. & Spillane, J. (2008) Distributed leadership through the looking glass, Management in Education, 22(1), 31-34.

Harris, A. (2011) Distributed leadership: Implications for the role of the principal, Journal of Management Development, 31, 7-17.

Harris, A., Day, C., Hopkins, D., Hadfield, M., Hargreaves, A. and Chapman, C. (2013) Effective leadership for school improvement, Routledge.

Harris, A. & Jones, M. (2019) Teacher leadership and educational change, School Leadership & Management, 39(1), 1–4.

Harris, A., Jones, M., Lewis, H., Lucas, N. and Thomas, J. (2020) Designing an integrated Programme of initial teacher education: Progress, considerations and reflections, Wales Journal of Education, 22(1).

Harvey, L. & Green, D. (1993) Defining quality, Assessment & Evaluation in Higher Education, 18(1), 9-34.

Harvey, L. (2002) Evaluation for what? Teaching in Higher Education, 7(3), 245-263.

Hattie, J. & Timperley, H. (2007) The power of feedback, Review of Educational Research, 77(1), 81-112.

Hattie, J. (2008) Visible learning: A synthesis of over 800 meta-analyses relating to achievement, Routledge.

Hattie, J. & Clarke, S. (2019) Visible learning: Feedback, Routledge.

Hawkins, P. (2021) Leadership team coaching: Developing collective transformational leadership, Kogan Page.

HCPC (2023) Standards of Proficiency for Regulated Professions (online). Available at www.hcpc-uk.org/standards/standards-of-proficiency (Accessed: 23/12/24).

Health and Safety Executive (HSE) (2022) Protecting mental health in the workplace (online). Available at: https://www.hse.gov.uk/stress/ (Accessed: 11/4/25).

HEBRG (2011) Professional, statutory and regulatory bodies: An exploration of their engagement with higher education, HEBRG.

Hénard, F. and Roseveare, D. (2012) Fostering quality teaching in higher education: Policies and practices, An IMHE guide for higher education institutions, 1(1), pp.7-11.

Hermawan, E. & Arifin, A. (2021) What expert say about empowering human resources in supporting leadership function in Higher Education in the 21st century, Journal Iqra': Kajian Ilmu Pendidikan, 6(2), pp.27-38.

Hernández-Torrano, D., Somerton, M. and Helmer, J. (2022) Mapping research on inclusive education since Salamanca Statement: a bibliometric review of the literature over 25 years, International Journal of Inclusive Education, 26(9), pp.893-912.

Hersey, P. & Blanchard, K. (2015) Management of organizational behavior: Leading human resources. Pearson India.

Herzberg, F. (1959) The motivation to work, John Wiley & Sons.

Hockings, C. (2010) Inclusive learning and teaching in higher education: A synthesis of research, Higher Education Academy.

Holland, A. & Ciachir, C. (2024) A qualitative study of students' lived experience and perceptions of using ChatGPT: immediacy, equity and integrity, Interactive Learning Environments, 1–12.

Hood, S. (1998) Culturally responsive performance-based assessment: Conceptual and psychometric considerations, Journal of Negro Education, 67(3), 187-196.

House of Lords Library (2024) Education for 11 to 16-year-olds: Recent curriculum reforms (online). Available at https://lordslibrary.parliament.uk/education-for-11-to-16-year-olds-house-of-lords-committee-report (Accessed: 13/12/24).

Hunsaker, P. & Hunsaker, J. (2015) Managing people, Dorling Kindersley.

IAEE (2023) The transformative power of mentorship (online). Available at: https://www.iaee.com/2023/09/05/the-transformative-power-of-mentorship/IAEE (Accessed: 16/4/25).

IBO (2024) Moderation (online). Available at ibo.org/programmes/middle-years-programme/assessment-and-exams/e-portfolios/moderation (Accessed: 20/12/24).

ICO (2023) Guide to the UK General Data Protection Regulation (UK GDPR) (online). Information Commissioner's Office. Available at: https://ico.org.uk (Accessed: 11/4/25).

IfATE (2023) Institute for Apprenticeships and Technical Education: Annual Report 2023-24 (online). Available at instituteforapprenticeships.org/media/c3tlqarc/ifate-annual-report-2023-24.pdf (Accessed: 23/12/24).

IfATE (2024) Apprenticeship Standards and Assessment Plans (online). Available at https://www.instituteforapprenticeships.org (Accessed: 23/12/24).

Igbokwe, I. (2024) Artificial Intelligence in Educational Leadership: Risks and Responsibilities, European Journal of Arts, Humanities and Social Sciences, 1(6), pp.3-10.

Imai, M. (1986) Kaizen: The key to Japan's competitive success, New York: McGraw-Hill.

Infosys BPM (2024) Predictive analytics in education (online). Available at https://www.infosysbpm.com/blogs/education-technology-services/predictive-analytics-in-education.html (Accessed: 2/1/24).

Ingersoll, R. & May, H. (2011) Recruitment, retention, and the minority teacher shortage, Consortium for Policy Research in Education.

Ingersoll, R. & Strong, M. (2011) The impact of induction and mentoring programs for beginning teachers: A critical review of the research, Review of Educational Research, 81(2), 201-233.

Ingersoll, R. & Merrill, L. (2017) A quarter-century of changes in the elementary and secondary teaching force: From 1987 to 2012, Phi Delta Kappan, 94(8), 75-79.

IRIS Connect (2024) Sharing good practice: Strategies to encourage teacher collaboration (online). Available at https://www.irisconnect.com/us/blog/sharing-good-practice-strategies-to-encourage-teacher-collaboration (Accessed: 16/4/25).

ISO (2018) ISO 21001:2018 Educational organizations (online). Available at https://www.iso.org/standard/66266.html (Accessed: 21/11/24).

Jennings, P., Frank, J., Snowberg, K., Coccia, M. and Greenberg, M. (2013) Improving classroom learning environments by Cultivating Awareness and Resilience in Education (CARE): results of a randomized controlled trial, School psychology quarterly, 28(4), p.374.

JISC (2023). Framework for digital transformation in higher education (online). Available at https://www.jisc.ac.uk/guides/framework-for-digital-transformation-in-higher-education (Accessed: 19/12/24).

Johnson, S., Blackman, D. and Buick, F. (2018) The 70: 20: 10 framework and the transfer of learning, Human Resource Development Quarterly, 29(4), pp.383-402.

Jones, K. & Tymms, P. (2014) Ofsted's role in promoting school improvement: The mechanisms of the school inspection system, Oxford Review of Education, 40(3), 315–330.

Jones, R., Woods, S. and Guillaume, Y. (2016) The effectiveness of workplace coaching: A meta-analysis of learning and performance outcomes from coaching, Journal of occupational and organizational psychology, 89(2), pp.249-277.

Joo, B. (2005) Executive coaching: A conceptual framework from an integrative review of practice and research, International Journal of Evidence-Based Coaching and Mentoring, 3(2), 1-13.

Jorgensen, M., Davis, K., Kotowski, S., Aedla, P. and Dunning, K. (2005) Characteristics of job rotation in Midwest US manufacturing sector, Ergonomics, 48(15), 1721-1733.

Kaner, S. (2014) Facilitator's guide to participatory decision-making, John Wiley & Sons.

Kaplan, S. (2025) Design Your Next Leadership Program Using AI Tools (online). Available at: https://www.sorenkaplan.com/leadership-development-design-ai-tools (Accessed: 29/3/25).

Karman, A. (2020) Understanding sustainable human resource management–organizational value linkages: The strength of the SHRM system, Human Systems Management, 39(1), pp.51-68.

Katzenbach, J. & Smith, D. (2015) The wisdom of teams: Creating the high-performance organization, Harvard Business Review Press.

Kelly, A. (2009) The Curriculum: Theory and Practice, 6th ed. Sage.

Khan, R. & Jawaid, M. (2020) Technology enhanced assessment (TEA) in COVID 19 pandemic, Pakistan journal of medical sciences, 36(COVID19-S4), p.S108.

Khan, I. (2024) The quick guide to prompt engineering: Generative AI tips and tricks for ChatGPT, Bard, Dall-E, and Midjourney. John Wiley & Sons.

Knowles, M., Holton, E. and Swanson, R. (2014) The adult learner: The definitive classic in adult education and human resource development, Routledge.

Kolb, D. (2014) Experiential learning: Experience as the source of learning and development, FT press.

Kotter, J. (1996) Leading change, Harvard Business Review Press.

Kouzes, J. & Posner, B. (2023) The leadership challenge: How to make extraordinary things happen in organizations, John Wiley & Sons.

Knight, P. & Yorke, M. (2003) Assessment, Learning and Employability, McGraw-Hill Education.

Kram, K. (1988) Mentoring at work: Developmental relationships in organizational life, University Press of America.

Krathwohl, D (2009) Methods of educational and social science research: The Logic of Methods, Waveland Pr Inc.

Kubicle (2024) How to implement a successful data literacy training initiative (online). Available at https://kubicle.com/implementing-a-successful-data-literacy-programme/ (Accessed: 4/1/24).

Labaree, D. (2010) Someone Has to Fail: The Zero-Sum Game of Public Schooling, Harvard University Press.

Lambert, L. (2002) A Framework for shared leadership, Educational Leadership, 59(8), 37-40.

Land, R. (2004) 'Educational development: Discourse, identity and practice', Open Learning, 19(3), pp. 223–232.

Lantang, D., Sumual, T., Usoh, E., Tuerah, P. and Sumual, S. (2023\0 Human resource management in special education, Interdiciplinary Journal & Hummanity (INJURITY), 2(4).

Laurillard, D. (2012) Teaching as a design science: Building pedagogical patterns for learning and technology, Routledge.

Learning Sciences Institute, Southern Methodist University (2024) Qualitative vs. quantitative data analysis in education (online). Available at learningsciences.smu.edu/blog/qualitative-vs-quantitative-data-analysis (Accessed: 3/1/24).

Learning A-Z (2024) Data in education (online). Available at www.learninga-z.com/site/resources/breakroom-blog/data-in-education (Accessed: 2/1/24).

LearnWise AI (2024) Empowering student success and decision-making in education with AI and Intelligent Analytics (online). Available at www.learnwise.ai/news-insights/empowering-data-driven-decision-making-in-education-with-ai-and-intelligent-analytics (Accessed: 3/1/24).

Legislation.gov.uk (2023) Equality Act 2010 (online). Available at: https://www.legislation.gov.uk/ukpga/2010/15/contents (Accessed: 11/4/25). Legislation.gov.uk (2023) Employment Rights Act 1996 (online). Available at: https://www.legislation.gov.uk/ukpga/1996/18/contents (Accessed: 11/4/25).

Leiter, M. & Maslach, C. (2017) Burnout and engagement: Contributions to a new vision, Burnout research, 5, pp.55-57.

Leithwood, K., Harris, A. and Hopkins, D. (2008) Seven strong claims about successful school leadership, School Leadership and Management, 28(1), 27-42.

Leithwood, K., Harris, A. and Strauss, T. (2010) Leading school turnaround: How successful leaders transform low-performing schools, Jossey Bass.

Leithwood, K. & Azah, V. (2016) Characteristics of effective leadership networks, Journal of Educational Administration, 54(4), pp.409-433.

Leithwood, K., Harris, A. and Hopkins, D. (2020) Seven strong claims about successful school leadership revisited, School Leadership & Management, 40(1), 5-22.

Lencioni, P. (2010) The five dysfunctions of a team: A leadership fable, John Wiley & Sons.

LessonBud (2023) The ethical implications of data-driven education (online). Available at https://lessonbud.com/blog/the-ethical-implications-of-data-driven-education/ (Accessed: 4/1/24).

Levi, D. & Askay, D. (2020) Group dynamics for teams, SAGE publications.

Lewin, K. (1947) Frontiers in group dynamics: Concept, method and reality in social science; social equilibria and social change, Human Relations, 1(1), 5-41.

Liker, J. (2004) The Toyota way: 14 management principles from the world's greatest manufacturer, New York: McGraw-Hill Education.

Lofthouse, M. et al (1995) Managing the Curriculum, Financial Times: EMDU.

Lovell, O., Sherrington, T. and Caviglioli, O. (2020) Sweller's cognitive load theory in action, John Catt.

Lucent Innovation (2024) Data-driven decision making (DDMM) in the education sector - an overview (online). Available at https://www.lucentinnovation.com/blogs/it-insights/data-driven-decision-making-in-education (Accessed: 3/1/24).

Luckin, R., George, K. and Cukurova, M. (2022) AI for School Teachers (AI for Everything), CRC Press.

Lumby, J. (1995) Managing the Curriculum in Further Education, EMDU.

Lumby, J. (2012) Disengaged and disaffected young people: Surviving the system, British Educational Research Journal, 38(2), pp.261-279.

Luthans, F., Avolio, B. and Walumbwa, F. (2004) Authentic leadership: Theory-building for veritable sustained performance, The Leadership Quarterly, 18(3), 222–238.

MacBeath, J. (2019) Leading Learning in Schools: A Handbook for Educational Leaders, London: Routledge.

Madaus, G., Scriven, M., Stufflebeam, D. and Stufflebeam, D. (1983) The CIPP model for program evaluation, Evaluation models: Viewpoints on educational and human services evaluation, pp.117-141.

Madavi (2024) Adaptive Learning in EdTech systems: Enhancing student performance (online). Available at https://madavi.co/adaptive-learning-in-edtech-systems-enhancing-student-performance/T (Accessed: 2/1/24).

Male, B. (2012a) Primary Curriculum Design Handbook, Continuum.

Male, B. (2012b) The Secondary Curriculum Design Handbook, Continuum.

Mandinach, E. & Gummer, E. (2016) What does it mean for teachers to be data literate: Laying out the skills, knowledge, and dispositions, Teaching and Teacher Education, 60, 366-376.

Mandinach, E. & Schildkamp, K. (2021) Misconceptions about data-based decision making in education: An exploration of the literature, Studies in Educational Evaluation, 69, 100842.

Marsh, C. & Willis, G. (2003) Curriculum: Alternative approaches, ongoing issues, Prentice Hall.

Marsh, J., Pane, J. and Hamilton, L. (2006) Making sense of data-driven decision making in education: Evidence from recent RAND research, RAND Corporation.

Marshall University Institutional Research and Planning (2023) Building a data-driven culture at educational institutions (online). Available at www.marshall.edu/irp/2023/10/19/builddatadrivenculture (Accessed: 2/1/24).

Martinho-Truswell, E. (2018) How AI Could Help the Public Sector. Harvard Business Review (online). Available at https://hbr.org/2018/01/how-ai-could-help-the-public-sector (Accessed: 29/3/25).

Maslow, A. (2023) A theory of human motivation, Zinc Read.

Massachusetts Department of Elementary and Secondary Education. (2015) An Interactive Planning Guide for Distributed Leadership (online). Available at doe.mass.edu/edeffectiveness/leadership/distributed-leadership-ipg.pdf (Accessed: 10/1/25).

McCauley, C. & Van Velsor, E. (2004) The Center for Creative Leadership Handbook of Leadership Development, Jossey-Bass.

McTighe, J. & O'Connor, K. (2005) Seven practices for effective learning, Educational Leadership, 63(3), 10–17.

Meacham, M. (2020) AI in Talent Development: Capitalize on the AI Revolution to Transform the Way You Work, Learn, and Live, Alexandria, VA: Association for Talent Development.

Meechan, D., Whatmore, T., Williams-Brown, Z. and Halfhead, S (2022) Why are we tracking reception-aged children? Teachers' and key stakeholders' perspectives on the reintroduction of national Reception Baseline Assessment, Educational Futures,13. 113-139.

Mentoring Complete. (2023) Why workplace mentorship is more crucial than ever in 2023? (online). Available at: https://www.mentoringcomplete.com/why-workplace-mentorship-is-more-crucial-than-ever-in-2023 (Accessed: 16/4/25).

Mercer, J., Barker, B. and Bird, R. (2010) Human resource management in education: Contexts, themes and impact, Routledge.

Merriam, S. & Bierema, L. (2013) Adult Learning: Linking Theory and Practice (2nd ed.), Jossey-Bass.

Metcalf, H., Rolfe, H., Stevens, P. and Weale, M. (2005) Recruitment and retention of academic staff in higher education, National Institute of Economic and Social Research.

Middleton, T. & Kay, L. (2019) Using an inclusive approach to reduce school exclusion: A practitioner's handbook, Routledge.

Miller, P. (2001) Theories of Developmental Psychology, Worth Publishers.

Miller, W. & Rollnick, S. (2013) Motivational Interviewing: Helping People Change (3rd ed.), The Guilford Press.

Mishra, P. & Koehler, M. (2006) Technological Pedagogical Content Knowledge: A framework for teacher knowledge, Teachers College Record, 108(6), 1017-1054.

Moon, J. (2013). A handbook of reflective and experiential learning: Theory and practice, Routledge.

MRC EdTech (2024) How AI revolutionizes Higher Education with predictive analytics (online). Available at https://mrccedtech.com/how-ai-revolutionizes-higher-education-with-predictive-analytics/ (Accessed: 2/1/24).

Mukhopadhyay, M. (2020) Total Quality Management in Education, SAGE Publications.

Munoz, J. & Naqvi, A. (2021) The AI Leader: Mastery of Humans and Machines in the Workplace, London: Anthem Press.

Murchan, D. & Shiel, G. (2024) Understanding and applying assessment in education, Sage.

National Center for the Improvement of Educational Assessment (2024) Strengthening ties between accountability and school improvement (online). Available at https://www.nciea.org/blog/strengthening-ties-between-school-accountability-and-improvement (Accessed: 2/1/24).

NEA (2025) National Education Association (online). Available at: https://www.nea.org (Accessed: 16/4/25).

Nicol, D. & Macfarlane-Dick, D. (2006) Formative Assessment and Self-regulated Learning: A Model and Seven Principles of Good Feedback Practice, Studies in Higher Education, 31(2), 199–218.

Nicol, D. (2020) The power of internal feedback: Exploiting natural comparison processes, *Assessment & Evaluation in Higher Education*, 46(5), 756–778.

Nicolini, D. & Korica, M. (2024) Structured shadowing as a pedagogy, Management Learning, 54(1), 3-22.

Nilholm, C. (2006) Special education, inclusion and democracy, European Journal of Special Needs Education, 21(4), 431-445.

Nkomo, L., Daniel, B. and Butson, R. (2021) Synthesis of student engagement with digital technologies: a systematic review of the literature, International Journal of Educational Technology in Higher Education, 18, pp.1-26.

Northouse, P. (2021) Leadership: Theory and practice, Sage.

NMC (2023) The Code: Professional Standards of Practice and Behaviour for Nurses and Midwives (online). Available at https://www.nmc.org.uk/standards/code (Accessed: 23/12/24).

Oakland, J., Oakland, R. and Turner, A. (2020) Total Quality Management and Operational Excellence, Routledge.

OECD (2020) Education at a Glance 2020: OECD Indicators, OECD Publishing.

OECD (2022) PISA 2022 Assessment Framework (online). Available at https://www.oecd.org/en/publications/pisa-2022-assessment-and-analytical-framework_dfe0bf9c-en.html (Accessed: 23/12/24).

OECD (2023a) PISA 2022 Results (online). Available at: https://www.oecd.org/pisa (Accessed: 21/11/24).

OECD (2023b) Skills Outlook 2023: First results from the survey of adult skills, Paris: OECD Publishing.

Office for Students (2023) Regulatory Framework for Higher Education in England (online). Available at: https://www.officeforstudents.org.uk (Accessed: 18 April 2025).

Office for Students (2024) Benchmarking (online). Available at www.officeforstudents.org.uk/data-and-analysis/benchmarking (Accessed: 2/1/24).

Ofqual (2020) Regulated Qualifications Framework (online). Available from https://www.gov.uk/find-a-regulated-qualification (Accessed: 20/12/24).

Ofqual (2022) Regulatory framework for GCSEs, AS and A levels (online). Available at https://www.gov.uk/guidance/regulating-gcses-as-and-a-levels-guide-for-schools-and-colleges-2022 (Accessed: 19/12/2024).

Ofqual (2023a) Corporate plan 2022 to 2025 (online). Available at gov.uk/government/publications/ofquals-corporate-plan (Accessed: 23/12/24).

Ofqual (2023b) Regulating Technical Qualifications (online). Available at https://assets.publishing.service.gov.uk/media/5b44bdcfed915d39ed011760/Technical_qualifications_policy_consultation.pdf (Accessed: 23/12/24).

OfS (2023) Teaching Excellence and Student Outcomes Framework (online). Available at: https://www.officeforstudents.org.uk (Accessed: 21/11/24).

Ofsted (2019) Early years inspection handbook, Ofsted.

Ofsted (2023) Education Inspection Framework (online). Available at: https://www.gov.uk/government/publications/education-inspection-framework (Accessed: 21/11/24).

Okon, R., Odionu, C. and Bristol-Alagbariya, B. (2024) Integrating data-driven analytics into human resource management to improve decision-making and organizational effectiveness, *IRE Journals*, *8*(6), p.574.

O'Leary, M. (2016) Reclaiming lesson observation: Supporting excellence in teacher learning, Routledge.

Oliver, B. (2019) Making Micro-Credentials Work for Learners, Employers and Providers, Deakin University.

Open University (2024) Quantitative and qualitative data (online). Available at Retrieved https://www.open.edu/openlearn/mod/oucontent/view.php?id=109325&section=2.2.1 (Accessed: 3/1/24).

Ologbosere, O. (2023) Data literacy and higher education in the 21st century, IASSIST Quarterly, 47(3-4).

Otus (2024) Using data dashboards to improve decision making (online). Available at https://otus.com/blog/how-administrators-are-using-data-dashboards-to-improve-decision-making/ (Accessed: 2/1/24).

Papaevangelou, O., Syndoukas, D., Kalogiannidis, S. and Chatzitheodoridis, F. (2023) Efficacy of embedding IT in human resources (HR) practices in education management, Journal of Infrastructure, Policy and Development, 8(1), p.2371.

Paradigm Press (2023) Aligning Teaching Strategies with Educational Quality Standards (online). Available at https://www.paradigmpress.org/rae/article/download/703/602 (Accessed: 31/12/24).

Parker, G. & Leat, D. (2021) The case of curriculum development in England: Oases in a curriculum desert? In Priestley, M., Alvunger, D., Philippou, S. and Soini, T. (Eds.), Curriculum making in Europe: Policy and practice within and across diverse contexts, Emerald Publishing.

Passmore, J. (2015). Excellence in Coaching: The Industry Guide. Kogan Page.

Passmore, J. (2020) The coaches handbook, Routledge.

Perryman, J. (2009) Inspection and the fabrication of professional and performative processes, Journal of Education Policy, 24(5), pp. 611–631.

Pink, D. (2011) Drive: The surprising truth about what motivates us, Penguin.

Podolsky, A., Kini, T., Bishop, J. and Darling-Hammond, L. (2016) Solving the teacher shortage: How to attract and retain excellent educators, Learning Policy Institute.

Pragmatic Institute (2024) Common types of data bias (online). Available at https://www.pragmaticinstitute.com/resources/articles/data/5-common-bias-affecting-your-data-analysis/ (Accessed: 4/1/24).

Prenger, R. & Schildkamp, K. (2018) Data-based decision making for teacher and student learning: A psychological perspective on the role of the eacher, Educational psychology, 38(6), pp.734-752.

Priestley, M., Biesta, G. and & Robinson, S. (2015) Teacher agency: An ecological approach, Bloomsbury.

PromptFrame (2005) AI Courseware (online). Available at http://promptframe.co.uk (Accessed: 4/5/25).

Przytuła, S., Sułkowski, L. and Kulikowski, K. (2024) Human Resource Management in Higher Education Institutions: An International, Routledge.

Pulakos, E. & O'Leary, R. (2011) Why is performance management broken?, Industrial and Organizational Psychology, 4(2), 146–164.

Quality Assurance Agency (2024) UK Quality Code for Higher Education (online). Available at: https://www.qaa.ac.uk (Accessed: 21/11/24).

QuestionPro (2024) Examples of qualitative data in education: How to use (online). Available at https://www.questionpro.com/blog/examples-of-qualitative-data-in-education (Accessed: 3/1/24).

Race, P. (2019) The Lecturer's Toolkit: A Practical Guide to Assessment, Learning and Teaching, Routledge.

Ragins, B. & Kram, K. (2007) The Handbook of Mentoring at Work: Theory, Research, and Practice, Sage Publications.

Ramsden, P. (2003) Learning to teach in higher education, Routledge.

Rath, T. & Clifton, D. (2004) How full is your bucket? Positive strategies for work and life, Gallup Press.

Redecker, C. (2011) The Future of Learning: Preparing for Change, European Commission: JRC Publications Repository.

Reeves, P. & Burt, W. (2006) Challenges in data-based decision-making: Voices from principals, Educational Horizons, 85(1), 65-71.

ResearchGate. (2024) The Role of Collaboration and Networking in the Digital Age: Students' Perspectives (online). Available at https://www.researchgate.net/publication/383829705_The_Role_of_Collaboration_and_Networking_in_the_Digital_Age_Students%27_Perspectives (Accessed: 16/4/25).

ResearchGate (2024) Collaborative Networking in Education: Learning Across International Contexts (online). Available at https://www.researchgate.net/publication/361591876_Collaborative_Networking_in_Education_Learning_Across_International_Contexts (Accessed: 16/4/25).

Rhodes, C. & Brundrett, M. (2012). Retaining leadership talent in schools, International Studies in Educational Administration (Commonwealth Council for Educational Administration & Management (CCEAM)), 40(1).

Rivkin, S., Hanushek, E. and Kain, J. (2005) Teachers, schools, and academic achievement, Econometrica, 73(2), 417-458.

Robinson, V. M., & Timperley, H. (2007). The impact of leadership on student outcomes. Australian Journal of Education, 51(3), 277-289.

Roffey, S. (2017) The Aspire principles and pedagogy for the implementation of social and emotional learning and the development of whole school well-being, International Journal of Emotional Education, 9(2), pp.59-71.

Rose, D. & Meyer, A. (2002) Teaching every student in the digital age: Universal design for learning, Association for Supervision and Curriculum Development.

Runde, C. & Flanagan, T. (2012) Becoming a conflict competent leader: How you and your organization can manage conflict effectively, John Wiley & Sons.

Ryan, R. & Deci, E. (2000) Intrinsic and extrinsic motivations: Classic definitions and new directions, Contemporary educational psychology, 25(1), pp.54-67.

Sadler, D. (2012) Beyond feedback: Developing student capability in complex appraisal, in Hatzipanagos, S. & Rochon, R. (2012) Approaches to assessment that enhance learning in higher education (pp. 45-60), Routledge.

Salas, E., Tannenbaum, S., Kraiger, K. and Smith-Jentsch, K. (2012) The science of training and development in organizations: What matters in practice, Psychological Science in the Public Interest, 13(2), 74–101.

Sallis, E. (2014) Total Quality Management in Education, Kogan Page.

Salovey, P. & Mayer, J. (1990) Emotional intelligence. Imagination, Cognition and Personality, 9(3), 185-211.

Santamaria, L. & Santamaria, A. (2016) Culturally responsive leadership in education: Promoting social justice and equity, Routledge.

Schein, E. (2010) Organizational culture and leadership, Jossey-Bass; Wiley.

Schildkamp, K., Lai, M. and Earl, L. (2012) Data-based decision making in education: Challenges and opportunities, Springer.

Schildkamp, K. (2019) Data-based decision-making for school improvement: Research insights and gaps, Educational Research, 61(3), 257-273.

Schön, D. (2008) The reflective practitioner: How professionals think in action, Basic Books.

Sembly (2025) 11 Best AI tools for competitor analysis in 2025 (online). Available at: sembly.ai/blog/best-ai-tools-for-competitor-analysis (Accessed: 30/3/25).

Senge, P. (2006) The fifth discipline: The art and practice of the learning organization, Broadway Business.

Serrano, O., Miranda González, F., Mourato, J. and Lourenço, R. (2024) Student contributions to quality assurance in higher education: a systematic literature review, Assessment & Evaluation in Higher Education, pp.1-17.

Serbati, A., Aquario, D., Da Re, L., Paccagnella, O. and Felisatti, E. (2020) Exploring good teaching practices and needs for improvement: Implications for staff development, Journal of Educational, Cultural and Psychological Studies, 2020(21), pp.43-64.

Shibiti, R. (2020) Public school teachers' satisfaction with retention factors in relation to work engagement, SA Journal of Industrial Psychology. 46. 10.4102.

Shore, L., Randel, A., Chung, B., Dean, M., Ehrhart, K. and Singh, G. (2011) Inclusion and diversity in work groups: A review and model for future research, Journal of Management, 37(4), 1262-1289.

Siemens, G. (2005) Connectivism: A Learning Theory for the Digital Age, International Journal of Instructional Technology and Distance Learning, 2(1), 3-10.

Siemens, G. (2020) Learning Analytics: The Emergence of a Discipline, Routledge.

Sinek, S. (2009) Start with why: How great leaders inspire everyone to take action, Penguin.

Skaalvik, E. & Skaalvik, S. (2011) Teacher job satisfaction and motivation to leave the teaching profession: Relations with school context, feeling of belonging, and emotional exhaustion, Teaching and teacher education, 27(6), pp.1029-1038.

Skaalvik, E. & Skaalvik, S. (2017) Teacher stress and teacher self-efficacy: Relations and consequences, Teaching and Teacher Education, 67, 152-160.

Skaalvik, E. & Skaalvik, S. (2020) Teacher burnout: relations between dimensions of burnout, perceived school context, job satisfaction and motivation for teaching. A longitudinal study, Teachers and Teaching, 26(7-8), pp.602-616.

Skills for Care (2023) The Care Certificate Standards and Implementation Guide (online). Available at https://www.skillsforcare.org.uk/Developing-your-workforce/Care-Certificate/Care-Certificate.aspx (Accessed: 23/12/24).

Smith, J. (2023) HR Planning: How to Balance Short-Term and Long-Term Need (online). Available at: https://www.linkedin.com/advice/0/how-do-you-balance-hr-planning-between (Accessed: 9/4/25).

Soliz, A., DeLoach, C. and Mesa, H. (2023) How do community and technical colleges build cross-sector collaborations?, The Journal of Higher Education, 94(6), pp.691-719.

Spady, W. (1993) Outcome based education, Workshop report No 5, Canberra: ACSA.

Spillane, J. P. (2006). Distributed Leadership. San Francisco: Jossey-Bass.

SRA (2024) Solicitors Regulation Authority (online). Available at www.sra.org.uk/ (Accessed: 23/12/24).

STA (2023) Assessment Frameworks for Primary Schools (online). Available at https://www.gov.uk/government/organisations/standards-and-testing-agency (Accessed: 23/12/24).

Stake, R. (1967) The countenance of educational evaluation, Teachers College Record, 68(7), 523–540.

Stenhouse, L. (1975) An introduction to curriculum research and development, London: Heinemann.

Stoll, L., Bolam, R., McMahon, A., Wallace, M. and Thomas, S. (2006) Professional learning communities: A review of the literature, Journal of Educational Change, 7(4), 221-258.

Stone, D. & Heen, S. (2014) Thanks for the feedback: The science and art of receiving feedback well, Viking.

Stratpilot. (2024). Best AI prompts for building leadership skills (online). Available at https://stratpilot.ai/best-ai-prompts-for-building-leadership-skills (Accessed: 30/3/25).

Sue, D., Alsaidi, S., Awad, M., Glaeser, E., Calle, C. and Mendez, N. (2019) Disarming racial microaggressions: Microintervention strategies for targets, White allies, and bystanders, American Psychologist, 74(1), 128-142.

Swap, W., Leonard, D., Shields, M. and Abrams, L. (2001) Using mentoring and storytelling to transfer knowledge in the workplace, Journal of Management Information Systems, 18(1), 95–114.

Tai, J., Ajjawi, R., Boud, D., Dawson, P. and Panadero, E. (2018) Developing evaluative judgement: Enabling students to make decisions about the quality of work, Higher education, 76, pp.467-481.

Taris, T., Le Blanc, P., Schaufeli, W. and Schreurs, P. (2005) Are there causal relationships between the dimensions of the Maslach Burnout Inventory? A review and two longitudinal tests, Work & Stress, 19(3), 238-255.

TeachFind (2024) 5 game-changing adaptive learning technologies: Revolutionizing K-12 education (online). Available at https://teachfind.com/teaching-strategies/5-game-changing-adaptive-learning-technologies-revolutionizing-k-12-education/ (Accessed: 2/1/24).

Terzi, L. (2005) Beyond the dilemma of difference: The capability approach to disability and special educational needs, Journal of Philosophy of Education, 39(3), 443-459.

The Conference Board (2023) Global executive coaching survey 2023 (online). Available at: https://www.conference-board.org/publications/global-executive-coaching-survey-2023-report (Accessed: 16/4/25).

The Data School (2024) Bias in data collection (online) Available at www.thedataschool.co.uk/morgan-a-rennie/bias-in-data-collection-I (Accessed: 4/1/24).

The Hechinger Report (2021) When using data to predict outcomes, consider the ethical dilemmas, new report urges (online). Available at hechingerreport.org/using-data-predict-outcomes-consider-ethical-dilemmas-new-report-urges (Accessed: 2/1/24).

The Learning Accelerator (2024) Leadership that moves you forward: Innovation, vision, and planning (online). Available at practices.learningaccelerator.org/insights/leadership-that-moves-you-forward-introduction-part-i-effective-district-leadership-innovation-vision-and-planning (Accessed: 23/12/24).

Thomas, L., Hill, M., O'Mahony, J. and Yorke, M. (2017) Supporting student success: Strategies for institutional change, Higher Education Academy.

Tickell, C. (2011) The early years: Foundations for life, health and learning, HM Government.

Tomlinson, C. (2001) How to Differentiate Instruction in Mixed-Ability Classrooms, ASCD.

Topping, K. (2009) Peer Assessment, Theory into Practice, 48(1), 20-27.

Topping, K. (2017) Peer assessment: Learning by judging and discussing the work of other learners, Interdisciplinary Education and Psychology, 1(1), 1-17.

Torrance, H. (2012) Educational assessment and evaluation, Routledge.

Torrington, D., Hall, L., Atkinson, C. and Taylor, S. (2020) Human resource management, Pearson UK.

Tyler, R. (2009) Basic principles of curriculum and instruction, The curriculum studies reader, pp.69-77.

Ueda, N. & Kezar, A. (2024) A systematic review: pedagogies and outcomes of formal leadership programs for college students, Cogent Education, 11(1), p.2314718.

UK Government (2010) Equality Act, HMSO (online). Available at https://www.legislation.gov.uk/ukpga/2010/15/contents (Accessed: 19/12/24).

UK Parliament (2017) The consequences of high stakes testing (online). Available at https://publications.parliament.uk/pa/cm200708/cmselect/cmchilsch/169/16908.htm (Accessed: 23/12/24).

UNESCO (2015) Education 2030: Incheon Declaration and Framework for Action, Paris: UNESCO.

UNESCO (2024) Global Education Monitoring Report: Education for All 2000-2015 (online). Available at: https://en.unesco.org/gem-report (Accessed: 21/11/24).

Universities UK (2024) Graduate employment: its limits in measuring the value of higher education (online). Available at https://www.universitiesuk.ac.uk/what-we-do/policy-and-research/publications/graduate-employment-its-limits-measuring (Accessed: 18/12/24).

University of Iowa (2022) Goal: Excellence in Teaching and Learning (online). Available at https://strategicplan.uiowa.edu/strategic-plan-2022-2027/goal-excellence-teaching-and-learning (Accessed: 31/12/24).

University of Iowa. (2024) The role of AI in modern education (online). Available at: https://onlineprograms.education.uiowa.edu/blog/role-of-ai-in-modern-education (Accessed: 1/4/25).

Valence (2025) An AI coach for every manager, tailored to your company (online). Available at: https://www.valence.co/ (Accessed 1/4/25).

Van Nieuwerburgh, C. (2019) Advanced coaching practice: Inspiring change in others, SAGE Publications Ltd.

Vangrieken, K., Meredith, C., Packer, T. and Kyndt, E. (2017) Teacher communities as a context for professional development: A systematic review, Teaching and teacher education, 61, pp.47-59.

Varma, A., Pereira, V. and Patel, P. (2024) Artificial intelligence and performance management, Organizational Dynamics, 53(1), p.101037.

Vedhathiri, T. (2022) In-house leadership development programs for high-potential and high-performing engineering faculty, Asia-Pacific Journal of Educational Management Research, 7(2), 17-32.

Vekeman, E., Devos, G. and Valcke, M. (2016) Linking educational leadership styles to the HR architecture for new teachers in primary education, SpringerPlus, 5, pp.1-19.

Verywell Mind (2023) Why leadership coaching Is the career hack you never knew you needed (online). Available at: https://www.verywellmind.com/benefits-of-leadership-coaching-8548209 (Accessed: 16/4/25).

Viscione, I., D'Elia, F., Vastola, R. and Sibilio, M. (2017) Psychomotor assessment in teaching and educational research, Athens Journal of Education, 4(2), pp.169-177.

Vorecol (2024) The Impact of AI on Test Validity and Reliability in Psychometric Assessments (online). Available at https://psico-smart.com (Accessed: 24/12/24).

Vorecol (2024) How AI algorithms can predict and enhance student performance (online). Available at https://vorecol.com/blogs/blog-adaptive-learning-pathways-how-ai-algorithms-can-predict-and-enhance-student-performance-196757 (Accessed: 2/1/24).

Vygotsky, L. (1978) Mind in society: The development of higher psychological processes, Harvard University Press.

Warren, M. (2005) Communities and schools: A new view of urban education reform, Harvard Educational Review, 75(2), pp.133-173.

Wenner, J. A. & Campbell, T. (2017) The theoretical and empirical basis of teacher leadership: A review of the literature, Review of Educational Research, 87(1), 134–171.

Wheatley, M. (2006) Leadership and the new science: Discovering order in a chaotic world (3rd Edition), Berrett-Koehler Publishers.

Whitfield, L. (2019) Moving beyond the 'initial' in initial teacher education: the role of ITE, Advancement Network Journal, 11(3), 15-24.

Whitmore, J. (2009) Coaching for performance: GROWing human potential and purpose - The Principles and practice of coaching and leadership, Nicholas Brealey Publishing.

Wiggins, G. & McTighe, J. (2005) Understanding by design, Association for Supervision and Curriculum Development.

Wiliam, D. (2011) Embedded formative assessment, Solution Tree Press.

Wilkins, C. (2015) Education reform in England: Quality and equity in the performative school, International Journal of Inclusive Education, 19(11), pp.1143-1160.

Williamson, B. (2021) Datafication and automation in education: Critical perspectives on AI and assessment, Big Data & Society, 8(1), 1-12.

Winstone, N. & Boud, D. (2019) Exploring cultures of feedback practice: The adoption of learning-focused feedback practices in the UK and Australia, Higher Education Research & Development, 38(2), pp.411-425.

Witherspoon, R., Goldsmith, M., Lyons, L. and Freas, A. (2000) Coaching for leadership: How the world's greatest coaches help leaders learn, San Francisco, CA: Pfeiffer.

World Bank (2022) Ending Learning Poverty: What Will It Take? (online). Available at: https://www.worldbank.org (Accessed: 21/11/24).

Yang, Z., Wu, J. and Xie, H. (2024) Taming Frankenstein's monster: Ethical considerations relating to generative artificial intelligence in education, Asia Pacific Journal of Education, pp.1-14.

Yar, M., Hamdan, M., Anshari, M., Fitriyani, N. and Syafrudin, M. (2024) Governing with Intelligence: The Impact of Artificial Intelligence on Policy Development, Information 15, no. 9: 556.

Young, M. & Muller, J. (2015) Curriculum and the specialization of knowledge: Studies in the sociology of education, Routledge.

Zeichner, K. (2003) Teacher research as professional development for P–12 educators in the USA, Educational Action Research, 11(2), 301-326.

Zhu, J., Liao, Z., Yam, K. and Johnson, R. (2018) Shared leadership: A state-of-the-art review and future research agenda, Journal of Organizational Behavior, 39(7), 834–852.

INDEX

360-degree feedback 122
70:20:10 model 117
Accreditation 22, 50, 242-244
Accreditation of Prior Experiential Learning 55, 60
Accreditation of Prior Learning 60
Active listening 28, 109, 113, 119, 120, 139
Adaptive assessment 73
Affective domain 57-58, 64, 284, 290
AI agent 214-226
Apprenticeships 48-51, 81, 86, 93, 208
Artificial Intelligence 72-73, 97, 153, 179, 194, 197, 212-215, 224, 230-234, 262-263, 273
Assessment bodies 47-55
Assessment cycle 40-41, 292-293
Assessment design 42-53, 59, 64, 71
Assessment for learning 35, 41, 272-273
Assessment manager 37-38, 46
Assessment of learning 34, 41
Assessment office 38
Assessment reliability 34, 45, 60, 63-66, 67, 70, 73
Assessment suitability 34
Assessment validity 34, 45, 60, 66-68, 73
Association for Supervision and Curriculum Development 107
Attracting talent 148-149, 152
Audits 69, 112, 204, 231, 241-246, 252, 280, 292
Bachelor of Education 92
Backward design 7, 9, 21
BambooHR 177
Bard 216
Baseline assessment 40-42, 292-293

Behaviourism 81-82
Benchmarking 9, 22, 36, 40, 46, 51, 53, 68, 85, 184, 193, 227, 237, 239-245, 252, 264, 267, 295, 320
Blackboard 9, 38, 78, 192, 311, 318, 320
Bloom's taxonomy 7, 57, 61-62, 282, 286-291
Bobbitt, Franklin 16
Bruner's spiral curriculum 18, 85
Burnout 94, 143, 150, 152, 157, 167-170
Butler Education Act 238
Callaghan, Jim 18
Cambridge Assessment International Education 53
Canvas 38, 78, 192, 195, 197, 311, 320
Cause-and-effect diagram 252
Center for Transformative Learning 80
Chartered Institute of Personnel and Development 52, 54
Chatbot 179, 219-230
ChatGPT 212-233, 317-318
City & Guilds 49-53
Civil Aviation Authority 52
Claude 217
CLEAR model 113
Coaching 12, 107-155, 229-230, 270, 274, 281, 296
Cognitive domain 57, 61, 64, 81-82, 84, 161, 226, 272, 284
Cognitivism 81-82
Collaborative learning 59, 106-108, 131, 219, 221, 294
Communication 27-29, 35, 61-62, 78-83, 92, 133, 140, 147, 160, 202, 228, 259
Computer Based Training 221
Conflict 15, 70, 92, 103, 120, 128, 130, 133, 136, 139, 146-155

Conflict management 130, 146-152
Connectivism 82, 86
Construct validity 66
Construction Industry Training Board 51
Constructivism 81-82
Constructivist approach 18, 295
Content validity 66
Continuous improvement 123, 256
Coordinated curriculum 26
Core skills 26
Course design 6, 9, 22, 219
Course evaluation 7, 9, 46, 264, 290
Course implementation 7, 28
COVID 65, 178
Credit Accumulation and Transfer Scheme 26
Credit transfer 26
Credly 52, 54
Criterion referenced assessment 34, 36
Criterion-related validity 66
Cross-marking 68
Curriculum 1-30
Curriculum accountability 13
Curriculum components 4-5
Curriculum design 6-30, 56, 84
Curriculum design cycle 6-8, 272
Curriculum framework 9, 21-22, 31, 286
Curriculum Impact 9
Curriculum Implementation 13
Curriculum Intent 7, 28, 236, 239
Curriculum leadership 10-15, 30-31, 271
Curriculum organisation 23-25
Curriculum Study Group 2
Dashboard 192, 194-196, 200, 278, 296, 320-322
Data analysis 9, 188-202, 248, 304-310
Data analytics 38, 73, 78, 177-178, 194, 246, 251, 256, 269

Data cycle 186-187
Data literacy 184-185, 196, 198-201, 206
Data source 121, 191, 192, 196
Data stewardship 203
Data-driven decision-making 183-209, 213, 246, 269
Dewey's Progressive Education Philosophy 56
Diagnostic assessment 34, 215
Differentiation 58, 266
Digital assistant 214
Digital Capabilities Framework 64
Diploma in Education and Training 93
Distributed leadership 11, 14, 16, 106, 119, 131, 143
Diversity 151
Domains of learning 55, 57-58
Duolingo 73
Dynamic assessment 36
E-assessment 72
Education and Skills Funding Agency 48, 51, 267
Education for All 239
EduPeople 177
E-leadership 212-232, 273-274
E-mentoring 124
Emotional intelligence 58, 105, 110, 120, 133, 136, 148, 154, 155, 237, 277
Employment law 173
Equity 64, 94-98, 172, 256
Essay 63
Ethics 74, 172-174, 202-204, 255
European Foundation for Quality Management 244
EU Aviation Safety Agency 53
Evaluation 7, 9, 18, 22, 34, 46, 62, 121, 123, 125, 165, 184, 188, 288
Every HR 177

Evidence-based decision making 181-211, 278

Experiential learning 55, 58, 63, 86, 103-104, 294

External review 39, 69

Facilitation 18-20, 88, 92, 130, 138-141, 152, 202

Fairness 48-50, 67-70, 172-173

Family Educational Rights and Privacy Act 196

Feedback 7, 9, 13, 34, 44, 46, 65-71, 118, 122-125, 131, 233, 296, 305, 321

FeedbackFruits 70

Formative assessment 29, 35, 39-45, 56, 61, 72-73, 193, 215, 246, 253, 273, 284, 292-293, 296, 299-301

Freire's critical pedagogy 17

Fronter 196

Functional skills 26

Games 64, 313

GCSE 20, 33, 35, 36, 45, 47, 67, 112, 266, 272

Generative AI 212-215, 222

Global Education Monitoring Report 239

Google Classroom 39, 78, 81, 311

Grade descriptor 65-67

Grading 45, 65-72, 273

Group coaching 124

Group work 42, 60-61, 69, 294, 304

GROW model 111

Health and Care Professions Council 52

Health and Safety at Work Act 174

Hidden curriculum 3, 6

Higher Education Subject Benchmarks 9, 23

High-stakes 44, 71, 237, 243

HR software 176-179, 311

Human resources 156-181, 279

Humanistic Model 18

Hybrid work 65, 69-70, 85, 139, 178, 222, 237

Independent learning platforms 85

Individualisation 58-59

Influencing others 126, 152

Informed consent 203

In-house staff development 102

Initial Teacher Education 101-102

Innovation 13, 54, 73, 130, 171, 196-198, 250, 295

Institute for Apprenticeships and Technical Education 49

Instructional leadership 11

Integrated curriculum 18, 26

International Baccalaureate 53, 69, 107

International Civil Aviation Organisation 53

International Standards Organisation 51

Inter-rater reliability 67

Interviews 62, 123, 186, 252, 285, 319

ISO standards 244

iTrent 177

JISC 63

Job rotation 101, 103, 104

Job satisfaction 169

Journal 62

Kaizen 248, 258

Keeping Children Safe in Education 174

Key skills 26-27

Khan Academy 73

Large language model 230

Leadership capacity 11, 14-16, 102, 118, 122, 143

Learned curriculum 5

Learner-centred education 19, 86

Learning experiences 4, 8, 17-19, 23-25, 36, 72, 78-79, 84, 95, 117, 132, 143, 158, 185, 197, 239, 263, 277, 285, 301

Learning Management System 9, 38, 75, 78, 81, 192, 195, 197, 246, 262, 263, 301, 311, 320

Learning objectives 10, 21, 35-36, 42, 57, 64, 66, 72, 183, 282-286

Learning outcomes 5-6, 21, 36, 42-46, 49, 56-57, 63, 64, 66, 71, 72, 79, 80, 87, 91, 95, 158, 162, 193, 197, 215, 239, 240, 246, 257, 261-265, 273, 282-285, 299

Level descriptor 45, 65-67

Levels of understanding 23

LinkedIn 52, 86, 149, 302

Lockwood Committee 2

Log book 62

Managing people 130, 152-154

Marking scheme 64, 67, 266

Maslow's hierarchy of needs 137

Massive Open Online Course 86, 222

Measurement bias 203

Mental health 151, 163, 167-170, 174, 256, 263, 298

Mentoring 81, 88, 91, 99, 100-101, 108-125, 136, 137, 151-152, 154-155, 157, 162-167, 180, 261, 271-275, 279, 281, 297, 310

Mentoring cycle 116-117

Micro-credentials 52, 74, 86, 302-303

Microsoft Teams 78, 274, 319

Middle management 19, 21, 23

Ministry of Defence 52

Ministry of Education 2

Mission 3, 10, 28, 78, 79, 141, 157-159, 163, 169, 171, 202, 225, 228, 246, 296-297

Moderation 38, 39, 62, 66-70, 266, 273

Modularisation 26

Moodle 9, 38, 78, 192, 311, 320

Motivation 34, 57, 58, 71, 72, 114, 127-133, 136-138, 140, 142, 152, 155, 157, 171, 225, 226, 253, 271, 278, 281, 285

National Curriculum 9, 13, 17, 18, 23, 27, 28, 68, 238, 286

National Education Association 107

National networks 102, 107

Needs analysis 6, 7, 9, 27, 285

Networking 77, 82, 86, 98, 102, 106, 107, 124, 130, 134, 142, 161, 162, 164, 170, 271, 302

Norm referenced assessment 35-37

Null curriculum 6

Nursing and Midwifery Council 52, 54

NVQ 52, 53

Objective test 63

Office for Students 244, 49

Official curriculum 5

Ofqual 47-50, 65

Ofsted 5, 7, 47, 48, 60, 236, 238-242, 244, 245, 259, 267, 320, 321

Ofsted Inspection Framework 7

One-to-one mentoring 124

On-the-Job training 93, 101, 103, 117, 143

Oral assessment 62

Organisational dynamics 129-130

Organising threads 25

Originality 217, 225, 226

OSKAR model 114-116

Outcome-based education 238, 240

Parental engagement 132

Pareto analysis 254, 255, 261

Pathways for leadership 143, 144, 152

Pathways into teaching 92, 94, 99

Pearson 52

Pedagogical agent 215, 219

Pedagogy 3, 9, 10-12, 16, 18, 19, 23, 28, 84-86, 104, 154, 217, 270, 271, 278, 301

Peer assessment 35, 42, 43, 58, 64, 70, 249, 268

Peer coaching 119, 124, 270

Peer observation of teaching 89, 91, 250

Peer review 67, 69, 70, 165, 179, 193, 241, 244, 273, 292, 296, 299, 322

Peergrade 70, 322

People leadership 129

PeopleSoft 177

Performance management 180, 181, 225

Performance metrics 242-252, 267, 321

Perplexity 217

Personalised learning 58, 72, 73, 80, 81, 143, 183, 194, 197, 216, 271, 296, 299

Personalising leadership 232

PGCE in Post-Compulsory Education and Training 93

Piloting 45-46

PISA 53, 74, 193, 239, 245, 320

Plan-Do-Check-Act 247, 258 269

Policy guidance 230-232

Portfolio 44, 45, 52, 55, 60, 62, 63, 70, 71, 75, 194, 300

Postgraduate Certificate in Education 92

Postgraduate degrees 102, 103

Power BI 195, 319, 320

Predictive analytics 178, 192, 194, 195, 196, 246, 322

Privacy 74, 185, 192, 196, 198, 199, 202, 203, 230, 232, 234, 255, 269

Problem-Based Learning 18, 81, 297

Process model 10, 18, 19, 20, 30, 31, 55, 85

Product model 16, 18, 20, 30, 31, 85

Professional associations 102, 107

Professional learning communities 168

Professional Standards for Teaching 92, 102

Professional, Statutory, and Regulatory Bodies 49-50

Project management 101, 105

Prompt 212-234, 317-318

Psychomotor domain 57, 64

Qualified Teacher Status 92

Qualitative data 184-193, 209, 251, 278-279, 304, 319

Quality assurance 37, 38, 49, 51, 53, 63, 68, 235-246, 256, 259-260, 263-269, 270, 276, 319-322

Quality Assurance Agency 5, 49, 63, 68, 240, 241, 267

Quality Code for Higher Education 49, 237, 267

Quality control 235, 240-244, 256, 268, 269

Quantitative data 182-186, 190, 193, 209, 248, 278, 279, 308, 319

Questioning 186, 266

Readymade prompt 212-234, 317-318

Reception Baseline Assessment 39

Recognition 13, 22, 88, 93, 121, 129, 148, 167, 168, 170-172, 183, 242, 264, 302, 303

Recruitment 148-161, 172-181, 278, 281

Reflective practice 64, 77, 80, 99, 101, 105, 110, 134, 241, 249, 250, 267, 276

Regulated Qualifications Framework 65

Remote work 178, 231

Reporting bias 203

Resistance 15, 77, 94, 97, 99, 200, 202, 246, 259, 260, 262, 268, 295

Review panel 68, 254

Reward 13, 49, 92, 111, 128, 141, 144, 170-172, 199, 202

Role play 218

Rubric 29, 44, 45, 54, 60, 62-69, 262, 273, 304

Safeguarding 232, 241

SAP SuccessFactors 177

SAT 20, 39, 45, 48

School Direct 92

363

School Information Management System (SIMS) 39, 177, 195, 311, 320, 321

School-centred initial teacher training 93

Schools Council 2

Sector Skills Councils 50

Selection bias 203

Self-development 129

Seminar 63

Senior management 16, 18, 19, 21

Sequence 24, 286

Shared leadership 12, 105

SIMS Personnel 177

Simulation 63, 293

Six Sigma 260-262, 269, 276

Skills for Care 50, 52

SMART 124, 165

Social and emotional learning 20

Staff development and training 161-164, 180

Standardisation 67, 204, 242, 266

Standards 22, 47, 48, 52, 53, 102, 240, 284

Standards and Testing Agency 47, 48

Statutory Framework for the Early Years Foundation Stage 23

Statutory SATs 20, 39, 45, 48

STEM 79, 148, 149, 150, 204, 208, 209

Stenhouse, Lawrence 10, 18, 55, 85

Stenhouse's Process Model 55

Strategic HRM 158

Student Information System 192, 197, 310, 321

Student voice 131

Stufflebeam's CIPP Model 7

Subject-based curriculum 25

Summative assessment 29, 41, 42, 193, 215, 293

Support systems 8

Supporting Inclusive School Leadership 95

SUSP ITE Programme 102

Synoptic assessment 36

Taba's model of curriculum development 18

Taught curriculum 5

Taxonomy 57, 61, 282, 287, 290, 291

Teach First 92

Teacher leadership 93, 98

Teaching & Learning 77-99

Teaching Assistants 93

Teaching excellence 78, 80-81, 85, 128, 169, 171

Teaching Excellence Framework 49, 260

Team building 130, 140, 152

Technology 25, 26, 38, 56, 63, 71, 72, 81, 96, 130, 154, 177, 194, 246, 263, 303, 304

Technology-Enhanced Assessment 71

Tested curriculum 6

Test-retest reliability 67

Think-pair-share 220

Thomas-Kilmann Conflict Model 147

Total Quality Management 256-260, 276

Transactional leadership 111

Transformational Leadership 10

Tyler, Ralph 7, 9, 10, 16, 17, 21, 23, 28, 29, 30, 31, 55, 85

Tyler's Objectives Evaluation 7

Tyler's rationale 17, 30, 31

UK Data Protection Act 196

UK General Data Protection Regulation 173

Underperformance 166

Understanding by Design 18

UNESCO Education 2030 Agenda 85

United Nations Educational, Scientific and Cultural Organisation 85, 239

Universal Design for Learning 95, 221, 297

Value added assessment 37

Vertical and horizontal relationships 24

Vision 11, 28, 86, 97

Vygotsky 18, 36, 64, 82, 131, 295

Wiggins & McTighe 7, 21

Work-based learning 50-51

Workday 177

Work-life balance 151, 153-157, 167, 169, 180

Leadership & Management Strategies for Education

BOOKS IN THIS SERIES

Volume 1: Core principles of educational leadership (November 2024)

Volume 2: Managing key institutional processes (June 2025)

www.ingramcontent.com/pod-product-compliance
Lightning Source LLC
Chambersburg PA
CBHW080213040426
42333CB00044B/2645